Un

The Political Context

The Open University
Faculty of Educational Studies

The Education and the Urban Environment Course Team

John Raynor (Chairman)
Merrill Evans
Alec Fleming
Elizabeth Harris
Peter Hart
Peter Raggatt
Rosalind Street-Porter

Gwynn Pritchard BBC
David Seligman BBC

Consultant:
Jack Barnes   Centre for Studies in Social Policy

Urban Education   3

The Political Context

Edited by
Peter Raggatt and Merrill Evans

Ward Lock Educational
in association with
The Open University Press

ISBN 0 7062 3639 4 paperback
    0 7062 3640 8 hardback

First published 1977

Set in 11 on 12 point Plantin by
Computacomp (UK) Limited, Fort William
and printed by
Robert MacLehose and Company Limited, Glasgow
for Ward Lock Educational
116, Baker Street, London W1M 2BB
A Member of the Pentos Group
Made in Great Britain

Contents

Acknowledgments

The Open University and publishers would like to thank the following for permission to reproduce copyright material. All possible care has been taken to trace ownership of the selections included and to make full acknowledgment for their use.

George Allen & Unwin (Publishers) Ltd for 'Forward Planning UK Style' by H. Glennerster from *Social Services Budgets and Social Policy* by H. Glennerster 1975; and for 'Participatory government – the place of the head' by J. Watts from *The Countesthorpe Experience* J. Watts (ed) 1976; Basic Books and Penguin Books Ltd for 'Schooling and Cognitive Inequality' by C. Jencks *et al* from *Inequality: A reassessment of the effect of family and schooling in America* C. Jencks *et al* 1972; The Bobbs-Merrill Company Inc. for 'Community control and political theory' by L. Fein from *The Ecology of the Public Schools* by L.J. Fein 1971; British Association for the Advancement of Science for 'Social inequality and social integration in modern Britain' by Dr. J.H. Goldthorpe from *Advancement of Science* 26 (28) 1969; British Educational Administration Society for 'Institutional autonomy and public accountability' by M. Kogan and 'A Response' by A. Ellis from *Autonomy and Accountability in Educational Administration* 1975; The Controller of Her Majesty's Stationery Office, for 'Political ends and educational means' by A.H. Halsey from *Educational Priority* Vol. I. 1972; and 'Positive discrimination in education, individual groups and institutions' by J. Barnes and H. Lucas from *Educational Priority* Vol. III 1975 and for extracts from the *Report and Memoranda, Select Committee on Expenditure, (Sub-Committee on Education, Art and Home Office)*; Fabian Society for 'Whose Schools?' by Anne Corbett from Fabian Research Series 328; *Harvard Educational Review* Winter 1968 for 'The concept of equality of educational opportunity' by J. Coleman; ILEA for 'Summary and conclusions of the Auld report' from the Report of the Public Inquiry into *Teaching Organization and Management of William Tyndale Junior and Infants' Schools* 1976; MacGibbon and Kee Limited/Granada Publishing Limited for 'Class inequality and meaning systems' by F. Parkin from *Class Inequality and Political Order* by F. Parkin 1970; David Mackay Co. Inc. for 'The case for the community control of schools' by H.M. Levin from *Schooling in a Corporate Society* M. Carnoy (ed) 1972; *New Society*, London, the weekly review of the Social Sciences, 20th September 1973 for 'A Blunt Instrument: a review' by J.W.B. Douglas; NFER Publishing Company Ltd for 'The allocation of curricular resources' by E.M. Byrne from *Planning and Educational Inequality* by E.M. Byrne 1974; *Phi Delta Kappan* December 1970 for 'Towards objective criteria of professional accountability in the schools of New York' by H.S. Dyer; *Secondary Education* Vol. 3, No. 2 1973 for 'Virement and the alternative use of resources' by E. Briault; *The Times Educational Supplement*, London for 'Whatever happened to positive discrimination' by A.H. Halsey (21 January 1977) and 'Servants or Masters? How the Civil Servants rule British Education' (9th May 1975); W. Williamson and D.S. Byrne for 'The effect of local education authority resources and policies on educational attainment' SSRC final report 1975.

General introduction

Three companion volumes of readings: *The City Experience*; *Schooling in the City* and *The Political Context*, have been prepared for the third-level course *Education and the Urban Environment* offered by the Faculty of Educational Studies at the Open University. As many people will now know, the Readers form only one component of Open University courses which also include correspondence texts, BBC radio and television programmes, personal tuition and summer schools. In the preparation of these Readers, we have deliberately excluded material which will appear in other components of the course. This accounts for the non-appearance of names and materials which might otherwise be expected.

Taken together the three Readers are designed to provide students with:

1 a sample of perspectives on the city and of the social processes at work within urban settings
2 an introduction to a variety of political and economic issues in urban education
3 a survey of some of the principal debates encountered in urban schooling.

It is only four years since the previous course, E351 *Urban Education*, was prepared with its two Readers: *Cities, Communities and the Young* and *Equality and City Schools* (published by Routledge and Kegan Paul, 1973) and in that short space of time it is interesting to note the differences in emphasis between the two courses. In the earlier course, one of our central concerns was the problem of urban poverty and the disadvantaged learners in our city schools, and the course preparation period coincided with the Educational Priority Area and the Community Development Programmes. Again, we were writing against a background of high truancy rates, high teacher turnover and the reported crises taking place within many of our large secondary schools. Not surprisingly therefore, our attention came to be focused on the process of institution-building within schools, on community relations and on alternative strategies for education. Today's educational picture has changed, and the new course reflects that change.

As might be expected at a time of cutbacks and economic stringency, considerable time is given to examining resource implications for urban schooling. Again, though the earlier course gave some attention to an understanding of urban processes, the new course contains even more material reflecting our greater awareness of the way in which the city serves as a distributive agency; of the plight of the 'inner city' areas, of cultural dislocation within different groups and the implications all of these have for urban schooling. Further, we are today much more conscious of the difficulties of searching for a multicultural education in a period of economic recession and unemployment, when the racism which lies so close to the surface manifests itself in hostility towards minorities.

This is not to suggest that Urban Education is nothing more than a loose collective title for a number of disparate topics conveniently gathered under one heading susceptible to whim, current concern or the crisis of the moment. In any course on urban education one would now expect to find students examining some, if not all, of the following issues:

1 *the urban setting* covering the main urban processes, not only in terms of location and structure but also in terms of interests, community and culture
2 *urban politics* introducing students to the questions raised by the priorities, activities and judgments of urban decision-makers in terms of physical planning, city governance and educational policies.

From these two basic considerations a whole number of issues branch out. Among these can be identified:

(a) *issues of equity* – the debates, the research and the programmes for equal educational opportunity; compensatory programmes multicultural education; bilingual education and affirmative action
(b) *management, finance and government* – the structure, plans, methods and budgetary considerations of urban education
(c) *institutional issues* – the most appropriate kinds of provision for education for different groups at different ages in different parts of the city. Here, too, is that debate on the nature of the curricular objectives that are being pursued in urban schools and the way they relate to parents and to community.

The three Readers in this series reflect the issues outlined above. They have been compiled to enrich the course which starts from a study of the urban experience, surveys a number of issues in urban schooling and concludes by examining various political and economic questions. However, each volume can be read separately from the course and give the reader a useful introduction to the field of study.

Reader 3 considers the choices available to educators and the decision-making process within the wider political context. The first section is concerned with the normative debate on inequality in society, carrying forward questions of social justice raised in Reader 1. It explores changes in the concept of equality of educational opportunity and of positive discrimination as a principal strategy for attacking inequality.

The second section turns to the system at work. It looks at how decisions are made and priorities established for the allocation of resources at both national and local level. The effects of resource allocation are discussed with respect to inter- and intra- LEA resource policies.

The third section explores the balance of responsibility between professionals in the schools and the lay public. Accountability is considered and the section concludes with a discussion of community control of schools.

1 Challenges and choices

Introduction

The many forms of inequality which exist in society have provided a rich source of theoretical and empirical study for social scientists. The first two articles (by Goldthorpe and Parkin) serve to remind us that inequality is not simply about economic resources but is deeply embedded in our social and cultural organization.

Because of the pervasiveness of structures of inequality of both condition and opportunity, Goldthorpe (1.1) argues that society is highly resistant to change. It is a 'man-made structure' with a 'substantially self-maintaining structure of social groupings differentiated multifariously and often extremely in terms of the power and advantage that their members enjoy'. Advancement of the ideal of social justice is regarded as a precondition for both the reconstruction of economic life and the reduction of social inequality.

Parkin (1.2) explores the relationship between class power and the moral framework of inequality. He argues that the interpretation of inequalities and the class structure is mediated by the meaning systems to which people have access. This promotes different responses to inequality and low status. The tension which exists between the abstract moral order, issuing from the dominant class, and the situational constraints of low status give rise to a subordinate value system − a negotiated form of dominant values. For the subordinate class, the discrepancies between abstract values and situational acts are more serious than for the dominant class, who find a closer fit between institutionalized values and their concrete situations.

These preliminary analyses suggest that social inequality cannot be attacked effectively on a single front. Nonetheless, the educational system has frequently been regarded as the most convenient and suitable instrument for such a policy. It is regarded as a major distributor of life chances in industrialized and developing nations. Thus, policies for social inequality come back to provisions for equality of educational opportunity. Coleman (1.3) describes changes in the concept of equality of educational opportunity over time. His work was influential in replacing a concern with equality of access to schooling with equality of outcomes for the average member of non-educationally defined groups. Halsey (1.4) carries on the discussion noting the contradiction between 'astronomical' (political) ends of efficiency and equality and the 'miniscule' (educational) means provided. The problem is clear, but the solutions uncertain or contentious.

5

Education thus becomes the repository for ambitious social reforms. Local analysis and the development of the community schools are offered as a hopeful approach for advancing some way towards social equality.

A theory of positive discrimination for the most seriously 'disadvantaged' areas was advanced in the Plowden Report. It was adopted in the EPA action research project and became Government policy in the late 1960s. Barnes and Lucas (1.5) in a detailed examination, argue that it is based on a serious methodological fallacy, which fails to distinguish between group averages and individual children. Nor does it distinguish between the sum of separate problems and the effects of cumulative disadvantage. The number of 'disadvantaged' children is greater outside EPAS than inside them. Even within EPAS, there are proportionately more children who are not disadvantaged, according to the criteria used, than are disadvantaged.

The assumption to date is that schools can have a significant independent effect upon educational attainment. This is attacked by Christopher Jencks (1.6) who finds no support for the view that schools can reduce cognitive inequalities or, more generally, that educational reform can bring about economic and social equality. Reviewing the work of Jencks and his associates, Douglas (1.7) criticizes the statistical methods used but draws similar conclusions for Britain.

1.1 Class inequality and meaning-systems

F. Parkin

Sociological accounts of the normative aspects of inequality reveal the absence of any general agreement concerning the distribution of values in the class hierarchy. One school of thought maintains that the values underlying major social institutions are held in common by all social classes, though perhaps with varying degrees of commitment. A different school of thought argues that values vary sharply and systematically between classes, so that one cannot speak of a unified moral order. Engels, commenting upon the class structure of nineteenth century England, felt that the proletariat had become a 'race wholly apart' from the bourgeoisie. 'The workers speak other dialects, have other thoughts and ideals, other customs and moral principles, a different religion and other politics than those of the bourgeoisie. Thus they are two radically dissimilar nations, as unlike as difference of race could make them ... '[1] Present day class contrasts are not normally drawn in quite such dramatic terms as this, but the 'two nations' view of the normative order continues as a powerful tradition in stratification studies. Accounts of working-class life in modern Britain often make explicit contrasts between working-class and middle-class values, so characterizing the moral order as highly differentiated.[2] This same approach is implied in the use of the term 'working-class subculture', suggesting as it does a sector of society having a distinct set of values and behavioural patterns. Similar contrasts are held to typify the normative systems of other Western societies. Hamilton suggests that in West Germany the middle and working classes 'constitute separate populations which have, for the most part, independent and relatively autonomous values'.[3] Similarly, for the United States, W. B. Miller has argued that: 'There is a substantial segment of present day American society whose way of life, values, and characteristic patterns of behaviour are the product of a distinctive cultural system which may be termed "lower class".'[4] Again, Hyman's much-cited paper, 'The Value Systems

Source: *Class Inequality and Political Order* (1971), pp. 79–102 and 189–90.

of Different Classes', also gives support to a class differentiated version of the normative order.[5]

The opposite approach is to emphasize the unity rather than the diversity of the general value system. The functionalist strand of thought in sociology, particularly as represented in the work of Talcott Parsons and his followers, draws heavily on the assumption of a unitary value system.[6] Merton, too, in his influential paper, 'Social Structure and Anomie', adopts a somewhat similar approach. Merton suggests that a major source of tension in modern society lies in the fact that members of the subordinate class internalize the same values as the dominant class, but lack the means for realizing them.[7] Mayer's analysis of social stratification in the United States also produces the observation that 'the working class shares a "white collar" style of life and accepts middle class values and beliefs'.[8] Contemporary political theorists have also been prone to focus on the extent of normative consensus found in the 'stable democracies'. Class variations in voting patterns and party allegiance notwithstanding, what we typically find, it is claimed, is broad agreement on values underpinning the political institutions of welfare capitalism. Thus, societies such as our own come to be labelled 'civic cultures' to distinguish them from societies characterized by sharp normative dissensus in the political sphere.[9]

The major problem raised by the class-differentiated view of the normative system is that of social control. If the subordinate class were to subscribe to a value system sharply distinguished from that of the dominant class, then the latter's normative control over the former would obviously be seriously diminished. In this situation, the dominant class would have to rely on physical coercion as a substitute for moral suasion. Thus, in societies where the use, or threatened use, of force does not appear to be the prevailing strategy of social control, we are bound to have reservations about the validity of a class-differentiated model of the moral order.

One of the main objections to the consensual model, on the other hand, is that it often fails to make clear the relationship between the normative and factual elements of stratification. Of particular relevance here is the connection between the distribution of power and the legitimation of values. All too often the assumption seems to be that common agreement on values betokens a kind of independent convergence in the moral outlook of different classes. But in fact, of course, the extent to which values are legitimized in society is largely a function of institutional power. Values are much more likely to flow in a 'downward' than an 'upward' direction; consequently, moral assumptions which originate within the subordinate class tend to win little acceptance among the dominant class. The reverse process, however, is much more marked, so that normative consensus is better understood in terms of the socialization of one class by another, rather than as independent class agreement or convergence on values.

It might be helpful if we approach this complex issue by looking at the normative order as a number of competing meaning-systems. Although there is a factual and material basis to class inequality, there is more than one way in which it can be interpreted. Facts alone do not provide meanings, and the way a person makes sense of his social world will be influenced by the nature of the meaning-systems he draws upon. So far as class stratification in Western societies is concerned it seems that we can quite usefully distinguish three major meaning-systems. Each derives from a different social source, and each promotes a different moral interpretation of class inequality. These are:

1 The *dominant* value system, the social source of which is the major institutional order. This is a moral framework which promotes the endorsement of existing inequality; among the subordinate class this leads to a definition of the reward structure in either *deferential* or *aspirational* terms.

2 The *subordinate* value system, the social source or generating milieu of which is the local working-class community. This is a moral framework which promotes accommodative responses to the facts of inequality and low status.

3 The *radical* value system, the source of which is the mass political party based on the working class. This is a moral framework which promotes an *oppositional* interpretation of class inequalities.

In most Western societies all three meaning-systems tend to influence the social and political perceptions of the subordinate class. Variations in the structure of attitudes of groups or individuals within this class are thus to some extent dependent upon differences in access to these meaning-systems. Any discussion of working-class values regarding the reward structure must thus concern itself both with the types of major meaning-systems 'available', and with social factors which help to account for variations in their adoption. Clearly, values are generally not imposed on men in any crudely mechanistic way. Men also impose their will by selecting, as it were, from the range of values which any complex society generates. At the same time, individuals do not construct their social worlds in terms of a wholly personal vision, and without drawing heavily upon the organizing concepts which are part of a public meaning-system. What now follows is a brief analysis of three such public meaning-systems which seem to be of major importance to the process by which men come to perceive the nature of inequality and the class structure. No claim is made that the three meaning-systems examined – the dominant, subordinate and radical – exhaust the range of normative complexity. Most societies will undoubtedly spawn a variety of subsidiary value systems which may cut across the major systems to be considered here. But given the problems and difficulties inherent in any discussion of values it seems advisable to limit the scope of the analysis to fairly broad and general categories. We begin, then, with a discussion of the dominant value system and its effect on perceptions of inequality among the subordinate class.

The concept of a dominant value system derives from Marx's celebrated statement that 'the ideas of the ruling class are, in every age, the ruling ideas'. This proposition rests on the plausible assumption that those groups in society which occupy positions of the greatest power and privilege will also tend to have the greatest access to the means of legitimation. That is to say, the social and political definitions of those in dominant positions tend to become objectified and enshrined in the major institutional orders, so providing the moral framework of the entire social system. It is not of course necessary to posit any monolithic social or normative unity to the groups which cluster at the apex of the dominant class. Undoubtedly they display variations in political and social outlook – as, for example, between aristocratic or traditional élites on the one hand and managerial or entrepreneurial élites on the other. However, these differences are not likely to be fundamental with regard to the values underlying class inequality and its institutional supports. With the partial exception of that group or stratum loosely defined as the intellectuals, almost all groups within the dominant class tend to define the reward system as morally just and desirable. Dominant values are in a sense a representation of the perceptions and interests of the relatively privileged; yet by virtue of the institutional backing they receive such values often form the basis of moral judgements of underprivileged groups. In a way, dominant values tend to set the standards for what is considered to be objectively 'right'. This holds not only for the rules governing the distribution of rewards but also for many other aspects of social life. In the sphere of culture, for example, the musical, literary and artistic tastes of the dominant class are accorded positive evaluation, while the typical cultural tastes and pursuits of the subordinate class are negatively evaluated. Thus in the allocation of national resources to the arts, or of honours to their practitioners, the claims of 'élite' culture will tend to have precedence over the claims of 'mass' culture. To take a somewhat similar example, the characteristic speech-patterns and linguistic usages of the dominant class are generally regarded as 'correct', or what counts as the grammar of the language; the usages of the subordinate class are often said to be 'incorrect' or ungrammatical where they differ from the former, even though such usages may represent the statistical norm. These examples serve to illustrate that what is essentially an evaluative matter can be transformed into an apparently factual one by virtue of the legitimating powers of the dominant class. And what applies to the evaluation of linguistic forms, or of artistic tastes, applies equally to evaluations of the reward structure. Thus, to accept Marx's proposition regarding the genesis of 'ruling ideas' is not to subscribe to a conspiracy theory of society; it is rather to acknowledge that moral and political rules hold sway not because they are self-evidently 'right', but because they are made to seem so by those who wield institutional power.

Now the more completely the subordinate class comes to endorse and internalize the dominant value system, the less serious will be the conflicts over existing inequalities. There is of course a good deal of variation in the extent to which lower strata come to accept the version of social reality held by upper strata. The caste system of traditional India provides an extreme case of a stratified order permeated throughout by values legitimizing the power and privilege of dominant groups. The subordinate class in industrial society does not generally subscribe so completely to a meaning-system which confirms its own inferiority. Nevertheless, certain tendencies in this direction are observable. Studies by McKenzie and Silver, and Eric Nordlinger have demonstrated that large segments of the British working class express moral commitment to many of the dominant class symbols and institutions which sanction inequality. Furthermore, there appears to be fairly widespread disapproval among the subordinate class for bodies such as trade unions which attempt to redress the balance of advantages in their favour.[10]

This phenomenon of a class, or at least a large segment of it, endorsing a moral order which legitimizes its own political, material, and social subordination is open to somewhat different assessments. On the one hand, it can be taken as evidence of a socially desirable political consensus – a social order free from disruptive class conflicts. Or, on the other hand, it can be understood as an example of a society in which the dominant class has been especially successful in imposing its own definitions of reality on less privileged groups. Thus, to equate political and social consensus with the good society, as so many contemporary writers do, is really to state a concealed preference for a system in which the dominant class has effectively translated its own values into a factual moral order binding on all. From this point of view, societies such as France or Italy, where the dominant class has been less successful in shaping the workers' perceptions, are regarded as somewhat inferior political species. Unlike the 'stable democracies' or the 'civic cultures' the subordinate class in France and Italy is prone to *incivisme:* that is, it puts a different interpretation upon inequality, and its own place in the social order, from that provided by the meaning-system of the dominant class. Thus, from the consensualist standpoint, a class-conscious proletariat is regarded as dysfunctional for the political system, in so far as it is less amenable to normative control by the dominant class than is a deferential proletariat.

Deferential interpretations of the reward and status hierarchy stem from acceptance of the dominant value system by members of the subordinate class. It should be emphasized here that deference as a general mode of understanding and responding to the facts of low status does not necessarily entail a sense of self-abnegation. Rather, it tends to be bound up with a view of the social order as an organic entity in which each individual has a proper part to play, however humble. Inequality is seen as inevitable as well as just, some men being inherently fitted for positions of power and privilege. To acknowledge the superiority of such people is not to demean or belittle oneself, since all must benefit from their stewardship of society. In their discussion of working-class Conservatives, McKenzie and Silver point out that:

> deferentials, although seeing themselves as subordinate, do not feel themselves inferior. English deferentials feel themselves the moral, if not the social, equals of the elite because they appear to accept the classic doctrine that all who properly fulfil their stations in life contribute worthily to the common good ... English working class deferentials are provided with a sense of esteem by the very ideas which justify and explain their social and political subordination.[11]

Acceptance of the dominant value system by members of the subordinate class does not necessarily promote deferential orientations. Equally consistent with such acceptance is a view of the reward structure which emphasizes the opportunities for self-advancement and social promotion. This aspirational model of reality endorses the class and status system as it stands, but also represents it as a relatively open order in which men of talent and ability can, with effort, rise above their present station. Thus, whereas the deferential version of the social world accepts the class system as a fixed, unchanging order, the aspirational version allows for the social exchange of personnel between classes, while accepting the necessity for classes as such.

Both deferential and aspirational models are extracted from the dominant value − or meaning-system; but whether one rather than the other is accepted as a workable moral framework seems, to some extent at least, to be related to structural variations within the subordinate class. There are, for example, various indications that deferential attitudes tend to be most marked among groups and individuals who directly experience the social influences and judgements of dominant class members. Included among these might be those whose occupations bring them into immediate face-to-face contact with employers; or those who live in rural communities and small towns with established local status systems. Under such conditions, nationally derived symbols of class and status are reinforced by becoming 'operationalized', as it were, through personal contact and regular social encounters with high-ranking members of the community. As Lockwood puts it:

> Local status systems, therefore, operate to give the individual a very definite sense of position in a hierarchy of prestige, in which each 'knows his place' and recognizes the status prerogatives of those above and below him. For the deferential traditionalist, such a system of status has the function of placing his work orientations in a wider social context. The persons who exercise authority over him at his place of work may not be the same persons who stand at the apex of the local status system, but the structural principles of the two social orders are homological; and from neither set of relationships does he learn to question the appropriateness of his exchange of deference for paternalism.[12]

Aspirational interpretations of the reward structure appear to flourish among those in a quite different social situation. We should, perhaps, expect such an outlook to be found most commonly among members of the working class who are downwardly mobile. Those who have had some experience of white-collar styles of life have access to a window on the social world which is closed to most of their class peers. Hence their symbolic meaning-system is likely to incorporate many of the elements common to the dominant class, while also differing sharply from the deferential view, which draws essentially upon the experience of inherited subordinate status. In addition to the downwardly mobile, it could be expected that those whose occupations make them somewhat marginal to the working class would also be prone to visualize the reward system as a fairly open opportunity structure. Those in positions such as foreman, policeman, supervisor, etc., are in the anomalous situation of exercising authority over members of the subordinate class without actually being part of the dominant class. There is not much reliable evidence concerning the general outlook and attitudes of those who are 'in' but not altogether 'of' the subordinate class; but we might speculate that working-class authority figures would, by virtue of their position, be committed to dominant values, but not to a deferential interpretation of them. As mentioned in the previous chapter, there are some indications that marginal members of the subordinate class are relatively successful in encouraging educational ambition and performances in their children. And this might be taken as one index of a general aspirational outlook similar to that held by the downwardly mobile. However, given the absence of information on this score we cannot get much beyond plausible hunches. Even less appears to be known about the extent to which Western societies vary among themselves in the distribution of deferential and aspirational norms. British society, for example, is said to be especially productive of deference, while in the United States aspirational values are said to be far more entrenched.[13] If this is in fact so, then it is clear that the interpretation of any given society's dominant value system is not simply a function of variations in the social location and attributes of different groups. Obviously, if American or Australian workers who are in face-to-face relations with their employers, or who live in small communities, do not tend towards a deferential outlook, then we cannot posit a general connection between images of society and structural factors. The stock of class symbols 'available' in a society must to some extent be influenced by specific historical and cultural factors; consequently, we should expect to find variations in the dominant value systems of different societies, and therefore certain variations in the meanings given to inequality, structural similarities notwithstanding.

The subordinate value system; the generating milieu of this meaning-system is the local working-class community. There is an abundance of studies of the patterns of attitudes and beliefs typifying what is sometimes called the working-class or lower-class subculture.[14] In so far as it is possible to characterize a complex set of normative arrangements by a single term, the subordinate value system could be said to be essentially accommodative; that is to say its representation of the class structure and inequality emphasizes various modes of adaptation, rather than either full endorsement of, or opposition to, the *status quo*. Hoggart portrays this underlying theme of the subordinate value system as follows:

> When people feel that they cannot do much about the main elements in their situation, feel it not necessarily with despair or disappointment or resentment but simply as a fact of life, they adopt attitudes towards that situation which allow them to have a liveable life under its shadow, a life without a constant and pressing sense of the large situation. The attitudes remove the main elements in the situation to the realm of natural laws ...[15]

The subordinate value system tends to promote a version of the social order neither in terms of an open opportunity structure nor as an organic unity; rather, strong emphasis is given to social divisions and social conflict, as embodied in the conceptual categories of 'them' and 'us'. This power or conflict model of the reward structure is clearly different from any which could be derived from outright endorsement of the dominant value system. Indeed, it is a general perspective which casts some doubt on the morality of the distributive system and the persistent inequities it generates. At the same time, however, it would be misleading to construe the subordinate value system as an example of normative opposition to the dominant order. Least of all, perhaps, should it be understood as exemplifying class-consciousness or political radicalism. Some writers have tended to overemphasize the political significance of the power or conflict model, and to see it as evidence for a highly differentiated normative system. Dahrendorf, for example, has leaned heavily on working-class notions of 'them' and 'us' to support a general theory of class conflict.[16] More recently, Newton's study of the social bases of the British Communist Party claims that there are 'elements in the British working-class culture which can be tapped by the BCP. Outstanding among these is the powerful class consciousness which is to be found in almost any working-class community.'[17] Again, 'At the purely local political level, class-conscious "them" and "us" awareness is expressed in the strong community spirit which is remarked on by almost every writer on working-class communities. The CP is fairly successful where it can draw on this expression of class consciousness ... '[18]

This is a fairly common interpretation of the political significance of the subordinate value system, or what most writers refer to as the 'working-class subculture'. But if we examine its content at all closely we are bound to be rather sceptical of such politicized constructions. To begin with, Hoggart's catalogue of working-class usages (which is the main empirical source of the power model so far as England is concerned) refers primarily to the experience of authority relations with such diverse figures as policemen, civil servants, local government officials, and petty bureaucrats, as well as with employers. Now resentment at bureaucratic officialdom is certainly likely to be more sharply felt among the subordinate than the dominant class. But this is hardly to be equated with political class consciousness in the usual meaning of that term. Nor, again, is the pervasive sense of communal solidarity which is typically found in the underclass milieu to be equated with a class outlook on politics and society. As Hoggart himself points out, the communal or solidaristic aspect of working-class life is largely confined to interpersonal relationships, and for 'most people it does not develop into a conscious sense of being part of the "working class movement" '.[19] Conventionally, to describe workers as class conscious is to refer to their commitment to a radical or oppositional view of the reward structure of capitalist society. Typically, of course, this type of outlook is associated with Marxist or socialist movements, and does not emerge of its own accord from the underclass milieu. Indeed, it could be said that the subordinate value system represents something of a bulwark to political class consciousness, in so far as it entails adaptive rather than oppositional responses to the *status quo*. As Westergaard has argued, the solidarities of class and the solidarities of community are antithetical rather than complementary.[20] Subordinate class communities throw up their distinctive value systems more or less independently of one another; there is no 'national' subordinate value system in the way that there is a truly national or societal dominant value system. The similarity in the normative patterns of working-class communities derives largely from the similarity of the conditions they are exposed to. They generate a meaning-system which is of purely parochial significance, representing a design or living based upon localized social knowledge and face-to-face relationships. A class outlook, on the other hand, is rooted in a perception of the social order that stretches far beyond the frontiers of community. It entails a macro-social view of the reward structure and some understanding of the systematic nature of inequality. In a way, becoming class conscious, at least in the ideal-typical sense, could be likened to learning a foreign language: that is, it presents men with a new vocabulary and a new set of concepts which permit a different translation of the meaning of inequality from that encouraged by the conventional vocabulary of society. In some social settings, and for many individuals, becoming class conscious must often amount to what is virtually a normative transformation; at any rate, it draws upon a meaning-system which is far removed from that embodying accommodative or adaptive responses to the facts of subordinate status.

In certain respects, accommodation to material insecurity or deprivation betokens a kind of fatalistic pessimism. Hoggart catalogues some of the many working-class expressions indicating the necessity for making mental adjustments to material hardship: 'What is to be will be'; 'that's just the way things are'; 'grin and bear it', 'y've got to tek life as it comes'; 'it's no good moaning'; 'mek the best of it ... stick it ... soldier on ... ' etc., etc.[21] Although fatalism and the reluctant acceptance of one's lot is a prominent theme of the subordinate value system, it is by no means the only major response compatible with adaptation. A no less important element in the accommodative outlook is the 'instrumental collectivism' typified by the trade union movement. Trade unionism is one of the few forms of socio-political organization which is indigenous to the subordinate class, and yet based upon society rather than community. And, in so far as men combine in the attempt to improve their material situation they could not be said to have a purely fatalistic outlook; commitment to trade unionism implies a belief that conditions should and can be improved, which is quite different from the pessimistic resignation enshrined in the popular sayings quoted above. However, the fact that unionism is closely geared to the moral framework of the subordinate value system is reflected in the movement's aims regarding the distribution of rewards. Collective bargaining and its attendant strategies imply a general acceptance of the rules governing distribution. Organized labour directs its main efforts towards winnning a greater share of resources for its members – not by challenging the existing framework of rules but by working within this framework.

In this respect it is reasonable to regard trade unionism and instrumental collectivism generally as an accommodative response to inequality. Collective bargaining does not call into question the values underlying the existing reward structure, nor does it pose any threat to the institutions which support this structure. Trade unionism could in fact be said to stabilize the modern capitalist order by legitimizing further the rules and procedures which govern the allocation of resources. At least, the fact that many modern capitalist states give legal protection to trade unions, and social honours to their leaders, suggests that the strategies of collective bargaining do not cause serious inroads to be made into the privileges of the dominant class. It was of course on these grounds that Lenin, among others, contrasted 'trade union consciousness' with 'class consciousness', arguing that only the development of the latter could lead to genuine social and political transformation.[22]

Trade union consciousness, as one of the emergent properties of the subordinate value system, exemplifies what is perhaps the defining characteristic of this meaning-system; namely, its uneasy compromise between rejection and full endorsement of the dominant order. Put in rather broad terms, it could in fact be suggested that the subordinate value system represents what could be called a 'negotiated version' of the dominant value system. That is to say, dominant values are not so much rejected or opposed as modified by the subordinate class as a result of their social circumstances and restricted opportunities. Members of the underclass are continually exposed to the influence of dominant values by the way of the educational system, newspapers, radio and television, and the like. By virtue of the powerful institutional backing they receive these values are not readily negated by those lacking other sources of knowledge and information. However, since such values are the moral representation of the interests and opportunities of more privileged groups, their 'appropriateness' as far as the less privileged are concerned is problematic.

The tendency among the underprivileged is not to reject these values, and thus create an entirely different normative system, but to negotiate or modify them in the light of their own existential conditions. This principle of negotiating the dominant value system in response to the pressures of underclass life is similar to what Rodman has referred to as the 'lower class value stretch'.

> By the value stretch I mean that the lower class person, without abandoning the general values of the society, develops an alternative set of values ...
>
> Lower class persons in close interaction with each other and faced with similar problems do not long maintain a strong commitment to middle class values that they cannot attain, and they do not continue to respond to others in a rewarding or punishing way simply on the basis of whether these others are living up to the middle class values. In this way they need not be continually frustrated by their failure to live up to unattainable values. The resultant is a stretched value system with a low degree of commitment to all the values within the range, including the dominant middle class values. This is what I suggest as the major lower class value change, rather than a change in which the middle class values are abandoned or flouted.[23]

Rodman's formulation draws attention to the fact that the subordinate class has two distinct levels of normative reference; the dominant value system and a 'stretched' or 'negotiated' version of it. We can perhaps add to this formulation by suggesting, further, that which of the two frames of reference is actually drawn upon will be situationally determined; more specifically, it could be hypothesized that in situations where purely abstract evaluations are called for, the dominant value system will provide the moral frame of reference; but in concrete social situations involving choice and action, the negotiated version – or the subordinate value system – will provide the moral framework. It may be useful to give one or two examples in illustration of this distinction.

Values associated with occupational success and material achievement are an important element in the normative system of the dominant class. As far as the subordinate class is concerned, there seems to be some evidence that achievement values are similarly endorsed in some abstract sense, but not as guides to action in existential situations. Thus, when working-class youths are asked to specify which occupations they would like to enter if they had a completely free and Utopian choice, they frequently mention positions which rank high on the scale of material reward and social honour.[24] In other words, their 'fantasy' aspirations tend to reflect the influence of the dominant, achievement values. Their 'realistic' expectations, however, are far more modest and tend to be based on the social knowledge of restricted opportunities: that is, in situationally defined contexts the subordinate value system will be more likely to provide the appropriate frame of reference.

To take a somewhat similar example, it is a common finding of social research that industrial workers often endorse middle class criticisms of the trade unions when asked to express an opinion. Cannon reports that only 33 per cent of a sample of skilled workers disagreed with the view that the trade unions have too much power.[25] A 1969 survey found that 67 per cent of trade union respondents agreed with the statement that their leaders' activities constituted a 'threat to the prosperity of the country'.[26] At the same time, however, there is little evidence that workers are opposed to trade union action in furtherance of their own particular demands, whatever they may say in answer to questions about trade unionism in general. Attitudes tapped by opinion polls or by interviews are likely to reflect the influence of the dominant value system, since generally the questions do not specify precise situational contexts. But day-to-day experiences at the workplace are likely to be more decisive in shaping a man's views of collective bargaining and strike activity than are the abstract moral precepts of the dominant value system.

One final illustration of this normative ambivalence will suffice. This concerns popular evaluation of the occupational status order. Members of the subordinate class tend to acknowledge the status superiority of dominant class positions, and the status inferiority of subordinate class positions. It is this apparent lack of sharp disagreement between classes in the evaluation of prestige which has encouraged many sociologists to speak of a consensual status order. However, it is equally well established that those who rank low in this 'factual' status order are also prone to elevate their own particular occupation to a higher social level than it publicly enjoys; and this they do while acknowledging the subordinate status of manual work in general. In other words, when asked to evaluate positions as an abstract moral exercise, the dominant value system furnishes the primary frame of reference; but when required to evaluate their own individual social worth, by assessing their own specific occupations, members of the subordinate class are much less securely bound by the moral criteria of the dominant class. Thus there is not necessarily a logical inconsistency in the fact that subordinate class members demote the social value of manual work while at the same time excluding their own particular manual occupations from this blanket evaluation.

All this serves to highlight the significant fact that the norms underlying many aspects of subordinate class behaviour do not come to be objectified into a positively sanctioned and over-arching moral system. Subordinate values cannot be transformed into an objectivated moral system because the generating milieu of these values is typically the local underclass community; and this simply lacks the institutional power to legitimize a normative system which is sharply at odds with the dominant value system. Consequently, members of the subordinate class are constrained to accept the dominant moral framework as an abstract and perhaps somewhat idealized version of reality, although their life conditions tend to weaken its binding force in the actual conduct of affairs. It is from this tension between an abstract moral order and the situational constraints of low status that the subordinate value system emerges. It is a system of meaning which cannot oppose the orthodoxies of the dominant class, although it may neutralize them to some extent. On these grounds, it is useful to regard subordinate values as a negotiated form of dominant values, rather than as a completely differentiated normative construct.

The fact that the subordinate class tends to have two levels of normative reference, the abstract and the situational, is highly relevant to the problem posed at the beginning of this chapter: namely, whether it is more plausible to speak of a common value system shared by all classes, or a class differentiated value system. To some extent the answer will depend on the level of generality at which the inquiry is pitched. Thus, studies of working-class attitudes which rely on questions posed in general and non-situational terms are likely to produce findings which emphasize class consensus on values; this is because the dominant value system will tend to provide the moral frame of reference. Conversely, studies which specify particular social contexts of belief and action, or which rely on actual behavioural indices, are likely to find more evidence for a class differentiated value system; this is because in situational contexts of choice and action, the subordinate value system will tend to provide the moral frame of reference. It should of course be said that members of any social class are often likely to distinguish between abstract values and concrete situations. But the reason why such a distinction is particularly crucial to our understanding of subordinate class behaviour is that the moral standards and evaluations which make up the abstract framework originate within another, more powerful, social class. Members of the dominant class, on the other hand, do not take their abstract standards from a different social class, and are therefore likely to experience less serious discrepancies between institutionalized values and situational acts. Thus it is not a simple distinction between concreteness and generality which is at issue here, but also the relationship between class power and the moral framework of inequality.

It is clear from the foregoing discussion that the conditions which favour the emergence and acceptance of the subordinate meaning-system are those associated with the growth of metropolitan areas of high population density. Engels, writing of conditions in nineteenth century England, noted the role of cities and large towns in loosening the normative bonds between bourgeoisie and proletariat.

> If the centralisation of population stimulates and develops the property-holding class, it forces the development of the workers yet more rapidly. The workers begin to feel as a class, as a whole ... [Thus] ... their separation from the bourgeoisie, the development of view peculiar to the workers and corresponding to their position in life, is fostered, the consciousness of oppression awakens, and the workers attain social and political importance ... Without the great cities and their forcing influence upon the popular intelligence, the working class would be far less advanced than it is.[27]

Engels similarly noted that paternalistic relations between workers and their employers were greatly undermined by the development of mass manufacturing processes and large-scale industry. Only when the 'sentimental bond between them ... had wholly fallen away, then only did the worker begin to recognize his own interests and develop independently; then only did he cease to be the slave of the bourgeoisie in his thoughts, feelings, and the expression of his will. And to this end manufacture on a grand scale and in great cities has most largely contributed.'[28] The heavy concentration of underclass populations in homogeneous communities could be said to produce a certain 'moral density' necessary for the development of a subordinate value system. However, it should again be emphasized that this type of social setting does not generate political opposition to the dominant order. Oppositional values are the creation of political agencies based on society rather than on community and are not derivative from the subordinate value system. So let us now consider the role of such political agencies, and more specifically the mass radical party, in shaping man's perceptions of class and inequality.

The radical value system; the social source of this meaning-system is the mass political party based on the subordinate class. The party's interpretation of the reward structure draws upon a set of precepts – typically of a socialist or Marxist variety – which are fundamentally opposed to those underlying the institutions of capitalism. It thus promotes a view of the social order which is quite unlike that which finds expression in instrumental collectivism or trade union consciousness. The radical value system purports to demonstrate the systematic nature of class inequality, and attempts to reveal a connectedness between man's personal fate and the wider political order. In order that the sometimes obscure link between cause and effect may be made manifest, a new set of political concepts and symbols is introduced. Thus, the subordinate value system restricts man's consciousness to the immediacy of a localized setting; and the dominant value system encourages consciousness of a national identity; but the radical value system promotes the consciousness of class European socialist movements based on an egalitarian ideology, and having their own distinct traditions, heroes, songs, slogans, and political imagery, have created a composite political culture in which class perceptions and evaluations occupy a central place. This type of class-oriented meaning-system is an important counterweight to that of the dominant order not only in an obvious political sense, but also at an individual level. That is, attachment to the ideals of socialism can provide men with a sense of personal dignity and moral worth which is denied them by the dominant value system. Judged by the standards of the dominant class, manual workers' contributions to society are not highly regarded, and they rank relatively low in the scale of social honour. The radical value system, on the other hand, affirms the dignity of labour and accords the worker a position of honour in the hierarchy of esteem. Members of the subordinate class who endorse radical values are thus provided not merely with a certain explanatory framework for the interpretation of social facts, but also with a more favourable social identity. Oscar Lewis has suggested that where socialism becomes the dominant ideology of the society it may have a positive effect on the morale of those formerly regarded as the subordinate class. This was indicated by his study of a poor community in Cuba, before and after the Revolution. Lewis found that in the post-revolutionary situation:

> The physical aspect of the slum had changed very little, except for a beautiful new nursery school. It was clear that the people were still desperately poor, but I found much less of the despair, apathy and hopelessness which are so diagnostic of urban slums in the culture of poverty. They expressed great confidence in their leaders and hope for a better life in the future. The slum itself was now highly organized, with block committees, educational committees, party committees. The people had a new sense of power and importance. They were armed and were given a doctrine which glorified the lower class as the hope of humanity.[29]

So far as Western capitalist societies are concerned, there seems to be a considerable range of variation in the extent to which radical values are disseminated among the subordinate class. The United States, for example, is one of the few industrial societies lacking a mass working-class party; and partly as a result of this, radical or class interpretations of inequality are not an important element in the normative make-up of that society. In France and Italy, on the other hand, political class consciousness is much more marked, partly because the mass working-class parties in these countries continue to espouse radical doctrines. Elsewhere in Europe, and particularly where Social Democrats form the mass working-class party, there seems to have been a long-term trend towards de-radicalization. Although at present it is only possible to speculate on the outcome of this trend, it seems quite likely that it could have a decisive effect on the political perceptions of the subordinate class. It seems plausible to suggest that if socialist parties ceased to present a radical, class-oriented meaning-system to their supporters, then such an outlook would not persist of its own accord among the subordinate class. Once the mass party of the underclass comes to endorse fully the values and institutions of the dominant class, there remain no major sources of political knowledge and information which would enable the subordinate class to make sense of their situaiton in radical terms.

This is really to assert that the mass party has a potentially more formative influence on the political perceptions and understanding of the subordinate class than is generally acknowledged. All too frequently it is assumed that the party's doctrines on issues related to inequality are in some sense an expression of its supporters' evaluations of these issues. Thus, a decline in the party's radicalism tends to be explained as the outcome of changing attitudes among its supporters, to which the party must respond. However, this approach may overestimate the extent to which political perceptions are formed independently of the party. Once established among the subordinate class, the radical mass party is able to provide its supporters with political cues, signals, and information of a very different kind from those made available by the dominant culture. To a considerable degree workers may look to their party for political guidance in the attempt to make sense of their social world. They themselves have relatively little access to knowledge, so that the political cues provided by their own mass party are of key importance to their general perception of events and issues. As Philip Converse has pointed out:

> Unless an issue directly concerns ... [uneducated lower strata] ... in an obviously rewarding or punishing way ... they lack the contextual grasp of the system to recognize how they should respond to it without being told by elites who hold their confidence ... If a communication gets through and they absorb it, they are most willing

to behave 'ideologically' in ways that will further the interests of their group.[30]

To see the party simply as a receptacle for the political views of its supporters is really to underestimate its potential influence in shaping the social consciousness of the subordinate class and in providing its members with a distinctive moral framework for interpreting social reality. If, as so many observers suggest, there has occurred a marked decline in working-class radicalism in the post-war period, this may be due at least as much to changes in the nature of the party as to changes among its supporters. Some of the factors associated with de-radicalization are examined in the next chapter; but what is of immediate relevance here is the possible long-term effect this may have on the normative aspects of stratification.

It was suggested at the beginning of this chapter that one way of conceiving the normative side of inequality was in terms of a number of different meaning-systems. Three such meaning-systems – the dominant, subordinate, and radical – were held to be of special significance in understanding the attitudes and responses to inequality on the part of the subordinate class. These three systems of meaning, each presenting social reality in a different light, are all to be found within the subordinate class in varying degrees. Put in metaphorical terms, the overall meaning-system of the subordinate class could be likened to a kind of 'reservoir' fed by three major 'normative streams', each flowing from a different 'institutional source'. Attitudes towards the social order held by any given members of this class would be likely to reflect the influences of this normative mix, rather than the kind or rigorous intellectual consistency which would be produced through exposure to only one major meaning-system. At the same time, we should expect to find patterned variations in a man's social outlook to be associated with differences in the degree of his exposure to the three meaning-systems in question. The implication of all this is that the general structure of attitudes towards inequality is likely to undergo a significant change if the radical value system should cease to be part of the overall normative complex. In terms of our metaphor, the reservoir of meaning would be seriously diluted if the normative stream represented by the radical value system should run dry at its source – namely, the mass working-class party.

One likely consequence of such an occurrence is that the subordinate value system would increasingly provide the frame-work of social meaning among the working class. That is, interpretations of, and responses to, class inequalities would probably be weighted more heavily in the direction of adaptation and accommodation. The realities of class would continue to be highly salient to man's construction of his social world; but the responses to these realities would be bounded by the moral categories of the underclass community and the instrumental collectivism of the trade union movement. This would promote an image of the reward structure in terms of a division between 'them' and 'us', in which certain limited gains could be made through bargaining techniques; but it would not promote an alternative moral view of society nor principled opposition to the subordinate status of the working class.

To accept the possibility that socialist parties might cease to be a major source of radical values is certainly not to claim that such values would then be expunged from the political culture. It seems altogether likely that they would continue to influence the outlook of certain groups, such as intellectuals and students, as well as small parties on the political fringe. But the decisive question here is the strength of the social links between these groups, the intellectuals in particular, and the subordinate class. Historically, of course, the system of values we call socialism was developed mainly by western intellectuals who then disseminated it among the industrial workers. As Kautsky pointed out in a celebrated passage:

> The vehicle of science is not the proletariat, but the *bourgeois intelligentsia*: it was in the minds of individual members of this stratum that modern Socialism originated, and it was they who communicated it to the more intellectually developed proletarians who, in their turn introduce it into the proletarian class struggle where conditions allow that to be done. Thus, socialist consciousness is something introduced into the proletarian class struggle from without and not something that arose within it spontaneously.[31]

If the radical value system continued to flourish among the intellectuals, they could, it might be argued, repeat the same task of political indoctrination described by Kautsky. However, it is important to bear in mind that intellectuals tend not to be successful in influencing workers unless there are strong institutional links between them. In nineteenth-century Europe those links were provided by the mass party. It was through the medium of the party that the radical intelligentsia were able to broadcast the ideas of socialism and so exert a powerful influence on the outlook of the industrial working class. In western societies today, however, radical intellectuals do not have the same degree of access to socialist parties; consequently there are now few, if any, institutional links between the socialist intelligentsia and the workers, so that the former's political influence on the latter is minimal. The de-radicalization of the party typically leaves the radical intellectuals politically isolated, as exemplified by the case of the New Left in various western societies.

B

Intellectuals, or students, may attempt to forge independent links with workers, but these tend to be fragile and short-lived. It would seem that the mass party is one of the very few social agencies which has the potential to condition the outlook of the working class in a radical direction. If, for whatever reason, it chooses not to utilize this potential, then we might expect a gradual de-radicalization of the working class to set in.

De-radicalization is not of course to be equated with the acceptance or moral endorsement of existing inequality. Resentments over the distribution of rewards are likely to persist, even in the midst of affluence. What this could mean is that the tensions generated by inequality would be directed into non-political channels. In particular, certain forms of 'subcultural deviance' might be expected to flourish more readily among groups which are both relatively deprived and de-politicized. Apolitical 'deviance' would perhaps be most likely to occur among those members of the subordinate class who fall outside the orbit of the organized labour movement. Unionized workers are able to accommodate themselves to the reward system through the collective bargaining process; and, as the American experience shows, this process is not impaired by the absence of a mass radical party or class ideology. But for those numerous groups which lack access to formal bargaining agencies, personal adjustment to the facts of low status may be somewhat more problematic.

References

1 ENGELS, F. (1892) *The Condition of the Working Class in England in 1844*, London, p. 124.
2 KLEIN, J. (1965) *Samples from English Culture*, London.
3 HAMILTON, R.F. 'Affluence and the Worker: The West German Case', *American Journal of Sociology*, September 1965, p. 152.
4 MILLER, W.B. 'Lower Class Culture as a Generating Milieu of Gang Delinquency', *Journal of Social Issues* (14), No. 3, 1958, p. 6.
5 HYMAN, H.H. 'The Value Systems of Different Classes', in BENDIX, R. and LIPSET, S.M. (1953) *Class Status and Power*, Glencoe.
6 PARSONS, T. (1951) *The Social System*, London.
7 MERTON, R.K. *Social Theory and Social Structure*, Glencoe.
8 MAYER, K.B. (1955) *Class and Society*, New York, p. 41.
9 Cf. ALMOND, G. and VERBA, S. (1963) *The Civic Culture*, Princeton.
10 McKENZIE, R. and SILVER, A. (1968) *Angels in Marble*, London; NORDLINGER, E. (1967) *Working Class Tories*, London.
11 McKENZIE and SILVER, *op. cit.*, p. 249.

12 LOCKWOOD, D. 'Sources of Variation in Working Class Images of Society', *Sociological Review*, November 1966, p. 254.

13 LIPSET, S.M. *The First New Nation*, London, 1964, pp. 110 *passim*.

14 KLEIN, *op. cit.*

15 HOGGART, R. (1958) *The Uses of Literacy*, London: (Pelican edition) p. 92.

16 DAHRENDORF, R. (1959) *Class and Class Conflict in Industrial Society*, London.

17 NEWTON, K. (1969) *The Sociology of British Communism*, London, p. 60.

18 *Ibid.*, p. 62.

19 HOGGART, *op. cit.*, p. 82.

20 WESTERGAARD, J.H. 'The Withering Away of Class: A Contemporary Myth', in *Towards Socialism*, London, 1965, pp. 107–8.

21 HOGGART, *op. cit.*, p. 92.

22 LENIN, V.I. 'What is to be Done?', *Collected Works*, Vol. I, Part I, Moscow, 1950.

23 RODMAN, H. 'The Lower Class Value Stretch', *Social Forces*, 1963, p. 209.

24 WILSON, M. D. 'The Vocational Preferences of Secondary Modern School Children', *British Journal of Educational Psychology*, June and November, 1953; STEPHENSON, R. M. 'Mobility Orientation and Stratification of 1,000 Ninth Graders', *American Sociological Review*, April 1957.

25 CANNON, I.C. 'Ideology and Occupational Comunity', *Sociology*, May 1967, p. 168.

26 Reported in *The Sunday Times*, 31 August 1969, p. 2.

27 ENGELS, *op. cit.*, p. 122.

28 *Ibid.*, p. 123.

29 LEWIS, O. (1968) *A Study of Slum Culture*, New York, p. 14.

30 CONVERSE, P.E. 'The Nature of Belief Systems in Mass Publics', in APTER, D. E. *Ideology and Discontent*, Glencoe, 1964, p. 216.

31 Cited in LENIN, *op. cit.*, p. 243.

1.2   Social inequality and social integration in modern Britain[1]

John H. Goldthorpe

The overall extent and pattern of social inequality in modern Britain has been recently reviewed by a number of writers[2] and research is providing a steady flow of new information on particular aspects of this inequality. I shall not attempt here to add to this detailed knowledge, nor to produce any new synthesis of the information that exists. I wish simply to make three points about the general nature of social inequality before turning to the problem with which my paper will be centrally concerned: that is, the problem of the *implications* of inequality for social integration. The three points are the following.

1   Social inequality, in societies such as ours, is manifested in a very wide variety of ways – wider than is usually recognized in public discussion of the matter. For example, inequalities in economic resources tend, relatively speaking, to receive a fair amount of attention. The finding reported by Meade that 5 per cent of the population own 75 per cent of all personal wealth[3] has figured quite frequently in recent political argument, as have data on the number of households whose members could be regarded as living in poverty – on incomes, say, below the 'National Assistance' level.[4] But far less is heard of the further marked inequalities that are involved in the ways in which economic rewards are actually gained – most importantly, in the content of work tasks and roles. There is, however, by now ample evidence to show that wide differences exist between occupations and jobs in the extent to which they offer possibilities of intrinsic satisfaction to the individuals engaged in them or, on the other hand, are a source of psychological or social deprivation.[5] To take an obvious contrast, the inequalities in reward between professional employment and factory work are clearly not confined to the differences in their income levels.

Again, one aspect of inequality in work which has of late been somewhat fashionable to point to, and to decry, is that of the status differences which

---

Source: *Advancement of Science* (1969,) 26 (128), pp. 190–202.

operate among different categories of employee in most industrial organizations; for instance, in such matters as methods of payment, 'clocking-in' and lateness rules, toilet, canteen or car-parking arrangements, and so on. But discussion of these questions has usually been carried on without any reference to the far more basic inequality represented by the steep gradient of authority within such organizations – which, in fact, status distinctions serve largely to symbolize.

The tendency here illustrated to conceive of inequality in a piecemeal manner, rather than as a multiform and pervasive phenomenon, results, I would argue, from a failure to appreciate in what, fundamentally, social inequality consists. This leads me to my second point.

2   Social inequality in all its manifestations can be thought of as involving differences in social power and advantage: power being defined as the capacity to mobilize resources (human and non-human) in order to bring about a desired state of affairs; and advantage as the possession of, or control over, whatever in society is valued and scarce. Power and advantage are thus closely related. Power can be used to secure advantage, while certain advantages constitute the resources that are used in the exercise of power. Moreover, different forms of power and advantage tend in their very nature to be convertible: economic resources can be used to gain status or to establish authority; status can help to reinforce authority or to create economic opportunities; positions of authority usually confer status and command high economic rewards, and so on.

In this perspective, then, the way in which inequality structures virtually the whole of social life can be readily understood. Differences in social power and advantage, simply because they imply differences across the whole range of life-chances, always tend, other things being equal, to become generalized differences. Furthermore, it is important to add that this effect operates not only from one area of social life to another but also through time. Inequalities of condition at any one point in time create inequalities of opportunity for future achievement. For example, the intergenerational aspects of this phenomenon could be said to constitute the central problem thus far for the sociology of education. The results of research in this field provide impressive evidence of how, notably through the agency of the family, the stability of social strata tends to be maintained – despite the growing importance of education to career chances and the development of policies aimed at reducing non-academic influences on educational attainment.[6]

3   It has, therefore, to be recognized that structures of social inequality of both condition and opportunity – or, in other words, systems of social stratification – are inherently highly resistant to change. The members of higher strata have the motivation and in general the resources to hold on to

their position and to transmit it to their children, while the members of lower strata are often caught up in vicious circles of deprivation. This is not, of course, to suggest that change in stratification systems cannot, or does not, occur; but rather than any significant reduction in the degree of inequality will require purposive, well-designed and politically forceful action to this end – that it is unlikely to come about simply as the unsought for consequence of technological advance, economic growth, or any such like secular trends.[7] Such developments may well modify certain forms of inequality; but they appear just as likely to accentuate others.

Indeed, far from industrial societies having 'built-in' processes which steadily diminish inequality – as some writers have claimed – what is striking, at least in the British case, is the frequently very limited effect of even the deliberate pursuit of equality through governmental action. For example, as already implied, the egalitarian aspects of educational policy over the last half century or so have resulted in only a very slight lessening in class differentials in educational opportunity – despite the fact that over the same period an enormous expansion of educational facilities has occurred.[8] In a similar way, major improvements in medical services and general standards of health have failed over a long period to produce any appreciable reduction in relative class differentials in infant mortality and in many kinds of morbidity.[9] And finally in this respect it may be noted that inequalities in incomes, after being somewhat diminished in the war and immediate post-war period, subsequently stabilized and then from around 1950 appear, if anything, to have widened again.[10]

In sum, one may say that social inequality, as observed in present-day Britain, takes the general form of a substantially self-maintaining structure of social groupings differentiated multifariously and often extremely in terms of the power and advantage that their members enjoy. What, then, are the consequences of this inequality for the integration of British society; that is to say, for the extent to which the actions of individuals and groups tend regularly to comply with recognized norms, and to be thus consistent with, rather than in conflict with or unrelated to, the expectations and actions of other individuals and groups?[11]

This question, in certain of its aspects, has in fact been examined by a number of recent writers, who have adopted a similar initial approach. They have started from the observation that in Britain considerable and abiding inequality does not apparently give rise to deeply divisive conflicts in which the existing social structure, political institutions included, is frequently and fundamentally called into question. They have then gone on to infer from this, not unreasonably, that the resentment of inequality among the less favoured sections of the population is neither particularly widespread nor particularly militant – and especially if comparisons are made with the situation in certain other societies. Thus, the somewhat more specific problem which emerges from this approach is the following: why is it that, given the prevailing degree of social inequality, there is no widely supported and radical opposition to the existing socio-political order, and that at all levels of the stratification hierarchy attitudes of acceptance, if not of approval, are those most commonly found? At this point, analyses tend to divide into two main types which one might conveniently label 'social psychological' and 'culturalist'. The first type is best displayed in the work of Runciman.[12]

Briefly, Runciman's argument is that to account for the discrepancy between the objective degree of inequality in British society and the actual awareness and resentment of this inequality, we must consider the 'reference groups' in terms of which individuals in the lower social strata assess their position. That is to say, we must consider the other groups in society – real or imagined – with which members of less favoured groups habitually compare themselves in evaluating their rewards, opportunities and social deserts generally, and in relation to which their expectations and aspirations are formed. If, for instance, the reference groups adopted by a certain membership group are located fairly closely in the stratification hierarchy to the membership group's own position, then the degree of felt inequality is likely to be quite slight, no matter what the overall range of factual inequality may be. A strong sense of grievance is only to be expected if reference groups are selected in a more 'ambitious' way so that considerable inequality is perceived and is then, on the basis of the comparison made, regarded as illegitimate and unjust. In other words, the degree of relative deprivation – deprivation which is subjectively experienced and which may thus influence political behaviour – is primarily determined *by the structure of reference groups* rather than by the structure of inequality itself as the sociologist might describe it.

Runciman's own research, using both historical and survey methods, indicates that among the British working class reference groups are, and generally have been, restricted in scope; and that while some variation in this respect can be traced over time and from one form of inequality to another, no consistent trend is evident towards wider-ranging comparisons. Consequently, the disruptive potential that social inequality might be thought to hold remains in fact suppressed: social integration is furthered through perceptual and conceptual limitations.

Turning secondly to the 'culturalist' type of analysis, it should be said that this has been chiefly elaborated by American social scientists interested in the question of the social bases of stable and effective democracy.[13] In treating Britain as one of the relatively few countries whose polity might be thus described, these investigators have been led to examine – with differing degrees of directness – such issues as the following: Why among lower social strata in Britain is there not far more alienation from a political system which is élitist in itself and under which many other forms of inequality persist? Why is there no longer in Britain, if indeed there ever was, a powerful class-based social movement seeking radical structural changes of an egalitarian kind, and prepared if necessary to challenge existing political institutions in pursuit of its objectives?

In the explanations that are offered for the absence of these possible threats to stable democracy, major emphasis is laid on the nature of British 'political culture'; that is, on the pattern or 'mix' of attitudes which research has shown to exist in British society towards political institutions and political life in general. Like other countries in which democracy flourishes, the argument runs, Britain has, in the course of her historical development, built up a political culture of a distinctive type. It is one characterized primarily by the balance that holds, even across lines of class and party, between participant, activist attitudes on the one hand and acquiescent, passive attitudes on the other; between emotional commitment to political principle and cool pragmatism; between consensus on matters of procedure and conflict over particular issues.

Through their socialization into this culture from childhood onwards, it is held that the majority of citizens come to feel a sense of unfanatical, but generally unquestioning, allegiance to the established political order, and one that is unlikely to be seriously disturbed by any grievances they may have over the distribution of social power and advantage. Such grievances do not lead to alienation from the political system since there is wide acceptance of the 'democratic myth' – the myth that the individual can influence political decisions and outcomes – and the system itself is not therefore seen as exploitive. Moreover, attitudes towards the poltical élite tend to be ones of trust, if not of deference, and the exercise of government authority is generally accepted as legitimate. For example, in one study survey data are presented to show that manual workers who believe that there are inordinately powerful groups in British society (such as 'big business') are as much prepared to allow government a wide sphere of authority as are workers who do not share in this belief.[14] In other words, grievances arising out of inequality do not tend to become so highly politicized that established political institutions and processes are themselves challenged. Political awareness is in any case at only a moderate level, and politics is only rarely a central life interest. Consequently, the availability of the ordinary citizen for involvement in 'unstabilizing' mass movements is low; the political culture effectively inhibits the radical political action which marked social inequality might otherwise be expected to generate.

Clearly, social psychological and culturalist points of view on the issue in question are not incompatible: they could, rather, be represented as complementary and mutually supportive on the following lines. Because the reference groups of lower strata have remained generally restricted, political issues stemming from social inequality have tended to be relatively 'mild' and capable of being resolved or accommodated by existing poltical arrangements. This has, therefore, helped a basically 'allegiant' political culture to form. Reciprocally, the development of such a culture has been inimical to the spread of ideological thinking – as, say, on the matter of social justice – which could lead both to a heightened awareness of inequality and deprivation, and to greater recognition of their political dimensions.[15] In short social psychological processes of the kind examined by Runciman could be seen as a necessary condition of the political culture of British democracy, while this culture in turn, once established, favours the persistence of these processes.

Despite the various criticisms with which they have met, the analyses I have reviewed do, in my opinion, go some important part of the way to explaining why the consequences of inequality in Britain are not socially divisive in an extreme degree. But what has to be kept in mind, and what I wish here to emphasize, is that for the most part these analyses treat the problem of inequality and integration only from one particular angle. As I earlier noted, the focus of interest is on the possible political implications of inequality; and what is in effect illumined is chiefly the question of why among the British working class there is found no significant support for political ideas and movements of a revolutionary cast, nor even the widespread *incivisme* which characterizes sections of, say, the French or Italian working class. However, there are other major aspects of the problem which may be distinguished, and ones which have been curiously neglected. In particular, I would advance the view – as the central thesis of this paper – that the most far-reaching implications of inequality for the integration of British society occur not in the political sphere but rather in that of economic life; and that they are manifested not in a situation of fundamental class struggle but rather in a situation of anomie; that is, in a situation in which, to stay close to the original Durkheimian notion, there is a lack of moral regulation over the wants and goals that individuals hold. This contention can best be elaborated by reference to two closely related topics of current public concern: industrial relations and incomes policy.

In a recent paper – entitled 'The Reform of Collective Bargaining: from Donovan to Durkheim' – two leading authorities, Fox and Flanders, have in fact argued explicitly and at length that the British system of industrial relations is now in an anomic state.[16] In the post-war period, these authors observe, the wants, expectations and aspirations of industrial workers have expanded notably, and not only in regard to wage levels but also in such matters as security of employment, job rights and control over work organization. At the same time, generally high levels of employment have given many groups of workers the power to pursue their new goals with some effectiveness. A frequent outcome has then been that such groups have broken through the regulation of work relationships imposed by collective agreements at a national level and have secured agreements of a more favourable kind at company, plant or shop level. Thus, Fox and Flanders argue, industrial relations have become disordered in two main ways: first, as a result of the problems involved in developing new normative systems, capable of accommodating the new issues of industrial conflict which now arise; and second, and more seriously, because the solutions arrived at have tended to be *ad hoc* and piecemeal ones of only limited, local application. This tendency has therefore given rise to a proliferation of normative systems based on often unrelated or divergent principles; and such a situation is one rife with anomalies, frustrations and rivalries which constantly generate new tensions and conflicts both between employers and workers and between different sets of workers: 'Disorder feeds upon disorder.' The consequences of this anomic state are then to be seen not simply in strikes and other dislocations of the productive process, but further 'in such things as chaotic pay differentials and uncontrolled movements of earnings and labour costs'. Thus, it is claimed, threats are posed to the long-term development of the economy (apart from the aggravation of short-term balance of payments problems) and there could, furthermore, be serious political implications: increasing disorder might generate popular demands for state intervention of an authoritarian kind which would mark the end of the present pluralistic and voluntary basis of industrial relations.

The analysis offered by Fox and Flanders is insightful and important. However, I would suggest that it is one that does not go far enough in revealing just how deeply rooted in the structure of British society is the 'disorderly' situation with which it is concerned; and, further, that this limitation results precisely from the fact that Fox and Flanders do not follow Durkheim in relating the problem of anomie to the problem of inequality. This argument can best be illustrated by reference to their recommendations for reform in industrial relations – that is, for the 'reconstruction of normative order'. Briefly, what they stress is the continuing need for an incomes policy, accompanied by the regularizing and rationalizing of collective bargaining from plant and company level upwards. In this latter respect, they point to the availability and usefulness of such tenchniques as productivity bargaining and job evaluation and other means of measuring and rewarding different kinds of work. Through a programme of reform on the lines in question, they see the possibility of achieving a more logical wages structure, greater control over earnings and labour costs, and industrial relations institutions which, through being more adaptable to change themselves, will be better able to manage the conflicts that change inevitably produces.

Fox and Flanders recognize that there is no guarantee that such objectives will in fact be achieved, and they refer to the 'Promethean character' of the task of reform. None the less, I would argue that they still underestimate the difficulties that are involved: in particular, in creating an area of relatively rational and orderly inequality in place of the present 'wages jungle' when this jungle is simply part of a wider structure of inequality which has no rationale whatsoever − other, perhaps, than the principle of 'to them that have shall more be given'. For example, at one point in their paper Fox and Flanders remark that 'The debate on incomes policy is often conducted within the trade union movement as if collective bargaining were simply a mechanism for pursuing social justice as between capital and labour, and its function of determining the relative fortunes of different groups of labour is ignored.' This may be fair comment, but it is still highly questionable if an incomes policy of the kind they favour can be effective in establishing a less chaotic and more equitable pattern of earnings *within* the working class in the context of the overall degree of economic inequality which statistics on the distribution of income and wealth reveal. An industrial worker seeking a wage increase might be prepared to recognize that his claim was weak in comparison with that of, say, certain of his lower-paid workmates; but he would have no difficulty in finding other groups, possibly outside the working class, in relation to whom his claim could be much better justified − even assuming that his range of reference groups was not extensive. Moreover, it should be emphasized here that while restricted reference groups may inhibit feelings of grievance over inequalities, this is not to say that they actually motivate individuals to hold back from attempting to improve their position, especially economically: limited social horizons are not, as Durkheim might have put it, a source of moral restraint.[17]

Now it must be said that Fox and Flanders are well aware − indeed, they emphasize − that the normative regulation resulting from collective bargaining is unlikely ever to rest purely upon consensus; it will also be a product of the balance of power between the parties concerned and that their calculation of what for the time being, is the most advantageous position they can achieve. What may further be involved, at least in initiating any reform, is some kind of third party intervention − 'the forceful articulation of common norms by some authoritative source'. However, to follow Durkheim's argument closely here, one has to insist that in so far as the normative order in economic life is not based upon consensus, but is rather founded upon coercion or expediency, then the threat of anomie and of chronic malintegration remains – no matter what degree of internal logic or coherence normative systems may be given. For as Durkheim stresses, unless in modern society the regulation of economic life – and, crucially, the regulation of inequality – does have some accepted moral basis, then it is unlikely to be effective in any continuing way. To the extent that the normative order is imposed by superior power, fundamental discontent and unrest persist if only in latent form; to the extent that it results from the calculation of advantage under given (non-moral) constraints, it is likely to be called into question as soon as these constraints vary.[18]

Thus, while proposals for reform of the kind that Fox and Flanders put forward might well endow collective bargaining institutions and procedures with a good deal more formal rationality than they at present possess, I find it difficult to believe that such measures could go very far towards ensuring stable normative systems, of either a substantive or a procedural kind, at any level of industrial relations. The absence of an accepted moral basis for economic life as a whole in our kind of society must always render precarious the forms which at any time prevail in any specific area – a plant, company, industry, etc. As but one illustration of this point, taken from Durkheim's own discussion of the problem, one may consider the implications of inequalities of opportunity for attitudes towards inequalities of condition. If the former are extreme and without effective legitimation, little consensus can be expected on the latter – even supposing that some hierarchy of social positions and roles is generally acknowledged. For, as Durkheim argued, 'it would be of little avail for everyone to recognize the justice of the hierarchy of functions as established by public opinion, if they did not also consider just the way in which individuals are recruited to these functions'.[19] While ever, then, British society is characterized by the present marked degree of inequality in educational and occupational opportunity, it is difficult to see that there is any basis for the achievement of what Fox and Flanders regard as the ultimate objective of industrial relations reform; namely, 'agreed normative codes regulating the production and distribution of wealth in modern industrial society' – or, at all events, agreement will for the majority remain highly qualified, reluctant or uncertain, and thus inherently unstable. One need not assume that rank-and-file industrial employees resent the inferior life-chances they have been accorded as keenly as the facts might warrant.[20]

My conclusion must then be that the reconstruction of normative order in British industrial relations which Fox anf Flanders pursue is something of an *ignis fatuus*. Within a society in which inequality exists as brute fact

– largely without moral legitimation – 'disorderly' industrial relations cannot, I think, be understood as a particular pathological development which will yield to particular remedies: rather, to maintain a Durkheimian perspective, this disorder must be seen as 'normal' – as a generalized characteristic of societies of the type in question.[21]

The structural features of British society which stand in the way of the reform of industrial relations are at the same time obstructive, as the foregoing discussion would imply, to the effective administration of an incomes policy. The aim of an incomes policy, within a market economy such as our own, is usually stated to be that of controlling the growth of incomes so that inflationary tendencies may be kept in check while still preserving relatively high levels of employment and utilized capacity.[22] However, it is essential to appreciate that an incomes policy is not, and cannot be, just another economic instrument – despite the attempt of certain technocratically minded economists to present it in this guise. Once a government attempts to regulate incomes, in no matter how piecemeal or partial a fashion, it is forced into the position of arbiter on particular wage levels or wage changes, and issues of social justice thus inevitably arise and have in some way or other to be resolved. Indeed, government spokesmen in Britain have been generally prepared to acknowledge this situation and even to claim that an incomes policy is, or could be, a means of enhancing social justice; for example, by ensuring a better deal for the lowest-paid workers. But, I would argue, it is basically on account of this normative aspect of incomes policy that its administration runs into serious problems, which have not as yet been overcome, and which may, for reasons I shall shortly suggest, be self-aggravating ones.

At the root of the difficulty is again the fact that not only is the existing distribution of income and wealth in British society unprincipled – in the strict sense of the word – but further that there appears to be little consensus on the principles which ought to apply when it is a question of maintaining or altering any specific income level or relativity. Survey data are of some relevance to this argument,[23] but more significant is the great variety of frequently conflicting considerations which are actually invoked when pay issues are debated. Some criteria, for example, would entail at least the possibility of significant change in the existing pay structure – increased productivity, job evaluation ratings, 'absolutely' low wages or persisting manpower shortages: but others, such as increases in the cost of living, the need to preserve a differential or maintain the social status of a particular group, are essentially conservative in their implications. Moreover, as Professor (now Lady) Wootton has pointed out, claims for more pay based on any of these often conflicting criteria can be, and usually are, couched in moral terms, or at any rate the economic arguments are related back to moral premises.[24] Thus, one is again forced to the conclusion that little basis for moral restraint is currently to be found in British society – that, in other words, a condition of anomie prevails. Given the diversity of moral positions that are tenable in the existing state of public opinion, virtually any occupational group seeking a pay increase is likely to be able to find some kind of legitimation for pressing its case.[25]

From this standpoint, then, it is to be expected that the amount of 'voluntary' support for an incomes policy will be insufficient to enable it to achieve its ends; and such an expectation seems to be generally in accord with British (and other) experience. Furthermore, even when control over incomes is in some way or other 'imposed', it still appears difficult, at least within the constraints on governmental authority that liberal democracy entails, for such control to be very effective for very long. A 'norm' for pay increases may hold up for a short-run period and even a complete 'freeze' may work under crisis conditions – as in Britain, in 1966–7. But in the longer term control seems invariably to break down, most notably at the level at which coercive methods are least feasible – that is, at the grass-roots level of the individual enterprise.[26] A tendency for the actual earnings of many groups of workers to rise above the intended norm, as a result of collective agreements or other less formal arrangements locally made, has to be reckoned as the besetting problem of incomes policy administration – and even, it seems, in 'centrally planned' economies such as that of the USSR.[27]

Thus, as one economist, John Corina, has recently pointed out, 'the unpalatable facts of wage drift', once recognized, pose a hard dilemma so far at any rate as Britain is concerned. Either an attempt must be made to extend the range and increase the stringency of income control, to the point at which voluntary collective bargaining ceases to exist, and at risk of building up a considerable pressure of opposition; or it must be accepted that, under existing conditions, incomes policy initiatives are inherently unstable in their effects, and that their progressive breakdown is to be anticipated as a matter of course. Unlike some of his colleagues, Corina is prepared to recognize that 'at bottom, the crucial tangles of incomes policy stem from the intangible concept of "social justice" in income distribution', and are inseparable from issues raised both by the existing structure of inequality and by the lack of accord on what form this structure should possess. As he pertinently asks, ' ... how can incomes policy create consent where social valuations of incomes, within a given incomes distribution, are confused and often obscure?'[28]

Moreover, one point which Corina does not consider is that attempts to implement incomes policy may have quite unforeseen consequences which in fact tend to build up the difficulties involved. It is not simply that a 'freeze' or period of tight control over incomes may be followed by heightened militancy in wage demands, threatening greater inflationary problems than before.[29] There is a further, yet more awkward, possibility: namely, that through increasing information about, and interest in, differences between occupational rewards and conditions, the actual operation of an incomes policy will serve to broaden comparative reference groups among the mass of the population, and at the same time bring issues of equity and fairness into greater subjective salience.[30] Thus, following Runciman's analysis, one would expect, in the case of the working class at least, a growing sense of resentment and grievance over the *status quo* and, in turn, a yet greater unwillingness to accept 'restraint' or to hold back in any way from the direct pursuit of their own maximum advantage. In other words, what are sometimes called the 'educative' functions of incomes policy may well have the effect of undermining the viability of such policy. To the extent that evaluations of income and other economic differences do become less confused and obscure, there is little reason to suppose that what will emerge will be greater consensus from one group or stratum to another: the far more likely outcome, given the prevailing degree of inequality, is that conflicts will become more clearly defined and more widely recognized – that the anomic state of economic life will be made increasingly manifest.

To recapitulate, then, my two central arguments have been the following: first, that social inequality in Britain appears to pose no direct threat to the stability of the political order – because this is, as it were, 'insulated' from the potentially disruptive consequences of inequality by a combination of social-psychological and cultural influences; but second, that the existence of inequality, of an extreme, unyielding and largely illegitimate kind, does militate seriously against any stable normative regulation in the economic sphere – because it militates against the possibility of effective value consensus on the distribution of economic, and other, resources and rewards.

Of these two arguments, it is, I imagine, the latter that will be the more likely to provoke dissent, and chiefly perhaps among social scientists with 'applied' interests in the field of industrial and economic policy; for it obviously suggests that much of their present endeavour will meet with relatively little success. However, as a way both of rounding off this argument and leading on to my own, concluding, observations on policy issues, I would like to draw attention to one further point – somewhat obvious but often neglected – with implications that may be still more unwelcome to those colleagues in question. This is the point that, in spite of frequent attempts, it has not proved possible to give a satisfactory explanation of the persisting degree and form of inequality, in Britain or in any advanced society, by reference primarily to 'external' constraints, and without reference to the purposive exercise of their power and advantage by more privileged groups and strata. In other words, it has not proved possible to explain social inequality otherwise than as a structure with important self-maintaining properties.

For example, attempts to relate social inequality or particular aspects of it – say, in incomes – to differences in the so-called 'natural' attributes of individuals have repeatedly failed; and chiefly because social variation is regularly found to be of a different order of magnitude from natural variation. In advanced societies the dispersion of even earned income has a proportionate range of as wide as 50 or perhaps 100 to 1: no conceivably relevant natural attribute has been shown to vary to such an extent.[31] Again, it is by now evident enough that established structures of inequality yield little to explanation in terms simply of the operation of 'impersonal' market forces – in terms, that is, of the interaction of supply and demand in regard to different types of labour service. Labour economists themselves, as much as educational sociologists, have demonstrated the considerable restrictions that occur on the 'supply' side, as a result of various forms of inequality of opportunity. Consequently, the existence of the essentially 'non-competing groups' which social strata form distorts the labour market into a highly imperfect condition; and the 'imperfections' themselves lie outside the scope of pure economic analysis.[32] Finally, one should note, attempts by sociologists to revamp classical economics in the guise of 'functional' theories of social stratification have scarcely been convincing. Even if one leaves aside the basic problems of how to determine the functional exigencies of a social system or the relative functional importance of positions and roles within it, a logical limitation of such theories must still be stressed: that is, they are adequate only to explaining why some degree of social inequality should occur – not why the actual pattern of inequality is as it is.[33]

In short, then, one may assert that attempts to account for observable social inequality in terms simply of constraints, whether stemming from genetics, economics or 'societal' imperatives, are at best of very limited value. Through their very inadequacies, such attempts point to the degree to which the phenomenon of social stratification must be seen as an autonomous one: as a phenomenon which has to be explained largely as the outcome of social action and interaction in the form of competition and conflict, the basis for which being always the inequality in power and advantage previously existing.

This being so, there are, I think, two implications of note. First, since prevailing patterns of inequality cannot be represented as the direct consequence of ineluctable exigencies, it is hard to see how they can be 'scientifically' legitimated as necessary features, either of the human condition in general or of the functioning of a particular type of society. In itself, of course, this fact is unlikely to be of much significance for the attitudes towards social inequality which are actually held among the population at large: it seems probable that inequality is indeed quite widely accepted as deriving either from 'natural' differences or from (what sociologists would call) 'functional imperatives'.[34] But this situation then points to the second implication which I see as important. Namely, that when concerned with problems arising out of competition and conflict, such as those found in economic life, applied social scientists must seriously ask themselves whether they do not have an obligation to state, clearly and insistently, that the context of inequality in which these problems typically exist is neither unalterable nor indisputably desirable, and need not, therefore, be taken as a 'given'. In other words, they must consider whether they are not obliged to emphasize what they know about the nature of social inequality, including its self-perpetuating but 'man-made' characteristics, and thus try to redress a situation in which, as Runciman has put it, 'from the moment almost of birth, attitudes to the social structure are conditioned by pressures in which the ideal of social justice plays little if any part'.[35]

If applied social scientists do act in this way, they may well of course make their task of piecemeal social reconstruction even more difficult than I have already suggested; that is, by increasing awareness and resentment of inequality, especially among disadvantaged groups and strata, and thus reducing further the likelihood of their willing cooperation. But if, on the other hand, our social and economic engineers keep silent on the matter of inequality – if they attempt rather to build on the fact that the full extent of inequality is often unrealized and its sources misunderstood – then they are, willy-nilly, applying their knowledge and expertise in a partial way. And on this account, whatever their intentions may be, they lay themselves open to the charge of acting as 'the servants of power'.

I am, then, arguing not only that attempts at reconstituting normative order in economic life have small chances of success under existing conditions of inequality, but further that these chances will be still smaller if social scientists acknowledge an obligation to propagate the findings of examinations of this inequality and to relate these findings to the issues in which they seek to intervene. For it can scarcely be denied that such knowledge is likely to be corrosive of those beliefs and attitudes which, it seems, contain grievances arising out of inequality to a level that is 'manageable' at all.

This, I recognize, may be thought a very negative position to adopt, and in certain respects it obviously is. However, I should like to observe that there is one conclusion with constructive possibilities to which my analysis does lead on directly; that is, that if the problem of anomie in economic life is to be attacked effectively, then the problem of social inequality must be attacked simultaneously. It can, I think be argued, as a matter of sociology rather than ideology, that in a society that is both industrial and democratic relatively stable normative order in economic life can only be created through norms being underpinned by some minimum degree of value consensus – as opposed to merely customary limitations on wants and goals. And such consensus in turn cannot be achieved without the distribution of economic resources and rewards, and indeed the entire structure of power and advantage, becoming in some sense 'principled' – becoming, that is, more capable of being given consistent rational and moral justification. In other words, the advancement of social justice has to be seen not as some lofty and rather impractical ideal, the further pursuit of which must wait upon the attainment of such basic objectives as 'getting the economy right', but rather as an important precondition of mitigating current economic difficulties. Such a lesson had to be learnt once in the nineteenth and earlier twentieth centuries, when governments were forced to recognize, as one historian has remarked, that social welfare policies were not 'mere sweeteners of the hard rigours of a system of individualist compulsions' but represented rather 'social provision against waste of life and resources and against social inefficiency – not concessions'.[36] Governments now apparently need to learn that in a society with a highly complex division of labour, in which the possibilities of malintegration are correspondingly great, social inequality which is extreme and without legitimation will continually frustrate the orderly and efficient conduct of industrial and economic affairs generally: or, as Durkheim more succinctly put it, that 'all external inequality compromises organic solidarity'.[37]

This is not the place to spell out in detail how the normative reconstruction of economic life and the reduction of social inequality might proceed together. But certain general possibilities are evident enough. For example, several writers have already observed that attempts to regularize industrial relations at enterprise level, so as to facilitate grievance procedures and checks on wage movements, inevitably raise afresh issues of industrial democracy: issues of the right of employees to participate in management and economic decision-making going beyond the scope of collective bargaining. And at least one economist has been prepared to recognize that effective answers to the key 'micro' problems of incomes policy may well entail 'changes in concepts of managerial structure, authority and control'.[38] Again, as regards incomes policy in 'macro' terms, Professor Wootton more than a decade ago argued the need for such a policy to be expressly related to egalitarian objectives, in order to counteract the self-reinforcing character of social inequality and to give the structure of earnings a clearer moral basis; otherwise, the support of large sections of the population could neither be asked for nor expected. Professor Wootton in fact points to the genuinely radical conception of an incomes policy addressed not simply to problems in inflation, but, more basically, to those of social integration and the furtherance of democracy. Such a policy, rather than being devised as an essentially economic instrument, would be framed as part of an overall social policy, with economic considerations being admissible only as and when their imperative nature could be actually demonstrated.[39]

In adumbrating such possibilities, there are two thing I should make quite clear. First, I do not for a moment underestimate the difficulties that would be involved in realizing them — not least as a result of the direct opposition which could be safely predicted from those whose power and advantage would be diminished. Second, I am not attempting here to argue for the desirability of developments of the kind in question in any absolute sense — though such a case might no doubt be made. What I am trying to establish is that these possibilities exist, and that unless and until something on these lines is accomplished, then the present anomic character of economic life will remain. I recognize that from a number of value positions the goal of greater equality may be given only low priority, or that inequality may even be regarded as a good in itself. Moreover, I do not believe that the sociologist *qua* sociologist is able to impugn such positions directly. But what can be argued sociologically is that those who are prepared to accept social inequality more or less as it presently exists must also be prepared to accept 'disorderly' industrial relations, the 'wages jungle' and the general economic 'free for all' more or less as they now exist — or, as the one remaining possibility, to support attempts at entirely authoritarian solutions to these problems. This last course of action, however, would be perhaps the most effective way of breaking down the insulation of the British political system from issues and grievances stemming from inequality — the insulation which the national political culture has hitherto provided. In other words, it would carry the very real threat of extending economic into political instability.[40]

Finally, to turn from possibilities to probabilities, one has, I think, to accept that for the foreseeable future by far the most likely outcome is the continuance of the present state of affairs; that is, of a situation of persisting, marked inequality and also of chronic industrial unrest and of general economic in-fighting between interest groups under the rules mainly of 'catch as catch can'. Such a forecast is indicated by the fact that the egalitarian restructuring of our society, which could only be achieved as a work of political will, expertise and force, does not now appear to be even on the agenda of any major political party. For those who find this situation an unacceptable one, the main hope, at this stage at least, must lie in attempts at analysis and persuasion; in attempts, that is, to demonstrate, as cogently and as widely as possible, just what the concomitants of existing social inequality are, and how they block the aspirations found in many groups and strata – and not only among the less privileged – for a society in which resources are more rationally and co-operatively used. The highest degree of optimism that egalitarians can permit themselves – the belief that the need for greatest equality will eventually prevail – is aptly expressed in one further passage which I take from Durkheim, from near the end of *The Division of Labour*.[41]

> The task of the most advanced societies is then, one could say, a work of justice ... Just as the ideal of less developed societies was to create or maintain as intense a common life as possible, in which the individual was absorbed, so our ideal is to invest our social relationships with ever greater equity in order to ensure the free development of all socially useful potentialities. When one thinks, though, that for centuries men have been content with a much less perfect justice, one begins to ask if these aspirations might not perhaps be due to fits of gratuitous impatience; if they do not represent a deviation from the normal state of affairs rather than an anticipation of the normal state of the future; in short, whether the way of curing the disorder they make manifest is through satisfying them or rejecting them. What we have already established ... enables us to answer this question precisely. There are no needs more firmly grounded than these impulsions, for they are a necessary consequence of the changes that have occurred in the structure of societies ... In the same way as earlier peoples needed, above all, a common faith to live by, we ourselves need justice; and we can be sure that this need will become increasingly exigent if, as seems in every way likely, the conditions that govern social evolution remain unchanged.

Notes

1 Presidential Address delivered to Section N (Sociology) September 1969 at the Exeter Meeting of the British Association.
2 See, for example the Introduction by R. M. Titmuss to the recent republication of R. H. Tawney's classic study, *Equality* (5th ed., London, 1964).
3 J. E. Meade, *Efficiency, Equality and the Ownership of Property* (London, 1964), p. 27.
4 See, for example, Brian Abel-Smith and Peter Townsend, *The Poor and the Poorest* (London, 1965).
5 For useful reviews of relevant literature, see Robert Blaunder, 'Work satisfaction and industrial trends in modern society' in W. Galenson and S. M. Lipset (eds), *Labor and Trade Unionism* (New York, 1960), and John Child, *The Business Enterprise in Modern Industrial Society* (London, 1969), pp. 64–76.
6 See the research findings and discussion presented in A. H. Halsey, Jean Floud, and C. A. Anderson, *Education, Economy and Society* (London and New York, 1961), Parts II, III, IV; and Olive Banks, *The Sociology of Education* (London, 1968) Chs 3 to 5.
7 It is also, of course, important that changes in the structure of social inequality should be distinguished from the processes of individual, or group, mobility within a given structure. Such mobility can occur without strata losing their identity as collectivities or 'quasi-groups'. Cf. Walter Buckley, 'Social stratification and the functional theory of social differentiation', *American Sociological Review*, 23 (1958).
8 Alan Little and John Westergaard, 'The trend of class differentials in educational opportunity in England and Wales', *British Journal of Sociology*, 15, 4 (1964).
9 J. N. Morris and J. A. Heady, 'Social and biological factors in infant mortality: V. Mortality in relation to the father's occupation 1911–1950', *Lancet*, i (1955), p. 554; and Morris, *Uses of Epidemiology* (2nd ed., Edinburgh, 1964) pp. 52–64.
10 John A. Brittain, 'Some neglected features of Britain's income leveling', *American Economic Review*, 50 (2) (1960).
11 I am thus concerned here specifically with 'social' as opposed to 'system' integration – to apply the important distinction made by David Lockwood. See his paper, 'Social integration and system integration' in George K. Zollschan and Walter Hirsch (eds), *Explorations in Social Change* (New York, 1964). It should further be noted that social integration is not taken as implying actors' moral

commitment to the norms they observe. As Cohen stresses, 'there is a fundamental difference between the recognition of a normative expectation and a commitment to uphold the norm.' (Percy S. Cohen, *Modern Social Theory* London, 1968, p. 113.) However, what will emerge as a central contention is that a state of social integration will be more stable, the greater the degree to which compliance with norms does derive from moral consensus rather than from calculation, coercion, or custom; i.e. the greater the relative importance of 'internal' as opposed to 'external' constraints.

12 W. G. Runciman, *Relative Deprivation and Social Justice: a study of attitudes to social inequality in twentieth-century England* (London, 1966).

13 The most important studies are Harry Eckstein, 'The British political system' in Samuel H. Beer and Adam B. Ulam (eds), *Patterns of Government* (New York, 1962); Gabriel A. Almond and Sidney Verba, *The Civic Culture* (Princeton, 1963) and Eric A. Nordlinger, *The Working Class Tories: Authority, Deference and Stable Democracy* (London, 1967).

14 Nordlinger, *op. cit.,* pp. 107–8. The effect in question was the same among Labour and Conservative voters.

15 In summing up his findings on the relationship between social inequalities and the feeling of relative deprivation, Runciman notes that 'of all its various determinants, one of the least powerful is the abstract ideal of social justice' even though 'the notion of social justice is somewhere implicit in every account of how people feel about social inequality' (*op. cit,* p. 247). He is further aware of the way in which dominant modes of political socialization within British society are inimical to a developed awareness of issues of social justice (pp. 292–4).

16 *British Journal of Industrial Relations,* 7 (2) (1969).

17 At one point at least Durkheim makes a quite explicit distinction between a 'moral discipline' and one maintained by 'custom', and stresses the greater effectiveness of the former. See *Le Suicide* (new ed., Paris, 1930), p. 278. Moreover, the distinction seems to me to be always implicit in, and crucial to, his analyses of the problems of the integration of economically advanced societies, in comparison with those having a less developed division of labour. The most frequent function of comparative reference groups in industrial negotiations would seem to be to help support claims that an improvement in pay or conditions is necessary in order for a particular group to maintain its relative position. See the discussion in S. M. Lipset and Martin Trow, 'Reference group theory and trade union wage policy' in Mirra

Komarovsky (ed.), *Common Frontiers of the Social Sciences* (Chicago, 1957). Lipset and Trow in fact advance the view that the extent to which workers feel that wage relationships are morally right will determine the comparative reference groups they adopt – rather than *vice versa* (pp. 400–1).

18 Cf. *De la Division du travail social* (7th ed., Paris, 1960) pp. 356–7; *Le Suicide*, pp. 278–9; and *Leçons de sociologie; Physique des moeurs et du droit* (Paris, 1950), ch. 1. Further, as already observed, consensus which reflects moral commitment to norms is in turn seen as more durable, in the context of modern societies, than that which reflects simply the customary observance of norms. Durkheim in fact makes it clear that to increase the integration of such societies and overcome the problems arising from anomie in economic life, it is not sufficient simply to have norms or rules articulated: the question of their basis is quite crucial. ' ... ce n'est pas assez qu'il y ait des règles; car parfois, ce sont ces règles mêmes qui sont la cause du mal'.

19 *Le Suicide*, p. 277. All translations from Durkheim are my own and differ, sometimes significantly, from published versions.

20 The one possible source would seem to be in the close and highly personalized relations between workers, and between workers and the employer, which may prevail in very small scale establishments. Cf. G. K. Ingham, 'Organizational Size Orientation to Work and Industrial Behaviour', University of Cambridge Ph.D. thesis, 1968. Durkheim himself noted how small enterprises might in this way escape the consequences of an anomic division of labour, *De la Division du travail social*, pp. 344–6. The major objective of the 'human relations industry' movement might in fact be described as that of recreating the characteristic quality of interpersonal relations in small establishments in the context of large scale, bureaucratized concerns. It has yet to demonstrate any widespread and lasting success.

21 Cf. *Les Règles de la méthode sociologique* (Paris, 1895) ch. III. Fox and Flanders argue that at the present day industrial relations are more disorderly than at any time since Britain became an industrial society. This claim is, I think, debatable; but in any case their explanation of why disorder was not greater in earlier periods is essentially in terms of 'custom' or imbalances of power, i.e. 'coercion'; and order thus based cannot be regarded as the converse of anomie. What Durkheim contrasted with the anomie of economic life in modern societies was the idea of a 'moral economy' such as was pursued, and in some measure realized, in pre-industrial Europe.

22 Cf. National Board for Prices and Incomes, *Third General Report, August 1967 to July 1968*, Cmnd 3715 (HMSO, 1968) pp. 6–7.

23 For example, results from an Opinion Research Centre study (February, 1967) showed that when members of a quota sample of electors were asked to choose the one most important objective of an incomes policy out of three suggested, significant differences emerged on class lines, and especially between 'AB' and 'DE' respondents: 71 per cent of the former selected 'that people with special skills are fully rewarded' while 52 per cent of the latter selected 'that lowest paid workers get a reasonable wage' and a further 10 per cent 'that incomes become more equal'. For a report on the survey, see.R. P. Kelvin, 'What sort of incomes policy' *New Society*, 6 April 1967.

24 *The Social Foundations of Wage Policy* (2nd ed., London, 1962) chs IV and V.

25 Nor can it be thought likely that many individuals will support control over incomes on a purely calculative basis – i.e. on the basis of understanding, or supposed understanding, of the interrelationships between money incomes, cost and prices, and thus of the nature of inflation. Survey research has demonstrated the not very surprising fact that the bulk of the population has little grasp of macro-economics. See Hilde Behrend, 'Price images, inflation and national incomes policy', *Scottish Journal of Political Economy*, 13 (November 1966), and Behrend *et al.*, *A National Survey of Attitudes to Inflation and Incomes Policy*, Edutext Publications, Occasional Papers in Social and Economic Administrations, no. 7 (London, 1966). In any case, no amount of macro-economic understanding could ensure general consensus on the actual application of an incomes policy, the crucial problems of which concern what shall happen to particular groups rather than to the aggregate of incomes.

26 See the recent valuable review of the working of incomes policies provided by John Corina, 'Can an incomes policy be administered?' in B. C. Roberts (ed.), *Industrial Relations: Contemporary Issues* (London, 1968).

27 See A. Nove. 'Wages in the Soviet Union: a comment on recently published statistics', *British Journal of Industrial Relations*, 4 (2) (1966).

28 'Can an incomes policy be administered?', pp. 284–8, 290–1. It may be noted that an earlier review of incomes policies in western societies arrived in effect at the conclusion that an essential condition of controlling wage drift was some measure of moral restraint: ' ... a willingness on the part of individual trade unions, groups of workers, and employers to sacrifice some autonomy in matters of wage fixing under circumstances which may be particularly favourable or

conducive to their exercise of it'. H. A. Turner and H. Zoeteweij, *Prices, Wages, and Incomes Policies* (ILO, Geneva, 1966) p. 142.

29 *Ibid.*, pp. 135–6.

30 Cf. Lipset and Trow, *art. cit.*, pp. 397–400; also the comments by Bob Rowthorn, 'Unions and the economy' in Robin Blackburn and Alexander Cockburn (eds), *The Incompatibles: Trade Union Militancy and the Consensus* (London, 1967) pp. 221–2.

31 See Wootton, *op. cit.*, pp. 51–4; and Harold Lydall, *The Structure of Earnings* (Oxford, 1968), pp. 68–88. It should of course be said that all human attributes that might be treated as 'abilities' or 'capacities' are determined by both genetic and environmental influences. Cf. J. M. Thoday, 'Geneticism and environmentalism' in J. E. Meade and A. S. Parkes (eds), *Biological Aspects of Social Problems* (Edinburgh, 1965).

32 Cf. Guy Routh, *Occupation and Pay in Great Britain 1906–60* (Cambridge, 1965); A. H. Halsey (ed.), *Ability and Educational Opportunity* (OECD, Paris, 1961); and J. W. B. Douglas *et al.*, *All Our Future* (London, 1968).

33 For a relevant collection of papers, see Reinhard Bendix and S. M. Lipset (eds), *Class, Status and Power* (2nd ed., New York, 1966), Part I: 'The Continuing Debate on Equality'. Also the paper by Buckley earlier cited.

34 Cf. the data referred to by John H. Goldthorpe, David Lockwood, Frank Bechhofer and Jennifer Platt, in *The Affluent Worker in the Class Structure* (Cambridge, 1969) pp. 154–5.

35 *Op. cit.*, p. 294.

36 H. L. Beales, 'The Making of Social Policy', Hobhouse Memorial Lecture, 1945, p. 9.

37 *De la Division du travail social*, p. 373. By *'inégalité exterieure'* Durkheim refers to all inequality resulting from sources other than differences in individual potentialities. Cf. also *Leçons de sociologie*, ch. XVIII.

38 Corina, *art. cit.*, p. 286.

39 *Op. cit.*, ch. VI especially. Particularly pertinent here, for example, would be the requirement that arguments on the functions of economic inequalities as work incentives should be precisely stated and empirically tested, rather than being merely asserted in the form of vague generalities.

40 Cf. Turner and Zoeteweij, *op. cit.*, p. 147.

41 *De la Division du travail social*, pp. 381–2.

1.3   The concept of equality of educational opportunity[1]

James Coleman

The concept of 'equality of educational opportunity' as held by members of society has had a varied past. It has changed radically in recent years, and is likely to undergo further change in the future. This lack of stability in the concept leads to several questions. What has it meant in the past, what does it mean now, and what will it mean in the future? Whose obligation is it to provide such equality? Is the concept a fundamentally sound one, or does it have inherent contradiction or conflicts with social organization? But first of all, and above all, what is and has been meant in society by the ideal of equality of education opportunity?

To answer this question, it is necessary to consider how the child's position in society has been conceived in different historical periods. In pre-industrial Europe, the child's horizons were largely limited by his family. His station in life was likely to be the same as his father's. If his father was a serf, he would likely live his own life as a serf; if his father was a shoemaker, he would likely become a shoemaker. But even this immobility was not the crux of the matter; he was a part of the family production enterprise and would likely remain within this enterprise throughout his life. The extended family, as the basic unit of social organization, had complete authority over the child, and complete responsibility for him. This responsibility ordinarily did not end when the child became an adult because he remained a part of the same economic unit and carried on this tradition of responsibility into the next generation. Despite some mobility out of the family, the general pattern was family continuity through a patriarchal kinship system.

There are two elements of critical importance here. First, the family carried responsibility for its members' welfare from cradle to grave. It was a 'welfare society', with each extended family serving as a welfare organization for its own members. Thus it was to the family's interest to see that its members became productive. Conversely, a family took

Source: *Harvard Educational Review*, special issue (winter 1968), 38 (1), pp. 7–22.

relatively small interest in whether someone in another family became productive or not − merely because the mobility of productive labour between family economic units was relatively low. If the son of a neighbour was allowed to become a ne'er-do-well, it had little real effect on families other than his own.

The second important element is that the family, as a unit of economic production, provided an appropriate context in which the child could learn the things he needed to know. The craftsman's shop or the farmer's fields were appropriate training grounds for sons, and the household was an appropriate training ground for daughters.

In this kind of society, the concept of equality of educational opportunity had no relevance at all. The child and adult were embedded within the extended family, and the child's education or training was merely whatever seemed necessary to maintain the family's productivity. The fixed stations in life which most families occupied precluded any idea of 'opportunity' and, even less, equality of opportunity.

With the industrial revolution, changes occurred in both the family's function as a self-perpetuating economic unit and as a training ground. As economic organizations developed outside the household, children began to be occupationally mobile outside their families. As families lost their economic production activities, they also began to lose their welfare functions, and the poor or ill or incapacitated became more nearly a community responsibility. Thus the training which a child received came to be of interest to all in the community, either as his potential employers or as his potential economic supports if he became dependent. During this stage of development in eighteenth-century England, for instance, communities had laws preventing immigration from another community because of the potential economic burden of immigrants.

Further, as men came to employ their own labour outside the family in the new factories, their families became less useful as economic training grounds for their children. These changes paved the way for public education. Families needed a context within which their children could learn some general skills which would be useful for gaining work outside the family; and men of influence in the community began to be interested in the potential productivity of other men's children.

It was in the early nineteenth century that public education began to appear in Europe and America. Before that time, private education had grown with the expansion of the mercantile class. This class had both the need and resources to have its children educated outside the home, either for professional occupations or for occupations in the developing world of commerce. But the idea of general educational opportunity for all children arose only in the nineteenth century.

The emergence of public, tax-supported education was not solely a function of the stage of industrial development. It was also a function of the class structure in the society. In the United States, without a strong traditional class structure, universal education in publicly-supported free schools became widespread in the early nineteenth century; in England, the 'voluntary schools', run and organized by churches with some instances of state support, were not supplemented by a state-supported system until the Education Act of 1870. Even more, the character of educational opportunity reflected the class structure. In the United States, the public schools quickly became the common school, attended by representatives of all classes; these schools provided a common educational experience for most American children – excluding only those upper-class children in private shcools, those poor who went to no schools, and Indians and Southern Negroes who were without schools. In England, however, the class system directly manifested itself through the schools. The state-supported, or 'board schools' as they were called, became the schools of the labouring lower classes with a sharply different curriculum from those voluntary schools which served the middle and upper classes. The division was so sharp that two government departments, the Education Department and the Science and Art Department, administered external examinations, the first for the products of the board schools, and the second for the products of the voluntary schools as they progressed into secondary education. It was only the latter curricula and examinations that provided admission to higher education.

What is most striking is the duration of influence of such a dual structure. Even today in England, a century later (and in different forms in most European countries), there exists a dual structure of public secondary education with only one of the branches providing the curriculum for college admission. In England, this branch includes the remaining voluntary schools which, though retaining their individual identities, have become part of the state-supported system.

This comparison of England and the United States shows clearly the impact of the class structure in society upon the concept of educational opportunity in that society. In nineteenth-century England, the idea of equality of educational opportunity was hardly considered; the system was designed to provide differentiated educational opportunity appropriate to one's station in life. In the United States as well, the absence of educational opportunity for Negroes in the South arose from the caste and feudal structure of the largely rural society. The idea of differentiated educational opportunity, implicit in the Education Act of 1870 in England, seems to derive from dual needs: the needs arising from industrialization for a basic education for the labour force, and the interests of parents in having one's own child receive a good education. The middle classes could meet both these needs by providing a free system for the children of labouring classes and a tuition system (which soon came to be supplemented by state grants) for their own. The long survival of this differentiated system depended not only on the historical fact that the voluntary schools existed before a public system came into existence but on the fact that it allows both of these needs to be met: the community's collective need for a trained labour force, and the middle-class individual's interest in a better education for his own child. It served a third need as well: that of maintaining the existing social order — a system of stratification that was a step removed from a feudal system of fixed estates, but designed to prevent a wholesale challenge by the children of the working class to the positions held for children of the middle classes.

The similarity of this system to that which existed in the South to provide differential opportunity to Negroes and whites is striking, just as is the similarity of class structures in the second half of nineteenth century England to the white — Negro caste structure of the southern United States in the first half of the twentieth century.

In the United States, nearly from the beginning, the concept of educational opportunity had a special meaning which focused on equality. This meaning included the following elements:

1 Providing a free education up to a given level which constituted the principal entry point to the labour force.
2 Providing a common curriculum for all children, regardless of background.
3 Partly by design and partly because of low population density, providing that children from diverse backgrounds attend the same school.
4 Providing equality within a given locality, since local taxes provided the source of support for schools.

This conception of equality of opportunity is still held by many persons; but there are some assumptions in it which are not obvious. First, it implicitly assumes that the existence of free schools eliminates economic sources of inequality of opportunity. Free schools, however, do not mean that the costs of a child's education become reduced to zero for families of all economic levels. When free education was introduced, many families could not afford to allow the child to attend school beyond an early age. His labour was necessary to the family — whether in rural or urban areas. Even after the passage of child labour laws, this remained true on the farm. These economic sources of inequality of opportunity have become small indeed (up through secondary education); but at one time they were a major source of inequality. In some countries they remain so; and certainly for higher education they remain so.

Apart from the economic needs of the family problems inherent in the social structure raised even more fundamental questions about equality of educational opportunity. Continued school attendance prevented a boy from being trained in his father's trade. Thus, in taking advantage of 'equal educational opportunity', the son of a craftsman or small tradesman would lose the opportunity to enter those occupations he would most likely fill. The family inheritance of occupation at all social levels was still strong enough, and the age of entry into the labour force was still early enough, that secondary education interfered with opportunity for working-class children; while it opened up opportunities at higher social levels, it closed them at lower ones.

Since residue of this social structure remains in present American society, the dilemma cannot be totally ignored. The idea of a common educational experience implies that this experience has only the effect of widening the range of opportunity, never the effect of excluding opportunities. But clearly this is never precisely true so long as this experience prevents a child from pursuing certain occupational paths. This question still arises with the differentiated secondary curriculum: an academic programme in high school has the effect not only of keeping open the opportunities which arise through continued education, but also of closing off opportunities which a vocational programme keeps open.

A second assumption implied by this concept of equality of opportunity is that opportunity lies in exposure to a given curriculum. The amount of opportunity is then measured in terms of the level of curriculum to which the child is exposed. The higher the curriculum made available to a given set of children, the greater their opportunity.

The most interesting point about this assumption is the relatively passive role of the school and community, relative to the child's role. The school's obligation is to 'provide an opportunity' by being available, within easy geographic access of the child, free of cost (beyond the value of the child's time), and with a curriculum that would not exclude him from higher education. The obligation to 'use the opportunity' is on the child or the family, so that his role is defined as the active one: the responsibility for achievement rests with him. Despite the fact that the school's role was the relatively passive one and the child's or family's role the active one, the use of this social service soon came to be no longer a choice of the parent or child, but that of the state. Since compulsory attendance laws appeared in the nineteenth century, the age of required attendance has been periodically moved upward.

This concept of equality of educational opportunity is one that has been implicit in most educational practice throughout most of the period of public education in the nineteenth and twentieth centuries. However, there have been several challenges to it; serious questions have been raised by new conditions in public education. The first of these in the United States was a challenge to assumption two, the common curriculum. This challenge first occurred in the early years of the twentieth century with the expansion of secondary education. Until the report of the committee of the National Education Association, issued in 1918, the standard curriculum in secondary schools was primarily a classical one appropriate for college entrance. The greater influx of non-college-bound adolescents into the high school made it necessary that this curriculum be changed into one more appropriate to the new majority. This is not to say that the curriculum changed immediately in the schools, nor that all schools changed equally, but rather that the seven 'cardinal principles' of the NEA report became a powerful influence in the movement towards a less academically rigid curriculum. The introduction of the new non-classical curriculum was seldom if ever couched in terms of a conflict between those for whom high school was college preparation, and those for whom it was terminal education; nevertheless, that was the case. 'The inequality' was seen as the use of a curriculum that served a minority and was not designed to fit the needs of the majority; and the shift of curriculum was intended to fit the curriculum to the needs of the new majority in the schools.

In many schools, this shift took the form of diversifying the curriculum, rather than supplanting one by another; the college-preparatory curriculum remained though watered down. Thus the kind of equality of opportunity that emerged from the newly-designed secondary school curriculum was radically different from the elementary-school concept that had emerged earlier. The idea inherent in the new secondary school curriculum appears to have been to take as given the diverse occupational paths into which adolescents will go after secondary school, and to say (implicitly): there is greater equality of educational opportunity for a boy who is not going to attend college if he has a specially-designed curriculum than if he must take a curriculum designed for college entrance.

There is only one difficulty with this definition: it takes as given what should be problematic — that a given boy is going into a given post-secondary occupational or educational path. It is one thing to take as given that approximately 70 per cent of an entering high school freshman class will not attend college; but to assign a partcular child to a curriculum designed for that 70 per cent closes off for that child the opportunity to attend college. Yet to assign all children to a curriculum designed for the 30 per cent who will attend college creates inequality for those who, at the end of high school, fall among the 70 per cent who do not attend college. This is a true dilemma, and one which no educational system has fully solved. It is more general than the college/non-college dichotomy, for there is a wide variety of different paths that adolescents take on the completion of secondary school. In England, for example, a student planning to attend a university must specialize in the arts or the sciences in the later years of secondary school. Similar specialization occurs in the German *Gymnasium*; and this is wholly within the group planning to attend university. Even greater specialization can be found among non-college curricula, especially in the vocational, technical, and commercial high schools.

The distinguishing characteristic of this concept of equality of educational opportunity is that it accepts as given the child's expected future. While the concept discussed earlier left the child's future wholly open, this concept of differentiated curricula uses the expected future to match child and curriculum. It should be noted that the first and simpler concept is easier to apply in elementary schools where fundamental tools of reading and arithmetic are being learned by all children; it is only in secondary school that the problem of diverse future arises. It should also be noted that the dilemma is directly due to the social structure itself: if there were a virtual absence of social mobility with everyone occupying a fixed estate in life, then such curricula that take the future as given would provide equality of opportunity relative to that structure. It is only because of the high degree of occupational mobility between generations – that is, the great degree of equality of occupational opportunity – that the dilemma arises.

The first stage in the evolution of the concept of equality of educational opportunity was the notion that all children must be exposed to the same curriculum in the same school. A second stage in the evolution of the concept assumed that different children would have different occupational futures and that equality of opportunity required providing different curricula for each type of student. The third and fourth stages in this evolution came as a result of challenges to the basic idea of equality of educational opportunity from opposing directions. The third stage can be seen at least as far back as 1896 when the Supreme Court upheld the southern states' notion of 'separate but equal' facilities. This stage ended in 1954 when the Supreme Court ruled that legal separation by race inherently constitutes inequality of opportunity. By adopting the 'separate but equal' doctrine, the southern states rejected assumption three of the original concept, the assumption that equality depended on the opportunity to attend the same school. This rejection was, however, consistent with the overall logic of the original concept, since attendance at the same school was an inherent part of that logic. The underlying idea was that opportunity resided in exposure to a curriculum; the community's responsibility was to provide that exposure, the child's to take advantage of it.

It was the pervasiveness of this underlying idea which created the difficulty for the Supreme Court. For it was evident that even when identical facilities and identical teacher salaries existed for racially separate schools, 'equality of educational opportunity' in some sense did not exist. This had also long been evident to Englishmen as well, in a different context, for with the simultaneous existence of the 'common school' and the 'voluntary school', no one was under the illusion that full equality of education opportunity existed. But the source of this inequality remained an unarticulated feeling. In the decision of the Supreme Court, this unarticulated feeling began to take more precise form. The essence of it was that the effects of such separate schools were, or were likely to be, different. Thus a concept of equality of opportunity which focused on effects of schooling began to take form. The actual decision of the Court was in fact a confusion of two unrelated premises: this new concept, which looked at results of schooling, and the legal premise that the use of race as a basis for school assignment violates fundamental freedoms. But what is important for the evolution of the concept of equality of opportunity is that a new and different assumption was introduced, the assumption that equality of opportunity depends in some fashion upon effects of schooling. I believe the decision would have been more soundly based had it not depended on the effects of schooling, but only on the violation of freedom; but by introducing the question of effects of schooling, the Court brought into the open implicit goals of equality of educational opportunity — that is goals having to do with the results of school — to which the original concept was somewhat awkwardly directed.

That these goals were in fact behind the concept can be verified by a simple mental experiment. Suppose the early schools had operated for only one hour a week and had been attended by children of all social classes. This would have met the explicit assumptions of the early concept of equality of opportunity since the school is free, with a common curriculum, and attended by all children in the locality. But it obviously would not have been accepted, even at that time, as providing equality of opportunity, because its effects would have been so minimal. The additional educational resources provided by middle- and upper-class families, whether in the home, by tutoring, or in private supplementary schools, would have created severe inequalities in results.

Thus the dependence of the concept upon results or effects of schooling, which had remained hidden until 1954, came partially into the open with

57

the Supreme Court decision. Yet this was not the end, for it created more problems than it solved. It might allow one to assess gross inequalities, such as that created by dual school systems in the South, or by a system like that in the mental experiment I just described. But it allows nothing beyond that. Even more confounding, because the decision did not use effects of schooling as a criterion of inequality but only as justification for a criterion of racial integration, integration itself emerged as the basis for still a new concept of equality of educaticnal opportunity. Thus the idea of effects of schooling as an element in the concept was introduced but immediately overshadowed by another, the criterion of racial integration.

The next stage in the evolution of this concept was, in my judgment, the Office of Education Survey of Equality of Educational Opportunity. This survey was carried out under a mandate in the Civil Rights Act of 1964 to the Commissioner of Education to assess the 'lack of equality of educational opportunity' among racial and other groups in the United States. The evolution of this concept, and the conceptual disarray which this evolution had created made the very definition of the task exceedingly difficult. The original concept could be examined by determing the degree to which all children in a locality had access to the same schools and the same curriculum, free of charge. The existence of diverse secondary curricula appropriate to different futures could be assessed relatively easily. But the very assignment of a child to a specific curriculum implies acceptance of the concept of equality which takes futures as given. And the introduction of the new interpretations, equality as measured by results of schooling and equality defined by racial integration, confounded the issue even further.

As a consequence, in planning the survey it was obvious that no single concept of equality of educational opportunity existed and that the survey must give information relevant to a variety of concepts. The basis on which this was done can be seen by reproducing a portion of an internal memorandum that determined the design of the survey:

> The point of second importance in design [second to the point of discovering the intent of Congress, which was taken to be that the survey was not for the purpose of locating willful discrimination, but to determine educational inequality without regard to intention of those in authority] follows from the first and concerns the definition of inequality. One type of inequality may be defined in terms of differences of the community's input to the school, such as per-pupil expenditure, school plants, libraries, quality of teachers, and other similar quantities.
>
> A second type of inequality may be defined in terms of the racial

composition of the school, following the Supreme Court's decision that segregated schooling is inherently unequal. By the former definition, the question of inequality through segregation is excluded, while by the latter, there is inequality of education within a school system so long as the schools within the system have different racial composition.

A third type of inequality would include various intangible characteristics of the school as well as the factors directly traceable to the community inputs to the school. These intangibles are such things as teacher morale, teacher's expectations of students, level of interest of the student body in learning, or others. Any of these factors may affect the impact of the school upon a given student within it. Yet such a definition gives no suggestion of where to stop, or just how relevant these factors might be for school quality.

Consequently, a fourth type of inequality may be defined in terms of consequences of the school for individuals with equal backgrounds and abilities. In this definition, equality of educational opportunity is equality of results, given the same individual input. With such a definition, inequality might come about from differences in the school inputs and/or racial composition and/or from more intangible things as described above. Such a definition obviously would require that two steps be taken in the determination of inequality. First, it is necessary to determine the effect of these various factors upon educational results (conceiving of results quite broadly, including not only achievement but attitudes towards learning, self-image, and perhaps other variables). This provides various measures of the school's quality in terms of its effect upon its students. Second, it is necessary to take these measures of quality, once determined, and determine the differential exposure of Negroes (or other groups) and whites to schools of high and low quality.

A fifth type of inequality may be defined in terms of consequences of the school for individuals of unequal backgrounds and abilities. In this definition, equality of educational opportunity is equality of results given different individual inputs. The most striking examples of inequality here would be children from households in which a language other than English, such as Spanish or Navaho, is spoken. Other examples would be low-achieving children from homes in which there is a poverty of verbal expression or an absence of experiences which lead to conceptual facility.

Such a definition taken in the extreme would imply that educational equality is reached only when the results of schooling (achievement and attitudes) are the same for racial and religious minorities as for the dominant group.

The basis for the design of the survey is indicated by another segment of this memorandum:

> Thus, the study will focus its principal effort on the fourth definition, but will also provide information relevant to all five possible definitions. This ensures the pluralism which is obviously necessary with respect to a definition of inequality. The major justification for this focus is that the results of this approach can best be translated into policy which will improve education's effects. The results of the first two approaches (tangible inputs to the school, and segregation) can certainly be translated into policy, but there is no good evidence that these policies will improve education's effects; and while policies to implement the fifth would certainly improve education's effects, it seems hardly possible that the study could provide information that would direct such policies.
>
> Altogether, it has become evident that it is not our role to define what constitutes equality for policy-making purposes. Such a definition will be an outcome of the interplay of a variety of interests, and will certainly differ from time to time as these interests differ. It should be our role to cast light on the state of inequality defined in the variety of ways which appear reasonable at this time.

The survey, then, was conceived as a pluralistic instrument, given the variety of concepts of equality of opportunity in education. Yet I suggest that despite the avowed intention of not adjudicating between these different ideas, the survey has brought a new stage in the evolution of the concept. For the definitions of equality which the survey was designed to serve split sharply into two groups. The first three definitions concerned input resources: first, those brought to the school by the actions of the school administration (facilities, curriculum, teachers); second, those brought to the school by the other students, in the educational backgrounds which their presence contributed to the school; and third, the intangible characteristics such as 'morale' that result from the interaction of all these factors. The fourth and fifth definitions were concerned with the effects of schooling. Thus the five definitions were divided into three concerned with inputs to school and two concerned with effects of schooling. When the Report emerged, it did not give five different measures of equality, one for each of these definitions; but it did focus sharply on this dichotomy, giving in chapter 2 information on inequalities of input relevant to definitions one and two, and in chapter 3 information on inequalities of results relevant to definitions four and five, and also in chapter 3 information on the relation of input to results again relevant to definitions four and five.

Although not central to our discussion here, it is interesting to note that this examination of the relation of school inputs to effects on achievement showed that those input characteristics of schools that are most alike for Negroes and whites have least effect on their achievement. The magnitudes of differences between schools attended by Negroes and those attended by whites were as follows: least, facilities and curriculum; next, teacher quality; and greatest, educational backgrounds of fellow students. The order of importance of these inputs on the achievement of Negro students is precisely the same; facilities and curriculum least, teacher quality next, and backgrounds of fellow students, most.

By making the dichotomy between inputs and results explicit, and by focusing attention not only on inputs but on results, the Report brought into the open what had been underlying all the concepts of equality of educational opportunity but had remained largely hidden: that the concept implied effective equality of opportunity, that is, equality in those elements that are effective for learning. The reason this had remained half-hidden, obscured by definitions that involve inputs, is, I suspect, because educational research has been until recently unprepared to demonstrate what elements are effective. The controversy that has surrounded the Report indicates that measurement of effects is still subject to sharp disagreement; but the crucial point is that effects of inputs have come to constitute the basis for assessment of school quality (and thus equality of opportunity) in place of using certain inputs by definition as measures of quality (e.g. small classes are better than large, higher-paid teachers are better than lower-paid ones, by definition).

It would be fortunate indeed if the matter could be left to rest there – if merely by using effects of school rather than inputs as the basis for the concept, the problem were solved. But that is not the case at all. The conflict between definitions four and five given above shows this. The conflict can be illustrated by resorting again to the mental experiment discussed earlier – providing a standard education of one hour per week, under identical conditions, for all children. By definition four, controlling all background difference of the children, results for Negroes and whites would be equal, and thus by this definition equality of opportunity would exist. But because such minimal schooling would have minimal effect, those children from educationally strong families would enjoy educational opportunity far surpassing that of others. And because such educationally strong backgrounds are found more often among whites tham among Negroes, there would be very large overall Negro – white achievement differences – and thus inequality of opportunity by definition five.

It is clear from this hypothetical experiment that the problem of what constitutes equality of opportunity is not solved. The problem will become

Figure 1 Patterns of achievement in verbal skills at various grade levels by race and region

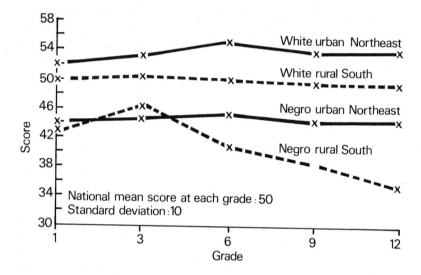

even clearer by showing graphs with some of the results of the Office of Education Survey. The highest line in Figure 1 shows the achievement in verbal skills by whites in the urban Northeast at grades 1, 3, 6, 9 and 12. The second line shows the achievement at each of these grades by whites in the rural Southeast. The third shows the achievement of Negroes in the urban Northeast. The fourth shows the achievement of Negroes in the rural Southeast.

When compared to the whites in the urban Northeast, each of the other three groups shows a different pattern. The comparison with whites in the rural South shows the two groups beginning near the same point in the first grade, and diverging over the years of school. The comparison with Negroes in the urban Northeast shows the two groups beginning farther apart at the first grade and remaining about the same distance apart. The comparison with Negroes in the rural South shows the two groups beginning far apart and moving much farther apart over the years of school.

Which of these, if any, shows equality of educational opportunity between regional and racial groups? Which shows greatest inequality of opportunity? I think the second question is easier to answer than the first. The last comparison showing both initial difference and the greatest increase in difference over grades 1 through 12 appears to be the best candidate for the greatest inequality. The first comparison, with whites in the rural South, also seems to show inequality of opportunity, because of the increasing difference over the twelve years. But what about the second comparison, with an approximately constant difference between Negroes and whites in the urban Northeast? Is this equality of opportunity? I suggest not. It means, in effect, only that the period of school has left the average Negro at about the same level of achievement relative to whites as he began − in this case, achieving higher than about 15 per cent of the whites, lower than about 85 per cent of the whites. It may well be that in the absence of school those lines of achievement would have diverged due to differences in home environments; or perhaps they would have remained an equal distance apart, as they are in this graph (though at lower levels of achievement for both groups, in the absence of school). If it were the former, we could say that school, by keeping the lines parallel, has been a force towards the equalization of opportunity. But in the absence of such knowledge, we cannot say even that.

What would full equality of educational opportunity look like in such graphs? One might persuasively argue that it should show a convergence, so that even though two population groups begin school with different levels of skills on the average, the average of the group that begins lower moves up to coincide with that of the group that begins higher. Parenthetically, I should note that this does not imply that all students' achievement comes to be identical, but only that the averages for two population groups that begin at different levels come to be identical. The diversity of individual scores could be as great as, or greater than, the diversity at grade 1.

Yet there are serious questions about this definition of equality of opportunity. It implies that over the period of school there are no other influences, such as the family environment, which affect achievement over the twelve years of school, even though these influences may differ greatly for the two population groups. Concretely, it implies that white family environments, predominantly middle class, and Negro family environments, predominantly lower class, will produce no effects on achievement that would keep these averages apart. Such an assumption seems highly unrealistic, especially in view of the general importance of family background for achievement.

However, if such possibilities are acknowledged, then how far can they go before there is inequality of educational opportunity? Constant difference over school? Increasing differences? The unanswerability of such questions begins to give a sense of a new stage in the evolution of the concept of equality of educational opportunity. These questions concern the relative intensity of two sets of influences: those which are alike for the two groups, principally in school, and those which are different, principally in the home or neighbourhood. If the school's influences are not only alike for the two groups, but very strong relative to the divergent influences, then the two groups will move together. If school influences are very weak, then the two groups will move apart. Or more generally, the relative intensity of the convergent school influences and the divergent out-of-school influences determines the effectiveness of the educational system in providing equality of educational opportunity. In this perspective complete equality of opportunity can be reached only if all the divergent out-of-school influences vanish, a condition that would arise only in the advent of boarding schools; given the existing divergent influences, equality of opportunity can only be approached and never fully reached. The concept becomes one of degree of proximity to equality of opportunity. This proximity is determined, then, not merely by the equality of education inputs, but by the intensity of the school's influences relative to the external divergent influences. That is, equality of output is not so much determined by equality of the resource inputs, but by the power of these resources in bringing about achievement.

Here, then, is where the concept of equality of educational opportunity presently stands. We have observed an evolution which might have been anticipated a century and a half ago when the first such concepts arose, yet one which is very different from the concept as it first developed. This difference is sharpened if we examine a further implication of the current concept as I have described it. In describing the original concept, I indicated that the role of the community and the educational institution was relatively passive; they were expected to provide a set of free public resources. The responsibility for profitable use of those resources lay with the child and his family. But the evolution of the concept has reversed these roles. The implication of the most recent concept, as I have described it, is that the responsibility to create achievement lies with the educational institution, not the child. The difference in achievement at grade 12 between the average Negro and the average white is, in effect, the degree of inequality of opportunity, and the reduction of that inequality is a responsibility of the school. This shift in responsibility follows logically from the change in the concept of equality of educational opportunity from school resource inputs to effects of schooling. When that change occurred, as it has in the past few years, the school's responsibility shifted from increasing and distributing equally its 'quality' to increasing the quality of its students' achievements. This is a notable shift, and one which should have strong consequences for the practice of education in future years.

Note

1 This paper was delivered at the conference on the *Equality of Educational Opportunity* report sponsored by the Colloquium Board of the Harvard Graduate School of Education, 21 October 1967.

1.4 Political ends and educational means

A. H. Halsey

To find a strategy for educational roads to equality! That has been a central theme of educational discussion from the beginning of the twentieth century. It has produced a prolific sociology of education over the last generation in which the centrality of educational systems to the structure and the functioning of industrial societies has become a commonplace. In the 1950s education in these societies was seen has having a crucial role for economic growth and change. More recently the emphasis has shifted to the part played by formal educational organizations in defining what is and what is not knowledge, and as selective agencies allocating individuals to social positions, moulding their social personalities and their definitions of the world around them. But the underlying question is whether, and if so under what circumstances, education can change society.

The answer, whatever its form, has been controversial in two apparently different ways. Debate has turned on the desirability of using educational means for political ends. But also, and much more fruitfully, it has turned on the feasibility of different educational means towards agreed ends. Thus 'keeping education out of politics' can be a crude evasion of the incontrovertible fact that, in a modern or a modernizing society, educational arrangements are an important determinant of the life and livelihood of individuals: education is a social distributor of life chances. In its more subtle forms, however, this political or moral stance may be a protest against narrow definitions of the social consequences of educational reform. As such it belongs neither to the political right nor to the political left. It is of course associated with such writers as T. S. Eliot,[1] Professor Bantock[2] and the authors of the Black Papers,[3] but there are equally important radical criticisms of narrowness in the sociological imagination; for example reform in the direction of meritocracy may fail to take account of those ramified consequences which Professor Bernstein has referred to

Source: *Educational Priority* (ed.) A. H. Halsey (1972) HMSO, vol. I, pp. 3–12.

as 'the individualisation of failure' and there is a good deal of current writing from an interactionist or phenomenological point of view which insists on the importance of education as structuring reality for those exposed to it in broader terms than that associated with a definition of schooling as the agency through which individuals are allocated to the labour force.

The problem of the entanglement of analysis with value assumptions is intrinsic to sociological study. To get it straight we must first distinguish the 'scientific' from the 'value' problem: to ask separately what is possible and thereby, with the issues and alternatives sharply defined, to decide on preferences and priorities. In this way the challenge to social science becomes clear and the task for the sociologist is, literally, to inform the political debate. Of course the distinction between sociology and politics is much less easy than a naive positivism would presuppose. It is necessary at every step to try to make explicit what are the implicit assumptions of political aims and the value premises of sociological analysis. There is no final ready-made procedure for either of these tasks. We have only imperfect aids beyond the injunction to constant vigilance.

One aid of particular relevance to our problem in this book can be taken from John Goldthorpe's discussion of futurology.[4] Goldthorpe distinguishes between futurology as prediction and futurology as design. Conventional futurology is essentially extrapolation to the future of trends from the recent past. It therefore tends to carry with it the value assumptions of the *status quo* and is in that sense conservative. That is why the book covers of this literature *USA 2000* are, as Raymond Aron has remarked, so much more exciting than the pages. The future is only the present, usually writ slightly larger. Futurology as design is quite another matter, and not only because it is inherently more radical in its political possibilities. It is scientifically much more challenging in that it directly requires the social scientist to state clearly what he knows or does not know about the possibility of moving from the present state to a postulated, presumably desired, future state.

Political aims and programmes in general and the aim of educational equality in particular, together with the various programmes for its attainment, lend themselves fairly readily to translation into futurology as design. The translation can be used to define the critical and constructive role of the social scientist, in this case with relation to the problems of educational reform through political and administrative action. And action-research, as we understand it, is an experimental or quasi-experimental version of futurology as design. Ends are stated together with means to their achievement. In this case the ends are greater social equality of educational opportunity and attainment and the means are Plowden's positive discrimination for educational priority areas. Ends and means are modified and explicated in a programme of action and the relation between them is analysed by research monitoring of the action programme.

A second and related aid to understanding the social science task is the Popperian distinction between holistic and piecemeal reform. The general arguments against holism cannot be rehearsed here. What is relevant however is not a debate over the dichotomy but over the appropriate scale of the piecemeal. It is not so much a question of whether education can change society: it is a question of the level of ambitiousness of social engineering which may be required to change an undesired state of affairs. The Plowden analysis of low educational standards in EPAs points to causes outside the school in the neighbourhood structure of life and therefore calls for a widely based programme of social reform alongside positive discrimination in education. Within this framework Plowden postulates that 'what these deprived areas need most are perfectly normal, good primary schools'. There is in other words a belief here in educational cures for educational evils. Some of the early American compensatory education programmes seem to have gone much further and approached the belief that poverty can be completely abolished through educational reform. Others take an opposing and more radical view of the changes necessary to ameliorate either poverty in general or educational poverty in particular. K. Coates and R. Silburn have expressed this view in a recent comment on the Plowden ideas:[5]

> The schools themselves could become, to a degree, centres of social regeneration: growth points of a new social consciousness among the poor, which might at last bring poverty under attack from its sufferers no less than from the all-too-small battalions of liberal welfare workers and social administrators.

Obviously many of these are sensible aims. Yet it is important at the same time to state baldly what these aims could not achieve. Education, in itself, will not solve the problem of poverty. The social structure that generates poverty generates its own shabby education system to serve it; and while it is useful to attack the symptom, the disease itself will continually find new manifestations if it is not understood and remedied. The solution to poverty involves, of course, the redistribution of effective social power. Self-confidence, no less than material welfare, is a crucial lack of the poor, and both can only be won by effective joint action. More contentiously, it seems to us that educational provision alone cannot solve even the problem of educational poverty, if only because in this sphere there are no purely educational problems.

Our own view in undertaking the EPA action-research was cautiously open-minded on the capacity of the educational system to reform itself, dubious about an educational approach to the abolition of poverty, but at least as optimistic as Plowden about the primary school and pre-schooling as points of entry for action-research aimed at inducing changes in the relation between school and community.

In principle action-research can approach the holistic end of the continuum. In practice it usually operates at the other extreme though often with implicit holistic expectations of the kind reflected in the early euphoria and rhetoric of the American Headstart programme. Perhaps it is mainly the confused contradiction between astronomical ends and minuscule means that underlies the asperity of such criticisms as Bernstein's 'education cannot compensate for society'. We have to know what is sociologically and politically possible. In part the answer to both questions turns on the willingness and power of a society to define education imperiously in relation to the other social organisations which carry educative or culturally transmitting functions, especially the family but also classes, neighbourhoods, ethnic groups and local communities. This depends again in part on economic and technical means. Obviously the feasibility of education as the dominant means to a particular social design is eased by wealth and growth, but the crucial factor here is political – the political structure and the will of political leadership.

Perhaps the importance of the economic and technical base for educational development is exaggerated. There are conspicuous variations in the level of educational development between countries of similar income and wealth per capita. And the remarkably durable success of classical China in using her educational system to create and maintain a ruling administrative class of mandarins was, it should be remembered, the invention of a pre-industrial society. Perhaps also the serviceability of education as an agent of social selection and distribution is exaggerated until one examines the evidence: for example it was shown in the Robbins Report that two-thirds of middle-class children with IQs of 130 + who were born in 1940–41 did not go on to a university education. Nevertheless it still remains a crucial question as to how seriously a society determines to realize the values in which the use of the educational system as a means is involved. That is the crux of the problem of educational inequality and the ultimate determinant of whether or not Plowden's positive discrimination will bring about its intended effects.

What, then, are the sought ends in the politics of education in modern Britain ? The dominant slogans are combinations of efficiency and equality. Efficiency for modernity. Equality for efficiency and justice. But both the meaning of these combined ends and the means postulated as adequate to their attainment remain dubious and confused. Thus the combination of equality of educational opportunity with the goal of national efficiency has led to policies designed to create and maintain a meritocracy – a principle which by no means commands universal acceptance.

However the essential fact of twentieth-century educational history is that egalitarian policies have failed. This must be the starting point for understanding the significance of our studies and to reach it we must review past principles and policies. There appears to us to have been a developing theoretical and practical debate in three stages about the way education can be used as a means towards the political and social end of equality.

In the first phase, from the beginning of the century to the end of the 1950s, the definition of policy was liberal – equality of opportunity. It meant equality of access to the more advanced stages of education for all children irrespective of their sex or social origin in classes, religious and ethnic groups or regions. It therefore expressed itself in such measures as building the scholarship ladder, abolishing grammar school fees, doing away with a system of separate secondary education for the minority and elementary education for the majority and substituting a system of common schooling with secondary schools 'end-on' to primary schools. In the later years of this phase it also meant expansion of higher education.

The logical end of the first phase, when equality of opportunity is combined with national efficiency, is meritocracy. In its most advanced educational expression this essentially liberal principle is to be found in the Preface to the Newsom Report written by the then Minister for Education, Sir Edward (later Lord) Boyle: 'The essential point is that all children should have an equal opportunity of acquiring intelligence, and of developing their talents and abilities to the full.' But the inexactitudes of psychometrics, the capriciousness of late developers, the survival of the private market in education along with the continuous renewal of non-educational avenues to higher social positions – all these factors together have prevented the emergence of an educationally based meritocracy.

The liberal notion of equality of opportunity dominated discussion at least until the 1950s. But it was never unchallenged by those who wrote in the tradition of R. H. Tawney and it was effectively lampooned in Michael Young's *Rise of the Meritocracy*. Writers like Tawney and Raymond Williams[6] always sought for an educational system which would be egalitarian in the much broader sense of providing a common culture irrespective of the more or less inescapable function of selection for different occupational destinies. There is a broad distinction of political and social aims here which, in the end, come to the most fundamental issue of the purposes of education in an urban industrial society and about which judgements are explicitly or implicitly made in any action-research programme of the type we have undertaken. One way of putting the distinction is that the liberal goal of efficient equality of opportunity is too restrictive: we have also to consider liberty and fraternity. Properly conceived the community school, an idea which we discuss in detail below, reflects the attribution of value to these other two great abstractions of the modern trilogy of political aims.

All this is to say nothing about the problem of feasibility of either narrowly or broadly conceived egalitarian aims. Tawney took it for granted that the processes of parliamentary democracy, serviced by the British type of civil administration, would be adequate as means to these ends. There is less confidence now and much more questioning as to what it might mean politically to achieve what Coates and Silburn have referred to as 'the redistribution of effective social power'. Questioning of this kind comes from many sources, but not least from recognition of the failures of past policies directed towards a greater equality of educational opportunity.

The essential judgement must be that the 'liberal' policies failed even in their own terms. For example, when, in a large number of the richer countries during the 1950s, a considerable expansion of educational facilities was envisaged, it was more or less assumed that, by making more facilities available, there would be a marked change in the social composition of student bodies and in the flow of people from the less favoured classes into the secondary schools and higher educational institutions. This has certainly not happened to the degree expected. While expansion of education was accompanied by some increase in both the absolute numbers and the proportions from poor families who reached the higher levels and the more prestigious types of education, nevertheless progress towards greater equality of educational opportunity as traditionally defined has been disappointing. It is now plain that the problem is more difficult than had been supposed and needs, in fact, to be posed in new terms.[7]

Too much has been claimed for the power of educational systems as instruments for the wholesale reform of societies which are characteristically hierarchical in their distribution of chances in life as between races, classes, the sexes and as between metropolitan/suburban and provincial/rural populations. The typical history of educational expansion in the 1950s and 1960s can be represented by a graph of inequality of attainment between the above-mentioned social categories which has shifted markedly upwards without changing its slope. In other words, relative chances did not alter materially despite expansion. No doubt, the higher norms of educational attainment contributed something towards raising the quality of life in urban industrial society – that, at least, is the faith of the educationist. But in terms of relative chances of income, status and welfare at birth, the impact of the educational system on the life of children remained heavily determined by their family and class origins. From the same point of view, what appears to have happened was a general adjustment of the occupational structure such that entry to it was in process of continuous upward redefinition in terms of educational qualifications. The traditional social pattern of selection remained remarkably stable. The school is only one influence among others, and, in relation to the phenomenon of social stratification, probably a fairly minor one. Attitudes towards schooling, and actual performance in school, reflect children's general social milieu and family background, and, probably most important of all, the expectations, built in by constraining custom, of his teachers. School reform helps but the improvement of teacher/pupil ratios, the building of new schools and even the provision of a wider variety of curricula have at best a limited effect as counterweights.

Moreover there has been a tendency to treat education as the waste paper basket of social policy − a repository for dealing with social problems where solutions are uncertain or where there is disinclination to wrestle with them seriously. Such problems are prone to be dubbed 'educational' and turned over to the schools to solve. But it was now increasingly plain that the schools cannot accomplish important social reforms such as the democratization of opportunity unless social reforms accompany the educational effort. And it also became more evident that the schools are hampered in achieving even their more traditional and strictly 'educational' purposes when, in societies changing rapidly in their technologies and in the aspirations of their populations, a comparable effort to make the required change in social structures and political organisation is lacking.

In summary, it may be said that liberal policies failed basically on an inadequate theory of learning. They failed to notice that the major determinants of educational attainment were not schoolmasters but social situations, not curriculum but motivation, not formal access to the school but support in the family and the community.

So the second phase began with its new emphasis on a theory of non-educational determination of education. In consequence of the experience of the first phase in trying to bring about greater equality of educational opportunity, there had to be a change in the meaning assigned to the phase. Its earlier meaning was equality of access to education: in the second phase its meaning gradually became equality of achievement. In this new interpretation a society affords equality of educational opportunity if the proportion of people from different social, economic or ethnic categories at all levels and in all types of education are more or less the same as the proportion of these people in the population at large. In other words the goal should not be the liberal one of equality of access but equality of outcome for the median member of each identifiable non-educationally defined group, i.e. the average woman or Negro or proletarian or rural dweller should have the same level of educational attainment as the average male, white, white-collar, suburbanite. If not there has been injustice.

This important social-cum-educational principle, with its radical implications for both social and educational policies, was graphically illustrated in the findings of the American Coleman Report[8] where educational attainments were compared as between Northerners and Southerners of white and non-white race. Research has shown that schooling between ages 6 and 18 (grade 1–12, in American schools) is associated with a divergence of the mean attainment of four categories of children who are not directly defined in educational terms.[9] The radical goal of educational equality of opportunity would, if realized, produce converging as opposed to diverging lines.

The Plowden Report belongs to this phase in the development of our understanding of the egalitarian issues in education and relates them to the social setting of the school.

With Plowden the close relationship of social deprivation, in neighbourhood and home, and educational attainment was well founded in research. Equally valid is the corollary that, if social conditions and parental interest could be improved, achievement might be expected to rise. One or two examples must suffice. J.W.B. Douglas in 1964 set the attainment scores of a large sample of upper primary children against a number of social factors.[10] From this survey certain extreme cases might be extrapolated. At eleven years of age and with 50 as the average mark, lower manual working-class children in unsatisfactory housing were scoring on average 46.66 as against the 56.91 of upper-middle-class children in satisfactory accommodation; as between the same groups divided by low and high levels of parental interest the scores were 46.32 and 59.26; polarized by 'very disturbed' and 'undisturbed' assessments, the two groups averaged 44.49 and 57.53; while the seventh child of the lower bracket of parents obtained 42.19 over against the 59.87 of the first child in the higher social category. Eleven per cent of the lower manual group and 54.3 per cent of the upper middle group obtained grammar-school places. Only 4.8 per cent of the children in a poorly assessed lower-working-class school as opposed to 53.22 per cent of those in a highly assessed upper-middle-class school obtained places in grammar schools. Just below the cut-off point for selection, 1.4 per cent only of the 'lower manual' children and as many as 42.9 per cent of 'upper middle' children were in grammar, technical or independent schools.

These admittedly are deliberately extracted extremes, but the EPA projects were planned to consider one of these extremes. A very disturbed child of unskilled parents, who showed no interest in his schooling and who lived in unsatisfactory accommodation, was, for example, no rarity in Liverpool 7. In 1967, the Ministry of Social Security reported that 7 per cent of families were at or below the poverty line. Either figure would include a large number of the study area's population; indeed, in 1968, the Merseyside Child Poverty Action Group found that one in three in Liverpool 8 were living in poverty as defined by the Ministry of Social Security while, in 1971, the Child Poverty Action Group claimed that one in every six children in the nation was on or below the poverty line.[11]

Professor Wiseman argued convincingly that ' "home" variables have, pro rata, twice the weight of "neighbourhood" and "school" variables put together' when correlated with educational attainment.[12] His research indicated that it was parental attitudes rather than social levels which were more important in the home. Again, the National Child Development Study showed that parents in the highest occupational grouping were much readier to initiate school contacts than those in the lowest grouping, and there was a similar social gap in terms of adjustment to school.[13] A recent examination of truancy suggests that gross absenteeism is solidly linked with unsatisfactory home life and uninterested parents.[14]

We are not here, it must be added, embracing the view that the pre-Plowden literature had overemphasized the part played by class in determining educational performance. On the contrary we agree with the sociological critique of the Plowden Report by B. Bernstein and B. Davies, in which they expressed the view that, by its concentration on child centredness, Plowden had underestimated class distinctions.[15] As these writers argue, 'evidence suggests a strong relationship between social class and the extent of the mother's preparation of her child for school' and that 'one would wish to guard against an argument that avoided including attitudes as a dimension of class differences'.

At all events, in reading the Plowden Report, one could hardly escape the view that equality of opportunity was, without equality of conditions, a sham. Home circumstances were obviously critical and these in turn were adversely affected by class and neighbourhood patterns. The school, where, after all, the children spent only five hours of the day, seemed comparatively powerless to alter matters radically of its own volition. Assuredly, a decision to consider the EPA school in its communal setting was a wise one, and the Plowden Committee had been well advised to recommend that community schools should be developed in all areas but especially in EPAS.

Our own definition of the problem in 1968 was consonant with the debate up to this point and was in accord with the Plowden approach accepting that positive discrimination held out the hope of further steps towards the new definition of equality of opportunity.

But in the early months of our work we began to realise that there were unsolved issues behind the equality debate even in its advanced formulation and especially when applied to the children of the educational priority areas. The debate could be taken beyond equality of educational opportunity to a third phase which involves reappraisal of the functions of education in contemporary society. Education for what? The debate over equality as we have summarized it – a movement from preoccupation with equality of access towards concern with equality of outcomes as between social groups – is essentially a discussion about education for whom and to do what. In planning our intervention in schools we were forced sooner or later to consider both questions and in doing so to question whether an EPA programme is anything more than a new formula for fair competition in the educational selection race.

What assumptions could or should be made about the world into which our EPA children would enter after school? Were we concerned simply to introduce a greater measure of justice into an educational system which traditionally selected the minority for higher education and upward social mobility out of the EPA district, leaving the majority to be taught, mainly by a huge hidden curriculum, a sense of their own relative incompetence and impotence – a modern, humane and even relatively enjoyed form of gentling the masses? Or could we assume a wide programme of social reform which would democratize local power structures and diversify local occupational opportunities so that society would look to its schools for a supply of young people educated for political and social responsibility and linked to their communities not by failure in the competition but by rich opportunities for work and life? Even short of the assumption of extra-educational reform how far should we concentrate on making recognition easier for the able minority and how far on the majority who are destined to live their lives in the EPA? And if the latter did this not mean posing an alternative curriculum realistically related to the EPA environment and designed to equip the rising generation with the knowledge and skills to cope with, give power over and in the end to transform the conditions of their local community?

It was, and is, commonly felt that a discriminatory boost was needed in the backward areas to bring education up to scratch so that, for instance, the thousands leaving school at fifteen who had the potential to benefit from advanced schooling might stay on. The Plowden Report argued this respectable and widely held thesis with admirable spirit. It detailed a programme of 'positive discrimination' and 'a new distribution of educational resources', through priority building and minor works, improved staffing and auxiliary help, supplemented salaries and so on. This was designed to cater for 'a great reservoir of unrealised potential', for 'what these deprived areas need most are perfectly normal good primary schools'. Twice over Plowden decreed that the EPA schools should be as good as the best in the land.[16]

Because the national system of education was seen not to operate efficiently in its uniform application across the country, it was accepted that a differential application would help close, to quote Plowden again, 'the gap between educational opportunities of the most and least fortunate children ... for economic and social reasons alike'. But, logically, an alternative existed. It was worth considering that what was wrong was a uniform system, and that differing areas required differing educational formats.

This viewpoint, Eric Midwinter insisted in our early conferences, does no disservice to the pioneers who campaigned for parity of opportunity. They doubtless imagined that equality of opportunity would beget conditions in which forthcoming generations would automatically start at par. This has not, unhappily, transpired. Those working in a deprived area are typically sympathetic to the egalitarian tradition and find the alarums and the postures of the anti-egalitarian commentators laughable.[17] They shout before they are hurt. One might recall the words of R. H. Tawney: of the nation's children, he wrote 'if, instead of rejuvenating the world, they grind corn for the Philistines and doff bobbins for the mill-owners, the responsibility is ours into whose hands the prodigality of nature pours life itself'.[18] Eventually an EPA community must stand on its own feet like any other and rejuvenate its world, and that is a dogma which might hold good on both political wings.

Notes

1 See *Notes Towards a Definition of Culture*.
2 *Education and Values*, 1965, Faber, especially chapter 7.
3 C. B. Cox and A. E. Dyson (eds) *Fight for Education*: T. E. B. Howarth, *Culture, Anarchy and the Public Schools*, Critical Quarterly Society, 1969.
4 J. Goldthorpe, 'Theories of industrial society: Reflections on the recrudescence of historicism and the future of futurology', *European*

Journal of Sociology, vol. 12, 1972, pp. 263–88.

5 'Education in poverty' in David Rubinstein and Colin Stoneman (eds), 1970, *Education for Democracy*, Penguin Education Special.

6 See, for example, Raymond Williams, 1966, *Culture and Society*, Penguin, *The Long Revolution*, Penguin, 1965.

7 Cf. Charles Frankel's and A. H. Halsey's Introduction to *Educational Policies for the 1970s*, OECD, 1971, pp. 14ff.

8 James S. Coleman *et al.*, 1966, *Equality of Educational Opportunity*, US Government Printing Office, Washington DC.

9 We found some evidence of similar patterns in our EPA schools (*Educational Priority*, vol., chapter 5).

10 J. W. B. Douglas, 1964, *The Home and the School*, MacGibbon & Kee.

11 R. Boyson (ed), 1971, *Down with the Poor*, CPAG.

12 S. Wiseman, 'The Manchester survey', App. IX, *Plowden Report*, ii.

13 1st Report of the National Child Development Study (1958 Cohort), April 1966, App. X, *Plowden Report*, ii, *Research and Surveys*, 1967.

14 M. J. Tyerman, 1968, *Truancy*, University of London Press.

15 B. Bernstein and B. Davies, 'Some sociological comments on Plowden', in R. S. Peters (ed.), *Perspectives on Plowden*, 1969, Routledge & Kegan Paul, pp. 58–77.

16 Plowden, *op. cit.*, ch. 5, especially paras 136–52 and 158–73.

17 For instance, C. B. Cox and A. E. Dyson (eds), *op. cit.*

18 R. H. Tawney, *The Acquisitive Society*, Bell, 1921, republished 1961 Fontana p. 81.

1.5 Positive discrimination in education, individual groups and institutions

J. Barnes and H. Lucas

The policy of positive discrimination

In this paper we report our attempts to clarify the nature and identify the possible outcomes of one series of policies which have been designed to promote greater equality in British primary education: 'positive discrimination in the allocation of educational resources ... in favour of areas and schools where children are most severely handicapped by home conditions'.

The policy was first proposed by the Plowden Council in 1967 in its report on 'primary education in all its aspects'. Their formulations were designed to encompass an extremely complex series of interactions, many of which they imply rather than specify. Children in educational priority areas were seen to be surrounded by a 'seamless web of circumstance', where everything was causing everything else. Individuals and institutions were interacting together in a downward spiral of deprivation, making identification of cause or consequence redundant – perhaps impossible. The basic dynamic appears to have been as follows: various non-educational characteristics of groups of children – the colour of their skin, the occupation of their father, the financial circumstances of their family – are determinants of their educational performance. The effect of combinations of these attributes on a child's capacity to perform successfully at school is cumulative. The Council identified this as 'cumulative deprivation', a situation which, they said, occurred when one deprivation 'reinforced' another. Children subject to these cumulative deprivations are not scattered at random across the population. They are concentrated in certain (primarily urban) areas and schools where their interaction together, and with an environment 'ingrained with the grime of generations', increased the cumulative effect of disadvantage. Situations in

Source: *Educational Priority*, J. Barnes, (ed.) (1975) HMSO vol. 3, 239–74.

the schools are thus a consequence, and then become a further cause of disadvantage for the children attending them. The concentration of disadvantaged families in poor neighbourhoods has consequences for their community institutions, which lack coherent organization and suffer from poor leadership. And to complete the circle, disorganization at the community and family level contributes further to the educational effects of initially non-educational circumstances: race, social class, income, etc.

In some respects the policy proposed by the Council to deal with this situation was clear and unambiguous. It was to be an educational policy; and one which had relatively moderate resource implications. Marginal increments to the total volume of resources available to education were to be diverted to educational priority areas and their children and schools. The main weapon in the attack on multiple deprivation was to be more effective schools. Secondly 'objective criteria for the selection of educational priority schools and areas' were provided. The policy would be focused on the poor; but it would not require poor people to identify, and to risk stigmatizing themselves in order to receive help. The target for the policy was to be disadvantaged areas and the schools in them.

In other respects the Council's recommendations are less easy to understand. In particular, although their concern for disadvantaged schools and areas is unequivocal, it occasionally becomes muddled with a further concern: for disadvantaged groups and individuals and their families. Certainly the Report moves very easily from one to the other without recognizing the consequences of the change of focus. And further, it is not clear what the effects of positive discrimination on its recipients are intended to be. The Council advised, for instance, that 'the first step must be to raise the schools with low standards to the national average. The second quite deliberately to make them better.' The target for the policy here is schools; but it is not clear whether 'better' refers specifically and only to the volume of resources going to the schools, to the opportunities available to, or to the actual performance of the children in them. Initial priority should, they urged, be given 'to the schools which by our criteria contain the ten per cent of most deprived children'; but for a long term programme they envisaged an extension of positive discrimination beyond 'an arbitrary figure of ten per cent of the population'. (Notice that the target for the policy has moved from schools to people.) Both in the long and the short term, a national policy of positive discrimination should 'favour schools in neighbourhoods where children are most severely handicapped by home conditions'.

Our analysis has been directed towards a clarification of these two issues: of who can be helped, and of what can be achieved by a policy of positive discrimination in favour of educational priority area schools. In the first section of text below we examine the concept of educational disadvantage itself. We attempt to identify the disadvantaged children in one inner city population. We ask whether the notion of disadvantage is a meaningful way to characterise their social and educational situation. And we attempt to place the phenomenon in the context of its social geography by exploring how far disadvantaged or poor children are concentrated in disadvantaged or poor areas. From this we are able to estimate possible upper limits to the scope of the policy expressed in terms of who can be helped. In the secand section of text we examine what effect a discriminatory policy can have. This necessarily involves an attempt to identify an effect from the social and educational context of schools which exists independently of the circumstances of individual children. Presuming that a discriminatory policy will operate in some way to counteract this contextual effect, we once again estimate the upper limits to the scope of the policy. The data we use were largely gathered at the individual level; and we would contend that such a heterogeneous concept as educational disadvantage can only be studied in this way. But at the same time our concern is largely with the policy consequences for groups of children and for schools. We would contend in this respect that, while educational policies might be designed to help particular groups of individuals (and these groups might be very small and homogeneous), policies can hardly be expected to accommodate the unique life situations of particular individuals. Teachers do this while teaching children; we are unsure what a policy for it would look like other than in some very general and perhaps rhetorical sense.

Sources of data

The data used were all derived from work undertaken by the Research and Statistics Group of the Inner London Education Authority (the ILEA) during the period 1968–71. It should be remembered that the original data were collected in order to provide the Authority with descriptive material on its primary schools and their children. Certainly the child data are in a number of ways unreliable and inadequate for our purposes. And our findings can only be applied with confidence to Inner London. We were aware of these limitations throughout the analysis, and have taken account of them when presenting our conclusions.

1 Information on the schools: from the index of relative institutional deprivation

During 1967–68 the Research and Statistics Group of the ILEA developed an Index to identify primary schools which answered to the Plowden Council's definition of educational priority area schools. The criteria included in the Index were either those recommended by the Plowden Council or conveniently near equivalents. The measures of each of the criteria were either school-based or collected for a notional catchment area for all primary schools in the ILEA. School scores on each of the measures were scaled to conform to a distribution between 0 and 100; and these scaled scores were summed to derive an equally weighted, composite, institutional score. Schools were then ranked, according to their composite score, to create an Index of Relative School Deprivation.

A basic premise of our analysis is that the logic of this Index is an adequate and acceptable way to identify educational priority area schools. We offer no defence of the Index, except to say that there was substantial agreement between the schools' rank positions on it and practitioner assessments of their relative positions. It was, and still is, used by the ILEA as one basis for allocating extra resources to schools thought to need help; and in spite of its limitations which are discussed in the account of its construction, it appears to have few rivals as an attempt to identify disadvantaged schools or areas as targets for positive discrimination.

2   Information on the children: from the ILEA literacy survey

At the same time as the construction of its Index of EPA Primary Schools, the ILEA conducted the first stage of a survey of reading performance in one age cohort of children in its junior schools. All junior schools in the authority were asked to test all children who were in their second junior school year on a reading test. In addition, class and head teachers were asked to complete a questionnaire giving a range of background information on each child. Towards the end of the school year 1970–71 all junior schools in the Authority were again asked to test all children in the same cohort on a parallel form of the original reading test. The cohort was then in its last year in primary school.

Table 1 (p. 82) shows the absolute size of that cohort of ILEA children from their birth year in 1960 to their year of transfer to secondary school in 1971. The table shows, firstly, that the cohort was growing smaller at a net rate of 2.7 per cent per annum for each year it was in ILEA primary schools and, secondly, that a reading test score was achieved for a very high proportion of the universe of children. We nevertheless need to be extremely careful when speaking about the performance of the whole cohort.

A file was created containing both school and child-based data. We set out the main data items placed on this file in Table 2. But briefly, all infant schools were excluded together with any junior schools on which there were no data from the schools' Index of Deprivation. As we had measures from the child data on only eight of the ten variables in the initial

Table 1   Changes in the size of the age cohort over time

Year		Size	Change	% Change
1960	Birth cohort	56,642		
			−18,499	−32.7
1965	Cohort 5 + years old	38,143		
			− 864	− 2.3
1966	Cohort 6 + years old	37,279		
			− 1,001	− 2.7
1967	Cohort 7 + years old	36,278		
			− 1,152	− 3.2
1968*	Cohort 8 + years old	35,126		
			− 977	− 2.8
1969	Cohort 9 + years old	34,149		
			− 980	− 2.9
1970	Cohort 10 + years old	33,169		
			− 803	− 2.4
1971†	Cohort 11 + years old	32,366		
Mean Net Percentage Change 1965–1971				− 2.7

* Time of initial reading survey: 31,308 children tested.
† Time of second reading survey: 31,731 children tested.
  Derived from ILEA Statistics.

schools' Index, a new eight variable Index of Schools was constructed for the file. To the new file, already containing both the school scores and their rank position on this new Index, were added equivalent variables for each individual child, together, where they were available, with the reading test scores. We then added three other pieces of data to characterize schools: the proportion of semi-skilled and unskilled workers' children in each school, the proportion of immigrant children in each school and the score and rank position of each school on the original ILEA Schools' Index of Relative Deprivation.

Disadvantaged children: the ecological fallacy

It is our conclusion that, in as far as they were concerned to help poor children or children in disadvantaged or deprived circumstances, the analysis of the Plowden Council which led it to advocate an educational priority area or school programme was based on a methodological fallacy. The fallacy occurs when ecological methods of analysis are used − when aggregated or averaged data are used to characterize areas or institutions. It is caused by a concentration on the principal or dominant pattern, and a failure to recognize the variation or heterogeneity. The fallacy in this

Table 2 Main data items used in the analysis

I	Data on the schools	Data we used

A *Source : ILEA Schools Index*

(i) School's scaled score on the EPA Index	
(ii) School's rank position on the EPA Index	To identify the EPA Schools and to arrange schools into Quartiles. (See Tables 4A, 4B, and 6.)
(iii) School's scaled score on the EPA Index amended by removing factors of overcrowding of houses and housing stress	To characterise schools for the regression analysis. (See Tables 9, 11 and 12.)
(iv) School's rank position on the amended Index	

B *Data from the Literary Survey averaged over all the children in the same school*

(i) Percentage of children whose parent or guardian was a semi-skilled or unskilled manual worker	To characterize schools for the regression analysis. (See Table 8.)
(ii) Percentage of children who were immigrant (i.e., stated country of origin not the United Kingdom or the Republic of Ireland)	To characterize schools for the regression analysis. (See Table 8.)

2	Data on the Children

C *Source: 1968 Literacy Survey*

	For the Index of Disadvantage. Tables 3, 4A, 4B, 6, 7A and 7B	For the regression analysis. Only if the following data were available. Tables 5, 8, 9, 10, 11 and 12
(i) Country of origin of the child	X	X
(ii) Number of schools attended by the child	X	
(iii) Number of teachers who had taught the child	X	

(iv) Number of absences during one term	X	
(v) Family size	X	X
(vi) Whether the child received free school meals	X	X
(vii) Occupation of parent or guardian (a proxy measure for social class)	X	X
(viii) Child's standardized score on the SRA Reading Test		(X)
D *Source: 1971 Literacy Survey*		
(i) Child's standardized score on the SRB Reading Test		
(ii) Child's rank position on a Verbal Reasoning Test completed prior to transfer to secondary school	X*	

* Children whose position was unknown were dropped for the analysis presented in Table 6.

particular case does not take account of the diversity within any group of educational priority schools, of the wide distribution of circumstances to which children outside any such group of schools are subject, nor does it recognize the logical jump between a counting of separate problems and the identification of a condition of cumulative disadvantage or deprivation. In advocating a priority area or school programme to meet the needs of poor children, the Council went beyond conclusions which could have been borne out by analysis of its data.

The policy consequences are that, as a device for helping poor children, positive discrimination through schools can only be disappointing. Most poor families do not live in poor areas; they are widely scattered throughout the population. A policy which discriminated in favour of the most disadvantaged 10 per cent of schools, could only help a relatively small proportion of the total number of poor or disadvantaged children. And trying to bring help to more of them by expanding the number of schools would run into diminishing returns: as more schools were added into the programme, so the rate at which relatively privileged children were included would increase faster than the rate for disadvantaged children. In effect, positive discrimination in favour of the most disadvantaged schools establishes for itself criteria which limit the number of disadvantaged people that can be reached.

1 Children at risk

We came to this conclusion once we had found the numbers and the various proportions of children, inside and outside priority area schools, who were at risk on criteria equivalent to those which had been used to identify the schools. Tables 3, 4A and 4B summarize our findings. For each of the school criteria on which we had individualized data, children were assigned an at-risk or not at-risk score; and these scores were added together to create a cumulative index. For analysis using the individual items, we said simply that children were either at-risk or not at-risk. For the analysis using the cumulative index, we said that children with high scores (five or more out of a maximum of eight) were at risk of being disadvantaged. For the sake of clear exposition we call these the disadvantaged children, but we think there should be more investigation of a 'condition of disadvantage' before a positive diagnosis is made. We said children with low scores on the index (zero or one) were not at risk. We call these the non-disadvantaged children. They cannot be called a privileged group because their 'objective' circumstances have been defined by a series of negatives: they were not immigrants, not unskilled or semi-skilled workers' children, they were not from large families, etc. Schools are grouped in two ways for Tables 3 and 4A and 4B. The 'Least Privileged Group' are those junior schools which were included in the 150 primary schools having the highest scores on the ILEA Index of Schools. We call these the EPA schools in the text below, because they are the group which conform most strongly to the Plowden Council's definition of education.¹ priority area schools. The second way in which schools are grouped (for Table 4B) is into approximate quartiles on the ILEA Index of Schools; this enables us to illustrate the effect, in terms of the individual children who would be encompassed, of extending the range of schools in any educational priority area programme.

The proportions of the total population at-risk on the individual items in the analysis varies from 16 per cent, in the case of high pupil mobility, to 50 per cent in the case of low social class (see Table 3). The overall pattern is that, in each case, between one in five and one in three of the cohort are at risk on these items, although the proportions are higher for social class and low verbal reasoning.

As could be expected, the proportions of children at risk in the EPA schools are higher than in the total population; but they only go above 50 per cent on those two items whose incidence in the population is also significantly high. On two items – pupil mobility and high absenteeism – the incidence in the EPA schools is similar to that which could be expected in any other group of schools in this population.

Although children with these individual at-risk characteristics are a

Table 3 Proportion of children at risk and not at risk on the single items of risk (%)

	Immigrant children	High pupil mobility	High teacher mobility	High absenteeism	Large families	Free meals	Low verbal reasoning scores	Low social class
Least privileged group of schools (EPA Schools) (N = 4,158)								
Not at risk	67.75	81.48	70.66	73.71	57.96	68.22	49.86	37.45
At risk	30.57 } 32.25	14.14 } 18.52	23.74 } 29.34	17.27 } 26.29	34.53 } 42.03	29.56 } 31.76	30.47 } 50.14	50.07 } 62.55
Don't know	1.68	4.38	5.60	9.02	7.5	2.2	19.67	12.48
All other schools (N = 26,338)								
Not at risk	83.55	84.20	81.65	76.67	67.46	82.79	64.09	52.11
At risk	16.45 } 16.45	13.03 } 15.80	15.15 } 18.34	17.59 } 24.33	27.59 } 32.53	16.57 } 17.21	17.80 } 35.91	38.40 } 47.89
Don't know	—	2.77	3.19	6.74	4.94	0.64	18.11	9.49
Total (N = 30,496)								
Not at risk	81.56	83.99	79.97	75.48	65.90	80.73	62.19	49.98
At Risk	18.22 } 18.44	13.05 } 16.00	16.53 } 20.03	17.52 } 24.52	28.55 } 34.10	18.42 } 19.27	19.52 } 37.81	39.96 } 50.20
Don't know	0.22	2.95	3.50	7.00	5.55	0.85	18.29	10.06
Number of cases of risk in the least privileged schools: all other schools	1:3.2	1:5.4	1:4.0	1:5.9	1:4.9	1:3.4	1:4.5	1:4.9

Table 4A   Individuals at risk on the cumulative child at-risk index of disadvantage in the least privileged group of schools
i by school group by level of risk
ii by level of risk by school group

level of risk	least privileged schools (%)	all other schools (%)	total (%)
i *least privileged group of schools: the EPA schools*			
0	6.0	14.5	13.3
1	15.4	25.5	24.1
2	22.1	24.7	24.3
3	21.8	18.0	18.5
4	17.9	10.6	11.6
5 +	16.8	6.7	8.1
Base = 100%	4158	26338	30496
ii *by level of risk*			
0 %	6.1	93.9	100
1 %	8.7	91.3	100
2 %	12.4	87.6	100
3 %	16.1	83.9	100
4 %	21.0	79.0	100
5 + %	28.2	71.8	100
Total %	13.6	86.4	100

higher proportion of the population of EPA schools than they are of the population generally, their total number is far greater outside the EPA schools. For instance we might wish to say that immigrant children are concentrated in under-privileged EPA schools; but from our evidence, for every immigrant child that is in an EPA school three are not. There are five times as many children at-risk because they come from large families outside the EPA schools than there are inside them. There are five times as many unskilled and semi-skilled workers' children, three and a half times as many children receiving free school meals and four and a half times as many children with low verbal reasoning scores outside the EPA schools than there are in them.

It might be argued that, although the incidence of individual situations of need is widely spread throughout the population, cumulative disadvantage is a phenomenon more common to the EPA schools. Tables 4A and 4B show our findings on this matter. In the total cohort

Table 4B Individuals at risk on the cumulative child at-risk index of disadvantage in the schools grouped into approximate EPA quartiles
i by school group by level of risk
ii by level of risk by school group

level of risk	least privileged quartile (%)	second quartile (%)	third quartile (%)	most privileged quartile (%)
i *schools grouped into quartiles*				
0	6.7	11.4	14.0	22.2
1	17.5	22.3	26.9	30.4
2	23.0	24.5	25.4	24.0
3	21.6	20.3	18.0	13.5
4	16.8	12.4	10.1	6.6
5 +	14.3	9.0	5.5	3.3
Base 100%	7029	9122	7670	6675
ii *level of risk*				
0%	11.6	25.6	26.4	36.4
1%	16.8	27.6	28.0	27.6
2%	21.9	30.2	26.3	21.6
3%	26.8	32.8	24.5	15.9
4%	33.6	32.0	21.9	12.6
5 + %	40.5	33.3	17.1	9.0
Total %	23.0	29.9	25.2	21.9

11,400 children – one in three – had scores of zero or one. We can say that these children are not disadvantaged. However, two and a half thousand children – one in every twelve – were multiply disadvantaged on our measures and according to our definition.

As with the single at-risk items, these children comprise a significantly higher proportion of the EPA schools than of the total population: 16.8 per cent as opposed to 8.1 per cent (Table 4A). Even so, even in the EPA schools, the disadvantaged group are outnumbered by children who are not disadvantaged: for every three children in these schools who are at risk of being disadvantaged, four are not.

Perhaps most significantly, less than one third of the multiply disadvantaged children are in the EPA schools. In other words, resources going to these schools reach 13.6 per cent of all the children in the cohort, but only 28.2 per cent (two out of every seven) of the disadvantaged children in it. It would clearly be unrealistic to expect all the disadvantaged children to be in the disadvantaged EPA schools. And it is an open question what proportion of them it would be regarded as satisfactory for any schools' programme to pick up. Indeed, given limited resources, a school or area policy acts as an effective rationing device.

But what seems to us to be important is that the logic of discriminatory school or area policies constrains the upper limit to their effectiveness seen in this way. The policy can only be discriminatory if some schools are excluded; but excluding some schools excludes some disadvantaged children. Table 4B illustrates the point. By encompassing half the schools in this analysis, a school programme of positive discrimination could bring benefit to 74 per cent of the disadvantaged children; but 40 per cent of the children who were not disadvantaged would also be included. By expanding to three quarters of all schools (78 per cent of all children), 90 per cent of high risk children could be reached but so also would nearly two thirds of the non-disadvantaged group. Nine per cent of disadvantaged children are in the most privileged quartile of schools, where they comprise 3 per cent of the population. To help this group, a schools' programme would need to include all schools and all children; it could hardly then be discriminatory according to the conventional definitions.

We believe that the results of this part of our analysis confront the policy of discrimination in favour of EPA schools with a paradox. It seems likely that the majority of disadvantaged children are not in disadvantaged areas, and the majority of children in disadvantaged areas are not disadvantaged. At the least this means the policies to assist disadvantaged schools or areas should not be seen as alternatives to policies which are focused on groups of children, whether these groups are to be identified in terms of single or combined indicators of need.

Further, we might wish to develop the policy by saying that any help for disadvantaged children which was channelled through a positively biased schools' programme should be differentially weighted according to the proportion of disadvantaged children in each school. But if such a programme were to be sensitively adjusted to the needs of different groups of children, it would need to take account of their relative positions within a school as well as the presence of their disadvantage measured on 'objective' indicators of need. In other words, once the policy moves from one which simply discriminates among schools to one which accommodates intra school differences, it must recognize other parameters. We illustrate something of what we mean by this in the text below, when we move from analysis of the children's circumstances to say something about their behaviour.

D

2 *Reading performance and objective and relative disadvantage*

We used performance on the reading test, given at the beginning of the children's second year in the junior school, to compare their objective and their relative situations seen in behavioural terms. We used this because, effectively, there was no other available measure of the children's behaviour. Clearly it provides a narrow view of a child's relative position in a school and other measures might have given different results. But every primary school tries to teach this skill, and its acquisition is seen to be particularly important for children of this age. Given this, it seems to us that reading performance is a powerful indicator of the degree to which a child is being assimilated into the main academic culture of the school.

Tables 5 and 6 provide basic descriptive statistics on the reading performance of the children in this analysis. For Table 5 groups of children are organized according to categorizations on need indicators. In Table 6 children are ranked according to their level of risk of being disadvantaged and by the previous school groupings. It is important to be clear what can be inferred from these tables. They represent the extant reading performance of groups of children: performances which are a consequence of the interaction of all kinds of factors. In the second section of the paper we attribute variations in reading performance to possible 'effects': but for the moment we wish to illustrate the actual situation, at one point in time, whatever the apparent reason for it.

Not surprisingly our broad findings are that, as children's objective circumstances become more disadvantaged, so their reading performance tends to be lower. But the actual size of the differences found between privileged and underprivileged children do seem to be disturbingly large. The performance of disadvantaged children in the EPA schools is slightly below that of similar children in the privileged schools. But at the same time, there are senses in which the relative position of disadvantaged children in privileged schools is actually worse than it is in EPA schools. In absolute terms disadvantaged children appear to be poor readers whatever sort of school they are in. In privileged schools, where average reading performances are high, low performing disadvantaged children are therefore relatively worse off.

Table 5 shows the average reading scores for groups of children as various home background factors or characteristics of family circumstance are controlled for. The average reading score for the whole group of children, for instance, is 95.5. When the occupation of the children's father (our proxy for social class) is controlled, the averages range from 107.4, for the children of professional and managerial workers, to 89.1, for unskilled workers' children. The range of average scores, controlled, is twenty six points of reading score (more than two years of reading age):

Table 5 Mean reading scores for groups of children

A according to social class
B for West Indian immigrant and groups born in the United Kingdom

	N	Mean score	SD
Total	22,614	95.5	15.28
A Social class			
Social class I	1,872	107.4	14.59
Social class II	3,539	100.4	14.43
Social class III	7,662	96.0	14.29
Social class IV	5,073	92.5	13.72
Social class V	4,468	89.1	13.95
B Non-immigrant and West Indian immigrant groups			
Non-immigrant			
Social class I	1,845	107.5	14.64
Social class II	3,425	100.7	14.45
Social class III	7,113	96.6	14.35
Social class IV	4,432	93.3	13.81
Social class V	3,793	90.2	14.19
West Indian immigrant			
Social class I	27	——	——
Social class II	114	91.8	13.78
Social class III	549	88.9	13.47
Social class IV	641	87.2	13.04
Social class V	675	83.1	12.55

between the average score of professional and managerial workers' children, who were born in the United Kingdom, who do not recieve free school meals and who come from small families and the children of West Indian immigrant unskilled workers, whether or not they receive free school meals and irrespective of their family size.

A simple comparison of mean scores does not recognize that, in every case, there is nearly as much variation in score within one of these groups as there is within the whole population. In order to illustrate the size of the differences among groups, therefore, we prefer to use a measure of the extent to which the various distributions of score overlap each other.

The reading performance of 50 per cent of the whole population represented in Table 5 falls below 95.5. The performance of 86 per cent of West Indian immigrant unskilled workers' children falls below this point. In other words, 86 per cent of this group of West Indian immigrant children score below the average for the population. Seventy-five per cent

Table 6   Individuals at risk on the cumulative child index of disadvantage: mean reading score and standard deviation
a   by the least privileged group of schools by level of risk
b   by the schools grouped into 'quartiles' by level of risk

a   least privileged group of schools

Level of risk	Least privileged group of schools (N = 3284)		All other schools in the index of privilege (N = 21360)		Total (N = 25952)	
	Mean	SD	Mean	SD	Mean	SD
0	98.8	12.7	104.1	13.3	103.8	13.3
1	94.4	13.2	99.6	13.6	99.1	13.7
2	90.6	13.3	94.9	14.4	94.4	14.3
3	85.7	12.2	90.3	13.9	89.6	13.7
4	82.5	13.3	85.7	13.7	85.0	13.7
5+	80.7	12.1	81.9	12.5	81.5	12.4
Total	88.0	14.0	95.5	15.2	94.6	15.2

b   schools grouped into 'quartiles'

Level of risk	least privileged quartile (N = 5581)		second quartile (N = 7292)		third quartile (N = 6291)		most privileged quartile (N = 5480)	
	Mean	SD	Mean	SD	Mean	SD	Mean	SD
0	99.6	13.3	101.8	12.9	103.9	13.3	106.5	13.1
1	95.6	13.1	98.1	13.1	99.2	13.6	102.2	14.0
2	91.2	13.5	93.1	13.9	95.3	14.1	98.2	15.0
3	86.6	13.0	88.6	13.3	91.3	13.7	94.1	14.6
4	83.1	13.3	84.8	13.7	85.9	13.5	89.6	14.1
5+	80.6	12.1	81.4	12.2	83.2	12.7	84.2	13.3
Total	89.2	14.4	93.0	14.7	95.9	14.8	100.4	15.1

of all West Indian immigrant children score below the average for the non-immigrant children in the analysis. Seventy-seven per cent of non-immigrant professional workers' children score above the average for all non-immigrant children. Ninety-seven per cent of West Indian immigrant unskilled workers' children score below average for non-immigrant professional workers' children; and 71 per cent of West Indian immigrant unskilled workers' children score below the average for non-immigrant unskilled workers' children. For whatever reason, differences in reading performance between privileged and disadvantaged children appear to be very large indeed.

A similar calculation from the mean and standard deviation of scores in Table 6 simply confirms this. The differences in mean score between zero risk children and children with a score of five or more on the index of disadvantage is of the order of twenty-two points (nearly two years of reading age); and 96 per cent of the high risk children score below the average for the zero risk group.

The average reading performance of high risk children in EPA schools is only one point of score below their average performance in all other schools, while high risk children in the most privileged quartile of schools do slightly better in an absolute sense: the difference of mean scores between disadvantaged children in EPA and in the most privileged quartile of schools is therefore of the order of three and a half points. In other words, 53 per cent of high risk children in EPA schools score below the average for high risk children in all other schools, but 61 per cent fall below the average for high risk children in the privileged schools. On the other hand, looking at intra school differences, high risk children in privileged schools are worse off relative to their classmates. Again the point can be illustrated with reference to distributions of score. Eighty per cent of high risk children score below the average for the total population; 70 per cent score below the average for EPA schools; and 86 per cent score below the average for the most privileged group of schools.

Clearly disadvantaged children in privileged schools have potentially more access to privileged children. But from this piece of analysis we do not know whether either of the groups take advantage of whatever opportunities this offers or whether, if they did, either would benefit from it. We do know that high risk children in privileged schools do slightly better than similarly defined groups of children in EPA schools. But it should be remembered that, in every case, the reading performance of groups of disadvantaged children is extremely low, that the differences between their scores in different sorts of school are relatively small, and that the performance of high risk children is more deviant for privileged schools and closer to the average in EPA schools.

We have previously demonstrated that there is only a loose correlation between the objectively measured and accepted distribution of disadvantaged schools and the spread of similarly identified groups of children. The geographical distribution of children at risk of being disadvantaged is not confined to a particular sample of schools; and school programmes of positive discrimination cannot be alternatives to other programmes of help for children in need. We can now also say with some confidence that educationally disadvantaged circumstances are themselves diverse. The behaviour – measured in terms of reading performance – of groups of disadvantaged children is different from that of privileged groups, and from groups that are not disadvantaged. But we have also illustrated that groups of children whose circumstances are identical on objective indicators (they are all at risk of being disadvantaged) can be in quite different social and educational situations. It may be that it is more pleasant in some way for disadvantaged children to be in privileged schools; it is certain that their group performance is low wherever they are. Once again we can ask what follows. At the very least programmes of positive discrimination must face the low performance of groups of disadvantaged children wherever they are: with concentrations of low performance in EPA schools and extreme diversities in performance between groups of children in privileged schools.

School context and family circumstance

The first stage of our analysis was focused on the concept of child disadvantage, and was concerned to establish upper limits to what school and area based programmes can achieve as devices for rationing and allocating resources. But there is a second proposition implied by the policy of positive discrimination in favour of schools: that disadvantaged schools themselves somehow affect performance irrespective of the home circumstances of children. Certainly there was some evidence for this from the first stage of our analysis; the average reading performance of disadvantaged children in privileged schools was slightly higher than their performance in EPA schools (see Table 6). In the text below we report our conclusions from an attempt to investigate this more directly. We first of all attempted to identify an 'effect' of school context on reading performance, which was independent of the family circumstances of children; and we secondly converted our findings into statistics which establish upper limits to the effectiveness of discriminatory policies to overcome this effect.

Schools in the United States

The question of how far differences among different school situations have independent effects on the distribution of educational performance is a matter of debate in the United States. The main source of data for the debate is the 1965 'Survey of Equality of Educational Opportunity' conducted and initially analysed by Coleman and associates. Many of the major findings of the initial Coleman Report have been confirmed by later re-analysis: the differences seem to have arisen over their interpretation and significance. Our findings, although similar to those on the American school system, are different in a number of important respects. A brief outline of the main evidence on inequalities of conditions and performance in American elementary schools may be helpful, therefore, to set our results in context.

It seems clear that the 1965 Coleman Survey was conducted in order to document that there were dramatic inequalities in school facilities in the United States, particularly for minority groups, and further, that these inequalities in resources were directly related to school performance. Analysis of the data revealed that there were inequalities in resources between regions and states; but that within regions, school resources were more similar than had been supposed. Since those regions which had relatively poor resources tended to be those with higher concentrations of minority group children, there were overall differences between the volume of educational resources available to minority group and to white children. But the larger part of the difference was accounted for by a regional effect. In any case it was found that differences in traditional resource levels bore little or no relationship to differences in school performance levels.

The average school performance of minority group or poor children was found to be lower at every stage of schooling than that of the average white pupil. Family circumstances were found to have the strongest explanatory power over performance levels. But the 'human resources' available to schools were found to have a significant impact on levels of performance, even when the family characteristics of individual children and levels of expenditure had been controlled. Subsequent re-analysis of the data has found that family background factors are, if anything, more strongly related to achievement levels than Coleman and associates originally asserted. But the re-analysis has not destroyed the main Coleman findings on the effect of schools – that it is the resources contributed to a school by the other people in it that most affect levels of performance. Further, the effect of schools on performance is strongest for those groups of children whose family circumstances are likely to be the most disadvantaged. Coleman has succinctly restated the case: ' ... the strongest inference that can be drawn from the results is that the resources most important for a child's achievement in school are the cognitive skills in his social environment in school, including his fellow students as well as his teachers, and that these effects are strongest for the children with least educational resources outside school ... Other resources, on which school systems spend much money, appear unimportant; and lower class students do better in absolute terms rather than worse (as one might have predicted) in schools where their relative achievement is low due to the presence of higher-performing middle-class students'.

The major American findings of interest to us for this analysis, therefore, are above all that we should be moderate in our expectations of what schools can do to overcome adverse extra-school circumstances. Secondly, we should expect evidence that variation in the human resources available to schools – in particular the mixture of pupils in the school – affect performance levels more than variations in more traditional expenditures or resources; and thirdly we should expect schools to have more effect on the performance of children from poor homes than they have on privileged children.

The effect of environmental disadvantage
Our concern was to identify the effect of poor environmental conditions on the school performance of groups of children. We used three measures of school environment for this the first two of which depicted characteristics of the pupils in each school (the proportion of immigrants and the proportion of unskilled and semi-skilled workers' children). The third was a composite measure of the relative circumstances of each school according to the logic of the original ILEA Schools' Index; we call this the measure of school context.

Children were included in the analysis to establish the school contextual effect only if four pieces of information were available on their family circumstance: the occupation of their father, whether they were children born in the United Kingdom or were immigrants from the West Indies, whether or not they came from large families and whether or not they received free school meals.

The method of analysis used was to compute how far the measured variation in reading performance for groups of children could be 'explained' by the measured characteristics of schools. We wished to avoid assuming that the effect of schools on different groups of children was the same or homogeneous. Indeed, given the American findings that schools have most effect on disadvantaged children and the argument of the Plowden Council that the effect of environmental disadvantage was most strongly felt by the most deprived children, this assumption was one we wanted to investigate. Therefore, the explained variation was computed separately for each group of children defined by social class, immigrant and family status, etc.

The regression coefficient given in the Tables is a line of best fit between the measured school characteristic and the reading score of each child, calculated separately within each group. In virtually all cases it has a negative value, indicating that as the school context becomes less advantaged so reading performance tends to deteriorate, even when various family characteristics have been controlled. The explained variance (the R^2 value) is a measure of the improvement that can be made in the prediction of a child's actual reading score by using the characteristic of the schools, rather than the average score of the group of children in that particular regression equation. It is, therefore, a measure of the strength of the independent effect of school context on the reading performance of children, when the various characteristics of family circumstance have been controlled for.

The proportion of the total variation in reading scores explained by any of the factors included in the analysis never reaches above 20 per cent and most of the time it is below 10 per cent. In other words we always fail to explain more than 80 per cent of the total variation in scores. We do not consider this to be surprising. The regression analyses were attempts to discover how far the derived, standardized distribution of scores was biased, or could be attributed to various family, or group, or institutional factors which educational policies might hope to affect. Included in the unexplained variances are errors in the measurement of reading scores, of child background characteristics and of school context. The unexplained variation would, in addition, be due to possibly random factors like the alertness and motivation of particular children on the day of the test, and also to variables which were not measured – the most significant of which would probably be the intelligence of individual and groups of children. More of the variation in reading performance could in principle be explained by the inclusion of more data in the analysis. But to repeat, we were interested in that part of the variation which can be explained or controlled; and which therefore, if they are to increase equality of opportunity or of performance, educational policies must do something about.

We found no significant pattern of independent effects on variations in reading performance from the social or immigrant mix of pupils in the school.

A proportion of the overall variation in reading performance could be explained by the concentration of unskilled and semi-skilled workers' children in schools. But this was reduced to between 1 and 2 per cent when occupation of father had been controlled (see Table 7). We doubt the educational significance of apparent 'effects' of this size.

There was virtually no independent effect on overall variations in reading performance from the concentrations of immigrant children. This is hardly a surprising finding when most schools have very few immigrant children in them. Sixty-five per cent of the non-immigrant children in the analysis are in schools where less than 10 per cent of the children are immigrant; 44 per cent of them are in schools where less than 5 per cent of the children are immigrant; and only 3.4 per cent are in schools which contain more than 40 per cent immigrant children.

We found that there was an effect on reading performance from the total school context. Reading performance was significantly lower the more disadvantaged the school – at least for groups of children from the United Kingdom.

It makes a difference to the reading performance of groups of non-immigrant children whether they go to schools which are privileged or disadvantaged on the measure we used. The differences exist irrespective of the family circumstances of the children. This independent contextual

Table 7 Reading score and social and immigrant mix regression series

Reading score regressed against:

1 Concentration of low social class children in the school
2 Concentration of immigrant children in the school

For groups of children controlling:

A *by social class (I and V only are displayed)*
B *by West Indian immigrant and groups born in the United Kingdom*

	1 Class concentration		2 Immigrant concentration	
	regression coefficient	R^2	regression coefficient	R^2
Total	− 0.18	0.0429	− 0.17	0.0229
A Social class				
Social class I	− 0.12	0.0203	− 0.11	0.0062
Social class V	− 0.10	0.0133	− 0.15	0.0227
B Non-immigrant and West Indian immigrant groups				
Non-immigrant				
Social class I	− 0.12	0.0195	− 0.09	0.0038
Social class V	− 0.10	0.0134	− 0.11	0.0085
West Indian immigrant				
Social class I	—	—	—	—
Social class V	− 0.07	0.0052	− 0.00	0.0000

We found that there was an effect on reading performance from the total school context. Reading performance was significantly lower the more disadvantaged the school – at least for groups of children from the United Kingdom.

effect is slightly stronger for United Kingdom children from non-manual workers' homes than for children from manual workers' homes: 6 per cent and 4 per cent respectively of the variation in reading performance is explained by it (see Table 8).

There is no significant school contextual effect on the variation in reading scores for groups of West Indian immigrant children. We had found that the average reading performance of West Indian immigrant children in this cohort was low irrespective of the occupation of their father (see Table 5). From this subsequent finding we must say, further, that whether they are in privileged or disadvantaged schools makes far less difference to the reading performance of West Indian immigrant children than it does to non-immigrant children.

With this evidence we can answer the first two of our questions concerning the justification for programmes to combat the effect of relatively disadvantaged school environments. There is an effect of relative institutional deprivation on the school performance of children. It does affect different groups of children in different ways: but in ways contrary to the forecast of the Plowden Council and expectations from the American data analysis. Across the whole population, the more privileged the home circumstances of groups of children, the more their performance is depressed by the apparent effect; and the less advantaged their home circumstances, the less children are affected by school context.

We can illustrate these points by establishing what, in principle, would be the upper limits to the impact of a programme of positive discrimination through schools. We can ask, first of all, what would be the impact on the distribution of individual scores of a policy which overcame the effects of the school context. Clearly the distribution of scores would be reduced by the amount now attributable to it. But the effect, in this case, would be to reduce the spread of individual scores in the population by a maximum of only 3.4 per cent. And so we must say that policies of positive discrimination which successfully overcame the total effect of school context would do little to reduce the spread of performance among individual children.

But the target for the Plowden Council's programme of positive discrimination was to be more specific than this. The programme was to bring help to the most disadvantaged 10 per cent of the population – initially raising them to the national average and subsequently improving their position even more. We might ask, therefore, what would be the effect of a policy which did this for groups of children in the bottom 10 per cent of schools – bearing in mind that the measured effect of school context is different for different groups of children.

We are speculating here about a possible future situation from evidence

Table 8   Reading score and school privilege regression series
Reading score regressed against relative privilege score of school for groups of children controlling:

A   *by social class*
B   *by West Indian immigrant and groups born in the United Kingdom*

	regression coefficient	R^2
Total	− 0.34	0.0674
A Social class		
Social class I	− 0.26	0.0378
Social class II	− 0.29	0.0485
Social class III	− 0.26	0.0418
Social class IV	− 0.18	0.0218
Social class V	− 0.27	0.0478
B Non-immigrant and West Indian immigrant groups		
All non-immigrant children	− 0.31	0.0579
Non-immigrant		
Social class I	− 0.26	0.0367
Social class II	− 0.26	0.0408
Social class III	− 0.24	0.0352
Social class IV	− 0.16	0.0163
Social class V	− 0.25	0.0409
All West Indian immigrant children	− 0.16	0.0140
West Indian immigrant		
Social class I	—	—
Social class II	− 0.02	0.0009
Social class III	− 0.19	0.0194
Social class IV	− 0.14	0.0118
Social class V	− 0.16	0.0148
Non-immigrant non-manual	− 0.30	0.0581
Non-immigrant manual	− 0.24	0.0366
West Indian immigrant non-manual	− 0.14	0.0098
West Indian immigrant manual	− 0.15	0.0135

on the present; we do not identify what could be done to bring about that situation. We are providing theoretical upper limits to the impact of discriminatory policies and not positive forecasts or practical recommendations.

To do even this we must assume that any transformation in scores brought about by a successful policy would be linear: that to make the most disadvantaged group of schools as good as the average would, in principle, be to make their effects on reading performance the same as those currently produced by the average schools. The validity of the assumption may be questioned; but it is necessary to ask what would be the consequences of not accepting it. All that could be said, if it were unacceptable, would be that improving schools will cause them to have as yet unknown effects on the performance of the children in them. Clearly in all policy there is an element of what we hope will happen in addition to what might reasonably be predicted. These transformations establish the reasonable predictions from evidence on schools as they operate at present; the creation of new futures is beyond their scope.

If, therefore, we say that the purpose of a programme of positive discrimination through schools was to overcome the disadvantages they currently impose on the children in them, then we can assess the maximum reduction in the spread of scores that would result from a successful policy.

Thus, policies of discrimination which overcame the effect of school context in the most disadvantaged 10 per cent of schools would narrow the gap in performance between groups of children in those schools, and similarly defined groups in the average school, by the following amounts:

For the children of non-immigrant non-manual workers	by 6.90 points of score or months of reading age
For the children of non-immigrant manual workers	by 5.28 points
For the children of West Indian immigrant non-manual workers	by 2.70 points
For the children of West Indian immigrant manual workers	by 2.93 points

The effect of such policies, far from tempering differences between groups which resulted from factors outside the school situation, would be to reinforce them. Positive discrimination which made the most disadvantaged schools as good as the average schools would increase the differences in performance between groups of children defined in terms of their family circumstances.

In order to provide a further framework within which the relative size of the overall independent school effects might be seen, we calculated the variation in reading performance which could be attributed to the measured characteristics of home circumstances. Table 9 presents our findings.

Table 9 Variations in reading scores independently explained by home background characteristics of groups of children

	Explained variation (%)
Occupation of father	9.35
Whether the child was of United Kingdom or West Indian immigrant origin	3.01
Contribution of all four family background characteristics: father's occupation, immigrant status, size of family, receipt of free school meals.	14.30
Cumulative child at-risk index	19.06

With school effects explaining between 4 and 6 per cent of the variations in reading score for groups of United Kingdom children and 1 per cent for West Indian immigrants, it is clear from Table 9 that the circumstances of families explain more of the variation in reading performance than do the circumstances of schools.

These again are perhaps not surprising findings but their implications for educational policy remain highly significant. To begin with, the measure of the socio-economic status of the children's father dominates the other measures – both of school context and of other family characteristics. Secondly, there is an effect of the immigrant status of groups of children which is independent of social class. The distinction in this cohort between West Indian immigrants and children born in the United Kingdom 'explains' a 3 per cent variation in reading performance which cannot be attributed to the father's occupation. Thirdly, once these two factors – social class and immigrant status – are taken into account, the remaining variance explained by the characteristics of home circumstances – family size and free school meals – appears far less important.

Making the same assumptions as were made over the calculation of the maximum impact of discriminatory policies operating against the apparent effect of schools on groups of children, we used the variances explained by family circumstance to estimate upper limits to the impact of policies on these effects. Thus in principle, the impact of policies which removed the effect of socio-economic status on the reading performance of groups of children would narrow the gap in performance between children in the bottom 10 per cent on that dimension of inequality and the average child in the population by 8.7 points of reading score: an amount equivalent to the same number of months of reading age. Similarly, the removal of differences attributable to a distinction between West Indian immigrant children and children born in the United Kingdom would mean that differences in reading performance between the bottom 10 per cent of children and the average child on that dimension would become smaller by 4.9 points. Policies operating against effects of all four family circumstance characteristics could have an effect of 10.8 points on the gap between the bottom 10 per cent and the average child; and the upper limit to a totally effective policy against cumulative disadvantage (as it was measured on the at-risk index) would narrow the gap in performance between the most disadvantaged 10 per cent of children and the average child by 12.5 points of score, or over a year of reading age.

Conclusions

In this paper we have reported our attempts to analyse data on one cohort of junior school children in Inner London, in order to say something more about educational disadvantage and about policies of positive discrimination through schools in order to meet it. In particular, we have tried to establish upper limits to those policies both in terms of their potential coverage and their possible effects. From the data available to us we have come to ten specific major conclusions:

1   Using single item indicators: between one in four and one in six of the children in need are in the EPA schools.

2   Using an indicator of cumulative disadvantage: for every two disadvantaged children who are in EPA schools, five are outside them. And in the EPA schools themselves, disadvantaged children are outnumbered by children who are not disadvantaged.

3   Irrespective of the schools they attend, there is about two years difference in the average reading age of disadvantaged and non-disadvantaged children, when those children are between eight and nine years old.

4   The average reading performance of disadvantaged children in

the EPA schools is approximately three months behind that of disadvantaged children in the most privileged schools. The two groups are nineteen months and sixteen months respectively behind a national norm, and eight months and sixteen months behind the average for their group of schools.

5 Once the occupation of father has been controlled for, there is no effect on variations in reading performance of either the low social class composition or the concentration of immigrant children in a school.

6 There is a pattern of independent effects on variations in reading performance from the overall context of a school. This pattern holds up even when groups of children are homogeneous with respect to the occupation of their father, their immigrant status, the size of their family and whether or not they receive free school meals.

7 Policies of discrimination which overcame this effect would do little to equalize performance between individual children.

8 Policies which overcame it would substantially reduce the gap in performance between identically defined groups of children in different sorts of school. The strongest impact of such a policy would be felt by the children of professional and managerial workers who were born in the United Kingdom. For that group, the gap between their performance in the most disadvantaged 10 per cent of schools and in the average school would be closed by 7 points of score or months of reading age.

9 The group of children least affected by discriminatory policies which overcame the effects of school context would be West Indian immigrants. This group is significantly less affected by its school context than are non-immigrant children.

10 The effect of school context on variations in reading performance is considerably less than the effect of characteristics of family circumstance.

The validity and general applicability of these findings can be criticized in a series of ways and it is instructive to list some of the main ones here. The data were only for one age group of children from Inner London, mainly for one point of time, five years ago. The information is in some senses faulty. It is also inadequate. In particular we must be careful of what can be inferred from measured performance on one reading test.

There is no information on intra school processes, or on teacher skills, or on schools which have effects on their children which are quite different from the measured dominant pattern. Quite possibly, policies which improved schools would change their impact on the performance of the children. For determined critics the list can go on. We think that these points should be considered carefully and we have tried to qualify our findings in the text without littering it with apologies.

At the same time two issues seem to us of overriding importance. The first comes from the logic of the data rather than from its precise quantification. Educational disadvantage is a very heterogeneous concept. School and area policies to tackle it set for themselves limits which prevent complete coverage. In order to bring discriminatory help to disadvantaged or needy children such policies will need to become substantially more complex, accommodating both intra school and area processes and other dimensions to the phenomenon. If school and area policies are to retain their original simplicity, they must be complemented with other, perhaps new and different policies which help the disadvantaged children who will inevitably be left out.

The other issue does rely on accurate measurement and correct analysis. But we think here that the questions we raise should be taken seriously even by those who may wish to question our findings. Consider the conclusions we derive from the analysis. Policies which successfully overcame the effect of school context and improved the performance of schools, would equalize performance between schools. But they would do little to equalize performances between individuals – perhaps nobody would expect them to; but also, therefore, equalizing the performance of schools could do little to equalize opportunities between individuals. In addition, because the effect of school context is stronger for privileged groups than for less privileged ones, equalizing the performance of schools would increase inequalities in performance between groups.

At the very least this raises questions about what it is appropriate and realistic to expect from schools. If what is desired is to maximize the opportunities available to all children irrespective of which school they go to, then, on this evidence, inequalities in performance between groups will increase. If what is desired is to reduce inequalities in performance between all children then, again on this evidence, more powerful policies than school reform will be needed. If what is desired is to reduce inequalities in performance between groups, then on this evidence, reforms will be needed which transform the relationships between schools and their social context. Further, a community of interest could not be assumed between all the families whose children attend the most disadvantaged schools; whether the policy is to improve or to transform those schools, again on this evidence, different groups will have different amounts to gain (and to lose) by it. It seems reasonable to ask the question, both of schools as they operate now and of a policy of positive discrimination to change them, who is expected to benefit?

1.6 Schooling and cognitive inequality

C. Jencks et al

The next five sections examine schools' effects on cognitive inequality. Before doing this, we must again remind the reader that we have defined cognitive inequality in fairly narrow terms, as the ability to use language easily and accurately, the ability to understand and make logical inferences from printed material, the ability to use numbers with facility, and the ability to absorb and retain miscellaneous information. These are the skills measured by standard tests of verbal ability, reading comprehension, arithmetic, and general information. Every school tries to teach these skills. There are other skills, such as the ability to speak French or the ability to do trigonometry, which some schools try to teach while others do not. Had we looked at these skills, we would probably have found more variation between the alumni of different schools. Conversely, we would have found that simply attending school affected these skills less often than it affected the basic skills taught in all schools. We have chosen to focus on verbal ability, reading, arithmetic, and general information because we believe these things are more important than things like French and trigonometry. Yet even the basic skills are far less important than many people imagine.

In analyzing the effects of schooling on basic cognitive skills, we will begin by trying to estimate the effect of staying in school as against dropping out.

The effects of school attendance
In order to assess the effects of school attendance on test scores, we must compare individuals who attended school at a given age to similar individuals who did not. This is relatively easy to do at the preschool level, where attendance is nothing like universal, and access is not yet defined as

Source: *Inequality. A reassessment of the effect of family and schooling in America* (1972), pp. 84–130.

a matter of right. It is much more difficult at the elementary school level, since virtually all American children attend elementary school, and those who do not are deviant in many other respects. In order to assess the effects of elementary schooling we must rely on a few 'natural experiments', in which children who would normally have attended school were denied this opportunity for some reason. At the secondary level, we can compare the eventual test scores of students who drop out to the eventual scores of students who remain in school, but it is hard to be sure that we have made the right adjustments for discrepancies in such students' initial ability and motivation.

Taken as a whole, evidence about the effects of school attendance on test scores is woefully inadequate. Such evidence as there is suggests that preschooling has few permanent effects, that elementary schooling is quite important to the development of the skills measured on standardized tests, and that secondary schooling and college also boost test scores to some extent.

Preschool
The reinvention of preschool is a perennial phenomenon in American education. The latest such cycle began in the early 1960s. Unfortunately, we have no surveys relating adult cognitive skills to preschool attendance. EEOS does, however, provide relevant data on children still in school.[1]

In northern urban elementary schools, four children in five said they had attended kindergarten. Once socio-economic differences were taken into account, there was a negligible difference in mean sixth grade achievement between schools with high proportions of kindergarten alumni and schools with low proportions.[2]

EEOS also asked students whether they had attended nursery school. Once socio-economic differences were taken into account, there were no significant differences in sixth grade achievement between those who said they had attended nursery school and those who said they had not. Given the probable inaccuracies in the data, this finding is hardly conclusive, but it is consistent with most other surveys and experimental research on preschooling.

Follow-ups of preschool alumni have a long history. They fall into a predictable pattern. The majority show that children who attend preschool do quite a lot better on standardized tests at the end of their preschool year than children who did not attend preschool. But children who do not attend preschool usually catch up with children who do attend by the end of the first grade. Only one or two small studies claim appreciable differences beyond first grade.[3]

The largest single follow-up of preschool alumni was the 1968

Westinghouse-Ohio survey of Head Start graduates. This study concluded that neither year-round nor summer Head Start programmes had a significant long-term effect on children's cognitive growth. When we re-analyzed this data, we found a few year-round centres in which the Head Start children's advantage over non-Head Start children persisted through first grade. Beyond first grade, however, the picture was gloomy. Overall, the evidence strongly suggested that Head Start's effects on children's cognitive growth had been quite transitory.

This is not surprising. Unlike politicians and parents, Head Start teachers and directors have not been primarily concerned with raising children's test scores. They have favoured 'supportive, unstructured socialization programmes rather than structured informational programmes'.[4] They have assumed that a child would get plenty of disciplined instruction when he reached first grade and that he would not do any better in first grade if he started such work a year or two early. The evidence suggests that the teachers and administrators were right.

Even if preschooling could be shown to provide long-term cognitive advantages, this would probably not reduce cognitive inequality. Head Start now excludes the middle classes, but this is only politically practical because most middle-class parents do not want their children in preschools with poor children. No study has yet suggested that preschool programmes do more for disadvantaged than for advantaged children. Thus, we cannot expect universal preschooling to narrow the gap between rich and poor or between whites and blacks. Universal preschooling might even widen the gap.

Elementary school

One way to estimate the effect of elementary schooling on cognitive skills is to look at situations in which schooling suddenly ceases to be available to a particular group for some reason. During World War II, for example, many elementary schools in Holland were closed. The IQ scores of children entering at least one secondary school after the end of the war appear to have dropped about 7 points as a result.[5] Also, the schools in Prince Edward County were closed by the local board of education during the early 1960s, in order to avoid integration. When schools were reopened, black children who had not attended school for several years scored substantially lower than most black children of their age.[6] We have not been able to discover whether any of these losses were permanent.

Schools are also usually closed during the summer months. Both the folklore among teachers and the available evidence suggest that children's test scores increase more slowly over the summer than during the school year. In some cases children's scores actually drop over the summer. A study of New York City, for example, found that the average child's reading scores improved almost three times as fast during the school year as during the summer. The average black child's scores improved nearly as fast as the average white child's scores while school was in session, but they hardly improved at all over the summer. This particular study concluded that only half the achievement gap between black and white children in New York City was attributable to differential growth during the school year. The other half was explained by differential growth over the summer.[7] This highly suggestive study has not yet been replicated.

These findings imply that if all elementary schools were closed down, so that growing up became an endless summer, white middle-class children might still learn much of what they now learn. Some of these children are taught to read before they enter school anyway, and some of them read a great deal at home, developing their skills without any help from school. But most poor black children would probably not learn to read without schools. The cognitive gap between rich and poor and between black and white would thus be far greater than it is now. Those who propose to abolish schools ought to ponder this possibility.

Secondary school

An extra year of secondary schooling or college is usually associated with a 3 or 4 point advantage on adult aptitude and intelligence tests. We cannot, however, conclude that schooling causes this advantage. Those who get a lot of schooling have higher test scores to begin with. To a large extent, schools and colleges simply screen out students whose cognitive skills are below par, conferring diplomas on those with high initial scores.

Only 2 American studies have tried to separate the effects of initial ability from the effects of schooling. A study in New York City before World War II found that each additional year of school increased boys' IQ scores by about 2.5 points over the level expected on the basis of their earlier school achievement scores.[8] The sample was far from ideal, but several Swedish studies also yield results in this range.[9] The other American study found, however, that additional schooling had no consistent effect on Stanford-Binet scores.[10] If we synthesize data from diverse sources, our best estimate is that each extra year of schooling boosts an individual's adult IQ score about one point above the expected level.

We are far from confident about the validity of these contradictory estimates. Surveys are likely to overestimate the actual effects of school attendance on test scores, because they seldom measure all the prior differences between those who stay in school and those who drop out.[11] No experimental evidence is available.

Despite our reservations, we tentatively conclude that if students leave school early in adolescence, their verbal and numerical skills do not develop as much as if they remain in school. We also infer that equalizing the amount of schooling people get might do quite a lot to equalize cognitive skills. This reflects the fact that although each extra year of schooling has only a modest effect on test scores, the benefits are now largely concentrated on those who are already advantaged. If everyone received the same schooling, the 'double advantage' phenomenon in this area could be eliminated.

Conclusions
The evidence we have reviewed supports three conclusions:

1 Preschools have little permanent effect on cognitive development.
2 Elementary schooling is helpful for middle-class children and crucial for lower-class children.
3 Secondary schools and colleges do less than elementary schools but more than most jobs or housework in developing the skills measured on standardized tests.

Perhaps the most astonishing feature of this whole inquiry is that virtually no research has been done on these issues, either by defenders of schools or by their critics. As a result, our conclusions are all based on problematic inferences of uncertain validity. The most we can claim is that such evidence is better than nothing.

Differences between schools
Nearly anything can happen in a place called a school. Some schools consist of a single room in which children of all ages are mixed with a barely literate teacher. Others are huge enterprises, with highly trained staffs from the world's leading universities. Some of these schools are run like prisons, with rigid routines that determine what every child is doing almost every minute of the day. Other schools are more like asylums, with constant battles to maintain order and no sequential activity that lasts more than a few minutes. A few schools are like permissive families, with children pretty much working out what they want to do, doing it on their own or in groups, and getting attention or help from adults only when they want it or when they 'misbehave'. Given this diversity, we did not expect all schools to have precisely the same effects on children's test scores. The differences are, however, surprisingly small. This suggests that public schools are more alike than parents and teachers think they are.

High schools

The best available evidence about high schools' effects on their students is found in survey data collected by Project Talent. The most relevant portion of this survey covered 5,000 students in 91 predominantly white comprehensive high schools. These students were given 49 different tests in 1960, when they were in ninth grade. They were given some of the same tests again in 1963, when they were in twelfth grade. We compared students' performance in ninth and twelfth grades on six of these tests: Vocabulary, Social Studies Information, Reading Comprehension, Abstract Reasoning, Mathematics, and Arithmetic Computation.

Predictably, ninth-grade scores largely determine twelfth-grade scores. Changes between ninth and twelfth grade have almost nothing to do with the school a student is in. If we look at vocabulary, for example, we find that all students' scores increase between ninth and twelfth grade. If we predict students' twelfth-grade scores from their ninth-grade scores, knowing nothing about their school, our predictions are never off by an average of more than five points for any school. In schools with enough students to yield estimates, the mean is always within three points of the expected level. Furthermore, the schools where students show unusual improvement on one test are not the same as the schools where students show unusual improvement on other tests.

If we average schools' effects on several different tests, the average twelfth grader's overall performance is within three points of what we would expect on the basis of his ninth-grade scores. Stating it slightly differently, we can say that if all high schools were equally effective (or ineffective) inequality between twelfth graders would fall less than one percent. This picture is reinforced by the EEOS data on high schools. The average difference between a high school's mean twelfth-grade scores and the twelfth-grade mean predicted from its mean ninth-grade scores was three points.[12]

Elementary schools

Children's test scores change in less predictable ways during the early years of elementary school than later on. We therefore expected differences between schools to have somewhat more effect on young children than on older children. We have found some evidence to support this expectation.

There have been no national longitudinal surveys of elementary schools comparable to Project Talent. This means we cannot actually follow children through elementary school to see how much their growth depends on their initial characteristics and how much it depends on the school they attend. In the absence of longitudinal data, we turned again to EEOS.

EEOS elementary schools whose entering students had low scores were appreciably more likely to have high scoring graduates than EEOS high schools whose entering students had low scores. This suggests that variations in school quality have more effect on young students than on older ones.

Nonetheless, the overall effect of elementary school quality on test scores appears rather modest. Suppose we rank schools in terms of their effects on test scores and then compare students who are in the most effective fifth of all elementary schools to students from apparently similar socio-economic and racial backgrounds who are in the least effective fifth of all schools. These students' sixth grade test scores will differ by about ten points. This implies that ten points is a maximum estimate of the average effect of attending an elementary school that ranks in the top rather than the bottom fifth. If we could compare sixth graders who resembled each other not only in terms of race and socio-economic background but in terms of initial ability, we suspect this estimate would be closer to five points than to ten. This implies that eliminating differences between elementary schools would reduce cognitive inequality by 3 percent or less.

We do not know how much of this difference is really explained by variations in what schools do, how much is explained by inadequate adjustments for variations in initial ability and in neighbourhood characteristics, and how much is due to various kinds of measurement error. One reason we suspect a lot of error is that schools' effects do not appear to be very stable from one year to the next. When we look at New York City elementary schools, for example, we find that in any given year there are some schools whose sixth graders do much better on reading tests than we would have predicted on the basis of the class's scores in earlier years. Each year there are also some schools whose sixth graders do worse than we would have expected on the basis of the class's performance in earlier years. This implies significant variation in schools' effectiveness. But on the average, schools which appear to have been unusually effective or ineffective with one class appear to have been only a third as effective (or ineffective) with the preceding and following classes. Perhaps these changes are real, reflecting mysterious changes in school 'climate' from one year to the next. We suspect, however, that a lot of the apparent variation in these schools' effectiveness is due to measurement error.

Cumulative effects of elementary and secondary schools
Suppose that we define a school's 'effectiveness' strictly in terms of its effect on students' test scores. The cumulative contribution of schooling to cognitive inequality will then depend on the extent to which students who start school with an advantage attend schools which are unusually effective, on the extent of variation in schools' annual effects, and on the extent to

which students who attend 'effective' schools in one year also attend effective schools in prior and subsequent years. If unusually talented students enter unusually effective elementary schools, if these elementary schools send their students to unusually effective high schools, and if these high schools then induce unusually large proportions of students to attend college, the cumulative impact of the educational system on an individual's test scores could be quite large, even though the effect in any one year is small. But if effective elementary schools send their students to ineffective high schools, and if high schools that are effective in boosting test scores do not send unusually high proportions of their students to college, the cumulative impact of the educational system on cognitive inequality will be much smaller.

Unfortunately, we do not have good data on cognitive 'value added' for individual students in American elementary schools. We can, however, use EEOS to see whether elementary schools whose students 'overachieve' relative to their socio-economic background feed into high schools whose students 'overachieve' in these same terms. At least in the urban North, they do not. If we judge an elementary school's effectiveness by whether its sixth graders do better or worse than sixth graders in other schools with a similar socio-economic mix, and if we judge high schools in the same way, the correlation between an elementary school's effectiveness and the effectiveness of the high school into which it feeds is almost nil. This means that a student who attends an elementary school which is good at boosting test scores is not especially likely to attend an equally effective high school. We suspect that this is because the observed differences between high schools are largely due to random measurement error.

We also estimated the effect of each northern urban EEOS high school on its students' chances of attending college. Students who attended an elementary school that seemed to boost their test scores were not especially likely to attend high schools that further improved their chances of attending college.

As a further check on the contribution of differences between schools to cognitive inequality, we investigated whether students with high initial test scores were likely to attend schools that were unusually effective in boosting test scores. At the secondary level, the answer seems to be no. There is no correlation between the mean achievement scores of students entering the 91 Project Talent high schools we studied and their rate of cognitive growth between ninth and twelfth grade. Unfortunately, we do not have data suitable for answering this question at the elementary level.

Conclusions
Overall, the evidence shows that differences between high schools

contribute almost nothing to the overall level of cognitive inequality. Differences between elementary schools may be somewhat more important, but evidence for this is still inconclusive. The average effect of attending the best rather than the worst fifth of all elementary schools is almost certainly no more than ten points and probably no more than five. The difference between, say, the top and bottom halves is even less.

Under these circumstances the reader should not be surprised to learn that it is very difficult to identify specific characteristics of schools that influence student achievement. The next section describes our futile attempt to identify resources that make one school more effective than another, and the following section summarizes our findings about the effects of a school's composition on the achievement of various kinds of students.

The effects of school resources

Expenditures

When legislators talk about school resources, they mean money. Taxpayers have a similar bias. Once the overall level of expenditure has been set, professional educators have the dominant voice in determining what the money goes for. In deciding whether to raise expenditures, then, laymen must assume that the money will mostly be used to buy the same things that money is now used to buy: higher salaries, smaller classes, more specialized personnel, lighter teaching loads, newer textbooks, better facilities, and so forth. This means that the best way to appraise the likely effect of, say, doubling per pupil expenditures is to assume that schools now spending $400 per pupil will become like schools now spending $800.

The evidence we have examined does not suggest that doubling expenditures would raise students' performance on standardized tests. A school's annual expenditure is, it is true, moderately related to the test scores of its alumni. But this is because affluent schools enroll students whose test scores are above average to begin with. When we compare schools with similar entering students, we do not find those with fat budgets turning out more skilled alumni that those with inadequate budgets.

In our analysis of Project Talent we found that when we compared an impoverished high school to one that spent twice as much, students in the rich school gained no more between ninth and twelfth grades than students in the poor school. EEOS measured only district-wide expenditures, rather than expenditures in each high school. Nonetheless, if expenditures influenced achievement, we would expect affluent districts to outscore indigent ones. In fact, each extra $100 of per pupil expenditure was associated with an extra point on the EEOS tests, but this was only because high schools with high expenditures had high scoring students to begin with. This finding is consistent with studies of 'value added' in high schools.[13]

When we turn to elementary schools, the data is less conclusive but equally discouraging. EEOS found no association of consequence between district-wide expenditures and mean achievement in elementary schools. Nor have other surveys found any consistent association between expenditures and elementary schools' effectiveness in raising test scores.[14]

In order to test the validity of inferences from survey research, it is useful to look at the effect of changes in expenditure on test scores in specific schools or for specific students. We know of no systematic efforts to evaluate the effects of increased state or local expenditures, but the failure of test scores to rise between 1960 and 1970 is discouraging, since expenditures rose sharply in those years. The federal government has also made sporadic efforts to determine whether the 'compensatory' programmes established in 1965 under Title I of the Elementary and Secondary Education Act were actually raising children's test scores. These evaluations are generally discouraging. The evaluators usually had inadequate information, limited co-operation from the schools, and limited technical expertise. Nonetheless, if additional Title I funds were raising children's test scores by substantial amounts, the evaluations ought to show this more often than they show the opposite. In fact, the results of evaluations appear to be virtually random. Students in Title I programmes do worse than comparison groups as often as they do better.[15]

There are two popular explanations for the fact that raising expenditures does not raise test scores.

1   Some critics argue that school administrators and teachers are not very interested in raising test scores. The way money is actually spent partly supports this argument. A superintendent often wants a new gymnasium because the high school basketball team is popular in the community – or because he used to be a basketball coach himself. He wants more money for teachers' salaries because otherwise the teachers will strike – and he will get an ulcer. He wants smaller classes because teachers prefer small classes and because small classes make it easier to keep order. The superintendent usually hopes these expenditures will raise achievement scores too, but if they do not, he wants them anyway.

2   Other critics assume that school administrators and teachers want to raise achievement but have no idea how to go about it. This theory has two variants. One version holds that the problem is intrinsically insoluble, at least with present knowledge and technology. According to this view, demands that schools raise achievement scores are like the demands that hospitals cure senility. A second version of the theory holds that test scores

can be raised if administrators and teachers use their resources wisely, but that they rarely do so.

We have not done any empirical research on what school administrators and teachers are really trying to do. We suspect that their primary objective is to teach children to behave themselves the way schools want them to behave. However, teaching the skills measured on standardized tests is probably a close second. We can see no evidence that either school administrators or educational experts know how to raise test scores, even when they have vast resources. Certainly we do not know how to.

Policies and resources
In hope of collecting some information that would help professional educators use their resources more efficiently, we have tried to identify schools that were unusually effective in boosting test scores, in order to see if they had any objective characteristics in common. We concentrated on school policies and resources that could be directly controlled by legislators, school boards, and administrators. This means we looked at things like physical facilities, libraries and library books, how much homework a school assigned, whether it had heterogeneous or homogeneous grouping, numbers and kinds of personnel, salaries, criteria for selecting teachers, and so forth. We did not look in any detail at things like morale, teacher expectations, school traditions, and school 'climate'. While these things may well be associated with unusually rapid or slow cognitive development, policy-makers cannot usually control them, social scientists cannot usually measure them, and no one can be sure whether they cause achievement or only result from it.

Survey data on the relationship of school policies and resources to student achievement has been gathered and analyzed by many different scholars. The results of such studies have been contradictory. Resources which are associated with high scores in one city are not associated with high scores in another city. Resources which have a positive relationship to the achievement of one kind of student have a negative relationship for another kind of student. Resources that look helpful when the data is analyzed one way look unimportant when the data is analyzed another way.

In an attempt to clarify some of these problems, we have re-analyzed the original data from three of the largest and most comprehensive school surveys: EEOS, Project Talent, and the Plowden survey in England. There has been a great deal of debate, often acrimonious, about the right way to analyze such surveys. Nonetheless, two general conclusions seem justified.

First, no measurable school resource or policy shows a consistent relationship to schools' effectiveness in boosting student achievement. The specific school resources that have a 'statistically significant' relationship to achievement change from one survey to the next, from one method of analysis to another, from one sort of school to another, and from one type of student to another. While it is always possible to invent explanations for all this after the fact, it is never possible to predict much about such differences in advance.

Second, the gains associated with any given resource are almost always small. In EEOS, for example, the presence of an important school resource is typically associated with a difference of no more than two to four months in mean sixth grade achievement. This is roughly equivalent to two to four IQ points. Thus, even if we were to persuade ourselves that resources had consistent effects, it would be hard to argue that they had pedagogically important effects.

Experimental studies of the relationship between student achievement and such things as school size, class size, ability grouping, and curriculum point to the same conclusion. Some show benefits, some show losses, and some show no effect either way.

The most plausible explanation for these findings is that school resources have small inconsistent effects on achievement. Experienced teachers are more competent than average in some systems, less competent than average in other systems. Teachers with high verbal scores help certain students to develop their verbal skills but inhibit others. Another complementary interpretation is that resource allocation responds to achievement in some communities but not others. Thus some communities allow experienced teachers to move to better schools, creating a spurious impression that experience causes high achievement. Other systems do not allow experienced teachers to move, so there is no association between teacher experience and student achievement. Both these interpretations have the same practical implication. Legislators, school boards, and school superintendents cannot expect that any general policy which simply provides more school resources will raise children's test scores.

In concluding this discussion we must again emphasize one major limitation of our findings. We have only examined the effects of resource differences among existing public schools. This tells us that if schools continue to use their resources as they now do, giving them more resources will not change children's test scores. If schools used their resources differently, however, additional resources might conceivably have larger payoffs. If, for example, principals or parents had control over the school budget and could spend their money on whatever they thought their school needed most, extra resources might affect test scores more than they now do. There is no way of testing this theory except by experimentation. Past history is discouraging, but the future is not always a re-run of the past.

The effects of segregation

This section will deal with the effect of segregation on students' test scores. We will look first at how school segregation affects blacks, then at how it affects poor whites and students with low initial test scores, and finally at how it affects 'advantaged' students. We will use the term 'advantaged' throughout the discussion to designate students who have what the majority defines as desirable traits: e.g. white skin, affluent parents, or high initial test scores.

Effects on blacks

The debate about racial segregation is by now so old that the theoretical arguments have all been made – and rebutted. In general they fall into four categories.

1   Advocates of desegregation say it gives black students access to school resources that were previously denied them: physics laboratories, small classes, experienced teachers, teachers who know their subject, and so forth. Critics reply that desegregated schools spend only marginally more than all-black ones, and in some cities they spend less. In addition, as we have seen, neither expenditures in general nor the particular things schools buy with their money have any consistent effect on black students' cognitive development.[16]

2   Advocates of desegregation argue that it will put black children in contact with classmates who have certain kinds of knowledge (e.g. knowledge of 'standard' grammar) that many black students lack. Critics answer that whether white schoolmates are a valuable resource to black students depends on how they actually relate to one another. If they become enemies or if their relations are mostly derisory, hostile, or violent, it is hard to see how either group will benefit.[17]

3   Advocates of desegregation often argue that teachers in desegregated schools expect more of black students than teachers in segregated schools and that black students learn more as a result. Unfortunately, we have no evidence on this point. Teachers in predominantly white schools often express distaste for black students,[18] but whether they expect more or less academically from black students we do not know.

4   Desegregation may convince a black student that he has a chance to make it in the larger society. This may make him work harder and learn more, even if the desegregated school is no better than a segregated one. But while the symbolism of desegregation may help convince a black student that he has a chance of making it in the larger society, direct exposure to teachers and students who put him down seems likely to have the opposite effect.

Educators and social scientists who have thought carefully about desegregation have usually concluded that its effects are unpredictable, depending on exactly how desegregation is initiated and implemented and how the participants view the process. This leads some experts to distinguish 'desegregation' from 'integration'. Desegregation is defined as having black and white students under the same roof. Integration is defined as knitting the two groups into a single social community. When desegregation leads to trouble or fails to raise test scores, this is attributed to the fact that there was no 'genuine integration'. When desegregation 'works', by whatever criteria someone judges relevant, it is hailed as an example of 'genuine integration'.

This explanation has considerable heuristic value. It does not, however, tell us when desegregation will raise disadvantaged students achievement scores, when it will lower their scores, or when it will leave them unchanged. In order to make predictions, we need some way of anticipating when desegregation will lead to integration and when it will not. No one has yet developed a method for doing this.[19]

The effects of desegregation on test scores have been studied in two ways. One approach has been to study 'natural experiments'. This has meant comparing the achievement of black students in all-black schools to the achievement of more or less comparable black students in desegregated schools. The difficulty with this approach is that the black student who enrolls in a desegregated school may differ in unknown ways from outwardly similar black students in segregated schools.

An alternative approach is therefore to study the effect of actually moving black students from all-black schools to desegregated schools. A number of northern cities have conducted such studies as part of desegregation efforts. Once again, it is hard to decide who the desegregated blacks should be compared to. Sometimes students' scores after a year or two of bussing are compared to their scores before busing. Unfortunately, this requires that we distinguish the effects of getting older from the effects of desegregation, which is not always easy. Sometimes the desegregated students are compared to supposedly similar blacks in all-black schools. Desegregation is seldom completely random, however, so it is always hard to be sure how comparable the two groups really are. Elaborate statistical techniques have been developed for dealing with all these difficulties, but none is foolproof.

These methodological difficulties would be of little concern if studies of desegregation yielded consistent results. Unfortunately, they do not. Virtually all surveys of natural experiments show that black students in desegregated schools score above apparently similar blacks in all-black schools. This pattern holds for a wide variety of tests and at all grade levels: But when black students are actually bussed from segregated to desegregated schools, their test scores do not always improve.

Two alternative explanations for this apparent contradiction come to mind. Those who believe in desegregation often argue that the bussing programmes have not been operating long enough to produce social integration, and that this accounts for their uneven effect on test scores. Those who oppose desegregation argue that the high test scores of blacks in naturally integrated schools reflect the greater motivation or resources of black parents who put their children in desegregated schools.

Given the importance of the issue, a brief review of the best available studies may be helpful. The most famous survey of 'naturally' desegregated schools is EEOS. James Coleman and his colleagues concluded from this survey that the socio-economic level of a student's school had more effect on his achievement than any other measurable factor except the socio-economic level of his home. Effectively, this meant that both blacks and whites were better off in predominantly white schools, since these schools were much more likely to be middle class.

Most re-analyses have supported Coleman's original conclusion. However, almost all these studies show that desegregation is associated with higher test scores only if it involves socio-economic as well as racial desegregation. There is little evidence that black test scores are any higher in schools where the whites are as poor as the blacks.

The most serious objection to these analyses is that black students in different types of schools were matched only on their socio-economic level, not on initial ability. Further analysis of EEOS has shown that there were substantial differences in initial ability between black students entering segregated and desegregated northern urban elementary schools in 1965. When we took these differences into account, we found that black improvement between first and sixth grade appeared to have been greatest in schools that were predominantly but not overwhelmingly white. Black first graders in schools which were 25–50 per cent black averaged two points below the northern urban black mean on the EEOS first grade tests. Black sixth graders in the same schools averaged three points above the northern urban black mean on the four sixth grade EEOS tests. The implied gain is 5 points. In 10–25 per cent black schools, the pattern was reversed. Black first graders in these schools were five points above the northern urban black mean, while sixth grade blacks in the same schools were no better than the black mean. The implied loss was thus five points. Blacks in predominantly black schools were equally far below national norms on both the first and sixth grade EEOS tests.[20]

Like its predecessors, this analysis of EEOS has several major limitations, the most important of which is that there were only 126 black children in the first grades of the 10–25 per cent schools, and 549 in the first grades of the 25–50 per cent black schools. Nonetheless, the fact that this analysis tries to take initial ability into account makes it slightly more persuasive than other analyses of EEOS data. In the absence of other evidence it would suggest that blacks benefited from elementary school desegregation so long as they were a large enough minority.

Re-analysis of the EEOS northern urban high school data shows that twelfth grade blacks in the forty-two predominantly but not exclusively white high schools score three points higher than would be expected from looking at ninth grade blacks in the same school. Since many blacks drop out of school between ninth and twelfth grades, it would be dangerous to draw many conclusions from this finding.[21]

The theory that desegregation boosts black test scores more often than it lowers them is supported by a 1966 survey of black adults.[22] The survey covered 1,624 northern urban blacks born between 1921 and 1945. Half were educated in the South, half in the North. Of those educated in the North, half said they had attended desegregated schools, a quarter said they had attended segregated schools, and a quarter said they had attended both. Those who had attended desegregated schools scored two or three points higher on a short verbal test than those who had attended segregated schools. The two groups did not appear to differ in socio-economic background. We do not know whether they differed in terms of initial ability.

Most local surveys have also found that blacks in desegregated schools score higher than blacks in all-black schools. The two best studies are by Alan Wilson and Nancy St. John. Wilson conducted a survey in Contra Costa County, California, and found that black students' scores rose faster in desegregated than in segregated schools. This held true even when initial test scores were controlled. Like EEOS, Wilson found that blacks benefited only when they attended school with middle-class whites, not when they attended school with whites as poor as themselves. He also found that school racial mix affected test scores, while neighbourhood racial mix did not. Racial mix had more effect in elementary than in secondary school.[23]

St. John conducted surveys of Pittsburgh ninth graders and Boston sixth graders. In Pittsburgh, black ninth graders did better in arithmetic, but no better in reading, if they were in desegregated schools.[24] The same thing appears to have been true in Boston.[25]

Taken together, these surveys suggest that black students educated in desegregated elementary schools score 2–3 points higher on standardized tests if they attend desegregated elementary schools than if they attend all-black elementary schools. If this estimate is realistic, we might also expect to find the following:

1 Black students in truly integrated schools, whatever they may be, might gain more than 3 points on standardized tests.[26]

2 Black students in schools which did not have meaningful social integration might not gain anything at all, or might even lose. This would be especially likely if desegregation was recent and had been accompanied by social dislocation and disruption of school routines. The same might hold for schools where blacks were a small minority.

3 Blacks from 'good' all-black schools might gain nothing from desegregation. They might even lose if they moved into 'bad' desegregated schools.

4 The benefits of desegregation might be confined to certain grade levels and to certain kinds of students, as well as to certain kinds of schools.

If this is the way the world works, we would also expect bussing experiments in diverse communities and grade levels involving small numbers of children to yield contradictory results. Some would show no gains whatever. Many would show gains so small they could reasonably be attributed to chance. A few would show losses. Such a mixed pattern would be particularly common when the 'receiving' schools in bussing studies were being desegregated for the first time. Studies that tried to identify changes in test scores after one or two years of bussing would also be likely to yield a lot of statistically insignificant differences, since short-term changes involve more random error.

The bussing studies we have surveyed conform to these expectations. Some show inconsistent gains. Some show no difference. Very few show (or at least report) losses.

In Hartford, Connecticut, Project Concern randomly chooses classrooms of black children for bussing to white suburbs. In 1970, children who had been in the programme three years had reading scores seven to eight points above the average for the all-black schools they had left. Others showed less improvement. There are a multitude of problems with this study, but in general it is encouraging.[27] In Riverside, California, on the other hand, a massive intracity bussing programme seems to have had negligible effects on black students' test scores.[28] In Evanston, Illinois, desegregation seems to have improved blacks' scores slightly in the early grades but not in later grades.[29] These findings could be expanded.[30]

Taken in isolation, none of these studies proves very much. When they are taken together, they seem consistent with our conclusion that if desegregation continues over a fairly long period it usually raises black students' scores slightly. But the gains are usually small, and they depend on factors that nobody fully understands.

When we turn from racial to economic segregation, the picture is equally murky. Analysts who try to disentangle the effects of racial and economic segregation on blacks generally conclude that economic segregation is far more important than racial segregation. This implies that poor blacks would benefit as much from going to school with middle-class blacks as from going to school with middle-class whites. It also implies that blacks do not benefit from going to school with poor whites. It seems reasonable to infer, although we have no direct evidence, that blacks also benefit primarily from going to school with students who have high test scores, not from going to school with students whose parents are merely affluent.

Effects on poor whites

The effects of desegregation on disadvantaged white students have not been widely studied. Coleman and his colleagues reported that white students' test scores were not much affected by the characteristics of their classmates.[31] This analysis was, however, flawed in several crucial respects.[32] Subsequent analyses of EEOS have implied that poor whites benefited from being in predominantly middle-class schools, but less than poor blacks. Unfortunately, the possibility that this was due to differences in initial ability was not ruled out.[33] But Wilson's study of Contra Costa County controlled initial scores and still found that working-class whites' scores rose more if they attended predominantly middle-class schools. Wilson also found that desegregation did not help whites as much as blacks, and that it only helped in elementary school.[34] In contrast, a study of Brookline, Massachusetts, found that economic segregation had no effect on test scores at the elementary school level.[35]

Project Talent shows that working-class whites gain as much between ninth and twelfth grades when they attend predominantly working-class high schools as when they attend predominantly middle-class high schools.[36] This is consistent with Wilson's study. A study of Nashville reached essentially the same conclusion.[37]

The weight of the evidence thus supports the assumption that poor white students benefit academically from desegregation at the elementary level but probably not at the secondary level. The evidence is not very weighty, however.

Effects on advantaged students

Advocates of desegregation are seldom very interested in its effects on advantaged students. Some actually hope that desegregation will depress advantaged students' achievement, so as to narrow the gap between them and the disadvantaged. Others expect desegregation to make advantaged students get along better with disadvantaged students. They assume that this is more important than academic gains or losses. Still others assume that advantaged students learn what they need to know at home, and that desegregation will not affect their test scores at all.

Opponents of desegregation naturally take a different view. Almost all the arguments usually advanced for believing that desegregation will help blacks or poor whites can be turned around to show that desegregation will also hurt middle-class whites:

1 Desegregation implies a more equitable distribution of scarce resources between the advantaged and the disadvantaged. If this raises the achievement of the disadvantaged, it may lower the achievement of the advantaged.

2 Desegregation implies that teachers will adapt their expectations to a new and more heterogeneous group of students. These new expectations are likely to be lower if the teachers are dealing with a mixed group of students than if they are dealing exclusively with advantaged students.

3 If desegregation leads to social integration, advantaged students will spend more time with disadvantaged students than before. This means advantaged students will spend less time with students who are likely to teach them the cognitive skills measured by standardized tests. (Disadvantaged students may well teach their advantaged friends other things of more value, but here we are concerned only with test scores.)

4 Desegregation may also lead to the creation of a new set of peer group norms, in which achievement may be less highly valued.[38]

5 If desegregation raises the self-esteem of disadvantaged students, it may also lower the self-esteem of advantaged students. Thus upper-middle class whites are fond of explaining poor whites' resistance to desegregation on the grounds that it leaves poor whites with nobody to look down on.

Advocates of desegregation have answers to all these arguments. They say that if students have the necessary advantages at home, they will achieve close to their maximum potential no matter what their school and schoolmates are like. They also say that teacher expectations and student culture are shaped by the modal style of the students, and that if a school is composed mostly of advantaged students, it can absorb a large minority of disadvantaged students without ill effects. This implies that there are 'tipping points' below which desegregation does not affect advantaged students' scores, but above which it does.

Let us begin by asking what effect racial desegregation has on the average white student's test scores. The original analysis of EEOS appeared to show that whites were not much affected by desegregation, but this was due to the peculiar method of analysis and certain technical errors.[39] Subsequent analyses of this data have focused primarily on elementary schools. These analyses have also found that white sixth graders scored lower if they were in school with blacks. But the reason for this seems to be that whites who are in school with blacks have lower scores when they enter. In predominantly black northern urban EEOS elementary schools, white first graders were as far below national norms as white sixth graders. In schools where blacks were a large minority (i.e. 25–50 per cent of the sixth grade enrolment), white sixth graders scored about three points higher relative to national norms than white first graders. Thus if desegregation has any effect on whites, EEOS suggests that it is positive rather than negative.

This tentative conclusion from EEOS is, however, contradicted by Wilson's California study. He found that whites who attended racially mixed elementary schools did worse than whites who attended all-white schools. He also found that the difference was not accounted for by his measures of initial ability or economic background. Fortunately, the size of the effect was generally small.[40]

None of the bussing studies we reviewed reported that white students' scores had declined when their schools were desegregated. In several cases, however, these studies only involved bussing blacks to previously white schools, not bussing whites to previously black schools. In some studies, the white students were not even tested. Even when they were, it could be argued that there had not been enough time for desegregation to bring social integration. This means that white students' scores might decline later on.

The effects of racial desegregation on whites, if they exist at all, also seem to depend on the economic background of the blacks whose schools they attend. Racial composition has no independent effect on white students once the economic characteristics of the student body have been taken into account.[41] Thus, there is no reason to suppose that middle-class whites suffer from exposure to middle-class blacks.

The effects of economic desegregation on whites are unclear. Wilson found that whites' scores did not improve as fast in working-class elementary schools as in middle-class elementary schools. But our re-analysis of the Plowden survey in England did not show any difference in rates of improvement for initially similar students in working-class and middle-class schools.[42] Our study of Brookline, Massachusetts, also found no differences.[43]

At the high school level, neither the racial nor the economic composition of a school seems to have much effect on white students' scores once their initial ability is taken into account. Our analyses of Project Talent show that white high school students' scores are not affected one way or the other by the racial, economic, or academic composition of their high schools. We find the same thing when we define advantage in terms of initial test scores. Those who score high in ninth grade gain as much in working-class schools as in middle-class schools and as much in schools with high ninth grade scores as in schools with low ninth grade scores.[44] Wilson's California study also shows trivial effects at the high school level.[45]

All in all, there is little evidence that desegregation has appreciable effects on initially advantaged students. This is a deliberately evasive conclusion. We cannot say for sure that desegregation never lowers advantaged students' test scores. All we can say is that if desegregation affects these students' scores, the effect must be fairly small and inconsistent.

Conclusions

We have reached four overall conclusions about the potential effects of desegregation on cognitive inequality.

1 About 80 per cent of all blacks were in predominantly black schools in 1965. They averaged 15 points below the white mean on standardized tests. Our best guess is that desegregation raises black scores by two to three points. Eliminating all predominantly black schools might therefore reduce the overall black-white gap from fifteen to twelve or thirteen points. Such a gain would not be completely trivial, but it would certainly not have much effect on the overall pattern of racial inequality in America.

2 Economic desegregation might raise poor whites' average test score by one or two points.

3 While desegregation would almost certainly reduce the overall amount of variation in test scores, the reduction would probably be quite small. Most cognitive inequality is within racial groups, within economic groups, and within schools. Desegregation will not affect these disparities much.

4 Finally, the case for or against desegregation should not be argued in terms of academic achievement. If we want a segregated society, we should have segregated schools. If we want a desegregated society, we should have desegregated schools. We suspect that most blacks, like most whites, want a mixture of the two, based on some degree of voluntarism at least among blacks. If this is so, we need a system of pupil assignment that reflects the preferences of individual black parents to some extent. The effects of segregation on test scores are certainly not large enough to justify overriding the preferences of parents and students.

The effects of tracking

We have argued that differences between schools have very little effect on test scores. Achievement differences between schools are, however, relatively small compared to achievement differences within the same school. If we compare the top fifth of all northern urban elementary schools to the bottom fifth, for example, the difference in mean sixth grade verbal scores is only two years.[46] But within the typical school, the top fifth of all sixth graders have verbal scores almost four years above the bottom fifth. From this it follows that even in the best northern urban elementary schools, the bottom fifth of the students are well below the northern urban average. Conversely, even in the worst schools, the top fifth of the students are above the northern urban average.

This means that every elementary school is nearly a microcosm of the larger society as far as cognitive inequality is concerned. This is even more true at the high school level. A strategy for reducing cognitive inequality must therefore be primarily a strategy for equalizing students in the same school. The difficulty of this task is obvious. But pretending that the main problem is parity between schools will not make it any easier. If by some miracle we were able to equalize the achievement of all American schools, leaving only differences between students in the same school, we would have reduced cognitive inequality by only about 20 per cent. If each school were able to eliminate inequalities among its students, leaving differences between them and students in other schools untouched, inequality would fall by about 40 per cent.[47]

Aside from differences in initial ability, the most obvious explanation for test score differences among students in the same school is that schools do not try to teach everyone the same things. At the elementary level, many schools put slow learners in slow classes and fast learners in fast classes. At the secondary level, they also put students in separate curriculums. If these differences do not affect students' test scores, nothing else is likely to do so.

We began our studies of tracking and curriculum placement with mixed expectations. We were used to finding that school policies and programmes had inconsistent and generally trivial effects on student achievement. Reasoning by analogy, some of us expected that tracking would have equally inconsequential effects. But we were also used to finding that segregation of advantaged and disadvantaged students into different schools increased cognitive inequality. Again reasoning by analogy, some of us expected that internal segregation would do the same. After an extensive review of previous research and re-analyses of four school surveys, we have concluded that if tracking affects test scores at all, the effect is too small to be pedagogically significant.

Research on tracking has a long history. The number of published studies boggles the mind. In 1968, the National Education Association reviewed what it regarded as the fifty best studies published in the previous eight years. The results are shown in Table 1. As with school resources, we have to conclude that ability grouping sometimes helps disadvantaged students, sometimes hurts them, and sometimes has no effect. The same appears to be true of advantaged students. Nobody knows when tracking will produce one effect or another.

Table 1   Number of studies showing various effects of ability grouping on achievement

ability level of students	favourable effects	mixed effects	unfavourable or insignificant effects
talented	18	11	17
average	11	12	10
slow	12	10	17

Source: National Education Association, Research Division, *Ability Grouping*, Research Summary 1968-Se (Washington, DC, 1968).

Unlike many previous researchers, we were not primarily interested in the average effect of tracking. We assumed it would be trivial. Our interest was in whether tracking affected the amount of variation in test scores. We thought it might well boost the scores of the students in fast classes, while lowering the scores of students in slow classes. Research of this kind poses serious methodological problems. We did, however, find one excellent body of data on English primary schools, collected by the National Foundation for Educational Research between 1964 and 1967. This study tested students when they were seven and again when they were ten, using the same tests. After correcting for unreliability in the initial tests, we found that students who were in fast streams ended up about two points ahead of initially similar students assigned to slow streams. We concluded that elementary school tracking had little effect on cognitive inequality.

We also investigated the effects of high school curriculum placement. We looked at ninety-one predominantly white comprehensive high schools throughout the United States that had tested their students for Project Talent in the ninth grade and had retested them in the twelfth grade. We compared students with initially similar scores on six different tests, some of whom said they were in the college preparatory curriculum and some of whom said they were in other curricula. We found that students in the college preparatory curriculum averaged one point higher when tested in the twelfth grade than students who had been in other curriculums. We also estimated the effects of curriculum placement on vocabulary and social studies information for students with both high and low initial scores. There was no difference between the two groups.

These analyses have convinced us that desegregating schools internally would not have much effect on students' test scores. We continue to favour internal desegregation, but we do not think it can be justified in terms of its effect on cognitive inequality.

Conclusions about cognitive inequality

The available data suggests that:

1　If we could equalize everyone's genes, inequality in test scores would probably fall by 33 to 50 per cent.
2　If we could equalize everyone's total environment, test scores inequality would fall by 25 to 40 per cent.
3　If we merely equalize everyone's economic status, test score inequality would fall by 6 per cent or less.
4　Equalising the amount of schooling people get might reduce cognitive inequality among adults by 5 to 15 per cent, although this estimate is very rough.
5　Equalizing the quality of elementary schools would reduce cognitive inequality by 3 per cent or less.
6　Equalizing the quality of high schools would reduce cognitive inequality by 1 per cent or less.
7　Eliminating racial and socio-economic segregation in the schools might reduce the test score gap between black and white children and between rich and poor children by 10 to 20 per cent.
8　Additional school expenditures are unlikely to increase achievement and redistributing resources will not reduce test score inequality.

Most differences in adult test scores are due to factors that schools do not control. It does not follow, however, that schools could not equalize people's test scores if they tried. They probably could. If, for example, we wanted everyone's reading scores to approximate the present national average, we could provide only one or two years of schooling to very bright youngsters, six years to youngsters who were a bit above average, twelve years to those who were a bit below average, and eighteen or more years to the very slow learners. This would, we suspect, greatly reduce inequality of reading scores. We do not, however, favour such a solution. We think of 'equal opportunity' as implying that everyone should get as much schooling as he wants. Equal opportunity, in this sense, guarantees inequal results.

If unequal performance on standardized tests were a principal cause of inequality in other realms, this traditional doctrine might need reexamination. The evidence discussed elsewhere does not, however, suggest that variations in cognitive skill account for much of the inequality among American adults.[48] There is nearly as much economic inequality among individuals with identical test scores as in the general population. Thus we can hardly suppose that making everyone's scores equal would appreciably reduce economic inequality in the general population.

While we reject the idea that schools should try to eliminate all variation in cognitive skill, it does not follow that schools need accept the present degree of cognitive inequality as inevitable. We have already argued that if people's cognitive skills are far below national norms they are likely to be at a significant disadvantage, not only economically but socially and psychologically. At least in a highly competitive society like ours, an individual who cannot read even simple instructions, or who cannot do enough arithmetic to tell whether he has been short-changed, is likely to be exploited in a variety of ways. Relatively few students leave school in this condition, but reducing their number still ought to be a high priority.

Unfortunately, few discussions of schooling and inequality focus on these extreme cases. When people talk about the schools' failure to prepare disadvantaged students for modern economic life, they are not usually talking about the handful of illiterates and innumerates, but about the much larger number of students who leave high school reading at the eighth or ninth grade level. As we shall see, these students are by no means unemployable. Nor are they automatically excluded from the main stream of American life. They are not likely to become physicians or physicists, but this would be true even if they were reading at the twelfth grade level. At least in economic terms, the cost of reading at eighth grade rather than twelfth grade level is quite small.

Notes

1 For details, see Coleman *et al.*, *Equality of Educational Opportunity*, and Jencks, *The Quality of the Data Collected*.
2 This analysis is reported in detail in Jencks, *The Coleman Report*.
3 See Weikart *et al Longitudinal Results*, and Gray and Klaus, *An Experimental Preschool Programme*.
4 See Smith and Bissell, *Report Analysis*, abd Boyd, *Project Head Start*.
5 See DeGroot, *War and the Intelligence of Youth*.
6 See Green *et al. Educational Status*.

7 See Hayes and Grether, *The School Year and Vacations*. It should be noted that this was a cross-sectional rather than a longitudinal study, based on school means rather than individual data.

8 The basic sample was the one described by Thorndike in *Prediction of Vocational Success*. The follow-up is reported by Lorge, in *Schooling Makes a Difference*.

9 See Harnqvist, *Relative Changes*, and Husen, *The Influence of Schooling on* IQ.

10 See Bradway and Thompson *Intelligence at Adulthood*.

11 See Harnqvist *Relative Changes in Intelligence*, and Jencks *The Effects of High Schools on Their Students*.

12 For details see Jencks *The Effects of High Schools on Their Students*.

13 See Burkhead, Fox, and Holland, *Input and Output in Large City High Schools*, on Atlanta high schools. See analyses of the Project Talent high school data that show an association between expenditures and output in Burrows *Some Determinants of High School Educational Achievement* and the National Center for Educational Statistics *Correlation and Regression Analysis*. Neither of these studies controlled input. See Goodman, *The Assessment of School Quality* and Kiesling *Measuring a Local Government Service* for analyses of New York State data that try to control initial ability and yield equivocal estimates of the relationship between district expenditures and value added. Additional expenditures are associated with gains for some students and with retardation for others.

14 The original EEOS findings are reported in Coleman *et al.*, *Equality of Educational Opportunity*. A re-analysis by Armor, in *School and Family Effects* reached the same conclusions, as did an analysis of northern urban elementary schools by Jencks in *The Coleman Report*. Boston elementary school data is reported by Katzman in 'Distribution and Production' while New York elementary school data is reported in First National City Bank *Public Education in New York City*.

15 See e.g. Piccariello, *Evaluation of Title I* and McDavid, *Innovations in Education*. These findings are not altogether surprising. These programmes have often been poorly managed. Sometimes the funds have been misspent. Often they have been widely diffused. Their aims are typically hard to pin down. Most announce improved reading or mathematics achievement as their principal goal, but many also seek to improve students' self-concept, eliminate truancy, prevent dropouts, improve school-community relations, increase parent involvement, or prevent falling arches. Very few of these programmes have done anything radically new. Most assume that what disadvantaged children need is pretty much what they have been getting, only more: more

teachers, more specialists, more books, more audio-visual devices, more trips to museums, and so forth. The quality of a child's experience is seldom changed, so we should not expect the results of change.

16 Some readers may wonder whether school resources might not have more effect on blacks than on students in general. We have found no evidence of this (see Mosteller and Moynihan, *On Equality of Educational Opportunity*).

17 See, for example, Katz and Greenbaum *Effects of Anxiety*.

18 The EEOS questionnaire data shows that teachers in white middle-class schools express a stronger preference for white, middle-class, academically talented students than teachers in black or lower-class white schools. It seems reasonable to assume that preference for whites is often accompanied by negative feelings about blacks.

19 Crain, in *The Politics of School Desegregation*, studied the process of desegregation in the North, but he did not try to predict when test scores would improve and when they would not.

20 See Jencks *The Effects of Desegregated Elementary Schools*.

21 See Jencks *The Effects of High Schools on Their Students*.

22 See Crain *School Desegregation*.

23 See Wilson *Educational Consequences*.

24 See St John and Smith *School Racial Composition*. The meaning of the findings is not entirely clear, since eighth grade IQ was controlled in all analyses. The finding seems to imply that desegregation raises achievement more than it raises IQ. Perhaps controlling IQ neutralizes gains in reading but not in maths. Blacks scored higher the longer they had been desegregated. The social class of their white classmates was not crucial.

25 See St John and Lewis *The Influence of School Racial Context*. Again, the 'gains' in maths but not reading may reflect the fact that the initial ability measure was more like the final reading test than like the final maths test.

26 McPartland in *The Segregated Student*, and Cohen *et al* in *Race and the Outcome of Schooling* found that where blacks were in the same high school classrooms as whites they scored slightly higher than when they were in the same schools but different classrooms. The direction of cause and effect is hard to determine, however.

27 See Mahan *Project Concern*.

28 See Gerard and Miller, *Factors Contributing to Adjustment and Achievement* and Purl and Dawson *The Achievement of Pupils*.

29 See Hsia *Integration in Evanston*.

30 For reviews of this literature, see St John *Desegregation and Minority Group Performance* and Weinberg *Desegregation Research*. See also

Armor *The Evidence of Bussing* for a very pessimistic appraisal.

31 See Coleman *et al Equality of Educational Opportunity*.

32 See Smith, *The Basic Findings Reconsidered*.

33 See Jencks *The Coleman Report*.

34 See Wilson *Educational Consequences*.

35 See Smith *The Brookline Study*. The data includes a measure of initial ability. No Brookline school is really poor by national standards.

36 See Jencks *The Effects of High Schools on Their Students*.

37 See Hauser *Schools and the Stratification Process*.

38 For evidence that achievement is not very high valued, even in middle-class schools, see Coleman *The Adolescent Society*.

39 See Smith *The Basic Findings Reconsidered*.

40 See Wilson *Educational Consequences*.

41 See Wilson *Educational Consequences*; Hanushek *The Education of Blacks and Whites*; and Jencks *The Coleman Report*.

42 See Acland *Social Determinants*.

43 See Smith *The Brookline Study*.

44 See Jencks *The Effects of High Schools on Their Students*.

45 See Wilson *Educational Consequences*.

46 Estimated from the northern urban EEOS data.

47 Estimated from Mayeske *et al A Study of Our Nation's Schools*.

48 See Jencks, C. *et al* (1972) *Inequality*, Chapters 6 and 7.

1.7 A Blunt Instrument*

J.W.B. Douglas

The message of this book, as given on the jacket, is 'that educational reform cannot bring about economic or social equality; that genes and IQ scores have relatively little effect on income; and that school quality has little effect on economic success in later life'. This is a fair statement of the conclusions reached by Jencks and his co-workers, after a re-examination of the main American studies of educational deprivation. Poverty, he finds, is not hereditary; there is almost as much inequality among those who score high on standardised tests as in the general population; there is no evidence that school reform can substantially reduce the extent of cognitive inequality; neither school resources nor segregation have an appreciable effect on either test scores or educational attainment.

Before we decide that all educational reform should be scrapped, and that the reasonable aim of the Department of Education and Science should be to provide the cheapest and, administratively, the most convenient service that can be devised, it is well to look at the assumptions that underlie this analysis, the adequacy of the data used in it and the appropriateness of the statistical method. This may help us to penetrate the grey fog which pervades the book and to see why so many aspects of American education and life take on the features of a lottery, in which ability, industry and family circumstances have little influence.

The first thing to realise is that Jencks is concerned with explaining inequality between individuals and not inequality between groups. This is playing God without having God's data bank to draw on. With many of the variables studied, variation within families is little less than variation within the whole population. We have, however, little opportunity to explain the variation within families, which may be partly genetic, partly environmental and partly random.

On genetic variation: ' ... our main conclusion after some years of work on this problem is that mathematical estimates of heritability tell us almost nothing about anything important'. On other causes of variation within

Source: *New Society* (20th September 1973), pp. 717–8.
* Editor's note: This is a review of JENCKS, C. *et al* (1972) *Inequality*.

families, adequate information is equally lacking and the only thing we can do is to regard it as random variation of unknown origin. This suggests that an analysis of group differences is likely to be more profitable than an analysis of individual differences. If we express results in terms of the proportion of total individual variation explained, we are likely to diminish the importance of differences which, though small in relation to total variation, may have important implications when related to the variation that can be explained between families or between groups.

With the method of analysis used (path analysis) it is important that the dependent (or outcome) variable should be reliable and that its intervals should be equal in the sense that a unit change in one part of the scale has an equivalent meaning to a unit change in any other part of the scale. This does not hold for any of the dependent variables used. Perhaps income comes closest to meeting this requirement, and it may be for this reason that the most satisfactory explanations are found in the income analysis. The independent (or explanatory) variables are even less satisfactory, and statements on the proportion of total population variance explained are likely to be highly inaccurate, if not misleading.

When the limitations of the variables available, and the over-simplification of even the most complicated path model, are taken into account, I would doubt that this was the right statistical method to use. But then I am more interested in trying to explain differences between groups than the differences between individuals. And Jencks himself admits that the path analysis approach can be criticised, though he still sees it as the best available. His comments on problems of statistical interpretation are relevant here: ' ... consider the following statements about the relationship of parental status and years of schooling, all of which are more or less true:

1 87 per cent of those high school seniors whose parents make more than $15,000 a year enter college, while only 20 per cent of those whose parents make under $3,000 per year do so.

2 Parental income explains 9 per cent of the variance in years of schooling, independent of IQ.

'The first statement might give a reader the impression that this problem was very large. The last statement might give a quite different impression. Since [both] statements are correct, it is hard to say whether the "big problem" response is more appropriate than the "trivial problem" response.'

While Jencks himself uses both types of statement in the book, he favours the latter. This is inherent in his interest in individual variation and in path analysis. It is largely responsible for the grey picture that he presents.

One of the more thought-provoking conclusions of this analysis of

American education is that 'differences between high schools contribute almost nothing to the overall level of cognitive inequality. Differences between elementary schools may be somewhat more important, but evidence for this is still inconclusive. The average effect of attending the best rather than the worst fifth of all elementary schools is almost certainly no more than ten points and probably no more than five.' Related to the 'overall level', differences of ten points of test score may appear small, but they are equivalent to the difference in score between fifteen year old pupils from middle class and manual working class homes, which many would regard as being far from unimportant. But the lack of influence of the high schools on cognitive ability stands; and the comment that 'we can see no evidence that either school administrators, or educational experts know how to raise test scores, even when they have vast resources at their disposal', is justified.

Would we, however, reach a similar conclusion in Britain? I think so. It is difficult to show that schools in this country play any effective part in reducing inequality in performance. There is no narrowing, between eight and fifteen years, of the gap in attainment between children from non-manual and from manual working class families. Children with many brothers and sisters arrive at school with poor vocabularies and, during the succeeding ten years, do not improve their position. Even when we compare the academic performance of boys from Headmasters' Conference ('public') schools and maintained schools, no differences are found, once we have roughly matched for measured ability and parental occupation and education. The results in A levels and university entry are the same, though the duller public school boys will have been encouraged to leave early and take their GCE examinations from a crammer or a technical college. The only difference is that public school boys are more likely to take only arts A levels, and the maintained school boys to take science only.

Differences can be found between the achievement of children in Scottish and English schools, and, having had two boys at Scottish schools, I can understand why. At the age of eight the standard of reading of children is higher in Scotland than in England. This holds equally in each social class and would seem to be a tribute to the persistence and determination of the Scottish infant school teachers. This early flowering does not, however, ensure a lasting advantage and, by fifteen the same Scottish and English pupils show closely similar scores in reading.

The early chapters on inequality in education are followed by chapters on occupational and income inequality. It is in the last of these that Jencks's greatest interest lies. If we wish to maximise the satisfaction of the population, he says, we should aim to make everyone's income the same, for people with low incomes value extra income more than people with high incomes. But do they? There is little association between job satisfaction and the level of earnings ' ... "bench workers" were as satisfied as professionals and managers, and they earned much less.' No strong case is made for believing that equalising incomes would increase satisfaction. Indeed, by removing an important and satisfying scheme of reference it might reduce it. As things are, the majority of individuals can compare themselves with others less well-off than themselves.

While we would all wish to eliminate poverty, we might not wish to attain the level of equality that Jencks hopes for, or be willing to accept the measures needed to attain it. By progressive taxation, income supplements, and free public services for some, we could 'make poverty (ie, having a living standard less than half the national average) virtually impossible'. A less remarkable reduction in the inequality of incomes – from 35 to 40 per cent – would be achieved, Jencks suggests, if all brothers and sisters were required to pool their incomes. This would, however, introduce a new dimension of inequality based on the size of families. As you will see, it is difficult to know how seriously to take these and other equally bizarre solutions to the problem of how to abolish income differences between individuals.

One thing is securely established by this book – education is not, and can never again be, an instrument of social policy. We can no longer accept the view of Edward Short that 'those responsible for the layout of the educational system and for allocating resources to it both locally and nationally can enlarge or restrict opportunity and so contribute in no small measure to, or retard, change in society'.

In a relatively illiterate society – in this country before the first world war, or in America between the wars – this may have been true. But today, education, when used as an instrument to alter society, is blunt, unpredictable and expensive. The public schools may have been effective in providing the district commissioners and governors of a great empire, but their pupils were wholly in their charge day and night, for eight months, or more, a year. The comprehensive school cannot compete with this. It is time that politics are taken out of education, and that we address ourselves to providing the sort of schools that best suit the needs of the child – not only educational needs, but the development of a wide variety of skills, social as well as practical and intellectual.

Jencks writes: 'Some schools are dull, depressing, even terrifying places, while others are lively, comfortable and reassuring. If we think of school life as an end in itself rather than a means to some other end, such differences are enormously important. Eliminating these differences would not do much to make adults more equal, but it would do a great deal to make the quality of children's (and teachers') lives more equal. Since children are in school for a fifth of their lives, this would be a significant accomplishment.' This is not, perhaps, the type of recommendation that one would expect to come from a statistical analysis of educational deprivation. It is none the less welcome for that.

1.8   Whatever happened to positive discrimination?

A. H. Halsey

We were not to know in remote 1966 that the cost of Plowden would, within a decade, look no more serious than an Arab Shaikh's laundry bill. Someone more prescient than I or HM Government might have seen that the failure of George Brown's plan for national economic growth was more than a temporary thwarting.

We live today under sentence of death by a thousand cuts (that is, of all things except the body of bureaucracy). In education the position is one of extreme relative deprivation, not only because of the financial background of a sudden halt to previously mounting largesse, but also, and more seriously, because of the collapse of belief in education either as the best investment for national production, or the great redistributor of chances to the traditionally disadvantaged.

In those days it was very different. Politicians and planners were still under the spell of belief in education as a prerequisite to growth, and growth as the road to distributional justice. Gaitskell's intention at the 1959 election to strengthen the social services primarily out of an accumulating gross national product was still the basic orthodoxy. In that sense the 1930s had been forgotten, and nowhere more than in education, with its established record, since Eccles, of a rising proportionate share of the public purse, was there such a mindless optimism that all good things would come in the not too distant fullness of time.

The then Secretary of State for Education, Anthony Crosland, remarked in irritation that it was all too easy to argue that any one of 1,001 good things would only claim 0.1 per cent of gross national product. But serious redistributional intention – that is, the redistribution which hurts because effected from static total resources – had somehow slipped out of the practical political intentions of the Labour Party.

Source: *The Times Educational Supplement*, 21 January 1977.

This point is of fundamental importance now that people of all political persuasions have to face the prospect of indefinite stagnation in the output of so-called developed countries. In the mid-1960s, positive discrimination came from the Plowden Report as a new phrase for an old principle. Looking back, I see it as the uncriticized social principle of the report. The critics, like Peters and Bernstein, addressed themselves more to the pedagogical assumptions of progressivism, of little interest to a ministry which had never trespassed on what is now called 'the secret garden' of education, other than through the peripatetic licence held by the Inspectorate.

The social principle was uncriticized because it was tacitly held to be no more than a convenient criterion for the allocation of marginal extras, which at some time would be likely to become available from a burgeoning education vote. And these assumptions were undisturbed by the fact that Plowden in general and EPA in particular were almost entirely rejected, or at least postponed, because of the latest sterling crisis (I forget now which one it was, but certainly we were firmly told that the time was not Treasury-ripe when Plowden landed on the DES desks).

By the end of the EPA projects and our report to the DES at the beginning of 1971, Mrs Thatcher had become Secretary of State. There was, none the less, considerable sympathy among DES officials and the new politicians for some elements of our new developed ideas of EPA. Our accent on preschooling, and on those aspects of community schooling which we linked to it in our advocacy of parent-teaching partnership, was in harmony with the widespread pressure for nursery schooling, and Mrs Thatcher's resolve to leave a new fourth tier of education as the monument to that stage of her political career.

The 1972 White Paper *Framework for Expansion* (though neither a framework nor expansive) incorporated bits from our EPA recommendations, but the package had been selectively picked over. Our elaborated idea of community schooling was, for example, too far-reaching in its implications for the traditional conception of function held by the DES. The Permanent Secretary could only shrug his shoulders and say that 'good ideas travel on their own legs'.

He was right in one way: Eric Midwinter, George and Teresa Smith and many other EPA enthusiasts carried the ideas through a thousand lectures and conferences in schools and colleges, making, I believe, a permanent mark on thought and opinion about the relation between education and upbringing, and especially about the nature of the partnership between parents and teachers. Yet the DES could have been brave enough to finance a national organization for the dissemination of the EPA experience it had commissioned. It failed to do so until long after the job had been done by private labour.

We learnt about the practicalities of social change from these experiences, but my own political education was accelerated most in conversations with the powers the following year. I was quickly taught by Mrs. Thatcher that the language of positive discrimination can readily translate into that of selective services. The latter is, after all, only a niggardly version of the former.

In *Framework for Expansion* there was vague reference to special help for EPA districts, alongside the opposite principle of 'first come, first served' in the programme for expanding pre-schooling. So the Tories in principle and Labour in practice accept positive discrimination, only to defeat it by taking away its generosity. Positive discrimination was, in any case, a shrouded issue behind the form of its presentation as a policy for discriminant treatment of different districts. In this sense Crosland did adopt a critical stance.

Is there, he asked, an authentic geographical theory of poverty? If there is, three cheers, because administration is so much easier for territories than for social categories. The Plowden Committee had, through its EPA proposals, linked positive discrimination to a geographical theory of poverty which rested on no better foundations than Lyndon Johnson's war on poverty in the United States. Both were a hotchpotch of appealing but unrigorous assertions that poverty and disadvantage were concentrated in city slums, ethnic ghettos and Appallachian (Yorkshire?) hamlets. Children were suffering (note the slide over to an individual appeal): they were being robbed of the opportunity to enter into full citizenship and something should be done immediately.

With the Victorian notion added that education was the instrument for full realization as a citizen of affluent democracy (and incidentally also the guarantee of continual national economic growth), it was politically natural that goodwill and Michael Young's persuasive prose overcame doubts about the intellectual soundness of a theory which pointed clearly to practical action. If the action itself was miniscule this was more because of immediate economic stringency, because of the other claims for educational expansion (especially the Robbins programme for higher education), and the Kathleen Ollerenshaw principle that only 2 per cent of next year's budget is actually available for redistribution, than because of any hesitation over the geographical theory of poverty itself.

Those like me who argued for a demonstration of what Plowden reform would look like through an action-research project were caught in a dilemma. Our theory was uncertain but, if the impetus of the report was not to be lost while the Chancellor was sorting out the foreign exchanges, then an earnest of good intention as well as an opportunity to learn by doing seemed to be a worthwhile immediate gain. Accordingly, we put our emphasis on experimental innovation rather than on critical analysis of the geographical theory.

But this did not mean that I or my colleagues committed ourselves to the fashionable theoretical assumptions of the day. In reviewing the transatlantic passage of poverty theory, I wrote: 'It is an open question as to how far British city slums resemble either those of Boston in the 1930s or Washington DC in the 1960s, though the signs that coloured immigrants are developing into a "thwarted social stratum" are clear enough'. Nor were we still bearers of the innocence of the 1930s, and the belief in education as the cure-all of inequality and social misfortune.

The anti-educationalist version of social reform is now heavily identified with Christopher Jencks, since he published *Inequality* in 1972. But by 1969, in the first year of the EPA project, when we repeatedly discussed the basis of our work, I wrote: ' "The Poverties" to which urban industrial populations are prone must be understood to have their origin in both the situational and the cultural characteristics of those minorities which suffer disadvantage and discrimination, and to have their cures in both economic and cultural reform, not only at the local or community level but also in the total structure of society.' Neither the optimism of war on poverty nor the pessimism of Jencks was unanticipated or uncritically accepted by British sociologists.

Nevertheless, there was an intellectual confusion which still dogs us. For example, in an otherwise excellent little book, *The Disadvantages of Inequality*, which appeared last November, Richard Berthoud asserts that: 'it has since been found that the concentration of "deprived" children in "deprived" areas is not sufficient to justify an area-based approach – most deprived children in such areas are not deprived'. The confusion is between two kinds of policy – the one aimed at individual and the other at social (in this case territorial) aggregates. The mistake is to conflate them: the remedy is to separate them, and then to pursue them as complementary elements of a wider strategy.

The social approach is vulnerable to the ecological fallacy, and the individual approach to the fallacy of composition. Lady Plowden and her colleagues described, with a good deal of evidence, the coincidence, in particular districts, of disadvantages in the social and economic environment and in the circumstances of schools. These conditions, internal and external to the school, are not randomly related but correlated, so that it was possible, using a combined index of social and educational disadvantage, to draw a map of deprivation. This showed the black spots of particular school catchment areas and districts, characteristically concentrated in the inner rings of the conurbations.

The average degree of education and social deprivation in such districts is undoubtedly high by national norms. In some EPA districts, levels of reading attainment are a whole standard deviation lower than the national norm. Thus, these geographically demarcated deprivations have a reality. Nevertheless, it is a fallacy to translate from average conditions to a prediction about individual circumstances and individual performance. It cannot be assumed that any particular child who grows up in an EPA area is doomed to low education attainment.

Moreover, however the map is drawn, the number of children who are deprived or disadvantaged is greater outside EPA districts than inside them. This apparent paradox is a consequence of failing to distinguish between group averages and individual children. This is the ecological fallacy (illustrated in the context of the EPA project by Jack Barnes in Volume 3 of the EPA studies. (See BARNES, J. and LUCAS, H., Chapter 1.5 in this volume. Ed.)

Nevertheless, it is just as easy to fall victim to the fallacy of composition by taking an individual approach. An important case in point is that of geographically concentrated racial and ethnic groups. The low performing black child is a fact. But the depression of a black community is not simply the sum of individual low performances. Theirs is a separate world within which individuals still vary, but around lower averages – a world socially determined by a complex set of discriminatory attitudes and policies which reinforce one another in limiting opportunities, effort and ambition.

As my colleague George Smith has argued, it is typical of EPA districts that the whole range of scores is depressed, and not one particular category. Thus, the weakness of an individual at-risk approach to deprivation is underlined. He insists it is necessary to analyse general social changes that create and sustain EPAs, and to pursue area-based policies in the light of such analysis.

A local education system has to be seen as only one of the educational resources of the area. Its development has to be planned in relation to other educative and anti-educative forces, including the characteristically low level of private and public investment, and the absence of social capital in transition areas with rapidly changing populations, poor housing and poor knowledge of the political and administrative skills required in securing a fair share of resources for the district.

There are, then, many different units and facets of poverty. Positively discriminatory policies must distinguish between regions, districts, schools and individuals. But there is no necessary opposition between work at the different levels.

Programmes which focus on the national organization of preschooling, or on realising the principle of the community school, or on psychological tests to predict the likelihood of failure in individuals, can all be fitted together coherently in educational approaches to the mitigation of disadvantage.

Positive discrimination is about resources. The principle stands, and is most urgently in need of application now that our total resources are both limited and forced to be idle.

2 The system at work

Introduction

The educational system is a major consumer of the nation's resources. Most of this expenditure is committed to maintaining the system – providing, for example, roofs over heads and salaries for those employed in the educational service – rather than with new policies. The section begins with an OECD (Organization for Economic Cooperation and Development) Report (2.1) on the Department of Education and Science, the most important single force in determining 'the direction and tempo of educational development'. This powerful position is maintained by 'combining the task of coherent planning with defensive tactics, excluding an open planning process, public hearings or even participation'. But the most serious charge is that the Department's planning is resource oriented, being primarily concerned with matters of scale, organization and cost, rather than with educational content. This leads it to adopt a principle of 'more not different', i.e. that there is little or no attempt to periodically review educational goals, and their relationships with other social and economic objectives.

The DES then presents its own view of the planning process (2.2) in a reading which also outlines the rate support grant – the major source of local authority funds.

Howard Glennerster (2.3) provides a detailed explanation of the origins of the present system of public expenditure controls and of departmental planning in the DES.

Eileen Byrne's research (2.4) reveals that the discriminatory patterns of allocating resources are based on widespread assumptions that owe little to the assessed educational needs of children. It is *assumed* that the less able need less spent on books and resources, fewer staff and lower paid staff than other children; that small schools are better for the less able child, while grammar school children require large schools in order to offer a wide choice of subjects; that the education of boys should be different from that of girls. The assumptions are built into the design, staffing and recurrent resource provision for schools. Many examples of these assumptions now appear to have changed or are changing, but the residues of such planning continue to influence educational provision. Williamson and Byrne (2.5) using their own researches in Sunderland, argue that the variation in resource provision between LEAS is correlated with educational attainment. This is in conflict with the findings of Jencks, who argued in 1.6 that there is no such consistent relationship.

Schools have certain needs in common with each other but individual schools will also have specific needs. The final paper by Briault (2.6) describes how one local authority has built this principle into its allocation of resources. Individual schools decide their own priorities and use of all resources additional to the basic ones provided directly by the local authority.

2.1   Servants or masters ?

OECD Report on Britain

I The planning process
Introduction

The planning in which a governmental body engages is not explicable in the abstract. It is intelligible only in relation to national institutions and habits and to an historical experience. Nowhere is this more obviously the case than in the United Kingdom, where government is conducted within a setting of understandings, restraints, and mutual forbearances that can only in part be codified. In Britain it is the habit of most people, high and low, to refer to 'the long history' behind any social practice under scrutiny. Sometimes, in fact, the history is a relatively short one. Nevertheless, a significant principle lies behind this phrase, even though it is normally left implicit.

It is meant to suggest that a society has organic qualities, that abstract schematisms cannot be imposed upon it without running great risks, and that if its institutions are to be managed successfully they must be approached from the inside, not the outside, felt in their concreteness and particularity, and understood as arrangements which people have worked out in the course of a common experience and which accomplish purposes too subtle to be written into a master plan.

Accordingly, it is best for people inside an institution to decide what to do with it, and it is always dangerous for outsiders to meddle. This is certainly true for people completely outside the society. But it is true even for the relations of a governing class to those it governs. A government must get results but it must do so without intruding into or disturbing the structures and habits of its subjects' intimate lives.

It has been in these terms that the British constitutional tradition has largely evolved, and that the British conception of limited government has been formulated. In the eyes of most observers outside the British Isles, this approach to the art of government has constituted the essence of the British political genius. There are very few countries in the West – perhaps

---

Source: *The Times Higher Educational Supplement* 9 May 1976.

none in the Organization for Economic Cooperation and Development – which, at some crucial point in their history, have not turned to British political philosophy and practice for instruction. Yet the British concept of limited government is not the only reason why British political institutions are objects of universal interest.

Britain is also the creator of a powerful Civil Service, and has pioneered for more than a century in the public examination of social problems and the attempt to use the tools of scientific investigation, law and central government to find remedies for them. It is the country of Locke and Burke, but also of Bentham and Chadwick, the Mills and the Fabians. And since the second world war it has been fairly steadily engaged in nationalization of key industries and services and in centralized planning.

There is nothing in the British tradition like the Napoleonic idea of treating the education of a nation as though it were a problem in centrally organising the distribution of manpower and recruiting and preparing an officer class. Yet within their more diffident tradition the British have been attempting to allocate limited resources to serve goals which involve the fairly thorough redesigning from bottom to top of their nation's educational structures. And although there is perhaps less tendency in Britain than elsewhere to envisage the transformation of human nature by new methods of pedagogy, the British have not lagged in the development and testing of new pedagogical methods and curricular designs. Modesty in the statement of educational purpose has been joined to accomplishment in educational practice.

For these reasons, an analysis of the educational planning process in Great Britain has unusual interest as a case study. Fundamental choices and dilemmas that planners face in most democratic countries are silhouetted in the British instance. In a single package are combined a sophisticated planning approach and a resilient tradition of limited government.

In this setting planners must lead but they must also follow. They must be thoroughly professional, and also at all times in the service of the political figure who heads the Department of Education and Science. They must resist the temptation and definitely avoid giving the impression of an attempt to control the content of education or the ultimate purposes lying behind its design. Yet they must allocate resources in accordance with some conception of national priorities and possibilities, and the line between doing this and making decisions about the goals of education is not everywhere clear.

The power of the Department of Education and Science
The educational planning process in Great Britain is part of a larger pattern

of received codes and mental habits.

At the start one is confronted by the position of the DES in the web of organizations and agencies that have educational responsibilities in the United Kingdom. It is true to say both that it has extremely limited authority and that it has great power. Although it bears the central responsibility for educational planning in the United Kingdom, and although it devises the overall plan, in so far as any exists, and takes such steps as lie within its powers to see that the plan is fulfilled, the mission of the department is nevertheless a restricted one. Not only do Scotland and Wales receive their educational allocations through the special Ministries for Scotland and Wales, but, more largely, the department is prohibited from determining the content of education anywhere in the United Kingdom.

The Government meets 60 per cent of the costs of primary, secondary and further education, but the department must leave to the local education authorities the final decision as to the way in which the monies it dispenses will be spent. In relation to institutions like the universities, the department's authority is similarly but even further restricted; it provides funds to the autonomous University Grants Committee, which makes the decisions concerning the distribution of these funds.

Even with regard to the need to provide for a measure of educational mobility and standardization in the United Kingdom as a whole, it is not the department but autonomous professional bodies which make the direct decisions relative to curricula, professional standards, and the content of examinations. Within this network of local authorities, autonomous committees and professional organizations, the department gives guidance but, except in certain specific areas defined by statute, it has little power of direct command.

In the distribution of teachers, for instance, it seeks to obtain a fair balance through persuasion and by indirect pressures on local authorities rather than by direct fiat. A large consensus on a second best solution is preferred to an assumed optimum obtained under duress. Decentralization of authority is characteristic of British political practice in general, but it is nowhere more evident than in the sensitive area of education, which touches the family and traditional mores intimately.

It should be noted, however, that this decentralization does not automatically signify a high level of participation in the administering and control of the system. The resulting virtual immunity of head teachers from external control, combined with the 'liberal pluralism' referred to above, allows innovatory initiatives to exist side by side with the most traditional of arrangements.

This, however, is only one side of the coin. The actual powers of the DES are nonetheless considerable. Since the Government is the largest single source of educational financing in Britain, the department's advice commands attention in any case, but it has powers that run beyond the purely advisory. It has direct control over capital expenditures at the local level, and thus has the final say with regard to the direction of educational growth. Further, its consent is required by statute in every case in which a local authority wishes to introduce or change a course at advanced level, to build a school or to close or change the character of an existing secondary school, for example by converting it from a grammar school into a comprehensive school.

The department also controls both the size norms and the price limits for school building. This latter is an area, it should be noted, where major innovations and economies have been achieved in the rationalising of school building provision accomplished by the developmental work of the architects and building branch of the department.

These powers, taken together with the general context of the Rate Support Grant System under which local education authorities receive their subsidies from the central government (averaging 58 per cent of educational expenditure in 1971/2) and the control over the total supply and the allocation of teachers, show up the important role played by economic reasoning and resource control (both positive and negative) exercised from the centre in the orientation of educational action at local levels.

They are enhanced by the fact that the ministry which possesses them is staffed by a corps of permanent civil servants, well-trained and experienced in practical efficiency. However restricted their jurisdiction, seemingly, may be, they do not waste what power they have. They exercise, in consequence, influence over the evolution of educational policy in their country at least equal to that of ministries of education that enjoy far more sweeping constitutional authority.

In sum, although the powers of government with regard to educational planning are formally limited, and British planning does not go so far as to be described even as 'indicative planning', the central Department of Education and Science is undoubtedly the most important single force in determining the direction and tempo of educational development.

It must adjust to economic and budgetary stringencies (such as those which led to the sharp cuts in December, 1973), to opinion in the educational and political worlds, and to the pressures of organised interest groups, most particularly the teachers. But the evolution of education in the United Kingdom cannot be charted without placing the planning function of the department at the centre of the story.

The bureaucracy

Further attention must be given to a particular characteristic of the planning process in the United Kindgom which invites and yet transcends the term 'paradox'. This is the role played by the Civil Service.

The permanent officials of the DES in the tradition of British civil servants, are non-political in their function. In no country, it is safe to say, does the Civil Service govern itself more closely by a code of loyalty to whatever government is in power. The protections in the British system against the Civil Service's being captured by a political party go very far.

In the DES, an incoming Secretary of State normally makes no appointments from the outside, though the Secretary of State in the present Labour Government has appointed an economist as a special adviser. Perhaps in no other democracy are ministers' powers of appointment so strictly limited.

To the Civil Service's own code of professional neutrality there are thus added stringent safeguards against political patronage. This means that the expression of politically-oriented points of view in the daily work of the ministries is exceptional. Nor do the political parties intrude in the service's selection procedures or internal communications. By means of these practices and traditions, the British nation has been served by a continuing stream of knowledgeable and experienced officials with a strong tradition for discipline, fidelity and morale, and chosen for their individual merits, not their political allegances.

But there has been a by-product. A permanent officialdom possessing such external protections and internal disciplines becomes a power in its own right. A British department composed of professional civil servants who have watched the ministers come and go is an entity that only an extremely foolish or powerful politician will persistently challenge or ignore.

The prestige, acquaintanceships, and natural authority of leading civil servants give them a standing in the civil forum often superior to that of their *de jure* political superiors. They are, in the continental phrase, *notables*, whose opinions must be given special weight, whether or not votes in the next election will be affected.

There has also to be taken into account the momentum of thought and action within a department composed of career officials who have long known one another, who have the same training and prospects, and who work within a common tradition and point of view. An essential part of their ethos is to serve their 'political masters'. They interpret this as imposing upon them the obligation to remain at all times sensitive to the changing realities of political pressures and to endeavour to identify in all

F

situations a social consensus as to the priority issues towards which policy planning could be directed.

Accordingly, it is a simplification to describe the planning process in the DES as a purely technical affair in which resources are canvassed and strategic alternatives weighed, but decisions about ends and goals are neatly partitioned off, and left to the politicians, the electorate, and the civic consensus. It is equally simplification, of course, to say that planning is entirely the Civil Service's doing.

For example, the White Paper under scrutiny in this examination bears the impress of the views on priorities, for example, nursery education and basic schooling, held by the Secretary of State under whom it was written. It further bears the impress of long-accepted goals in the United Kingdom such as the raising of the school-leaving age to 16 – something the British of all political complexions have contemplated since the second world war, and which was in fact envisaged in the Education Act of 1944.

Written under a Conservative minister it received initial criticism by the Labour Party as a statement of overall educational policy; none the less this does not appear to conflict with the decisions of the Labour Government to implement the main proposals contained in it. The immediate instrument of continuity was the permanent officialdom of the Department of Education and Science.

The inertial power of historically enshrined goals and the power of bureaucracies to guide the policies of their political masters are facts of life in all democracies, and in non-democracies as well. The phenomenon of Civil Service predominance in educational planning is in fact partly attributable to the circumstance that the civil servants in the DES remain within the confines set for them by law and their professional code. Their influence, like that of respected scholars or judges, derives from their justified reputation for neutrality and professional integrity. It might be said of them that they become powers by seeking not to be powers. But this does not make the role they play in planning any the less decisive. They do not make the plan in answer to their own beliefs and desires alone. But neither do they make it simply as passive respondents to the political process or the general will of the community.

In sum, the cohesiveness of the department and its enduring presence results in a continuity which provides a solid base and a guarantee of some stability to the other interests involved in the formulation and implementation of educational policy. On the other hand, the very clarity of its defined role has certain other implications to which we return later in this report.

II Characteristics of planning

Other features of the received structures and habits of British government are also pertinent to a consideration of educational planning as it takes shape in the United Kingdom. One of these, which is bound to strike the eye of observers from the outside, is the comparatively private character of the department's deliberations regarding the plan.

The examiners have had the privilege of reviewing documents and studies (particularly the *Programme Analysis and Review on Higher Education and Schools Expenditure*) that give the evidence for the factual propositions on which the White Paper is based, that rehearse in careful detail the options considered by the department, and that suggest the grounds for its final decisions. To us – and we repeat that we are acutely aware that we speak as outsiders – it seems that these excellently reasoned analyses would, if released, demonstrate to the public that the department has gone about its planning tasks in an unusually responsible way.

The habits of British government preclude letting down the bars of confidentiality, but it cannot be doubted that groups outside the department believe that departmental decision-making is not conducted sufficiently in the open, and, moreover, that secrecy at central levels may impair the coordination between central and local administration.

The separation of the planning process from other forms of supervision and control is also worthy of note. No standing committee of Parliament exists to which the department reports. Nor are there formal institutions of consultation requiring officers of the department regularly to exchange views with the various constituencies affected by their plans or to defend their decisions against criticism. Where basic questions of the plan are concerned, the principal means of consultation are informal, and are largely determined by the department's view of its needs.

The feeling exists strongly within the department that when it comes to planning leading to policy decisions for which resources have to be secured and allocated, such informal methods, utilised by sensitive and fair-minded government servants, are superior to highly structured formal procedures which invite half-baked and politically sectarian opinions, and encourage demagogy, confrontation, and publicity battles, leading to a lot of waste of time.

Widespread consultation could be more profitably applied to a different kind of planning input, as has been the case with the major educational reports of the 1960s and 1970s – Crowther, Newsom, Robbins, Plowden, James and Russell – an unprecedented series of analyses and statements which constituted a formative influence on general attitudes on the most important issues in educational objectives and philosophy.

This feeling may be well grounded, but the fact remains that the United

Kingdom offers an example of educational planning in which the structures for ensuring public participation are limited. This has at least two consequences. One is that in certain cases policy is less likely to be understood and therefore less likely to be wholeheartedly accepted when the processes which lead up to its formulation are guarded as arcane secrets. The second is that goals and priorities, once established, may go on being taken for granted and hence escape the regular scrutiny which may be necessary for an appropriate realignment of policy.

This latter consequence is discernible in the White Paper's posture of acquiescence towards existing goals. The method of planning it evinces, as it sets forth its programme for the allocation of resources, directed towards effecting incremental improvements within existing structures, derives from the assumption that the basic directions of educational development are largely foreclosed; determined, one infers, by historical circumstances, demographic trends, and changes in public attitudes.

Demographic trends and changes in educational preference are projected five or ten years ahead. General guidance is taken from the educational community's 'consensus' on good educational practice. A judgment about the overall movement of opinion in the country at large — for example, that policy should be skewed in favour of the disadvantaged — is made, and the result of that judgment introduced as a premise for the plan.

Finally, the probable availability of resources and funds is canvassed.

It lies beyond the province of the authors of the paper to query basic goals or new directions in education, except, perhaps, insofar as they create competing claims on resources or lead to financially unreasonable expectations. The question of the role of policy planning in appraising the controlling structures and purposes of an educational system and in initiating structural change rather than merely following or extrapolating existing trends thus presents itself as a major issue in this examination.

This method of planning has persisted even though in the 1960s, as Britain reached many of its post-war educational goals and began to taste greater material prosperity, educational discussion came to be significantly influenced by competing educational philosophies and ideologies and by political divisions in society at large. It persists, undoubtedly, not only by force of habit but because it reflects the professional belief that the appraisal of basic ends and goals is not a proper business for a non-political planning group. Underlying this belief there may also be the classic notion that if intermediate goals are sensibly sorted out, ultimate goals will take care of themselves.

It is redundant to say that these ideas contain much wisdom. Nevertheless, a great variety of planning strategies exist that lie between the passive absorption of the *Zeitgeist* and the laying down of a master plan for the rebuilding of society. Planners may, for example, take note of incongruencies between emerging problems and the received educational assumptions and structures employed to deal with them. They may set forth, from their professional point of view, alternative hypotheses for dealing with such problems, even while leaving the ultimate choice, needless to say, to political leaders and the electorate.

In the United Kingdom, for example, the social costs of deciding to expand nursery education as against attempting to create new facilities to provide for the 16–19 age group are relevant matters for analysis and weighing. A fundamental question for the present examination is whether this kind of analysis and weighing should have a place in the planning process, and we proceed in this light to a consideration of the White Paper as an example of the department's planning procedure, concentrating on the weaknesses which have struck us while attempting to formulate our criticisms in a constructive way.

The White Paper: a critique

It will be clear from what we have said above that, as a governmental planning operation, we consider the White Paper and the planning effort that went into its preparation undoubtedly to represent a most interesting and ambitious example of its kind, both in time scale and in scope. This is the more remarkable as it is not only concerned with a highly complex system of societal structure in which development largely depends on individual decisions and choices, but is also the product of a national political executive in a system in which policy and decision-making are shared to a singularly large extent by the various layers of public administration right down to the individual community, university, and – indeed – school.

It is obvious that *A Framework for Expansion* of the 'British educational service' which is drafted by the Government must take account not only of the uncertainties inherent in long-range forecasting political priorities, but also of certain responsibilities and weights that an independent body might have disregarded – though even in that case the price would be a loss in realism and validity, however 'neater' the outcome might be from the point of view of methodological coherence and comprehensiveness.

The aim of the remarks which follow is not, then, to evaluate the White Paper systematically, and completely by the rod of planning theory, nor to question its status as a ground-creating innovation in improving the tool of governmental policy. Our remarks will rather concentrate on certain critical issues with regard to scope and coverage, approach and technique, on the omissions rather than the merits. We shall relate this to the special conditions created by the existing political and administrative structure and the planner's place in it, as these have been explained above — in fact, one or two of the critical questions arise from just that consideration.

Scope, purpose and coverage

The White Paper is concerned with the 'British educational service'. It is designed to provide a 'framework for expansion', though it seems to be rather more a 'framework of expansion' for certain pre-selected areas. The problems of the areas chosen are treated with admirable clarity, technical expertise, and straight-forwardness. There seem, on the other hand, to be certain other areas — such as provision for the age group of 16–19 and for adult education — which have been wholly or partly omitted, without adequate explanation of the selection criteria and procedure.

At no point does the White Paper bring the structure of the educational function into perspective, either for the individual, over the whole of his life-span, or for innovation to meet economic, technical and social change. We miss a balanced analysis of persisting and new trends in society, in technological development and the role in the state and of the place of education and science in the process of evolution. Consequently, the perception which comes through is that of a static framework for what appear to be arbitrarily selected priority areas, without presentation of the analysis or open admission of the indeed problematic nature of such short-cuts.

The White Paper is, in its own words, concerned with 'matters of scale, organization and cost rather than educational content'. Consequently, it appears to adopt the principle 'more not different' without due consideration of the fact that long-term planning exercises, such as this, as well as having repercussions in other sectors, are bound to produce changes in quality, in content and in standards.

Thus, some of the main issues of educational goals and social purpose — individual promotion versus selection as functions of the age of pupils, the organization of schools and of educational content — have been deliberately left out of consideration. There seems to be a defensive strategy behind this, exemplified by the absence of any comment whatsoever on the issue of the comprehensive schools for the 12–16–18 year old: it is, after all, surprising that a large-scale planning exercise of this nature should omit any reference to what was perhaps the dominant educational issue of the last decade and one which is by no means extinct. Similarly missing is any discussion of general education versus vocational training, of recurrent education or life-long learning and of participation.

There is, in sum, no attempt at a new identification and formulation of educational goals in a world where the traditional canons of knowledge, values, attitudes and skills are continually questioned. There are hints to the effect that this might not be within the proper realm of government activity. On the other hand, there is no doubt that the department has to be and in fact is concerned with questions of content and goals (*vide* the power of the DES in deciding the scale and kind of educational operations) and with optimising resource utilization.

Insofar as the White Paper concentrates on the 'educational service' as provided for or controlled by the DES, it inevitably gives the impression of putting forth a defensive strategy of departmental interests in this field. In fact, the PAR document on which the White Paper is based disavows any claim to be 'a synoptic review of the whole field of education'. Though this document explicitly admits the interrelationship between educational and other social and economic objectives, these are nowhere instrumentalised and made operational for the active shaping of the educational service and system, or for the diversification of the character and quality of the provision.

Moreover, the role of the educational system is not reviewed or related to the functions of different departments concerned with educational matters, such as the Secretary of State for Scotland, the Department of Employment, the Civil Service Department, the Home Office, the Ministry of Defence, or the Department of Health and Social Security. Instead, the 'educational service' is identified institutionally and equated with the services provided by the DES, in spite of the fact that the branches of this service cannot be taken as static and stable phenomena.

For instance, the rapid expansion of nursery education may well create conflicts *vis-à-vis* other departments and interests outside the educational field. In contrast, the approach to the problems of young people beyond compulsory fulltime schooling is strictly passive: this may even be a case of conflict of negative interests since none of the relevant departments appears to be concerned with the educational problems of the 16–19 year old.

The White Paper is a document addressed to local authorities and to the educational service. Furthermore, it is a document backed in terms of resources by the Prime Minister and the Treasury. But it does not address itself to the function of education in its relation to tasks such as vocational or industrial training. It seems surprising that neither the rapid expansion of resource needs for education in the 1960s nor the specific problems of economic growth and social progress in the United Kingdom impelled the Government or the other departments to develop an integrated, or at least coordinated, approach to this vital challenge to industrial society.

III Lack of provision for the 16–19 age group and the academic/vocational dichotomy

It is stated in the PAR documents that the aim of the selection of priority areas has been 'to include those [options] that represent choices of major importance which are, on a realistic assessment, open to ministers and which would produce significant results from the point of view of resource allocation within the review period'.

One would have thought that provision for the 16–19 age group, in view of its increasing tendency to stay on into some form of further education, would have merited serious attention. Section 12 of the White Paper, *After School and Beyond*, contains no discussion of relevant plans, although it does express, in a footnote, the expectation that the educational service will play a major part in the new Training Opportunities Scheme (which is being shifted from the levy-grant system of some 30-odd industrial training boards, by sectors of the economy rather than by vocational functions, to a less influential levy-grant-exemption system).

Figures provided to us by the DES show that in 1972/3 the proportion of the age groups receiving full-time or part-time education ranged from about 60 per cent of the sixteen-year-olds to about 30 per cent of the nineteen-year-olds. Of those who entered employment in 1973 about half the sixteen-year-olds and a third of the seventeen-year-olds were receiving formal training of one sort or another.

It is estimated that of all the sixteen-year-olds in 1973 half were receiving full-time education and about a quarter some kind of further education and/or training. These participation figures would decrease considerably for the age group 17–19.

These figures are quoted here to show how significant the distance still is from the objective envisaged in the 1944 Education Act which provided for some kind of compulsory education and/or training for every young man and woman up to eighteen.

The rise in the number of births up to 1964 will, in any case, mean a high proportion of sixteen-year-olds in the 1980 school population, even if staying-on rates do not go up. One cannot calculate what percentage of this age group will be encouraged to go into non-school education. The sheer size of this group, assuming proportionately increasing importance and peaking in 1980, would lead one to support that its needs should be considered in detail.

In addition, the policies adopted, or assumed as continuing, for this group will in any case have a considerable impact on both the sectors bracketing it – that is, secondary school and higher education, and the plans for these sectors are correspondingly contingent.

The end of the compulsory stage puts a full stop to the education of most disadvantaged children. Therefore, a whole-hearted attempt to contribute to the improvement of this situation by educational services requires considerable attention and resources to be devoted to the educational prospects of those who leave full-time school at this age and enter the industrial sector where some vocational training is provided, but no compulsory further education as is the case in continental systems up to the age of eighteen or nineteen.

The department, and following its deliberations the Cabinet, did apparently consider the interrelationship between education and other social and economic objectives, as outlined in the PAR document, as not of over-riding importance. The exclusion of non-advanced further education from extensive consideration within the planning process contributes to the impression of the departmental and general education perspective which the White Paper planning conveys.

We understand from our discussions in the United Kingdom that the relative disregard for the issue of the 16–19 age group seems to have been a more or less unconscious decision resulting from the concentration on apparent policy priorities at that time. We venture to suggest that this might be taken as an indication of the risks or limitations of a 'closed' planning procedure.

During our discussions we were also given to understand that a reappraisal of objectives and structures for this age group has recently been initiated within the department. The question, however, remains of how any decisions which may result from this planning appraisal, and which will probably involve additional expenditures, can be implemented over the next ten years or so, considering that there is already a policy commitment to devote the considerable additional resources which have been made available to the specific areas charted out in the White Paper.

In fact, it is one of the strongest features of the White Paper planning that decisions, once various options within the selected areas have been carefully analysed and weighed, are backed up by a commitment to meeting their cost implications.

The omission of this area from the White Paper is the more significant since the choice of some sectors and the exclusion of others can hardly have been directly deduced from a very clear statement of objectives which is contained in the PAR document.

A policy designed to achieve two of these objectives, 'to develop powers of reasoning and the capacity for adapting to changing circumstances', and 'to provide systematic guidance and help so as to develop the power of making informed choices', must specify the content of the 'initial' and 'universal' education of children, as well as the age up to which it shall be provided. How can such objectives be achieved without reference to or outside the context of, industrial and vocational training?

It would also be essential to suggest structural plans which will facilitate the prescribed adaptability, thus trespassing on the self-imposed restraint on curricula and breaching the constraint of present departmental borderlines. In other words, there would need to be recognition of the problems of the actual or possible polyvalence of education and training in terms of the skills and knowledge, as well as the attitudes which both should be able to transmit in organised pedagogical processes.

'Educational service' as well as 'general education' – in their purpose, method and criteria – should be understood not institutionally but functionally. Otherwise, one would be blocked from seeing both of them as component parts of one system to 'develop the capacity for adapting to changing circumstances'.

One must, of course, be aware of the factual situation in which this omission occurred: general education was to be raised to sixteen, and there was a long and proven system of ladder rungs through vocational professional diplomas and degrees from local, area or regional colleges right up to the university – a system so 'typically British' in its flexibility and empiricism which makes it hard to describe as a 'system'.

Traditional English trust in the integrative powers of community and society as a whole, beside and beyond organized education, may also come into consideration. Still the question remains whether in our days society and, indeed, the economy can afford to stop educational concern for a large part of its youth at the age of sixteen.

Adult education

The stated objectives of the educational process clearly include 'to develop the attitude that education is a lifelong process'. It is equally clearly stated that the planning behind the White Paper 'refers only incidentally to further education below the higher educational level and not at all to adult education'. This exclusion seems to carry the risk of relegating adult education to a very minor position in the overall educational structure.

The educational service seems to be perceived as consisting of certain institutions offering full-time or part-time educational provision; consequently, the issues of paid educational leave and of the selection of target groups in society as part of a strategy for the extension of educational supply to minority groups, and such like, are not dealt with.

One answer to this multiple question refers to the unfortunately delayed Russell Report, another to the lack of funds. But the question appears not to have been thought of as being of particular relevance to the 'constituency' of the DES or as being sufficiently urgently pressed by groups in society.

One may in this context also refer to the Open University. Its original aim was to provide an answer to the demands for adult education. As has been the experience with institutions aimed at similar purposes in other countries, the ones that were most eager to grasp this chance were not the most strikingly underprivileged, but the ones with relatively high educational achievement already, such as late dropouts, or, indeed, former graduates of higher education.

We understand that in its second phase the Open University is putting the emphasis on programmes designed for adults without prior experience which will increase even more the importance of this unique and admirable venture also for the other countries facing similar questions. In view of these considerations it is surprising to find no mention of the Open University in the White Paper.

Binary higher education

While in the case of comprehensive schools the White Paper abstains from comment altogether it states that the Government have 'a contribution to make to the current debate about the objectives of higher education' (p 30). It is here that the paper is also quite outspoken on the system of units and credits as well as on the construction of university courses.

The absence of any statement on plans for the 16–19 age group makes estimates of demand for higher education more unreliable than they would be anyway. Admitting the need that in any long-term planning exercise some provisional figures are needed to be set as targets if buildings and staff are to be provided in time, it is none the less certain that such exercises should refrain, as far as possible, from plumping for exact figures and should instead concentrate on delineating the structure of future developments.

The proposed cutback from 835,000 higher education students by 1981 in Planning Paper No 2 to 750,000 in the White Paper (1) will take place entirely within the university sector which may create problems of selection and of binary balance.

This reduction, and the further reduction to 640,000 announced in November 1974, was based on evidence of a less buoyant demand for education than in the 1960s. But even the lower figure comfortably exceeds the Robbins Report's projection (in 1963) of 596,000 places in 1981.

There appears in this even split in higher education between the university and the polytechnic sectors more of elegance and formal parity than of rational estimation of social demand or of long-term projections for highly qualified personnel in the state, the economy and society. The reasons given to us include the apparent coincidence of organic expansion estimates and wishes on the side of existing universities.

The White Paper is silent on the long-term perspective for the higher education institutions under the control of local authorities both in terms of status and competition with other further education or compulsory school provisions, as well as on the issue of the viability of the existing rate support grant system to local authorities.

The DES, however, seems to have become aware that political pressures will ultimately push the present higher education system towards a unitary structure, but feels that only a continued period of long-term preservation of the present structure will eventually produce full 'parity', including greater similarities in status, which is a prerequisite to such a consummation.

The university sector appears to be excluded from active consideration for various reasons, among them its sacred autonomy and 'distance' from practical problems, while the polytechnics are considered as instruments for conscious shaping of future higher education.

This trend is backed by the handling in the White Paper of the future of colleges of education. There is here in fact a paradox in the general long-term planning perspective of the White Paper and the urgency with which the transformation of the colleges of education, and their effective affiliation into the binary system, is pressed.

Local authorities were given an effective maximum of nine months to submit their plans, which may appear to be an unrealistically short space of time for such an important structural mutation; especially in the absence of an explicit background of the new institutional structure against which to work.

Innovation and research
As the White Paper approach is largely restricted to quantitative projections and proposals for resource allocation, and is based on the existing institutional framework, it leaves little room for questions of educational purpose, content or method. Departmental perspectives, the self-interpretation of the role of civil servants as apolitical, or in any case neutral, servants of the state, and the views of the content of education as a matter for local self-government, that is for teachers or local authorities, seem to preclude the possibility of interpreting the role of education as an agent for innovation and social progress.

These factors also seem to inhibit any widespread interest in DES to foster research and experimentation for educational innovation beyond its indirect interest in these matters through the mechanism of the Schools Council.

Only in the cases of preprimary education and higher education is there recognized a (limited) necessity for research in educational matters. It appears thus to be left entirely to the educational community and to the initiative of the local authorities whether or not they engage in these vital questions.

The record of the system so far and its capacity to innovate have been good, as is universally attested; but the question arises whether the forces now at play are not such that in the not too distant future the need may not be felt for stronger involvement from the centre in the more esoteric matters of the educational process (including a more pronounced view on the promotion versus the selection role of education) similar to the one which exists in resource planning and allocation.

Improving the quality of basic education

If there is one explicit overall priority which comes out in the policy enunciated in the White Paper it is that which relates to improving the quality of basic education. This is to be achieved by action in two main areas — improved staffing standards and teacher training and an expanded provision of facilities for early/childhood education.

On both these areas, the plans and the resources to be committed for their implementation are admirably elaborated in the planning documents we have seen. Accepting the essentially political nature of the decision to focus priority on these two areas, we wish to limit our comments to a few points relating to nursery education.

Though the educational justification for the expansion of the nursery sector is considered paramount, the measures proposed in this area are not seen as serving narrowly defined educational ends. The White Paper, however, contains no initiative for involving the whole range of agencies and services which deal with this age group – even though the need for such involvement is highlighted in Circular No 2/73 which gives guidance to local education authorities on the implementation of the policy measures.

There is the same constraint, in other words, imposed by departmental barriers which, if it had been possible to break, might have led to inter-departmental sharing of the financial burden, which in itself might have given more impetus to genuine coordination of a practical nature which this field, more than any other perhaps, calls for.

We would also have liked to have seen more explicit references in the White Paper as to positive plans of how effective links with the primary school are to be established without which the monitoring of the 'effectiveness of nursery education in reaching its several goals', on which research studies are proposed, cannot be meaningfully undertaken.

There are other aspects of the problem – such as the relations between part-time provision and the consequent need for the promotion of part-time jobs for mothers; how demand will be stimulated among certain population groups, especially the disadvantaged around which a discussion of the implications of the White Paper provisions for the under fives could be illuminating to an international audience.

IV Concluding summary

The White Paper, as critically reviewed in this section, reflects an active bureaucracy, largely in the position to determine itself the framework and the nature of its activity. Within this definition of its role, the organization and articulation of this bureaucracy are particularly effective, especially in diffusing the location of planning work within the sectors which carry substantive responsibility for the implementation of decisions.

An effective network of communication has also been established within these various sectors, though we were not in a position to assess whether this network adequately covers the needs of the sectors concerned with the content and methods of education, except insofar as the interests of these sectors are represented by Her Majesty's inspectors located within the DES.

The chief features of the bases for its policy formation seem to be characterized by attempts to: minimize the degree of controversiality in the planning process and its results; reduce possible alternatives to matters of choice of resource allocation; limit the planning process to those parts of the educational services and functions strictly controlled by the DES; exploit as fully as possible the powers, prerogatives and responsibilities given to the DES under the 1944 Education Act; understate as much as possible the full role of the government in the determination of the future course of educational policy and even minimize it in the eyes of the general public.

The preservation of this powerful position, by combining the task of coherent planning with defensive tactics, excluding an open planning process, public hearings or, even, participation, seems to an outside observer as a mixture of strength and weakness.

The stress laid on the 'input' function of governmental policies, with matters of educational 'output' left to others, and the emphasis on control rather than on identifying problems severely constricts the role which planning for education could play in the general social development of the country.

Within this limitation, it should be recognized that one of the great merits of the White Paper lies in its bold attempt to tackle the problem of the overall balance of resource allocation as between the claims of preprimary, primary, secondary and tertiary education.

One of the crucial issues here is the rate at which staffing standards in schools should be improved, since teachers' salaries represent about half of all, and 70 per cent of recurrent, expenditure in education. In this, we believe there are important general lessons to be learnt by close study of the analysis of needs – based on the triple objective of improved in-service training, extending teacher training to three years, and reducing the pupil/ teacher ratio to 18.5/1 by 1981 – which led to the precise targets laid down in the White Paper.

Final observations and list of questions

In the previous two sections we have endeavoured, albeit at a level of generality which we felt inevitable in an exercise of this kind, to portray the planning process operating within the DES, both against the general background of national tradition and institutions and in the specific context of one concrete and major example of its policy output, the 1972 White Paper.

The effectiveness of the planning method is in fact to be measured not by some abstract *a priori* standard, but in relation to the concrete problems and pressures the planners face and, increasingly, the capacity of planners to anticipate and adjust to new problems in a rapidly changing society.

From this point of view, this examination comes at an apt moment. British educational planning, like educational planning in most other OECD countries, is at a watershed. However considerable its demonstrated virtues, its capacity to cope with gathering new pressures and problems is still to be seen.

The British economy has lagged in its development. To the extent that this is due to educational inadequacies, for example in the recruiting and training of workers and managers at the higher levels of skill, large changes of a fundamental structural kind will be needed. The question they raise is whether planning that is essentially acquiescent in relation to dominant opinion is sufficient.

Ethnic and racial problems, and what in the United Kingdom goes by the name of 'community relations', are increasing in severity in the United Kingdom as elsewhere. They pose particularly acute difficulties for education. Will planning methods based on informal consultative procedures and confidential determination of fact and attitude render these difficulties more or less severe?

This is only one side of the broader social strain which is becoming evident in England, as in other countries, resulting from egalitarian pressures within static or near static economies. The trend towards regionalization is one aspect of this strain, a trend which if it continues might lead to new configurations in the political map of the British Isles to which the organization of education will have to respond.

Yet a further sign of the strain is to be seen in the current difficulties with the rates system which threatens to undermine the capacity of local authorities to finance the educational services under their control. If this situation were to become aggravated, the implementation of social objectives including education is likely to require stronger intervention and support from central authority.

The DES might thus find it increasingly difficult to preserve its present position of total detachment with regard to purely professional education matters, even within the context of its current responsibility for the oversight of standards and for value for money. It will be a challenge to planning how to reconcile the problems arising from the need for such strengthening of central authority with traditional local autonomy seen as essential to the British way of life and politics.

The role of teachers' unions in the evolution of educational practices at the primary and secondary levels is already considerable. It appears probable that unions will become more and more involved in further and higher education as well.

The White Paper recognizes that professional opinion must be considered in the development of an educational policy, and also says – correctly in the opinion of the examiners – that it cannot be the sole determinant of the final result.

Are the methods now employed for canvassing professional opinion adequate to the task of striking the proper balance? Do they permit the unions, educational officials at local levels and the planners in the central government to reach understandings not based on economic and political power plans? Can methods better designed to achieve understandings based on acceptance of common goals and constraints be envisaged?

At the very least, the nature of the problem of 'alienated youth' needs analysis from the point of view of its susceptibility or otherwise to governmental remedy. Even with respect to existing planning methods, better understanding is needed.

Educational projections are currently being made in Britain based in part on recent shifts in the attitudes of the young towards remaining in the educational system. But without better knowledge of the causes of these attitudinal shifts it is not easy to know whether they presage a new trend or are mere 'hiccups' in existing ones.

Another long-term problem whose existence casts doubt on the viability of certain inherited educational structures is that created by the emergent 'world of work'. The need, for example, for the recurrent retraining of people is being met to some extent by industry and by the institutions for further education provided by public authority.

But the recognition that recurrent retraining has become a structural requirement of an advanced technological society raises questions as to the content and orientation of primary and secondary education, whose function is different if a large proportion of those who receive such education will spend their lives unlearning old skills and learning new ones.

Moreover, the relation of the school to other institutions, and activities in society needs also to be reviewed in a time when attitudes towards both work and leisure appear to be undergoing substantial modification.

What we said above, and in the earliest sections of this report, leads us to one final summative observation of the planning in the White Paper: given the vagaries of quantitative projections (exemplified yet once more by the recent school population forecasts, revised sharply downwards), we consider that an exercise of this nature, while inevitably built around figures – and we do not underestimate the need for quantitative assessment if only as a basis for altering priorities in the course of the implementation of the plan – should lay greater emphasis on the structural future of education; that is, in kinds of development which will be responsive to changes in the population, in staying-on rates, and so on, but which will be essentially viable even in the face of such changes.

What we miss in this respect is the use of greater daring in the delineation of new paths of learning and of new institutional and administrative developments which would allow education to respond and at the same time contribute to changes in society.

2.2 Policy making in the Department of Education and Science. Extracts from the tenth report of the Expenditure Committee

The system and process of formulating educational priorities and of decision-taking

Memorandum by the Department of Education and Science

1   The responsibilities of the Secretary of State for Education and Science stem in large part from the Education Acts, notably the Education Act of 1944. This Act made it his duty 'to promote the education of the people in England and Wales and the progressive development of institutions devoted to that purpose, and to secure the effective execution by local authorities, under his control and direction, of the national policy for providing a varied and comprehensive educational service in every area'. Some responsibilities, such as the provision of an adequate supply of teachers, are precisely defined; many others require foresight backed up by statistical projections. Thus the Department has always been involved in planning in the sense of resource allocation, although until about the mid-1960s this tended to be done in self-contained areas of policy.

2   The Labour Government returned in 1964 was concerned to plan national resources and to attempt to relate its own policies, particularly in the social services, to the likely growth in the economy. Although many of the hopes of the National Plan of 1965 were dashed by subsequent events, those which were incorporated in the education chapter of the Plan do not look unreasonable in retrospect; despite the succession of economic crises

Source: *Tenth Report of the Expenditure Committee* (1976). (Education Arts and Home Home Office Sub-Committee). Paragraphs 1–8 and 11–16 are included here.

since 1965, most of the major objectives set for education were achieved, only the raising of the school leaving age having to be significantly delayed – by two years. Among these objectives were a planned increase in the number of teachers in primary and secondary schools, in the number of students receiving university education, and in the number of students in colleges of education. All were achieved in line with the Plan.

3 A further important development was the acceptance by the Government in 1961 of the Plowden Report on the management and control of public expenditure which has led since the early 1960's to the annual preparation of five-year forecasts of expenditure. This in turn has highlighted the need for a more systematic and resource-oriented approach to decision-taking and educational planning.

4 The Public Expenditure Survey Committee (PESC) forecasts are prepared for each year of the five-year period beginning with the current year. These forecasts are made by all Departments, aggregated centrally, and presented in a report to Ministers in the summer. This report serves as a starting point for collective consideration by Ministers of the level of public expenditure that can be sustained, and of how the available resources are to be distributed. The decisions taken in the course of the examination form the basis of the annual White Paper on public expenditure, usually published in December.

5 These Ministerial decisions on the PESC forecasts provide the framework for the preparation of the detailed expenditure estimates for the following year, and second year of the review period. They also settle expenditure plans for the following years, subject of course to review in succeeding years.

6 Responsibility for the educational element in the public expenditure survey rests ultimately with DES and the other education departments, but the Rates Support Grant (RSG) system provides an opportunity to examine jointly with representatives of local authorities the data on which forecasts of local education authority current expenditure can be based. DES makes no grants to local education authorities in respect of their current expenditure and exercises no direct control over its level, though the RSG settlement exerts a strong influence on the totality of local authority expenditure, of which expenditure on education is the largest component.

Decision taking, implementation and planning
8 Decisions that have to be taken by Education Ministers can be divided into three main groups, categorized by the time-scale of their implementation:

(*a*)   those relating to the longer term, up to 10 years ahead, needed in order to plan the resources required over the PESC period – these decision are often registered in the annual public expenditure White Paper, or are the subject of separate announcement (e.g. the 10 year planning figures for the size of the teaching force and of the higher education student population);

(*b*)   those which fall within the five year span of the Survey and are shown in the White Paper as planning figures, consistent with the longer term projections, and converted into resource requirements – included in this group are decisions on whether the policies and priorities agreed the previous year should still stand, or should be modified in the light of subsequent developments;

(*c*)   operational decisions, relating usually to the forthcoming financial or academic year within the agreed PESC framework – for example the allocation of building programmes for schools, further education and universities; and the size of the entries to teacher training – these being decisions that have to be taken and announced every year in order that the educational institutions concerned can get ahead with their own planning.

9   All of these decisions must be negotiated through the public expenditure machinery and the Treasury has to be associated with the planning process of the Department before the product of that process can be finalised and announced. These negotiations involve officials and Ministers at various stages before final decisions are taken by the Cabinet. It must be pointed out however that in the present economic climate, the emphasis is very much on the short-term decisions and their consequences.

10   Two major considerations apply to the decision-making of Education Ministers. The first is that their plans must be compatible with general government plans, as set out in the annual expenditure White Paper; the second is that responsibility for detailed execution of educational plans and policies is devolved from central government, the principal groups in the institutional network through which the education service operates being governmental (the local authorities) and academic (the schools, colleges, polytechnics and universities).

11   Local authorities have their own resources (the rates), responsibilities, powers and discretions; and the universities have a great deal of influence and freedom. This is not to say that these powers and freedom are used to cause the education system to develop in directions contrary to those intended by central government. But they do mean that DES cannot control

the detailed execution of decisions taken centrally. For example, although there has been wide agreement on the priority to be given to pre-school education, the way in which it should be provided – whether in nursery classes in primary schools or in separate nursery schools – is largely a matter for local decisions. Thus local authority willingness to accept central government guidance on priorities has to be borne in mind in Departmental planning and represents a significant consideration in the decision-taking process.

12   For this reason, contacts with local education authorities collectively and individually are important to the Department in order to keep in touch with local authority thinking. DES is also well aware from experience that it is a mistake to confine narrowly within the Department the thinking that underlies the plans before they are published. This is a particular problem of planning in the education service, where the balance of power and influence between central government, local government and the academic and professional world has been carefully drawn. The Department therefore recognises the importance of associating these other parties and the local authority associations closely with the planning process, the results of which are often vital to their interests. There are difficulties about this – not least the fact that decisions arising from the need to reduce the rate of growth of public expenditure often have to be taken on a short-time scale. This points to the importance of developing further the process of consultation whether formal (e.g. through the Consultative Council on Local Government Finance, and the Council of Local Education Authorities) or informal (e.g. through involvement in the Rate Support Grant negotiations).

13   Three things follow from the distribution of power already referred to. First, the pace of development at the 'points of consumption', e.g. the more than 30,000 schools, colleges etc. in England and Wales, inevitably varies from place to place. Second, at these points, the consequences of decisions already taken are often still being worked through, e.g. raising of the school leaving age whereas the planners and central government are concerned with the next round of decisions. Third, developments on the ground have their own 'fly-wheel' effect, so that they can be changed in direction, pace or scale only slowly e.g. local planning may still be concerned with teacher shortages even at a time when it is becoming clear that the planned growth of the teacher force several years ahead may have to be slowed down to match the lower-than projected school population resulting from a continuing decline in the birth rate.

14   The Department does not plan education itself; curricula, pedagogical and professional matters are, by a long tradition in this

country, matters which the central Government does not control. Essentially DES planning for education covers in scope, public sector education programmes and policies from nursery to postgraduate education financed from public funds; in geographical terms, England and Wales, except for universities (which are dealt with on a Great Britain basis) and schools in Wales (which are the responsibility of the Welsh Office); and in time, a ten-year period ahead. DES planning, as undertaken by the Departmental Planning Organisation (see paragraphs 9–16 of the second Memorandum), is thus resource-oriented, being concerned primarily with options of scale, organization and cost rather than educational content. It should however be emphasized that the Departmental Planning Organisation is not responsible for all planning within DES; comprehensive reorganization for example, being primarily the responsibility of a single policy branch and deriving from a specific political commitment, is handled by that branch without reference to the policy groups.

15   The resources whose scale and distribution DES is planning are needed for $10^{1}/_{4}$ million consumers, just over 9 million in maintained schools and nearly $1^{1}/_{4}$ million in post-school institutions. The key resources are just over 31,000 institutions and about 600,000 teachers, representing in 1974–76 a total resource expenditure of £4,890 million. This was 6.7 per cent of the gross domestic product and about 12 per cent of all public expenditure.

The education White Paper
16   With the planning machinery described in the second Memorandum, it was possible in 1971–72 to undertake a major reappraisal of educational policy, which culminated in the education White Paper 'Education: a Framework for Expansion' (Cmnd. 5174).* There was hardly a branch in the Department which was not involved in this operation to some extent, although naturally the heaviest load fell on the main policy Branches and on Finance and Statistical Branches. The starting point for the operation was the known political commitments of Ministers, but a variety of options was explored in the course of the exercise, and the package which finally made up the education White Paper took account of constraints on public expenditure generally. A reference framework against which alternative strategies could be examined was provided by the Department's 'programme budget'.

---

* A parallel operation in Scotland led to the White Paper 'Education in Scotland; a Statement of Policy' (Cmnd 5175)

17   This planning operation, which lasted for eighteen months, was new of its kind – in depth, in scope, and more especially in the way the emphasis was on reallocation of resources to match new policies, but without adding to the overall growth of total expenditure on education provided for in the expenditure White Paper. Because planning needs to issue in decisions and, as has already been mentioned, decisions must be negotiated through the public expenditure machinery, the Treasury was closely associated with the Department's planning operations. So too was the Central Policy Review Staff, among whose functions is that of challenging spending Departments to consider new approaches and alternative methods of achieving objectives which their traditions or thought and procedure might otherwise rule out.

18   The five main features of Cmnd. 5174, which looked ahead to 1981, were proposals for an expansion of nursery education broadly on the lines recommended in the Plowden Report; a systematic programme for the improvement and replacement of old schools; the development of induction and in-service training of teachers following the report of the James Committee; a continued but moderated improvement in staffing standards which, together with induction and in-service training, called for an increase to 510,000 by 1981; consequentially, the deliberate contraction of the teacher-training system, and the integration of its colleges into the higher education system; and a further expansion of higher education, particularly in the polytechnics. These proposals commanded a wide measure of support in political as well as education circles, and the changes of government in 1974 did not itself result in major departures from them; changes in the demand for education and in the economic situation were more important in this respect.

19   It will be seen from this summary that two of the five major policy initiatives taken in the White Paper had their origin in reports of outside advisory bodies. Such bodies (other examples are the Robbins Committee on higher education, and the Warnock Committee on the education of the handicapped, which has not yet reported) in effect enable the Department to consult widely on matters of major interest, and to obtain a consensus of informed opinion in the educational world.

20   The White Paper stressed that progress with the implementation of its policies would be dependent both on changes in the demand for education, and also on the resources available. It may be helpful to illustrate briefly the way in which subsequent developments have caused the quantitative objectives set out in Cmnd. 5174 to be revised since it was published.

21 As an example of quantitative planning much influenced by demography, teacher supply is the most important. For the past 30 years, educational planning has been dominated by an ever-increasing school population and an ever-growing requirement for teachers. With the prospect of a substantial decline in the school population, until the mid-1980s at least, from a peak of 9.2 million in 1977, a planning figure for the teaching force of 510,000 (full-time equivalent) qualified teachers to be employed in maintained schools by 1981 was adopted in the White Paper. Each year, this figure is reviewed in the light of updated projections of the school population. These, together with the adverse economic climate since the White Paper was published, have led to the reductions in the planning figure. The DES Report on Education No. 82 (not printed) sets out the statistical projections and calculations involved.

22 Higher education provides another example of quantitative planning, but one which is heavily influenced by changes in the demand for education. The upward trend in the number of students qualifying for and entering higher education has slowed down in the last three years. As indicated in Cmnd. 5879 (the public expenditure White Paper published in January 1975), the plans for the expansion of higher education then rested on a revised planning figure of 640,000 full-time and sandwich students in Great Britain in 1981, which replaced the planning figure of 750,000 assumed in Cmnd. 5174. This new planning figure is itself under review in the light of the latest information about the demand for higher education and the resources likely to be available. Looking beyond 1981, the fall in the birthrate since 1964 will be reflected in a steady decline in the size of the eighteen-year old age group and this may more than offset any growth in the proportion of the age group qualifying for higher education. This has to be taken into account in planning, in order to avoid wasteful over-provision.

23 As to resources, successive reductions in the planned growth of public expenditure announced in December 1973, January 1975 and April 1975 have made it necessary to reappraise all the planning figures for 1981 set out in Cmnd. 5174. The Department's planning machinery has therefore had to devise less expensive programmes – a task made much easier by the reduced birthrate and the decline in the demand for higher education – while still preserving as far as possible the main features of the White Paper. This process is still continuing, and the next Public Expenditure White Paper, to be published at about the end of 1975, will record the decisions reached. Meanwhile, guidance on where economies might be made has been given, in response to local authority requests, in a

joint DOE/Home Office/DHSS/DES Circular 'Local Authority Expenditure in 1976–77 – forward planning'.

Conclusion

24 As this paper shows, education is a service in which – perhaps more than in any other – many policies can be expressed in terms of numbers because of the strong dependence on the size of the age groups being catered for. But educational planning is concerned with more than logistics; equally important is the need to secure organizational structures that will make for efficiency and value for money. Furthermore, although heavily dependent on numbers – and the collection of reliable and useful data has been highly developed – the degree of uncertainty and therefore of risk-taking and the need for judgment in educational planning remains substantial and projections must be constantly revised and extended. Again, because of the time-lags, resistance and frictions in the system, major changes of direction and pace can be achieved only slowly – most of what is going to happen in the next five years is largely determined already; and in a ten-year look-ahead, the real room for change lies only in the second five years – in the next Parliament but one. In the present economic climate, however, attention has to be concentrated on the short-term problems of resource distribution.

25 The paper has also referred to the importance the Department attaches to maintaining close contacts with the other elements of the education service, both to keep itself informed about developments in their thinking, and to involve them more closely in the planning process.

26 Finally, not all areas of decision-taking are susceptible to the planning process. It has always to be recognized that educational planning by central government is necessarily concerned more with quantity of input than with quality of output – in part because educational content is the preserve of the local authority and the individual situation, and in part because there is no satisfactory way of measuring the quality of the output in its totality. Consequently the judgment regarding the effects, on quality, of decisions about quantity is a subjective matter where the experience and opinions of a wide range of people must be brought to bear. In central government, this means the officials, HM Inspectorate, and Ministers – drawing on accumulated experience and awareness of the changing trend of demand. Outside central government it means local authority officials and their advisers, elected representatives in the local authorities, teachers and their representatives, and parents, students and pupils.

Basic organization, functions and planning machinery
Second Memorandum by the Department of Education and Science

1   The Department of Education and Science was created as a single Department, responsible for education, science, and the universities, in April 1964 when the Ministry of Education and the Office of the Minister for Science were amalgamated and took in various responsibilities from other Departments; in particular responsibility for the University Grants Committee (ie to be the channel for grants and to look after its establishment) was transferred from the Treasury.

2   The Department now exercises functions in the following main areas:
- (*a*) schools, including nursery and special schools, in England and certain ancillary services eg. school transport, meals and milk
- (*b*) universities in Great Britain
- (*c*) teacher training
- (*d*) further and higher education
- (*e*) awards to students
- (*f*) teachers
- (*g*) adult education
- (*h*) arts, libraries and museums
- (*i*) science
- (*j*) international relations.

3   The Department is essentially a policy-making body, not an executive agency. It does not run any schools or colleges, or engage any teachers (except for those who teach in European schools) or prescribe any text books or curricula. Its policy-making functions extend from defining, from time to time as necessary, specific policies, some large, some small, to establishing a general framework governing the direction, pace and scale of developments in the education service as a whole. It is because of these functions of policy formation that the Department has sought to develop an effective planning organisation.

4   Although the Department has no substantial executive functions, policy formation itself involves a good deal of administration and the education statutes place other duties of a regulatory kind upon it. For example, the Department:
- (*a*) sets minimum standards of educational provision
- (*b*) controls the rate, distribution, nature and cost of educational building
- (*c*) in consultation with local authority associations, forecasts the level of local authority expenditure on education to be taken into account in determining the size of the Exchequer Grant (ie the Rate Support Grant)

(d)   supports financially, by direct grant, a limited number of institutions of a special kind

(e)   determines the numbers and balance of teachers in training, and decides the principles governing recognition of teachers as qualified

(f)   administers a superannuation scheme for teachers

(g)   supports educational research through the agency of the National Foundation for Educational Research, university departments, and other bodies

(h)   settles disputes, for example, between a parent and a local education authority, or between a local education authority and the managers of a school

5   Control under the Education Act is exercised and guidance is given by means of regulations, orders and circulars, and by pamphlets and handbooks.

Functional organization

6   The Department is now organized into seventeen Branches; ten are policy branches (eight concerned with education) and seven are service branches. Each policy branch (and most of the service branches) is headed by an Under Secretary who is responsible to one of the four Deputy Secretaries or direct to the Permanent Secretary. The total staff of the Department in April 1975 was about 2,800. The booklet 'How the DES is organised', attached not printed, summarizes the functions of the branches of the Department and indicates their relationship to each other.

7   The Department has no regional organization, although several of the policy branches are internally organized on a regional (referred to within the Department as territorial) basis where this is seen to be advantageous.

HM Inspectorate

8   HM Inspectorate in England is led by the Senior Chief Inspector supported by six Chief Inspectors, fifty-seven Staff Inspectors, eight Divisional Inspectors and about 400 HMI; three-quarters of its members deal mainly with schools, special education and teacher training and the remainder mainly with further education. Scotland and Northern Ireland each has its own inspectorial arrangements; the Welsh inspectorate of about fifty, headed by a Chief Inspector, is seconded from HM Inspectorate and answers to the Secretary of State for Wales in matters concerning schools and to the Secretary of State for Education and Science for further education and teacher training. The inspectorate organizes its work indpendently. It seeks to monitor educational developments and standards

and to advise all partners in the service. The result of its activities are available to the Department.

11   This planning machinery is concerned with two things basically. First it tries to establish what is going on; and secondly it tries to help Ministers to decide what they would like to have going on. By 'what is going on' is meant the facts of the present situation and present policies. Some of the facts are easily established; for example the number of pupils and teachers and consequential pupil/teacher ratio or the present cost per place of new school building. Some are not so easy to establish; for example, the unit costs of keeping sixteen–nineteen year olds in, respectively, schools and further education establishments. Planning is also concerned with the implications as well as the facts of the present situation and present policies. What will be the pupil/teacher ratio in, say, 1981 as the known birth rates affect the size and composition of the school population, and as wastage and teachers in the training pipe-line change the size of the teaching force? In terms of forward projections, this is a relatively easy question. A more difficult one, for example, is to estimate the recurrent unit cost per student in higher education five years ahead as new buildings in the pipe-line come into use, as old ones change their function, as the various kinds of institution admit students in proportions that DES cannot know in advance, and as attitudes of pupils to staying on in higher education change.

12   The second function, that of trying to help Ministers to decide what they would like to see going on, is the territory of 'objectives', 'options', and 'priorities'. In these matters, the political background to the planning process, for example undertakings in election manifestos (see Annex 2), is clearly important. It is also obvious that work on these matters will be largely futile unless DES knows what is going on now under present policies and trends, and where these policies and trends will take the education service if no deliberate changes are made. For this, the Department's programme budget is a useful tool. This was developed to show the determinants of educational expenditure – how much of it is needed to maintain standards in the face of population increases; how much is needed to cater for the growth in the numbers choosing to participate in education; how much is needed to accomplish planned improvements in the service, etc. Other analyses within the programme budget show the relative importance of various institutions at each level of education, and the share of expenditure attributable to various resource inputs (teachers, other staff, buildings etc). It thus serves as a useful guide to relative magnitudes in the educational expenditure field.

13 On 'objectives', the main difficulty is the general terms in which they are usually defined. For example, the education White Paper gave as an overall objective for the educational system 'to guide each generation of children into a full appreciation of our culture, to quicken their social and moral awareness, to enhance their intellectual abilities to the highest standard of which each is capable, and to develop their practical and human skills so that each may be enabled to make his or her maximum contribution to the health, wealth and harmony of a democratic society'. (Cmnd. 5174, paragraph 57). Statements of this kind are usually unexceptionable, but the experience of the Departmental Planning Organization has been that instead of trying to work from the general to the particular, it is more productive to start with particular options and to evaluate them against such strategic aims as are current at the time.

14 'Options' present altogether firmer ground and much of DES planning activity is concerned with them. There are options of scale – what are the implications of 650,000, 750,000 or 850,000 students in higher education by 1981; or should the nursery education target be 90 per cent of the four-year olds and 50 per cent of the three-year olds or on some other scale. There are options of means – should financial support for students be through grants or loans. There are options of form – should there be a binary or unitary system of higher education; or should sixteen year olds take their education in schools covering the whole secondary age range or in sixth form colleges or in further education institutions.

15 For the planner, the problem is to decide when to discard options without wasting time on them because they are unrealistic; and when not to discard options just because they are unpleasant or uncomfortable to live with – for example, should the Government have more say in curriculum? For the last four years, the DES planning organization has been engaged in examining a variety of options of scale, means and form of the kind mentioned. Consideration of these options by officials and by Ministers involves choices and priorities.

16 Priorities, certainly in the present economic climate, are more related to optimizing resource distribution within predetermined limits than with the relative importance of additional commitments. Of course, a planning organization must take account of the ideas of enthusiastic reformers and pressure groups. But planning that simply adds these ideas together is not very practical. It could perhaps be said that the most important function for a planning organization to perform is to maintain itself in a position to assess with some assurance the likely resource and educational implications of a variety of options or alternative policies. This is particularly the case at

a time of restraint in public expenditure when it is essential to be clear what the implications of making economies in different sectors of the educational system will be; and also to ensure, as far as possible, consistency in the successive decisions that are taken.

Examination of Witnesses*

Sir William Pile, KCB, MBE, Permanent Secretary, Mr J. A. Hudson, CB, Deputy Secretary, Primary and Secondary Education, Mr E. H. Simpson, Deputy Secretary, Higher and Further Education, Mr J. D. Brierley, Accountant General, Mr J. R. Jameson, Head of Programmes and Planning Branch, and Miss S. J. Browne, Senior Chief Inspector of the Department of Education and Science, called in and examined.

Chairman

1   I am certainly not minded to preside over a witch hunt. On the other hand, we do want to make it as thorough a probe as our collective intelligence and time will allow. We realise that we have chosen, perhaps, rather a difficult study on which to embark, but it is one which we think is of particular interest. I believe that you may have one or two more points that you would like to add to the two memoranda which you have already kindly sent us. I would be grateful of an opportunity to make a few points. I really only wish to make very brief reference to five points which perhaps have not been brought out sufficiently in the documents before you. The first is that objectives, priorities and decisions are settled by ministers and not by civil servants. The second is that many of these objectives and priorities are settled politically, for example, in manifestos, before an administration comes into office. The third is that it is the job of civil servants to serve the government and ministers of the day. Quite rightly, we are not free agents. Fourthly, ministers, I think, expect civil servants to concentrate on means where ends have already been determined and on options where ends remain to be determined. The last point is that the Departmental Planning Organisation has been deliberately designed not to be a back room activity of a few specialists. It is, if I can put it this way, the whole of the DES with its thinking cap on. The 1972 White Paper 'A Framework for Expansion' stated that it was focused 'on matters of scale, organization and cost rather than educational content'. It has been inferred from these words that the DPO is only concerned with matters of scale, organization and cost, and I should like, if I may say, to take this very early opportunity to say that this is not so. The DPO is something more than a calculating machine. What that something more is, or what it should be, is a matter which the Committee may well want to take up, and my

* Editors' note: only paragraphs 1–14; 29–31 and 71–77 are included here.

colleagues and I will readily try to answer your question on that subject.

2   I think that the latter points are of particular interest to us. I think that perhaps items 1 to 4, which I have listed, of what you said are what we would expect you to say? – Not in self-defence, but simply as facts.

3   Yes, indeed. If we may turn to the Memorandum which you have produced, the first part, paragraphs 1 to 7, explains how the Public Expenditure Survey Committee forecasts work. I wonder if you could tell us something more about the machinery of this Survey Committee, as I think that most of us are a little vague as to precisely how it works? – Perhaps it is wrong to start by thinking that there is a committee, as such, or that that is its most important characteristic. What we are really talking about is the public expenditure survey system. This was introduced in the early 1960s. It is an exercise carried out each year by each department, setting out its forecast of expenditure over five years to come, against any background which the Cabinet of the time might set, in the form of restraints on general expenditure or whatever else they may decide. Each department prepares its forecasts in figures and accompanies these with fairly lengthy descriptions of what the programmes are intended to cover and the results of these departmental submissions are aggregated, usually in the early summer and are presented to ministers.

4   By whom are they aggregated? – They are aggregated by the Treasury and coordinated. A fairly substantial document is put before ministers, and that is the document on which the ministers of the day conduct the public expenditure survey for that year. They take such decisions as they do take. They are inevitably rather firmer in relation to the early years of the five year period than they are with regard to the later years. It is usually the late autumn before they have finalized their consideration and taken their decisions, and the results have usually been set out in a Public Expenditure White Paper towards the very end of the year, usually in early December. I can answer any more questions in detail that you want. Perhaps the only other connecting point to make is that at some stage in the process all the various expenditures that are covered by the review that relate to local authorities, are taken together and from these ministers take a specific decision about the level of resource expenditure that they wish to see local authorities abiding by in the next, coming year. It is this decision that basically determines the level of relevant expenditure, which is a technical term used in the rate support grant negotiations which are opened with the local authorities during the late summer and autumn and which culminate in decision meetings between ministers and representatives of the local authorities towards the turn of the year. Those decisions, which, of course,

entail other decisions relating to the level of rate support grant that the Government will provide towards the total of local authority expenditure, are taken roughly parallel with general public expenditure decisions and in time allow the local authorities to make their financial arrangements, particularly their rate calls, for the financial year that starts in the following April.

5   I think that we should like to pursue the question of rate support grant negotiations a little later but, remaining still with the public expenditure survey, you mentioned at the outset that you acted within certain restraints imposed by general government policy. Are those specifically spelt out to you in the form of any memoranda or instructions, or is it simply a question of feeling the atmosphere and knowing that certain things would, or would not, be acceptable? How specific are these restraints? − The normal tradition of the public expenditure reviews has been that one costed current policies forward. More recently, and I think only more recently, the Cabinet has set conditions of various kinds upon that exercise, sometimes, for example, asking for costed options − options, that is, simply to the continuation of current policies − and at other times fixing a desirable limit to the total, or suggesting formulae of various kinds. Wherever they have taken specific decisions, those decisions are made known specifically to the departments before the exercise is started.

6   Can you give a specific example of a recent one that you have had to take into account? − Not in terms, of course, because I think that they must remain confidential, but I have given you examples of the sort of restraints or conditions that can be applied − sometimes what is required are alternatives at, say, minus 5 per cent or plus 5 per cent on what you put in last year or, as I have already said, a finite limit on the total, or perhaps a particular growth rate or a reduction in the growth rate. These are the forms, that vary from time to time, of the conditions that are placed upon the carrying out of the exercise.

7   So far as these decisions are reached within the Department, how many officials would be involved in this exercise? Does it take the form of a series of meetings? − It certainly does, amongst other things. These are very important decisions for the Department and, of course, for the Secretary of State, so that a great deal of activity goes on. The finance branch is first involved in receiving the instructions and in making sure that they are entirely understood by the Department, and they then launch the necessary studies through the branches. At the same time usually I myself take the necessary number of meetings to preside over the collection of information and the judgements that have got to be made about this. At the

same time I keep my Ministers fairly fully informed of everything that is going on. Where the exercise requires difficult choices and decisions I certainly keep Ministers informed and seek their guidance. As they give us their guidance, *ambulando*, as it were, we build this into our thinking and planning and the whole intra-departmental process culminates in a document which we certainly clear with the Secretary of State. This is, in fact, the document that is our submission to the Treasury both as regards the tabulations that are called for and the narrative explaining the policies and any other facts that need illumination. That is the document that, as I say, we submit and which – certainly the prose elements of it – are repeated verbatim in the document which the Treasury consolidates and sends to Cabinet. Some of the tabulations, of course, are further tabulated. Scotland is wound in with England and various other tabulations are provided, so that sometimes the exact figuring is changed – in presentation, not in form.

8   At that stage there is no consultation with the Treasury or with any other spending department that might have any kind of overlap? – Yes, indeed, wherever necessary.

9   Is this constant or occasional in this exercise? – It is automatic where it is necessary. It is just a way of life that we automatically follow. If we had an expenditure programme that is linked with another department, we should always be very closely in touch with them. Certainly the Treasury is always anxious to see what we are submitting. We usually clear the texts of our submissions with them to make sure that they understand them, but the proposals are the proposals as from the Department within whatever terms the exercise is limited to.

10   How long does this exercise take? How time consuming is it? – I suppose that the exercise, strictly speaking, starts some time before Easter. We are usually required, as other departments are, to put our submissions in to the Treasury not later than perhaps mid-June, I should say, and the Treasury then has the job of consolidating this and hopes to get the consolidated document before ministers certainly before mid-summer or certainly before the summer recess.

11   For the White Paper to come out at the end of the year? – It is customary I think, for ministers collectively to start looking at the documents before the summer recess, and to commission other studies as necessary during the holidays, and they come to grips with it Septemberish time. As I say, they do not usually finish their consideration of it until the late autumn and early winter. Hitherto, at all events, the results have been made public round about the first week or the second week of December.

Mr Bates

12   Before the document is submitted to the Treasury, you will have had a number of discussions with Treasury officials, will you? – Yes, I would say so. Usually they are about the terms of the exercise. The Treasury knows that the proposals that go forward are ones for the Department to make. They are not entitled to substitute their views for ours.

13   But there will have been consultation about likely submissions before the appropriate Secretary of State decides to make a submission? – I am not sure that I want to give the impression that we can only move, as it were, with the agreement of the Treasury. That would not be so, but it is the practice that we keep the Treasury informed of what we are putting into our submission.

14   You would keep other departments informed as well, would you, or would you be having consultations with them? – Only, I think, where the interests of other departments are affected by our programme.

Chairman

29   I wonder if we could turn to the rate support grant system and negotiations attaching thereto. You did remind us in your Memorandum that you had reported in 1971 to a previous manifestation of this Committee about these negotiations, but I think that it would be helpful in view of the change in membership if you would outline again for us how these negotiations work? – I will give the most up to date description of how it works because some important changes have been made only recently. The starting point currently is the Government's decision about the level of expenditure which it would like to see the local authorities observe, in all their activities in the financial year that is immediately ahead. At this point in time, for example, the negotiations are concerned with the level of local authority expenditure in the financial year 1976–77 starting next April. The composition of that expenditure is known to ministers through the public expenditure survey. At the same time the machinery which is used for the rate support grant negotiations starts off with joint committees between the departments concerned and the local authority associations for each of the main local authority services. So that for education there is such a joint committee. They work out in their own ways the estimates of expenditure under various heads and currently they are trying to bring these out at a level that is as near as possible to the education component that the Cabinet will ultimately approve. In the fullness of time these various estimates from the joint committees for each service are aggregated, and so there is built up a total of expenditure, again to be matched against the one which ministers have in mind. The expenditure when finally settled as between the Government and local

authorities, is called the total of relevant expenditure for the purposes of the grant. This is expenditure, and that total is settled by means of a series of negotiations firstly built up in the aggregate way that I have just mentioned, then discussed in some new machinery of officials – an official committee which is part of the new Consultative Council on local government finance – and finally discussed (it has not yet been discussed) with local authorities' representatives and ministers of the Government. That is the first act that has to be performed in the rate support grant negotiations – the determination of the total of relevant expenditure. There are basically two further actions which are of critical importance. The first is the percentage of that expenditure which the Government will meet through the form of rate support grant. Last year that figure was $66^{1}/_{2}$ per cent, the remainder having to be met in the main by calls upon the rates. That itself is subject both of decisions within the Government and negotiations with representatives of the local authorities. The third element, after the total relevant expenditure and the percentage of the rate support grant are settled, is the various components which affect the distribution of that grant as between the grant receiving authorities. The elements of the grant, such as the resources element, the needs element, the domestic element and other characteristics of this kind, are again the subject of negotiations between the Government and representatives of the local authorities. All that process should be completed desirably as I think I said earlier on, certainly before the end of the year preceding the April to which the expenditure relates.

Mr Hardy

30   Who makes the arrangements for interim payments? Sir William mentioned that last year the Government gave $66^{1}/_{2}$ per cent of the reckonable expenditure. There have been interim payments since, or interim payments have been negotiated since, certainly during 1974–75. Substantial payments were made during that year. What about the monitoring of educational expenditure during 1974–75? – May I make one addition to what I said before I try to answer Mr Hardy's question? So far I have spoken about the main grant settlement, but provision is made, or has been made, for increase orders – that is, increases in the amount of money, not the percentage, that may be paid out; or perhaps more accurately, the total of relevant expenditure may be increased and on that increase the original percentage rate of grant may be paid. These are approved by increase orders and hitherto have been made subsequent to a financial year, arising from later information about prices and inflation and changes in policy since the main settlement was made. It is, of course, in connection with increase orders of this kind that the Government has made information available about possible changes in future in connection with

the introduction of the system of cost limits. That, I think, is an additional statement of the way that the system works. Mr Hardy asked how education features in particular in that process. I took the story as far as saying how the education component was built up within the Government and built up within the local authorities, the joint machinery, but at the point at which educational expenditure is aggregated with social service expenditure, local environmental service expenditure and law and order expenditure to constitute the total relevant grant, education figures are no longer separate. The whole essence of the rate support is that it is a block grant on the total of relevant expenditure. The grant that is distributed is not distributed specifically in relation to education or social services or environmental services. It is a general grant, and it is for the local authorities in the light of Government policy on the one hand and their own discretion on the other, and also, of course, in the light of the amount of grant that they have received from the rate support grant and as a consequence of decisions that they have taken themselves about the level of rates that they are prepared to raise, to constitute their own programmes at the other end. So that you may say there is something of a discontinuity in this system between the intentions of the Government at the starting end of the process and the actual outcome of a series of aggregate decisions, by, in our case, I think, 101 local education authorities at the other end.

Chairman

31 I think that I would call it a contradiction, but does it in fact work, or is that a question which it is not suitable for you to answer? — It works in some ways astonishingly well, that such a discontinuity can be overcome. In general the Government finds that its policies are the ones that generally appear on the ground. The speed is broadly what the Government had in mind and on the out-turn the expenditures are within reasonable distance of the original estimates. Until recently one was talking about an out-turn that was only varying by one or two per cent. on some very substantial sums of money. Given that there is this indirect element or this discontinuity in the system, until the full blast of inflation hit the local authorities I would say it was a miracle that it worked as well as it did. Inflation, of course, has had an enormously disruptive effect upon these expenditures, as it has on expenditures everywhere.

71 May we go back a little more closely to the criteria that you would adopt within the schools building branch? You have mentioned one, which would be priority for primary schools. I take it that another criterion that you would adopt would be roofs over heads, if I may use the well worn phrase, but after that it would be a subjective judgment, very largely? It would be bound to be? — 'Subjective' is not a word that I would have

used. It reflects the educational policies of the minister responsible for the time being and of the government of which he is a part, and different governments at different times have obviously had different priorities. There was a period when, for example, a very high priority attached to getting rid of the remaining all-age schools and completing the Hadow reorganization. It was a judgment of priority reflecting partly educational opinion and partly the views of the ministers that formed that particular government. So that it is a judgment. I would not call that subjective.

72   I did not use 'subjective' in an unpleasant way. I just wondered whether there was any other way in which you could do it? – (*Sir William Pile*) There is no formula that you could sensibly apply to it. The basic need of roofs over heads is the nearest you get to a formula, in the sense that if you have additional children and you have done the arithmetic as to the spare capacity, you ought to get your share of whatever is available for basic needs on that footing.

73   If, for example, you needed a new secondary school because of basic need at a time when replacing primary schools was the other top priority, presumably the secondary school would still feature, would it? – (*Mr Hudson*) I think that Sir William's answer really brings it out. The need to provide roofs over heads is an enduring and an inescapable priority for all governments. To the extent that there are resources available to do more than that, governments have some freedom of action as to the priorities that they choose.

74   When these choices are being made, how much regard is given to what I might call geographical spread, so that one area could not claim that it had been discriminated against, and so forth? – There are two aspects of geographical distribution. There are, as it were, geographical factors in the sense that population may be shifting in a particular way. The history and economic development of different parts of the country means that they do not all start from the same position. Some may have many more new schools or many more old schools. So far as we can do so, we reflect those factors in the allocations. Over and above that, of course, there is a general feeling, that I think ministers share with other people, that there should be some equity in the distribution between different areas.
Mr Gardiner

75   You said earlier that you would like to find some better indicators of local authority need. We try to fix, for the main programme, an allocation to an authority and tell them that they may identify the projects that they want to carry out within that allocation, but we cannot do so without scrutinising the case that they make out for individual projects. One would like to be able to cut out that first stage and to find some indicators which would

enable the allocation to be fixed without scrutinising cases for individual projects, and we shall continue to try to do this.

Sir Anthony Meyer

76   Are you aware of a constant conflict between the purely educational demands for buildings, investments, and so on, and what you might call the educational–social demands? I am thinking of areas where it is Government policy to pursue a policy of positive discrimination, in particularly bad housing areas. Does this, within your Department, cause a conflict between what you regard as educational imperatives and the quasi-social imperatives which are imposed on you from outside? – I am aware of some aspects of this. I might perhaps take one example of what I think is a real and serious dilemma. It may, or may not, be a good example of the sort of thing that you have in mind. I said that the economic development of areas differs in different parts of the country and also that one has to regard the provision of roofs over heads as a first claim normally because there is a statutory obligation to have children in school. This means that if one takes one area, perhaps an old industrial area which has had a static or a declining population, it will obviously have little or no claim for the provision of schools to meet new population. If, at the opposite end of the spectrum, you take a flourishing area, a growth area, where the population is increasing and where it is shifting and where new housing estates are being built, there will be a relatively large claim for new schools to place roofs over heads. If those two areas follow the same pattern for a long time, there is a risk that in one you will have nothing but old schools while the other one has nearly all new schools. Therefore the qualitative difference between the two areas is not only great but is growing, and it is difficult to redress that imbalance unless the amount available nationally for building programmes is large enough to do appreciably more than meet the aggregate demand for roofs over heads.

77   I am trying to compress you into having to make a choice within a given sum of money available. To take the particular example that you stated, the old industrial area with the decaying schools is likely also to be an area of growing social problems. There is therefore on the grounds of general policy, a strong case for equipping that area with better schools, even though the strictly educational need may not be manifest. Is this a problem about which you feel it your responsibility within the Department to give an answer which is socially biased, or is this one of those cases where you would expect the pressure to come from outside, from some other department? – I think that the correct answer is that as a Department we would carry out whatever is the policy of the government of the day on this. The room for manoeuvre in that situation is limited.

Probably there would be a good deal of agreement amongst ministers on this, that you squeeze out all you can for the deprived area, but that given your statutory responsibilities to provide education for children of compulsory school age, you cannot slant your building programmes towards the deprived areas to an extent which makes it impossible to provide schools in the other areas. *(Sir William Pile)* The basic needs allocations, which are much the largest, go .where the arithmetic leads, where the extra children are. The money for improvement projects at the moment has been mainly concerned with old primary schools, and the allocations and distributions of whatever sums we can get for that really go with the arithmetic of where the old schools lie, but there is a political judgment that is necessary and is applied. That is that if all the basic needs are tending to go, say, to the counties, ministers are going to say 'Where there are counties and city areas with old schools, Victorian schools, let us bias the distribution of any improvement resources in favour of the urban areas'. On nursery schools, it is fair shares against a definite policy of applying such resources we have got for the nursery capital programme to areas of the greatest social need, so that you do bias out, or bias in perhaps, such areas, and then, as far as possible, a fair shares distribution of what is available goes on that footing. The remaining programmes are special schools. The programmes are smaller. It is much more possible for the Department to have an intimate knowledge of the individual special school situation in each area. To take another case, the recently introduced SPAR programme – the Special Programme for Assisting with comprehensive Reorganisation – it is by now well enough established which authorities have run into a road block. The buildings that are easily usable have been used up and they cannot get much further unless some minor improvements are possible. So that group of authorities is identifiable and the SPAR programme can then be distributed amongst them on a fair shares basis. To take the last example, education for a £4 million programme, but this was pre-empted by the terms of the exercise for areas which had high levels of unemployment, so that we identified those areas and within that, broadly speaking the criterion was fair shares, always, of course, alongside the capacity of an authority, and the willingness of authorities, to take on the additional programme. By and large, other than the basic needs programme there are various devices that we try to use to get as objective a distribution as possible, always allowing for the fact that there will be legitimate biases that ministers will bring to it. Within that it is, I think, fair shares, but this does not amount to a formula application. That we have not got, but it is not as bad as just being any Tom, Dick or Harry's decision in the Department, of 'Let us give Birmingham a lot or nothing or Kent everything or nothing'.

2.3   Forward planning – UK style

H. Glennerster

In Britain, the introduction of a government-wide system of public expenditure control has had profound consequences for the planning of individual social services. The reforms were largely prompted by a desire to constrain the growth of government. They were introduced in a gradual way, with very little publicity or political bally-hoo, and have evolved gradually and continuously ever since. Initially they laid very little emphasis on the role of analysis in determining choices or indeed on the process of choice at all. However, as the system evolved, larger claims were made for it, its inventors and practitioners as well as independent commentators have come to praise and publicize its achievements.

Containing growth
The origins of the new system of public expenditure control lie in the frustrations experienced by the Treasury and its Ministers in the late 1950s. Earlier in that decade the Conservative Government had managed to contain the growth of public expenditure. Indeed, in real terms, it had been allowed to grow at less than one half of a per cent a year between 1952 and 1958. As a proportion of the Gross National Product it had fallen steadily from 47.0 per cent in 1952 to 41.6 per cent in 1958. As a consequence the Conservatives had been able to reduce taxation steadily throughout the period. How had this been achieved? The main contribution had been the run-down in Military expenditure following the end of the Korean War, but the social services had played an important part too. From the beginning of the period the National Health Service was held sharply in check and took a declining share of the GNP until the middle of the decade, council house subsidies were substantially reduced, and local authorities were confined to the residual and, as it was thought, temporary role of slum clearance just as they had been in the 1930s. A

Source: *Social Service Budgets and Social Policy* (1975), pp. 117–149.

Table I Growth rates in public expenditure in the UK – 1952–74. Annual average rates of increase – per cent

Social Services

	1952–8	1958–60	1960–5	1965–8	1968–70	1970–74
Education	6.0	6.3	8.1	6.9	2.6	5.9
National Health Service	2.3	7.0	4.8	8.4	4.7 ⎫	
Local Welfare Services	3.5	12.1	10.0	10.4	3.4 ⎬	6.4
Child Care	2.5	0.0	7.9	10.1	2.9 ⎭	
School meals, milk and welfare foods	—3.2	2.6	5.2	2.3	—0.3	—
Social Security Benefits	5.1	3.5	6.5	7.1	1.9	4.7
Total Social Services	4.3	5.1	6.6	6.6	2.7	5.5
Housing	—6.4	7.1	10.7	2.2	—2.6	20.7
Total Housing and Environment	—3.6	6.7	9.9	4.3	0.0	15.3
Military Defence	—3.6	2.2	2.3	0.5	—5.2	1.6
Total Public Expenditure	0.4	4.6	5.2	5.2	0.1	6.5

Sources: Sir Samuel Goldman *Public Expenditure, Management and Control* Table Aii and *Public Expenditure to 1978–9* (Cmnd 5879). Constant prices with relative price effect attributed. The 1970–74 figures are for Great Britain.

series of restrictions were imposed on local authority spending and the percentage grants system for local services was replaced in 1958 by a General Grant, the purpose being to instil a more 'responsible' attitude to spending on the part of local councils and so check the rising demands on the national exchequer. Food subsidies had been abolished and family allowances were allowed to decline in purchasing power.

The 1959 Graduated Pension Scheme was essentially an attempt to gain larger graduated contributions and reduce the expected contribution from general taxation. So much of the government's social policy was designed to reduce or contain the growth of government expenditure and, at least until 1957, it had some success despite suggestions to the contrary. But after 1957 the strategy did begin to fail.

The last three years of the 1950s are an important turning point in the management of public expenditure and for social welfare too. They deserve a detailed study which we cannot give them here, but a number of factors are clear. The armed forces could not be scaled down indefinitely at least without a fundamental reappraisal of Britain's international role especially in view of the deficiencies Suez had shown up. So defence spending begins to rise again in real terms. The pressures within the social welfare sector were growing too. The Guillebaud Committee, set up to help the government economise on health expenditure, showed instead that the service was being neglected. Hospital building was running far below the levels reached in the 1930s. 'No hospital built since the War' became an election propaganda weapon. There was a limit to the extent to which economies could be demanded from a service without unacceptable political costs being incurred. The same held with council house building. Demographic trends were also against the government. The size of the pensioner population was rising. The large post war cohort of school children were passing through secondary school and steadily increasing numbers were staying on at school, the birth rate began to rise for the first time since 1948. Moreover the Labour Party was switching more of its attention to social welfare policies and away from a more traditional emphasis on industrial policy.

In 1957 and 1958 the Conservative government was highly unpopular if Gallup polls and bye-elections were any guide. It was against this background that the spending ministers began to win more battles. The strategy of the early 1950s was collapsing. At the end of 1957 the Cabinet rows and the Treasury's unease broke the political surface. The Chancellor Thorneycroft and his two junior ministers – one of whom was Enoch Powell – resigned ostensibly because the cuts they insisted on in Cabinet had not been accepted. In fact the resignations had been prompted by a series of defeats for the Treasury ministers in Cabinet and in its 'sub-committees'. The Treasury might have concluded that there were strong underlying political reasons for this state of affairs and that it should accept the new situation. It did not. It concluded that the system it was operating was at fault.

The result was not an independent committee but an internal group chaired by an outsider from industry – Lord Plowden. The group consisted of senior officials from various departments including the Treasury and a number of other 'outsiders'. It was appointed in mid-1959 shortly before the General Election.

The Plowden Committee's report, published two years later in July 1961, became a key document.[1] The contents almost entirely derived from the Treasury. It makes very clear how the Treasury saw the basic issues and it is worth quoting at some length:

The system of control of public expenditure depends upon the attitude to public spending both of Parliament and of public opinion. In former times, there were strong external pressures on the Government to reduce both expenditure and taxes, and every Minister who wanted to spend had to run the gauntlet of severe criticism from his Cabinet colleagues, from Parliament and from the public. The system was then effective at keeping expenditure down. This was the instrument, indeed, by which an austere discipline was maintained throughout the public service for generation after generation up to World War I in marked distinction to many other countries' experience. In the inter-war period, although public attitudes were changing, there was still a strong body of critical opinion which served as a check on the growth of public expenditure.

In our judgment, the social, political and economical changes of the last twenty years have created a new situation. First, the scale of public expenditure is far greater .... Second, public expenditure has become more complex including, as it does, the cost of the most advanced technological projects and of scientific research; the financing of commerical risks that the private sector cannot take; aid of many different kinds to a variety of under-developed countries; and social insurance schemes of unprecedented scope. All of these activities involve commitments, contractual or moral, extending several years ahead. Third, there has taken place a great change in economic thought; the Keynesian revolution in the role of public finance and its relationship to the national economy as a whole ....

These, and above all the fact that the main weight of Parliamentary and public pressure, central and local, is for innovation, or improvements which cannot be brought about without increases in public expenditure, have created a situation in which, in our opinion, the traditional system of decision-making can no longer be expedted to be effective in containing the growth of expenditure within whatever limit the Government have set. If, as must be expected, these changes are permanent, the system needs to be reconstructed accordingly.

The report then proceeded to outline what was called 'a reconstruction' based on four particular objectives.

The first was that regular surveys be made of public expenditure as a whole over a period of years – five were recommended. All decisions involving substantial future expenditure should be taken in the light of these surveys. Expenditure should be 'properly aligned with prospective resources'. This was in fact the crux of the whole report. It could be seen to constitute a 'counter strategy' to those employed by the spending departments. If the long-term implications of policy proposals were fully examined they would often be seen to have large consequences on the future levels of public expenditure. Sudden impulsive decisions to expand or adopt an expensive policy might then be put off, or made to wait until 'room could be found' for them. If all ministers could be persuaded to adopt and hold to a certain 'optimum' rate of overall expansion in public expenditure the strategies employed by individual ministries could merely determine their share of the cake not its absolute size. Therein lay the essence of the strategy.

The second objective outlined in the original Plowden report was to seek the greatest possible stability in public expenditure decisions – to prevent the sudden cuts in school or house-building projects that had recurred several times in the 1950s. To stop and start capital projects was a costly business, and to be avoided as far as possible. Valid as the point was it has the appearance of being something of a cover for the essential purpose of the new system. The last two objectives were to improve the statistical tools for controlling expenditure and to improve the arrangements which would enable ministers to 'discharge their collective responsibility for the oversight of public expenditure as a whole'.[2]

There is at this stage little emphasis on choice, so long as constraint is secured. Even the final reference to ministers 'discharging their collective responsibility' was a veiled way of suggesting that the spending ministers should be put in their place and that a committee of non-spending ministers be given the task of vetting departments' bids.

The apparatus was gradually assembled, growing in detail and sophistication as the years passed. It significance and impact came to be felt gradually, as did public knowledge of its operations.

The Treasury was reorganized to carry through the changes. The existing supply divisions each kept a close watch on spending departments. They were retained and renamed 'expenditure' divisions to indicate that their proper concern extended beyond a single year's 'supply cycle'. The real innovation was the creation of two new divisions, one to oversee the Nationalized Industries and the other to handle the new long-term Public Expenditure Survey. Further changes have followed but the broad organizational outlines remain.

The reorganization of the Treasury was accompanied by the creation of a new political post: the Chief Secretary. He assumed responsibility for the whole survey system. The results are reported to the Public Expenditure Survey Committee. It is popularly known by its initials – PESC – and the whole process is often referred to as the PESC system. This committee has the task of agreeing on a document that can be presented to Ministers showing how much it would cost to maintain current policies over the coming five-year period. These expenditure forecasts can then be compared with the medium term assessment of the country's economic growth potential for the same period. The Cabinet must decide on the appropriate growth rate in public expenditure for the period in the light of these two pieces of information. The process of control is not confined to this 'single cosmic operation'. From time to time economic crises require sudden reassessments and emergency cuts. Moreover, there are monthly reviews of the way the expenditure figures are developing within each department as well as day-to-day contacts between those in the Treasury and their opposite numbers in the spending departments. But the strategy is broadly decided in these summer exercises and what is more that cycle of events has broadly held ever since the Plowden changes were formalized. It is in content and sophistication that the whole process has developed to such a remarkable degree. One enormous technical task has been to produce a consistent set of statistics where so many different sources and categories are involved – local authority grant returns, the House of Commons Estimates, the National Income accounts, none of which agreed with one another at the outset. The first surveys only included the next year's expenditure and the figures for five years hence. By the end of the sixties figures for each of the five years were included. The first three are relatively firm estimates, the last two more speculative. An elaborate series of conventions has been adopted to measure the impact different programmes have on effective demand in the economy. A whole treatise could be written on the adoption of an appropriate price basis for the forecasts. The surveys began with the use of a simple constant price concept. But as real incomes rise in the rest of the economy so will public sector salaries. In labour intensive social services raising real salaries means raising costs relative to less labour intensive services or industries. To look at the same point another way, even if the amount of education or health provided increases at the same rate as the economy expands they would still end up taking a larger share of the GNP because their relative prices rose. Hence, the Treasury began to add on a 'relative price effect' first to expenditure overall, then to individual programmes and then to parts of programmes. It is a sophistication which works to the detriment of the social services in particular. It makes social service spending appear to increase at a faster rate than hitherto. One further development began at least in part response to the complications of trying to cope with the longer term consequences of building programmes and policy developments in the social policy field. It became obvious that five years was too short a period to consider the impact of many new policies especially social policies. The Hospital Plan of 1962 was, even at that stage, concerned with plans for ten years ahead. The Committee on Higher Education made recommendations for student numbers twenty years ahead, so did the advisory committee on teacher supply and the Royal Commission on Medical Education. Although none of these recommendations were accepted in detail that far ahead, once the principles on which they were based became accepted they did have very long term implications. Even more difficult was the Labour Government's National Superannuation Scheme. It would take over twenty years to come to fruition. Hence the Treasury came to see the need to forecast the impact of current policies even further ahead. Long term surveys covering the next fifteen years are now conducted from time to time.

If the process is now more complex it is also more public. How did this come about? Plowden had argued:

> It is therefore doubtful whether any government will feel able to place these surveys before Parliament and the public. To do so would involve disclosing the Government's long-term intentions for a wide range of public expenditure; and also explaining the survey's assumptions about employment, wages, prices and all the other main elements in the national economy. It would be surprising if any Government were prepared to do this.[3]

However, in 1963, in response to a pre-election challenge by the Labour Opposition, The Government published a summary of the results of the PESC survey that was mentioned earlier. In September 1965, the Labour Government published a much more detailed account as part of its *National Plan*.[4] Chapters 18 to 22 of that document were devoted to a discussion of the new Government's public spending plans up to 1969–70. In 1966 the White Paper *Public Expenditure: Planning and Control*[5] not only outlined the forecasts in more detail but also gave an account of the Survey process as it had then evolved. It was only when devaluation caused the Government to rethink their programme in January 1968 that another White Paper was produced covering the last two years of the cycle – up to 1970.[6] It was a very slim document, comprising no more than the same basic table of figures that the 1963 White Paper had contained. However, by this time the Treasury officials seem to have concluded that publication of the forward plans, and some Parliamentary scrutiny of them, might help to hold the line against the spending departments more effectively. During the session 1968–9 the House of Commons Select Committee on Procedure discussed Parliament's scrutiny of expenditure. This had become little more than a charade. The House only considered expenditure estimates for the year ahead. But it did not

Table 2 The public expenditure survey timetable

Month	Survey Procedure	Economic Assessment	Parliamentary Timetable
December	Instructions on the conduct of Survey sent out by Treasury giving guidelines for expected growth.		
End February	Departments send to Treasury estimates of the cost of existing policies for next five years and possible additional programmes.		
March/April	Discussion between Treasury and Departments to agree policy assumptions and statistics. Draft report drawn up by Treasury agreed by PESC.	Medium term assessment drawn up on prospects for the economy.	
June	Report to Ministers.	Report to Ministers.	
July–October	Decisions on total public expenditure targets over the next five years; and on functional split.		
November/December	White Paper including the basis of agreed figures published.		
February			Discussion by the House of Commons Expenditure Committee of broad principles. Debate in Parliament on White Paper.
February/March			Publication of Estimates which relate to the next year's expenditure.
April–July			Debates on Estimates by the House of Supply Days.
End July/August			Appropriation Act passed giving Crown Authorisation to spend sums requested.

Table 3   The Basic Programme Categories

As in 1972/3

		£ millions	1963 categories
Defence and external relations			
1	Defence budget	2,842	Defence
2	Other military defence	75	
3	Overseas aid	275	Aid and other overseas
4	EEC and other overseas services	_ 198	
Commerce and industry			
5	Agriculture fisheries and forestry	572	Assistance to industry
6	Research Councils etc.	137	Transport and agriculture
7	Trade, industry and employment	1,615	
Nationalized industries			
8	Nationalized industries' capital expenditure	1,741	Investment by national-ized industries
Environmental services			
9	Roads	971	Roads
10	Surface transport	283	
11	Housing	1,417	Housing and environment
12	Miscellaneous local services	1,159	
13	Law and Order	818	Police and prisons
14	Arts	41	
Social services			
15	Education and libraries	3,375	Education
16	Health and Personal Social Services	2,814	Health and welfare
17	Social Security	5,050	Benefits and assistance Children's services
Other services			
18	Financial Administration	431	Administration and
19	Common services	298	other services
20	Miscellaneous services	97	
21	Northern Ireland	694	
Total programmes		24,903	

Source: Public Expenditure Handbook (1972) and Cmnd 2235 (1963)

examine them in detail, it merely rubber stamped them. Supply days were used by all Oppositions to debate issues having nothing to do with the estimates. Even the few days of debate set aside to discuss the estimates themselves were, and still are, debates on general issues not the details of spending. The Select Committee on Estimates had concerned itself with intensive studies of very narrow topics – such as school building controls – one per year. The development of the new long term control system within Government had not been paralleled by any comparable changes in Parliamentary procedure. As a result:

The House has no machinery for scrutinising this complicated process and has had little opportunity to debate the forward projections of expenditure produced during recent years.' (Para. 9 H.C. 410 1968–9.)

In evidence to the Committee, the Government announced that it intended to publish annually a White Paper giving the results of the survey together with projections of tax revenue and an assessment of the prospects for growth in the economy, which provided the rationale for the limits imposed. Beginning in December 1969 that government and its successors met the first of these promises. A White Paper outlined spending plans. Latterly, White Papers have given some indication of growth prospects but have not yet found it possible to produce projections of tax revenue.

The Select Committee recommended that the House should debate the White Paper as a whole House and that the old Estimates Committee be abolished and a new Expenditure Committee be set up to consider the White Paper as a whole in more detail. To do this it should have sub-committees paralleling broad areas of Departmental responsibility and a General Sub-committee. This recommendation was carried through in 1970 and has been operating ever since. The General Sub-committee, at least at the beginning of its life, had gone a long way to prising out the assumptions that are made in drawing up the surveys and in illuminating the whole process. The 'functional' sub-committees have disappointingly spent most of their time on small scale issues. They have, for example, produced reports on probation and aftercare, NHS facilities for private patients, planning the scale of further and higher education, urban transport planning, and several more. They have not sought to delve deeper into the separate sections of the White Paper, perhaps because they would raise too many sensitive party political issues.

2 The system at work

The achievements

There is no doubt that those who invented the system and those who are currently operating it are very proud of their handywork. Sympathetic observers too are convinced that the British Treasury has produced perhaps the most successful expenditure management systems in the world. In purely logistical terms this is probably true for the reasons we have just elaborated. In psychological terms too, PESC has bitten deep. Not only civil servants in spending departments but ministers and ex-ministers tend to think in terms of a given allocation within which they must work. Even the Labour Opposition in 1973 conducted its own amateur PESC exercise on its election manifesto proposals. Without doubt decisions about expenditure priorities have to be taken far more explicitly than ever before. The implications of these decisions are more public and therefore more debateable than they were. So far so good. How far has it met the objectives set out originally in the Plowden Report? How appropriate were these anyway?

It will be recalled that Plowden had four aims:

1 Planning public expenditure on the basis of five-year rolling programmes so that the long-term rate of expansion was 'properly aligned with prospective resources'.
2 Achieving greater stability in public expenditure decisions.
3 Improving the tools for making choices.
4 Improving the collective responsibility of ministers.

The first was the central objective, but in assessing it a great deal turns on the interpretation of the words 'properly aligned'. It is absolutely clear from the context within which Plowden used the phrase, and from statements made to the Expenditure Committee, that 'aligned' with economic growth meant 'equated with' or 'slower than'. One test of success may therefore be total public expenditure expressed as a percentage of GNP. If this percentage rises then on its original terms the system is failing. If it is static or falling the system is succeeding.

In the light of all this the actual post 1961 record comes as something of a surprise. The rate of increase in public spending after Plowden was significantly faster than the scale of the increases which had been the very reason for its creation. Moreover, the subsequent increases were far bigger than had been permitted in the 1950s without any such sophistication. By 1968 the ratio of public expenditure to the GNP was a full 10 per cent higher than ten years earlier. However, the figures also illustrate why Treasury officials explained to Heclo and Wildavsky that the system really only began to 'work' after 1968 for it was only then that the growth was virtually halted. 'By early 1970', Goldman writes, 'the system had reached full maturity, and shown a capacity, in determined hands, to deal with widely varying situations.'[7]

What went wrong? Goldman produces two reasons: First, 'indicative planning', i.e. the attempt to set a target or a hoped for growth rate for the economy. Public expenditure was hitched to that target which in the event proved unobtainable. Second, he blames the stupidity of politicians, or as he more delicately put it 'the dominance of the political over the intellectual factor'.

The whole survey procedure had the misfortune to begin in the run up period to a general election, when the Government of the day was in real political trouble, and when the Opposition had made its main election plank the Galbraithian theme – 'public squalor amid private affluence'. It was also a period dedicated to achieving a high growth rate or bust – the 'take off' or 'Maudling' strategy. The consequence was that as the 1964 election approached more and more large scale public expenditure programmes were entered into. The December 1963 White Paper made it clear that the Conservative Government had gambled on being able to attain a 4 per cent growth rate. Total expenditure was to rise at this rate in the long term. Yet between then and the election even more commitments were entered into. The new Labour Government, whose policies entailed even higher public spending, was also faced with a large balance of payments deficit. A major review of the previous government's commitments was undertaken. As a result the Cabinet agreed that the total growth of the public sector (excluding the nationalized industries) should be limited to $4^1/_4$ per cent per annum rate of increase between 1964–5 and 1969–70. Again, like its predecessors, the new Government was pinning its hopes on achieving roughly a 4 per cent growth rate and basing its expenditure limits on that. What the Chancellor actually said was:

> Meanwhile the government have decided that the growth of public sector expenditure between 1964–5 and 1969–70 will be related to the prospective increase in national production, which in our present judgment means limiting the average increase in public sector expenditure, taking one year with another, to $4^1/_4$ per cent a year at constant prices. (Hansard 22 Feb. 1965.)

This sounded as if they hoped the growth rate in the economy would be $4^1/_4$ per cent, but it preceded the detailed work in the new Department of Economic Affairs on an appropriate growth target. When this was produced it was rather less optimistic. The National Plan aimed at an eventual 4 per cent target with an average of 3.8 per cent per annum in the whole five year period. The government did not, however, alter their public expenditure target. As a result the National Plan propounded the government's judgement that the public sector should grow slightly faster over the whole period than the whole economy − 4.25 per cent compared to 3.8 per cent per annum. The White Paper in 1966 stated that the rate of expansion in the public sector was to be even faster than $4^1/_4$ per cent in the first few years, before the proposed cuts in defence spending could take full effect.

What actually happened was very different. The balance of payments failed to go right. Emergency measures in July 1965 and especially in July 1966 finally made the attainment of even the average 3.8 per cent growth impossible. The hoped for target for output was reduced to 3 per cent per annum, and the eventual outcome for the whole period was nearer 2 per cent. Nevertheless, the Government did not, for a long time, make any drastic changes in its strategy for the public sector until forced to do so by the November 1967 devaluation. Now it is possible to argue that such stubbornness merely proves how stupid the Labour politicians were. On the other hand these decisions represent a series of deliberate political choices. They meant that the Government's social programmes were to be sustained and that the consumer would have to bear the major consequences of the failure to achieve a faster growth rate. They ensured that the share of the public sector in the economy grew faster than had been intended in 1965. These planning decisions were entirely legitimate and for many people laudable political stances.

Goldman and other Treasury critics are possibly nearer the mark when they criticise the actual trend of expenditure between 1965 and 1968. Compared to the average rate of expansion laid down in the National Plan − $4^1/_4$ per cent up to 1969−70 − the actual rates of increase were higher, double those forecast in 1967−8. Finally when public expenditure was cut back after 1968 and PESC really began to bite, it did so only because the Cabinet had been convinced by the severity of the economic crisis that resources had to be forced into exports. This, too, is an illustration of the fact that the system depends for its success not on its sophistication but upon political support. In short the Treasury only succeeded in its public sector strategy through the failure of its economic management. There must be a temptation, to put it no higher, for the Treasury to exaggerate the impact that savings in public expenditure can make to help resolve an economic crisis. Nevertheless after the 1967 crisis the Treasury finally managed to convince Labour ministers that in the long term the growth rate for public expenditure should be equal to the likely increase in national output − about 3 per cent a year. The average rate of expansion agreed for public expenditure between 1968 and 1972 was indeed 3 per cent per annum. The Conservative Government revised this target downwards in each of their expenditure reviews, first to 2.6 per cent, then 2.2 per cent, then 2 per cent. In the outcome public expenditure rose faster in the seventies than for many years (Table 4)

Table 4   The growth of public expenditure* 1952–74

	1952	1958	1960	1965	1968	1970	1974
Public expenditure as a percentage of GNP at Factor cost	47.0	41.6	42.2	45.9	51.7	49.8	50.5
	1952–8	1958–60	1960–5	1965–8	1968–70	1970–74	
Average annual growth in total public expenditure per cent	0.4	4.6	5.2	5.2	0.1	6.5	

*With relative price effect attributed

Source 1952–70: Sir Samuel Goldman, KCB, *The Developing System of Public Expenditure Management and Control* 1970–74: Cmnd 5879 (1975) *National Income and Expenditure* 1963–73.

Whether the survey system should have 'succeeded' in reducing public expenditure growth after 1968 raises what is or ought to be the major issue in British politics. The experience of the period between 1952 and 1957 suggests that services cannot be held back below the general economic growth rate for very long without serious political repercussions. International experience suggests that nations have tended to spend a higher proportion of their resources on the social services the more their incomes rise. Indeed the relative price effect alone makes this probable. To a limited extent, and for a finite period, the circle can be squared by reducing foreign and defence commitments but sooner or later the issue has to be faced. To hold down the percentage of resources devoted to the public sector either means holding back a well-established historical and international trend towards higher social service spending or it means the services must be 'reprivatised'. The justification for either course of action is contentious to say the least.

What of the second of Plowden's objectives – *stability* in expenditure decisions? The period since 1961 has not been noticeably freer of the kind of emergency economy cuts of which Plowden was so critical. The January 1968 cuts were as damaging as anything which occurred in the 1950s.

The early seventies saw an even more serious break with the Plowden tradition. The new Conservative Government in October 1970 has proposed spending £330 million less in 1971-2 and £1,500 million less in 1974-5 than the Labour Government had been proposing to do. Yet within a year, clearly frightened by the prospect of a million unemployed, the Government once again *increased* its spending plans, replacing in cash terms over a half of the cuts it had imposed so recently. A year later (December 1972) the Government's White Paper showed that it had raised its limits once again. By now the total spending in real terms was to be higher in 1974-5 than it would have been under Labour's plans. Then six months later the Chancellor announced *cuts* of over £90 million in that financial year and more the year after. The White Paper which came out in December 1973, showing moderate cuts was followed the same day by announcements of further cuts amounting to over £1,000 million in the following year. A few months later the minority Labour Government raised the targets once more. Nothing remotely like this bedwildering set of changes had occurred in the 1950s. What had happened was that the Treasury decided both to introduce some short term measures to boost employment in the form of capital expenditure for the regions and to revise its judgements about longer term programmes too.

The former were to last for only two years, the latter were more difficult to fit into that time span. It is not our purpose to discuss the appropriateness of these measures for the economy – The House of Commons Expenditure Committee was 'strongly critical of these decisions taking them as a whole'.[8] But it is quite clear that the Treasury was now using the expenditure control system as a demand management tool in a way that is quite contrary to what Plowden recommended. Plowden essentially argued that if public expenditure were linked to the long run growth rate of the economy it could avoid being used as a short-term regulator. This has proved unduly optimistic. The last six years have two lessons. First, that now the Treasury has forged an effective mechanism of control it will not be able to resist the temptation to use it for medium and short term demand management with all the diseconomies that are involved. Second, economic crises will interfere with forward planning whatever the good intentions of the planners, just as political pressures will.

Social Services Departments
The overall strategies
The 1964 Labour Government accepted the Conservatives' plans for education adopting an identical growth rate. They did go for a rather higher growth rate for the Health Service and a considerably higher one for housing. This was to be 'paid' for by stabilizing defence expenditures.

When that Government was forced to recast its spending strategy in 1968 all the social programmes were pulled back and there was to be a more even pattern of growth between them. Indeed it was in that year that we see education and health given *equal* growth targets compared to the much higher rate that education had enjoyed in the 1950s and early 1960s. It is no accident that in the later White Papers these two growth rates have been identical. It does not reflect any sophisticated, or perhaps one should say spurious, attempt to judge different 'needs' between the two services. The demographic factors affecting each are quite different, for example. What it does illustrate is that the political weight of these two departments, the DES and the DHSS, is now roughly equal and that during this period they agreed to play for a draw. This balance of power held under both the Labour and Conservative Governments. However, the Conservative plans did differ sharply when it came to housing and social security policy. Housing expenditure, on new building and subsidies, was to fall slightly and then rise very sharply after 1972 compared to the steady increase Labour had planned. The Heath Government was also planning for a far slower growth rate in social security expenditure. In short, an explicit and quite coherent set of priorities can be traced in social spending intentions since the mid-sixties. They were not as muddled or incoherent as some commentators have suggested. What happened was not entirely what was intended.

The Conservative Government's housing subsidy policy went seriously wrong. Also the exceptionally high level of unemployment meant that far more went on unemployment benefit than had been anticipated. On other counts the economic climate was partly to blame for the divergence between plan and outcome.

Clearly as economic difficulties grow the shocks which the social services are going to have to absorb will be more frequent and more painful. We may soon come to look back on the past decade of 'planned growth' with a strong sense of nostalgia. We turn now to the evolution of planning within the separate departments.

The Department of Education and Science
Capital planning
One of the few direct financial controls the Ministry of Education, or later the DES, has had over the education system has been its power to approve building projects. This power extends to all local authority building for education purposes – not only schools, but colleges of further education and polytechnics. Probably the first piece of post-war capital planning was the emergency building programme mounted to house the extra children who would be staying on at school until fifteen in 1947. The 'hutted

operation for raising the school leaving age' (HORSA) – a name which evokes memories of D-Day and post war emergency restrictions.

After 1949 the Ministry introduced a system of cost limits under which all school building proposals from local authorities had to cost less than a specified sum per place. However, it was not until the mid-1950s that the deliberate forward planning of building programmes began. The White Paper 'Technical Education' proposed not merely that a series of new Colleges of Advanced Technology should be created but, in some ways more important, it announced a five-year building programme for the whole of Technical Education. Then two years later came another White Paper, this time on school building. It set out a five year programme from 1960–1 to 1964–5 which was designed to eliminate 'all age' schools – the old elementary schools which took children from the ages of five to fifteen and which the 1944 Act has said all local authorities should replace by separate primary and secondary schools. Science facilities too were to be improved – another post-Sputnik response. The Government announced, in effect, that it would accept bids from local authorities under these two headings up to a total value of £60 million a year. In 1963 a new three-year programme was announced, and authorities were asked to submit all their school building proposals covering the years 1965–8. Once again indications were given of the criteria that would be applied in judging the requests. Most of the allocations, the Treasury had agreed, would go on new school places to meet the rising birth rate, and on sixth form places to meet the larger numbers who were staying at school. These programmes were then rolled forward.

In 1968 the control was made even more elaborate. The Department introduced a system of 'programming'. It was to have three distinct phases. First, authorities must submit a 'preliminary list' of projects which they would like to have permission to begin work on – securing sites and gaining planning permission. The proposals must conform to criteria set by the Secretary of State. In the early 1970s, apart from new population needs, this mainly meant the replacement of pre-1902 primary schools. The lists were approved seven to five years ahead of actual building, but even this is not far enough ahead for a large urban authority like the Inner London Education Authority. One year before the authority is ready to start building it must submit a 'design list' with most of the design complete and with costs. Even then the DES only gives an amber light. A project next has to get on to the 'starts list'. Only then can building begin. At each stage the Government can hold the process up or defer permission on all or some of the projects if the Treasury demands cuts in the total capital programme that year.

In short, the loan sanction procedure has been developed so that the

Central Department aims not merely to promote economy and ensure minimum standards, but also to set a limit to the size of the programme well into the future, to determine priority needs it will meet, and to keep a close and continuing control over each stage of the process from site acquisition to the laying of the foundations.

Informal promotional planning

The mechanism of the advisory committee has been important in the formation of British education policy for more than a century. The 1870 Elementary Education Act which created a comprehensive pattern of state education had been preceded by a series of committees of enquiry which also prompted reforms in the private sector. A series of famous reports by the Consultative Committees on Education between the wars laid the intellectual foundations for the 1944 Act and, perhaps even more important, for the way it was administered. But it was in the decade between the mid 1950s and the mid 1960s when the practice reached its peak. It was used as vehicle for a series of separate investigations on different sections of the education system. The growth rate in education expenditure during and immediately following this decade is a partial testimony to its success. There were three types of advisory committees operating at this time. The statutory advisory council, the specialist National Advisory Council on the Training and Supply of Teachers and *ad hoc* committees set up for particular and limited purposes.

Under Section 4 of the 1944 Act the Minister, now the Secretary of State, is required to appoint two central advisory councils, one for England and one for Wales. Although they began with a general overview function, after 1951 the strategy changed and the members were to be appointed for three years to study specific areas of concern identified by the Minister. All the subsequent reports did this. Early Leaving (1954), Crowther (1959) Newsom (1963) Plowden (1967).[9] Crowther and Plowden especially were important planning documents. The first discussed the educational needs of the 15–18 age group. Apart from the impact made by its social surveys, it drew attention to the steady upward trend in voluntary staying on which was to have important repercussions on the planning of higher education. Above all it marshalled economic and social arguments for raising the school leaving age to sixteen. It estimated the additional demands for teachers and it recommended a time, seven to nine years afterwards, when the demographic trends would be favourable. It recommended an early announcement of the government's intentions and the laying of plans for buildings and teacher supply well in advance. Yet another report (Newsom) was needed to finally tip the political balance four years later. In the pre-1964 election period the Minister Edward Boyle did make such a declaration of intent. The staff work for this committee and all the statistical and planning work was undertaken in the Ministry of Education.

Plowden is in many ways an even better example. The period when it reported was one of recurrent economic crisis rather than the days of heady optimism in which the Crowther report was drafted. Consequently Plowden was very modest in its proposals all of which were carefully costed. The priority area proposals are the ones for which it is perhaps most remembered. Yet more important in resource terms were its proposals for introducing universal part-time preschool education. Plowden's planning assumptions here were accepted largely unaltered once the principle was agreed nearly six years later. For example, the government incorporated Plowden's assumptions about the proportion of children whom parents would wish to give part-time schooling, and the numbers of fulltime places that would be needed for working mothers. Yet the figures had been made on the most flimsy and out-dated social survey evidence. They were all Plowden had, yet they became enshrined in the Government's 1972 White Paper.[10]

Perhaps the best known and the most important report was that of an *ad hoc* committee appointed to examine higher education under the Chairmanship of Lord Robbins.[11] The methodology that the committee's advisers, with DES help, evolved for forecasting the demand for higher education, and the rationale it used for deciding on the total number of places that were needed, has been adopted by governments ever since as the basis for planning and financing higher education. Other *ad hoc* committees have contributed to the debate about policy and organization – most recently the Public Schools Commission (1970), the James Report on teacher training (1971) and the Russell Report on Adult Education (1973). The third type of committee, an on-going specialist committee on the supply of teachers, played a very important part in expanding teacher supply in the 1960s. The detailed projections and the assumptions about 'demand' largely derived from the Department, but they were discussed on the Committee by representatives of the teaching profession, and local authorities, and they were public knowledge. Their recommendations were the subject of fierce tussles with the Treasury and the professional and public support that the reports gained certainly helped in these battles.

This series of reports illustrates both the strengths and the weaknesses of this kind of 'disjointed' planning. Its strengths were that the committees educated and informed their specialist, interested publics as they worked. They called for evidence. About 110 different bodies gave evidence to Plowden as well as about 200 individuals in key positions. As all these bodies held their own meetings and did their own background reading and research in order to write their evidence so they became increasingly well-informed about the issues. Then, having completed it, these organizations would typically publish their evidence and this would be used as the basis for discussions at local NUT or AUT branches, at meetings of local parents who were members of Committees for the Advancement of State Education and so on through all the network of educational interest groups. Each committee was carefully balanced to include representatives of all the many interests and organizations within the education system. Many came with clearly formed views. Some went away with the same ones afterwards, but for most membership itself was an enormously educative process. Members became aware of information, arguments, and attitudes they may have barely perceived or even knew existed. Even the DES observers or 'assessors' sometimes found themselves in this position. Moreover, the committees generated much original research. As a consequence a kind of feed-back process operated and the members in turn educated their own 'constituencies' both before the reports were published and afterwards as they went round the country explaining and justifying the report they had signed. These reports themselves had astonishingly high sales, especially considering their length. Their contents were summarized and discussed particularly in the specialist press. In short, an elaborate educative process took place during and after the time the reports were published. Opinion within the universities on the desirability of expansion moved a long way while the Robbins committee was actually sitting, for example. The interested parties were not only educated, they were mobilized; if some degree of consensus emerged this put the Minister in a far stronger position with his Cabinet colleagues when it came to arguing with the Treasury.

If these were the strengths, there were also weaknesses. They became particularly obvious after the Robbins report had been accepted. If there were to be any constraints on education expenditure at all, the commitments made by the Conservative Government to expand higher education on demand pre-empted funds on an unprecedented scale. It meant that other options were effectively closed – for example the option to devote significantly more resources to primary education or to expand nursery education or to go ahead with comprehensive reorganization. Certainly from the Treasury's point of view they were an embarrassment. It could also be argued that education was beginning to pre-empt too large a share of resources which the social services as a whole were likely to gain. None of the other Ministries had used their advisory councils to such effect. But in the mid-sixties Departmental and Ministerial opinion ceased to favour the advisory committee approach and turned instead to internal planning arrangements. It is not entirely clear why this was so. The factors we have mentioned no doubt played some part. There was the view that they slowed up the decison making process, they took time and resources, and there was a feeling that, as Crosland put it, if the Department could not do its own planning it ought to pack up. But more than this the Department was probably unhappy with many of the Committee's proposals. This was certainly true of Robbins thoughts on the public sector of higher education and on Ministerial responsibility. The DES fought both and won. It was by no means enthusiastic about Plowden's priority area proposals and differential salaries for teachers in stress schools. With teacher supply the officials in the Department were feeling their way towards an unpopular as well as an important shift of policy, and probably did not welcome the idea of having it exposed to public gaze. Perhaps the Treasury had had enough. Whatever the precise reasons the change of approach is very clear. After Plowden no new Central Advisory Council was appointed for over seven years, contrary to the Secretary of State's clear statutory duty to keep one in being. The National Advisory Council on the Training and Supply of Teachers, too, was disbanded and not reappointed throughout the period when the Department was formulating its proposals to cut back the number of teacher training places and close many Colleges of Education. Only when this had been decided was the Committee reconvened and then all the statistical reasoning that lay behind the Departments conclusions on the future supply and demand for teachers was presented as confidential documents and no report was published. When Mrs Thatcher did appoint a committee with instructions to produce a rapid report on the education of teachers (James 1972)[12] it proved to be the very antithesis of what had gone before. No research, nothing on resources, no costs of its proposals, an after-dinner-speech kind of a report. A period of openness in educational planning had been replaced by baffling silence, secrecy and evasion.

Only in 1974 with the appointment of the Warnock committee on special education and the reconvening of the Teacher Supply Committee did the older tradition appear to be returning.

Formal departmental planning – model 1
In the mid-sixties various people had called for a National Plan for education, and Crosland as a new Minister had set up a Planning Branch within DES and some saw this as the body to formulate such an overall set of proposals and priorities. This never happened. The Branch was set up against strong opposition from senior officials in the Department. Crosland's own account illustrates this. The Department argued that 'it did not need a central planning division because the planning function was already being carried out in the separate operations branches – teacher supply, school building, further education and so on. I didn't agree.'[13] He

had to insist on his proposal. 'I sent a polite minute to Herbert Andrew saying, "I would be grateful for your final advice on this matter as I propose to make a public announcement in a fortnight's time." An experienced civil servant can always tell when the argument is over and he's lost the battle.'[14]

However it is far from clear that Crosland had won. The Branch was never given the resources or the status to perform effectively. It was not a unit superimposed above the other branches which were responsible for schools, or teacher supply or further education. It could not give advice on the respective merits of these other branches' claims on resources. Such an innovation would have run counter to the structure and traditions of the whole of the civil service. Instead it was created as a parallel branch and a weak one too. The statisticians were brought within it but they continued to do broadly what they had done before – produce a comprehensive series of historical statistics and make projections. Then two economists were brought in – the first the department had ever employed. The branch serviced the needs of other branches. The Branch was never allowed to compete with or in any way challenge the specialist or 'policy' branches.

Formal planning – model 2
When the Conservative Government came to power in 1970 The Planning Branch was abolished and a new arrangement was introduced in 1971 called the Departmental Planning Organization. It was offically said to consist of a 'flexible network of committees and working groups'. The first principle upon which it rested was that 'planning must directly involve those who must administer the policies that have to be planned'. What this meant was that the policy branches were officially included in the planning system. Nor were they to be dictated to by a separate breed of 'planners'. 'Specialist skills must be built into the machinery in such a way as to ensure that they can make a creative contribution to policy formation without being able to determine it single handed.'[15]

The Planning Organization since then has consisted of:

1 A Policy Steering Group under the Chairmanship of the Permanent Secretary which includes the heads of the most important branches. It determines the planning programme in consultation with Ministers. It sets particular studies in motion and receives the reports when they are complete, before submitting them, if they are accepted, to Ministers.
2 Beneath this are specialist policy groups each chaired by a Deputy Secretary covering a particular programme category or field of activity, e.g. schools or further education. On these groups will be Under-Secretaries, HM Inspectors, specialists like architects and statisticians. It may well break

down into small subgroups.

3   To service these groups is a Planning Unit to ensure that consistent planning, population and cost data are used.

It was this machinery that was employed to conduct a comprehensive assessment of resource priorities and plans for the 1970s. The results eventually emerged as the White Paper: *Education a Framework for Expansion* in December 1972. The whole exercise was dominated by the need to keep education expenditure within the new constraints that were being applied to public expenditure overall.

The White Paper does even so represent an attempt to view the system as a whole and to make explicit decisions about priorities between the different sectors of education – preschool, primary, secondary and higher education. The declining birth rate made it possible to consider realistically alternative strategies and the White Paper proposed tipping the balance more towards the preschool/primary school sectors and away from higher education in the next decade. Part time nursery education for all children by the early 1980s was balanced by a reduced expansion in higher education. The way the proposals were evolved indicates very clearly how the whole planning process has now become subordinated to or contained within the public expenditure control process we have described. The informal pluralist system of advisory committees was at least temporarily abandoned. An open system had been replaced by a more closed one. A diffuse system by a more centralized one.

Notes

1   *Control of Public Expenditure*, Cmnd 1432 (1961).
2   *Ibid.*, para. 31.
3   Cmnd 1432, para. 17.
4   Cmnd 2764.
5   Cmnd 2915.
6   Cmnd 3515.
7   Sir Samuel Goldman, *The Developing System of Public Expenditure Management Control*, Civil Service College Studies, No. 2 HMSO London 1973 p.9.
8   Fifth Report from the Expenditure Committee Session 1972/3, HC 149 (1972–3), para. 11.
9   Central Advisory Council for England: *Early Leaving*, 1954; 15–18

(Crowther) 1959. *Half our Future* (Newsom), 1963; *Children and their Primary Schools* (Plowden) 1967 HMSO.

10 *Education: A Framework for Expansion*, Cmnd 5174.

11 *Higher Education*, Cmnd 2154 (1963).

12 *Teacher Education and Training.* A Report of a Committee of Enquiry appointed by the Secretary of State for Education and Science (under the chairmanship of Lord James of Rusholme), HMSO, 1972.

13 Boyle and Crosland, p.177 ed. M. Kogan, *The Politics of Education*, Penguin 1971.

14 *Ibid.*, p.183.

15 Sir W. Pyle *Public Adminstration*, Spring 1974.

2.4 The structure of educational provision and patterns of educational attainment: a local authority case study

W. Williamson and D.S. Byrne

The question of how far well-known social and spatial inequalities in patterns of educational attainment can be attributed to equally well known inequalities among local authorities in the distribution of resources for education has received a great deal of attention in recent years.[1] Our own work occupies one position in these debates and emphasizes the centrality of resource and provision variation among local education authorities as explanatory variables for social and spatial patterns of educational attainment.[2] Counterposed to such an explanatory position are those which attach prime importance to patterns of inequality in the distribution of various forms of cultural competence so that some groups of children are well placed to succeed at school, almost irrespective of the quality of the school itself, while others are not.[3] The implications of these two contrasting positions in the field of social policy in education are very different; the first position places a heavy emphasis on the massive redistribution of educational resources if the educational system is to become more equal while the second approach places much more emphasis on engineering changes in social attitudes to education and forms of socialization.

It is a caricature of both positions to set them out in this way and, of course, they are not necessarily mutually exclusive although it is in fact the case, that, so far at least, each position has come to have a quite different political significance.[4] To the undecided, the essential tension between these two positions is not easily resolved and two main problems, each

Source: 'The effect of local education authority resources and policies on educational attainment.' SSRC final report 1975.

extremely complex, stand in the way of an easy and productive reconciliation. The first and fundamental one is theoretical and concerns the significance of class-stratified inequalities in education in a capitalist society for the continuation of a capitalistic mode of production. The second is a methodological problem and relates firstly to the reliability of certain statistical procedures and secondly to the adequacy of some official statistics as indicators of essentially theoretical concepts. Adding to the difficulties is, of course, the paucity of controlled research in this area.[5]

In the following discussion, we wish to make a small empirical contribution to these debates by examining some results of work we carried out in one local education authority in the north-east of England in 1974 just before the reorganization of local government in England and Wales. As part of our work on the significance of resource and provision variation among local authorities at the national level, we planned a smaller study for one local authority to assess the significance of variations among schools within a given area on patterns of educational attainment. Our national data on attainment, resources and provision variables had been aggregated at the level of the local authority and was therefore capable of being criticized on several grounds. The most important of these concerned the way in which such aggregated statistics concealed important variations among schools within local authorities and the way in which the attainment measures used (i.e. measures of rates of staying on at school beyond statutory minimum leaving age)[6] failed to get close enough to educationally meaningful notions of attainment such as test scores or examination results. For both reasons, among others, the national results would be deceptive. What was needed, we felt, was a study of a single local authority in which the historical aspects of class structuration through education could be examined and the significance of resource and provision variation among schools themselves carefully measured and analysed. We felt, in addition, that a local study would make it possible to spell out the political character of decision-making in education in such a way that the theoretical model of class relationships we were working with could be seen to generate a new set of questions about the social structure of educational attainment. What we hoped to demonstrate in this respect was that class differences were at the root of inequalities in education but that such differences were best thought of in economic and political terms and not in social and cultural terms. We had made out this case, we felt, in the national study but in a way which was removed from the realities of educational policy and politics, of schools and of children – in short, from the point where most earlier writers had located their arguments about inequality in education, the point at which different groups of children actually experience the educational system itself.

H

Selecting a local education authority

There were four strategic considerations which led us to select Sunderland as the site for our study. Firstly, we both knew the town quite well and it was, in any case, nearby. The second was that Sunderland had already been the subject of an impressive study by Robson in which the theoretical case which we wished to criticise, or, at least, assess, namely the socio-cultural explanation of educational inequalities, had been impressively set out and documented.[7] Thirdly, Sunderland was a good example of a particular type of authority which we had identified in the national study on the basis of cluster analysis namely, of urban, industrial working class county boroughs with their distinctive profiles of educational problems.[8] We felt that an intensive study of one such typical authority would, in a way, speak for them all although, of course, what was really required was a much more extensive programme of research into a variety of local authority areas of the sort we were proposing for Sunderland. Finally, Sunderland is a relatively homogenous town socially, where social class differences among the population have relatively clear spatial boundaries. In this situation a research design which aims to control the importance of social class factors on educational attainment in order to evaluate better the importance of provision and resource variables, especially those under the control of the local authority itself, is, in principle, at least possible. The technical difficulties of such a study are still very great as we shall show, but the social homogeneity of the town with its heterogenous educational provision affords interesting opportunities for the kind of study reported here.

The historical background to education in Sunderland

Sunderland is an industrial town still struggling against the legacy of its nineteenth-century development. Robson says of the place:

> Sunderland is a town which is living on the dwindling fat of its Victorian expansion. The legacy of the industrial revolution is apparent in its appearance, its industrial structure, its population growth and in a host of social and economic characteristics. Even attitudes are coloured by its past heritage. The Depression Years, the final death spasm of the nineteenth century in a pre-Keynsian era, are still a real memory amongst much of the town's population and impinge upon the attitudes of the working population.[9]

Despite industrial diversification after the Second World War and the declining fortunes of coal and shipbuilding and the growth of some light industries in the area, Robson is still able to claim that:

... it is still a town of heavy industry and subject to the economic fluctuations of economic fortune and the distress and poverty which this implies in the present economic situation.[10]

Sunderland, then, is not an ostentatious town. It is an unemployment blackspot in the Northern Economic Planning Region. Sunderland is nonetheless attempting to overcome the scars of its historical development. Slum clearance programmes, rebuilding of houses and industrial plant, new road building, central redevelopment are all, for better or worse, forging ahead.[11] Changes in the educational system are also being actively pursued and very hotly disputed in a context in which political battle lines are very sharply drawn. The educational background which Sunderland is seeking to escape from is one in which the historical differentiation of schools into grammar and secondary modern types is firmly rooted.

In the cluster analysis which formed part of the data analysis for the national part of the research project, Sunderland was located in cluster three. The characteristics of the cluster as a whole are those of urban, industrial, working-class county boroughs. Rates of staying on at school beyond sixteen and seventeen years of age are below the national average and secondary school provision is, in the main, comprehensive. These authorities are not poor but they could not be described as affluent; a large percentage of the population resident in them live in council houses and the quality of the housing stock measured in terms of the kinds of amenities available is below average. Sunderland is a typical example of the authorities in this group, but, as we shall make clear, there are aspects of the local social structure which require that generalizations about the group as a whole have to be carefully qualified. The pattern of educational provision and resource distribution in Sunderland is the outcome of an historical situation and it is against the background of this situation that education must be understood.

It is clear, however, from even a cursory glance at Table 1 that Sunderland performs less well than many other authorities grouped into cluster three. On the crude overall figures for staying on at school, Sunderland is not only below the national average but also below the average for the cluster. This is true of all the measures listed except for the production of school teachers. In terms of educational policy, and insofar as this can be inferred from the data presented, Sunderland is below the cluster average in the field of comprehensive provision, and its figures are below both national and cluster averages.

At the end of the Second World War, Sunderland had a school pattern based upon two non-denominational grammar schools and eighteen unreorganized senior schools for children between nine and fourteen years

Table 1 Characteristics of Sunderland LEA

Social Class

	high social class (%)	middle class (%)	low social class (%)	manual (%)	non-manual (%)
Sunderland	9.7	59.2	28.9	74.8	23.0
Cluster 3	12.0	55.4	29.4	69.8	27.0
national average	14.6	55.3	26.8	65.3	31.2

Characteristics of the area

	low r.v.	% owner occupiers	% council tenants	% private tenants	% households with all amenities
Sunderland	95.5	33.2	46.3	18.0	70.0
Cluster 3	92.8	44.2	29.4	22.7	68.5
national average	83.5	47.9	25.5	21.8	72.0

provision

	pupil : teacher ratio		teachers' salaries		total expenditure (costs per pupil)	
	primary	secondary	primary	secondary	primary	secondary
Sunderland	29.6	19.1	59.8	98.57	88.74	157.89
Cluster 3	27.5	17.8	63.0	129.3	98.5	187.6
national average	27.3	17.8	66.3	115.2	102.4	188.2

Policy

	proportion of 13 yearolds in: secondary modern	comprehensive	grammar (1)	grammar (2)
Sunderland	41.6	49.3	9.2	4.4
Cluster 3	5.6	89.5	6.8	3.5
national average	44.1	32.2	24.3	16.4

Attainment

	staying on beyond		uptake of awards to			
	16	17	university	F.E. 1	F.E. 2	teacher training
Sunderland	26.8	15.5	54.0	63.1	18.9	66.8
Cluster 3	29.9	16.1	58.3	57.9	20.0	55.6
national average	33.0	18.3	71.9	72.1	25.0	57.9

of age, and eight junior and senior schools for the seven to fourteen age groups.

The local authority response to the *1944 Education Act* was a positive rejection of multi-lateral schools. The outline development plan of April 9th 1946 set out the policy in the following way:

> Taking everything into consideration it is recommended that single bias schools should be adopted as the policy of the Authority. The chief arguments against the multilateral school in this area are the necessity for 'atmosphere', particularly in Technical Schools, and the inevitable unwieldy size which must be conducted in order to provide adequate sixth forms. The number of post-war primary pupils are so large in the town that it ought not to be difficult to make a selection at 11, and reconsideration of every pupil at the age of 13. Provided an easy system of transfer is operated and the schools work closely together, separate types are preferable.

The reasons given publicly for these decisions were reasons of space; Sunderland could not expand its schools because of new building regulations.

New schools have, of course, been built and in the 1960s Sunderland built three comprehensive schools and in the early seventies committed itself to a programme of full comprehensive reform to remove the last vestiges of official 11 + selection, but the political conflict over reform plans has been intense. Conservatives in Sunderland, while supporting comprehensive reorganization, cling ferociously to the idea of retaining the character of the town's most famous school – the Bede School, the jewel in the town's educational crown. It is clear, although this is not the place to write the history of secondary school education in Sunderland, that the town is only now beginning to escape from the tri-partism of the last twenty-five years, but the historical residue of small, differentiated schools will be difficult to overcome.

School resources[12]

There are twenty-three secondary schools in Sunderland including denominational schools. The schools are at different stages in the development towards fully comprehensive schooling; nine of the schools are still described as secondary modern schools and three of the schools have hardly lost their identity as grammar schools. Sunderland therefore, has still a long way to go before the secondary school system can be regarded as fully comprehensive. Indeed, 25 per cent of Sunderland children still have to face an 11 + test. In addition, 70 per cent of

Sunderland schools have less than 1,000 pupils, and in this respect may be thought of as being too small to constitute comprehensive schools.

Sunderland schools are not particularly salubrious in terms of facilities. Eight of the schools do not possess a separate gymnasium or playing fields. Five schools have no separate library. Twelve schools have no facility for A level science. Such figures are in no way surprising. They reflect the pattern of tri-partite educational provision which developed in Sunderland since the *1944 Education Act* and also the fact that such development took place within some very old buildings. Nine of the schools were built before the Second World War and four of the schools included in this survey had main buildings dating from the 1890s. Earlier forms of educational differentiation thus persist in the architecture of the schools themselves. But such a differentiation is not confined simply to the buildings; such patterns are also reflected in the character and distribution of the teaching labour force.

The distribution of graduate and non-graduate teachers in Sunderland schools reflects the character of secondary school provision. Some of the older secondary schools have very few graduate teachers while former grammar schools have a great many. It is still the case, however, that there are only three schools in Sunderland where more than half of the teaching staff are graduates. The typical secondary school teacher in Sunderland is a non-graduate, college trained teacher with less than eight years' teaching experience and, in any given school, with less than eight years' service and employed on Grade One of the Burnham scale. The staff turnover figure for Sunderland secondary schools is not large – 13.2 per cent – but there are eight schools where the staff turnover figure exceeds 12 per cent and in one school the figure has been as high as 36.2 per cent. There is therefore a very slight indication of staff turnover above national average.[13] The typical Sunderland teacher is therefore one who seems to be constantly on the look out for a job change. We have no direct evidence of this problem but the relative paucity of high grade posts and the age structure of the teaching labour force combine to create a situation in which legitimate demands for career advancement can only be met by changing schools. Such a conclusion can only be taken very tentatively; the whole question of staff turnover needs to be studied in much greater detail.

The resources of schools vary too. Expenditure on secondary school pupils in Sunderland is below national averages. Per capita expenditure in the schools themselves through the school capitation allowance is also quite small. We have no comparative data on this particular measure but in 1971/72 the mean figure was £7.04. From this money the school must finance stationary, books and equipment.

The cash fund upon which a school can draw is, however, likely to be very variable since schools can, through fund-raising activities, boost funds beyond the minimum represented by the annual capitation allowance.

Of much greater significance, therefore, are the range of courses which can be offered and are being offered in the schools. Only eight schools in Sunderland can offer all three major examinations i.e. A level, O level and CSE. The remainder can only offer courses up to CSE and O level and the capacity to provide these courses varies too. Of those which do not offer A level courses i.e. twelve schools in all, seven can offer only CSEs.

Variations in attainment

The effects of such differentiated patterns of provision on school attainment is very difficult to establish. Apart from anything else, attainment figures change over time so that controlled studies are difficult. The national average figures for the two main attainment measures which concern us have been consistently above those of Sunderland for the past few years as Table 2 makes clear. Sunderland has also had below average figures for English county boroughs as a whole.

Table 2   Rates of staying on at school to 16yrs and 17yrs; Sunderland, England and Wales

	Sunderland 16 +	17 +	English county boroughs 16 +	17 +	national average England & Wales 16 +	17 +
1967	19.4	11.1	—	—	—	14.9
1968	19.8	10.5	—	—	30.2	16.1
1969	26.4	14.0	27.8	14.4	32.1	17.4
1970	26.8	15.5	28.9	15.4	33.2	18.5
1971	25.0	15.7	29.3	15.8	34.0	18.9
1972	27.2	15.7	30.5	16.3	35.5	19.6
1973	25.3	14.5	35.6	19.9	30.2	16.5

Source: Department of Education and Science. *Schools Vol 1* 1967–73 London HMSO

Of far greater significance is the variation in staying-on rates among the Sunderland schools themselves. In seven schools the figure is greater than 50 per cent and in six schools less than 20 per cent. There is, therefore, considerable variation in rates of staying on among the schools.

For those children who do stay on to take O level examinations the chances of gaining a minimum of five passes varies, too. The mean percentage of pupils gaining five or more O levels is 16.3 per cent. In five schools, however, the figure is over 50 per cent. The same pattern emerges for A level passes. The mean percentage of pupils who gained two or more A levels was, for the town as a whole, 19.7 per cent. In four schools (out of the eight who are able to offer A level examinations) the figure is over 50 per cent. There is, then, clearly a concentration of academic excellence in the secondary school system reflecting once more the historical roots of educational opportunity in the area.

The older grammar schools are still the jewels in Sunderland's educational crown. Even within this network of concentrated opportunity there are variations. Seven schools in the survey sent pupils to University. Nearly 6 per cent of sixth-form pupils on average went to university in 1972. In three schools, however, the figure was over 20 per cent and in one school the figure was 40.0 per cent. The school in question is the Saint Aidans Roman Catholic Grammar School which selects its intake from a wide area beyond Sunderland. But the figure for Sunderland's most famous non-denominational school – the old Bede Grammar School – is 31.0 per cent. This school's record of academic success explains and is at the same time the outcome of, the political importance of the school in the town.

Such patterns of provision and attainment form the essential backcloth to comprehensive planning in Sunderland. The extent to which the obvious inequalities we have described can be reduced will be the measure of success of comprehensive change. The obstacles which need to be overcome to achieve such ends are, however enormous and educational debate in the town highly politicized.

One of the greatest current constraints on educational policy in Sunderland is, however, central government expenditure restrictions. The controlling Labour group of Sunderland council have, rightly or wrongly, insisted that full comprehensivization required new building in Sunderland but successive Ministers of Education, beginning with Mrs Thatcher, have denied them the necessary building permission.

The correlates of provision

The educational system of Sunderland is historically differentiated into those schools which stimulate children to high levels of educational attainment and those which do not. It is also differentiated according to the amount and quality of resources available in the schools. As we have seen there are very large differences among Sunderland schools according to criteria of educational provision. The question we need now to raise is how far differences in provision explain the differences in various measures of educational attainment of school children in Sunderland.

In order to examine this question we collected data on provision and attainment from Sunderland secondary school head teachers and calculated the product moment correlation coefficients among the variable set in Table 3.[14]

In the light of our earlier work we expected to show that social class variation in rates of educational attainment are to a large extent the outcome of variation in the structure and quality of educational provision. Unfortunately the limitations imposed upon our data by the research design we employed do not allow us to examine this proposition as fully as we might. We do not have adequate measures of the social class variable available and do not have data – despite our early optimism that census returns might provide us with it – of the social class composition of the schools in the survey. To collect such data would have involved a research programme far larger than that which was possible, given our resources.

Some of our results do cast light on the question, however. If what Ronald King has subsequently called the differential provision theory has any validity then we might expect the two following propositions to hold true:[15]

(a) Schools which are well provided for in terms of physical plant and human capital will offer a wider structure of opportunity for pupils.

(b) Schools which have high levels of provision will also show correspondingly high levels of educational attainment.

If such propositions can be shown to be valid then it is a short step to the further proposition that working-class children at well-resourced schools will do better than those working-class children at less well-resourced schools. Taken alongside research findings from other studies that working class children are more likely to attend schools less well provided for than middle class children; the evidence would then amount to a convincing *prima facie* case that the relative differences in educational attainment among children from different social class backgrounds are to a considerable degree attributable to differences in the level and quality of available educational resources.

Table 3 sets out the inter-correlations among some of the provision variables used in the Sunderland survey. While few of the correlations are high a number of important observations can be made.

Firstly, it is clear that larger schools provide a wider range of opportunities than smaller schools. The correlation between the current size of the school (measured in terms of numbers of pupils) and the number of advanced level courses the school can offer is 0.78. The correlation between number of forms of entry and number of ordinary courses available is 0.71. These figures reflect the historical development

Table 3 Product moment correlation coefficients between provision variables

	2	3	7	9	10	11	16	17	27	30	38	40	41	42	13	34	39
2	—	0.23	0.83	−0.05	−0.11	0.03	0.50	−0.05	0.10	−0.14	−0.08	0.71	0.58	0.58	0.2	0.38	−0.37
3		—	0.33	−0.17	0.09	−0.07	0.12	−0.12	−0.09	0.03	0.04	0.11	0.78	0.30	0.06	0.09	0.21
7			—	−0.19	0.19	0.02	0.63	−0.08	0.05	−0.27	0.09	0.78	0.81	0.55	0.09	0.50	−0.41
9				—	0.11	0.25	0.28	0.09	−0.13	−0.08	−0.06	−0.02	0.07	−0.25	−0.32	0.14	0.01
10					—	0.12	0.31	0.10	0.03	0.24	−0.03	0.05	0.29	0.09	−0.00	0.21	−0.52
11						—	0.25	−0.26	−0.42	−0.23	−0.11	0.37	0.28	−0.33	−0.14	0.30	−0.42
16							—	0.02	−0.02	−0.16	0.12	0.63	0.74	0.03	−0.19	−0.55	−0.40
17								—	0.77	0.46	0.09	−0.36	−0.18	−0.03	−0.01	−0.25	0.33
27									—	0.42	0.01	−0.20	−0.15	0.20	0.34	−0.20	0.27
30										—	−0.00	−0.20	−0.15	0.20	−0.03	−0.24	0.57
38											—	0.02	0.26	0.02	−0.42	0.18	0.19
40												—	0.86	0.44	0.13	0.71	−0.80
41													—	0.40	−0.16	0.82	−0.95
42														—	−0.45	0.35	−0.11
14															—	−0.20	−0.12
34																—	−0.49
39																	—

Variable names are set out in the Appendix.

226

of the secondary school system in Sunderland. Grammar schools in the town have been larger than secondary modern schools.

Secondly, the proportion of graduate teachers on the school staff is highly correlated with the provision of ordinary and advanced level courses, the correlations being 0.63 and 0.74 respectively. In addition the proportion of graduate teachers in a school is related to the size of the school. The correlation between the size of school staffs and proportion of graduates is 0.63.

Thirdly, there is a high inter-correlation between the number of ordinary and advanced level courses in Sunderland secondary schools. This suggests a pattern of concentrated opportunities. Advanced level courses are available in schools with ordinary level courses – a point which in itself is perfectly obvious – but the correlation suggests that ordinary level courses are more likely to be provided in schools with advanced level courses. This means that large numbers of children in Sunderland are being taught in former secondary schools without any real opportunity to study towards ordinary level examinations. Possibilities of school transfer do, of course exist, but the academic culture of the school without ordinary level examinations is conceivably very different from the school with such examinations available.

Finally, it seems to be inevitable that correlation studies of this kind will always produce figures which contradict some conventional wisdom. The variable, pupil-teacher ratio is not significantly correlated with anything and a measure of staff turnover, long thought by educationists to be an index of the quality of a school, is not correlated strongly with any of the provision variables used in this study. There is only the slight indication that staff turnover is higher when the career opportunity of the school is relatively poor and when the staff are young. The logic of these slight correlations is perfectly obvious; young teachers are likely to move to better jobs.

There is, therefore, some evidence that proposition (a) above holds true. To that extent the claim often made of comprehensive schools that they should be large enough to provide a wide range of courses is accurate in the Sunderland case.

The correlates of attainment

The second proposition that schools with higher levels of provision will have higher rates of educational attainment is much more contentious. The implication is clearly that high levels of provision cause high levels of attainment. Put another way the proposition suggests that variations among the attainment rates of working class children are attributable to variations in the quality of what is provided for such children. If this argument is valid then it has very important implications for social policy in education. Unfortunately the kind of analysis we have carried out so far is not adequate to explore the proposition fully.

Table 4 sets out the zero order product moment correlation coefficients for some of the provision variables included in the analysis with the attainment variables we employed. The results are in no way unexpected. Five observations can be made about the correlations.

Firstly, as we might expect in the light of what has already been said, there are strong correlations between the size of schools and the attainment measure, staying on at school to sixteen and seventeen. The correlations are 0.56 and 0.66 respectively.

Secondly, rates of staying on are highly correlated with the proportion of staff who are graduates. The measure, proportion of children gaining five or more ordinary level passes is also highly correlated with the proportion of staff who are graduates. The correlation in this case is 0.62. We have already seen that larger schools are correlated with attainment so once again these figures simply reflect the historical character of the Sunderland school system. The older grammar schools and purpose built comprehensives have a monopoly of the kinds of educational resources – courses and teachers – which are related to achievement in school.

Thirdly, there seems to be some correlation between the stability of school staff and the attainment rates of the school although the correlation is not a strong one. The proportion of children gaining five or more ordinary level passes is negatively correlated with our measure of staff turnover, and also negatively correlated with the proportion of staff on Burnham grade one. Once again, however, these figures reflect the resource pattern (this time as it affects the establishment of schools) and historical nature of the schools. The smaller secondary schools do not have establishments which provide a career structure for teachers and it is precisely these schools which do not offer the range of ordinary level course for children to take.

Fourthly, the importance of the provision of courses is underlined in the correlations between measures of staying on at school and the number of ordinary and advanced level courses provided. The correlations are not significant for certificate of secondary education courses. In addition, there is a negative correlation between the number of CSE enrolments and the number of ordinary level courses available. This suggests that schools which offer conventional school certificate courses are less likely to enrol children into CSE courses. It thus appears that the examination structure of Sunderland schools works very much in the favour of those who would otherwise take only ordinary level courses.

Finally, the only measure which we have which indicates something of

Table 4 Product moment correlation coefficients between education provision and attainment

	43	44	45	58	59	60	62	63	65
2	−0.23	0.37	−0.36	0.20	0.45	0.08	0.41	0.30	−0.13
7	−0.18	0.60	−0.41	0.56	0.66	0.30	0.63	0.46	−0.20
16	−0.06	0.65	−0.47	0.46	0.76	0.62	0.75	0.66	−0.24
17	−0.20	−0.21	0.13	−0.23	−0.18	−0.13	−0.16	−0.16	−0.29
19	−0.30	0.29	−0.01	0.18	0.31	0.45	0.31	0.44	−0.49
22	−0.26	0.10	−0.01	−0.20	0.11	0.22	0.16	0.23	−0.43
24	0.21	−0.09	0.04	0.11	−0.03	0.06	0.02	0.04	−0.21
27	−0.32	−0.25	0.12	−0.16	−0.22	−0.33	−0.23	−0.27	−0.37
30	0.39	−0.29	−0.16	−0.19	−0.27	−0.56	−0.29	−0.54	0.18
32	0.10	0.33	−0.41	−0.02	0.34	0.30	0.38	0.30	−0.06
40	0.02	0.70	−0.38	0.67	c.76	0.55	0.70	0.68	−0.25
41	−0.07	0.88	−0.46	0.72	0.94	0.64	0.89	0.76	−0.27
42	−0.53	0.11	0.09	0.08	0.18	−0.12	0.07	0.02	−0.26
39	−0.15	−0.49	0.23	−0.55	−0.52	−0.59	−0.49	−0.61	0.17
14	−0.20	−0.38	0.22	−0.20	−0.28	−0.26	−0.33	−0.16	−0.08

the social class make up of the school i.e. the proportion of those children receiving school meals who receive them free of charge, is negatively correlated with all the attainment variables. This result is consistent with conventional expectations that working class children do less well at school and are more likely to leave at the statutory leaving age. The pattern of correlation for the free school meals variable does support the general observation that children from low income families are more likely to attend smaller, less well-provided for schools offering negligible examination opportunities. They are also more likely to be taught by young, less experienced staff. There is therefore, some slight evidence of a spatial correspondence between the catchment area of a school and its quality which works to the disadvantage of working class children.

The cluster analysis

The data discussed so far lends weight to the overwhelming suspicion that the schools in Sunderland fall into a number of distinct types. At one extreme are the successful, large schools and at the other the smaller under-resourced former secondary modern schools. To describe these groups more effectively we subjected the data to cluster analysis. As we have already explained this is a procedure which groups together the cases in a survey – in this case schools – so that a number of distinct groupings of cases which most resemble one another are distinguished. The results of this procedure were not unexpected; the schools grouped themselves into three main groups or clusters and they can be described in the following way.[16]

Cluster one

This cluster contains the larger schools with the higher rates of educational attainment. They are the schools in which a large proportion of the teaching staff are graduates. The staff of these schools is slightly more experienced in terms of numbers of years' teaching than staff in other schools, although their service record within the schools is almost identical to that of school staff in other clusters. The staff of these schools are more likely to be placed on the higher grades of the Burnham scale than staff in other schools. The parents of the children who attend the schools in this cluster are more affluent than those in other clusters. The mean figure for the proportion of children receiving school meals who receive them free is 33.19 per cent. For schools in cluster one the mean figure is 15.13 per cent. These schools provide a wide range of examinable courses at all levels and have twice the overall average of children staying on at school beyond statutory minimum leaving age. A high proportion of the children attending these schools acquire university qualifications – 45 per cent gain two or more advanced level subjects compared with a mean figure of 19 per cent for the town as a whole. The total number of ordinary and advanced level passes per pupil is much higher than the average for all other secondary schools. These figures are also reflected in the patterns of higher education entrance. These schools are oriented towards university education sending proportionately more pupils to university than any other form of higher education. These generalizations apply to cluster one whether the measures in the survey applicable only to schools with sixth forms are excluded from the clustering or not.[17]

Cluster two

This cluster includes a small number of schools and the overall cluster averages are therefore considerably distorted. An inspection of the cluster variables reveals these schools tend to be medium-sized moderately successful schools with a much less than average proportion of children from low income families. These results cannot be taken seriously, however, since the number of cases in the cluster is too small.[18]

Cluster three

Whether sixth-form variables are masked or unmasked makes little difference to the schools in this cluster.[19] They are the small former secondary modern schools. They do not have a sixth form. Paradoxically, they have small classes. Over 50 per cent of the children receiving school meals receive them free of charge. A very small proportion of the staff have graduate qualifications and a slightly higher than average number of staff have less than one year's teaching experience. Staff turnover in these schools is higher than for the town as a whole. This is no doubt explained by the absence of a career structure for staff in these schools. Although some ordinary level courses are offered in these schools the range is small and enrolments low. The main examination is the secondary school certificate. A very small proportion of children stay on beyond the statutory minimum leaving age. Of those staying on an insignificant number gain ordinary level examination passes although these schools have slightly above average successes in the CSE examinations. It is significant therefore, that a much higher than average proportion of pupils from these schools go on to local colleges of further education and industrial employment.

Conclusion

These results need to be interpreted from two points of view; firstly, from the point of view of sociological theories of educational attainment and secondly, from the point of view of educational policy in Sunderland.

From the point of view of sociological theory, such results lend further weight to the general and well-known association between educational attainment and social class but they do so in a way which implicates the structure of schooling itself as a decisive explanatory variable. Robson noted in 1968 a close correspondence in Sunderland between the test performance of children at the infamous 11 + examination with their social class background and place of residence. Children from working class areas had, on the whole, lower IQscores than children from better-off areas in Sunderland. Patterns of educational aspiration, too, followed the same logic of distribution as IQ scores. Robson attributed a substantial amount of the variation in IQ scores among children to a number of 'areal forces' which, in his opinion were more significant than the summary variable, social class, in explaining test scores. He described these areal forces in the following way.

1 Community ethos

Pointing to the absence of grammar school oriented attitudes among working class communities in Sunderland Robson writes:

> The geographical immobility of the working class is perhaps a reason for its parochialism and conservatism. With this geographically based sense of community, the local secondary modern school, built within the local area, falls naturally into a neighbourhood role; a role which the grammar school usually built outside the immediate area of residence, cannot as easily play. That the grammar school is built at a distance from the working class area is partly a reflection of the social class for which it caters and also of the small but widely scattered, non-local population which it serves. Such physical distance has, for the working class area, a connotation of foreigness which it has not necessarily got for the middle class area. Without labouring the theme, it would seem that the middle class parent can more easily accept the grammar school as 'their' school even though it is not built within their own neighbourhood. For the working class population, the fact of its physical distance merely reinforces the fact that the grammar school disseminates middle class standards anyway.[20]

He reinforces this point a little later in an observation which has a significance far greater than that which he attributes to it, when he says,

> This isolation of the working class areas and the stultifying effects that it can have on the development of attitudes towards education is

exacerbated by the fact that the catchment areas of the various schools tend to follow the socio-economic pattern of the town.[21]

Here Robson is noting a historical correspondence in the development of both primary and secondary schooling in both Sunderland and the country as a whole. It is a correspondence which is also reflected in the kind of education patterning contained in cluster three which has already been described. Working class children are structurally destined to attend the older, poorer schools.

2 Overcrowding

Under this heading, Robson makes the point that living in overcrowded conditions can produce 'apathy and sluggishness'. He expands the argument with the comment:

> The urban child in certain environments can then become ill-suited to the demands made on him by education...[22]

3 Age structure

Where there are large numbers of working class children playing on the streets (a cultural characteristic of many working class areas which in itself is related to poor housing) there are tendencies which Robson claims 'work against the development of self-sufficiency'.[23]

The kind of observation which Robson makes of Sunderland are based upon a close analysis of survey data on attitudes towards education in selected areas of the town. The more important point, however, is that the concepts which have informed his data collection and interpretation of his results are derived from a conventional sociology which can be criticised for failing to examine the structure of opportunities in education. At no point in his account of attitudes to education does Robson attempt to assess the historical role of the opportunities, the school or parental attitudes. He is well aware of the localism in the working class attachment to the secondary modern school and the symbolic distance of grammar schools from such parents. The extent to which such attitudes are the outcome of an historically based and realistic assessment of the kinds of opportunities which actually exist in education in different areas of Sunderland is not measured.[24]

While not wishing to deny the validity of Robson's description of parental attitudes the results we have obtained suggest that such attitudes may very well be related to the kinds of results schools for the working classes in Sunderland have been historically able to deliver. It is easy to see why the old Bede Grammar school has become the focus of local pride and politics – it produces results. At the time when the Sunderland Education Committee announced (in 1972) the possible closure of the town's secondary modern schools as a step towards comprehensive reorganization nobody leaped to their defence. They were not at the centre of anyone's aspirations.

Unfortunately, however, the results we have at this stage do not allow us to answer these kinds of questions. If schools can, irrespective of the social class and neighbourhood background of their children, prime the pump of educational achievement, then their capacity to do so needs to be examined with different research procedures from those employed in this part of our research. Our results do not allow us to ask the important question of just how far levels of provision make a difference. We have no adequate measure of social class background and we have not had the resources to relate data about schools to data about children in schools.

The correspondence which we have observed, however, between social class, quality of school and various attainment measures is too strong to be dismissed.

From the point of view of local education policy the results we have obtained vindicate the general lines of change being pursued. There can be little justification in retaining small former secondary schools. However, given the current financial constraints on school building and the small likelihood that Sunderland, again for historical reasons, will be able to afford an ambitious building programme, there is no justification whatsoever in marking time with the present structure of educational provision which adds the insult of selection at eleven to the ignominy of unequal opportunities.

Appendix
Variable List Continuous Variables

Variable Number Name and Measurement

1 Length of existence of school in current form
2 Number of forms of entry
3 Total current size (pupils)
4 Percentage of school in 5th year
5 Percentage of school in 6th year
6 Percentage of school in 7th year
7 Numbers of staff including Head
8 Proportion of part-time staff
9 Percentage of vacancies on staff
10 Class size 1st year

11 Class size 5th year
12 Class size 7th year
13 Pupil teacher ratio 1st year
14 Pupil teacher ratio 5th year
15 Age of main school building
16 Percentage of staff graduates
17 Percentage of staff with 0–1 years teaching experience
18 Percentage of staff with 1–3 years teaching experience
19 Percentage of staff with 4–8 years teaching experience
20 Percentage of staff with 9–12 years teaching experience
21 Percentage of staff with 13 + years teaching experience
22 Percentage of staff with 0–1 years service in school
23 Percentage of staff with 1–3 years service in school
24 Percentage of staff with 4–8 years service in school
25 Percentage of staff with 9–12 years service in school
26 Percentage of staff with 13 + years service in school
27 Average percentage staff turnover. Calculated over four year period and excluding retirement
28 Percentage of staff on Deputy Head grade Burnham scale
29 Percentage of staff on Senior Master grade, Burnham scale
30 Percentage of staff on grade 1 Burnham scale
31 Percentage of staff on grade 2 Burnham scale
32 Percentage of staff on grade 3 Burnham scale
33 Percentage of staff on grade 4 Burnham scale
34 Percentage of staff on grade 5 Burnham scale
35 Capitation Allowance per pupil 1968/69
36 Capitation Allowance per pupil 1969/70
37 Capitation Allowance per pupil 1970/71
38 Capitation Allowance per pupil 1971/72
39 Percentage of children taking school meals who take them free of charge
40 Total number of ordinary level courses offered
41 Total number of advanced level courses offered
42 Total number of secondary school certificate courses offered
43 Average ordinary level enrollment i.e. All O no. 5th year pupils
44 Average advanced level enrollment i.e. All A no. 7th year pupils
45 Average secondary school certificate enrollment i.e. All CSE no. 5th year pupils
46 Percentage female entrance as proportion of total examination entrance ordinary level science
47 Percentage female entrance as proportion of total examination entrance advanced level science

48 Average female entrance as porportion of total examination entrance CSE science

49 Average female entrance as proportion of total examination entrance ordinary level languages

50 Average female entrance as proportion of total examination entrance advanced level languages

51 Average female entrance as proportion of total examination entrance CSE level languages

52 Average female entrance as proportion of total examination entrance ordinary level humanities

53 Average female entrance as proportion of total examination entrance advanced level humanities

54 Average female entrance as proportion of total examination entrance CSE level humanities

55 Number of years in which the school has offered ordinary level subjects

56 Number of years in which the school has offered advanced level subjects

57 Number of years in which the school has offered CSE level subjects

58 Percentage of 4th year pupils in 1970/71 entering the 5th year in 1971/72

59 Percentage of 5th year pupils in 1971 entering the 6th year 1972

60 Percentage of 5th year pupils in 1972 gaining five or more ordinary level passes

61 Percentage of 7th year pupils in 1972 gaining two or more advanced level passes

62 Percentage of 5th year pupils in 1972 gaining five or more CSE level grade one passes

63 Total number of ordinary level passes per 5th year pupil 1972

64 Total number of advanced level passes per 7th year pupil 1972

65 Total number of CSE grade one passes per 5th year pupil 1972

66 Percentage of those in 1972 gaining places at University who were male

67 Percentage of those in 1972 gaining places at University who were female

68 Total percentage of 7th year pupils in 1972 who gained places at University

69 Percentage of 7th year pupils in 1972 who went to Polytechnics who were male

70 Percentage of 7th year pupils in 1972 who gained places at Polytechnics who were female

71 Total percentage of pupils in 7th year 1972 who gained places at Polytechnics

72 Percentage of both 5th & 7th year students who gained places in further education in 1972 who were male

73 Percentage of both 5th & 7th year students who gained places

74 Total percentage of pupils in 1972 who gained places in further education

75 Percentage of 7th year pupils in 1972 who gained places at teacher training colleges who were male

76 Percentage of 7th year pupils in 1972 who gained places at teacher training colleges who were female

77 Total percentage of 7th year pupils in 1972 who gained places at teacher training colleges

78 Percentage of 5th year in 1972 who gained apprenticeships

Notes

1 During the nineteen sixties it became increasingly clear that the expansion of education provision from 1944 onwards had been uneven and had not changed substantially older patterns of spatial inequality among regions of the country and among local education authorities. Indeed, one of the many underlying forces leading to local government reorganization in the early seventies was a belief that larger units of local government would be more effective in allocating resources for education on a more equal basis. In this respect local government reorganization in the seventies must be seen to have its roots in the nineteen thirties when many demands were made for reorganization to increase the tax base of some of the poorer urban boroughs. The importance of such inequalities as part of the structure of persisting wider social inequalities was documented by C. Taylor and N. Ayres in *Born and Bred Unequal* London Longman 1969. Some of the more intractable problems of such inequality were examined in the report of the Plowden Committee, *Children and Their Primary Schools* London HMSO. Central Advisory Council for Education 1969. Much of this work was not particularly analytical. In an early paper, *The Myth of the Restricted Code*, University of Durham Working Papers in Sociology No. 1. David Byrne and I tried

to relate such inequalities to educational life chances. We followed up this work with a book, D.S. Byrne, W. Williamson and B.G. Fletcher, *The Poverty of Education: A Study in the Politics of Opportunity* London, Martin Robertson and Co. 1975. Meanwhile, in the United States of America a similar debate had been opened up by the so-called Coleman Report, i.e. J.S. Coleman *et al. Equality of Educational Opportunity*, Washington, US Office of Education 1966 and by C. Jencks *et al.* in *Inequality: A Reassessment of the Effect of Family and Schooling in America* London Allen Lane 1973. Both Coleman and Jencks argued that resource inequalities in education were not the significant determinants of social class inequalities in educational performance. This view contradicted the position we had taken but the airing of these arguments represents in itself an important departure in this field of study.

2 Our own work was financed by the Social Science Research Council. It had three components: a national study of local authorities in England and Wales which, using the techniques of correlation analysis attempted to measure the degree of variation in patterns of educational attainment which could be attributed to variation in resources and patterns of educational provision; secondly, a study of one local education authority which is reported here, and finally, a study of the way in which school children come to make decisions about staying on or leaving school. Within the overall resources of the research grant the second two enquiries were rather more limited in their scope than we had wished them to be. Our overall thesis was that social class inequalities in educational opportunity and attainment were to a considerable degree the outcome of the way in which children from different social class backgrounds were given differential access to educational resources. We argued, therefore, that the class structuration of educational inequality operated through the mechanisms of resource distribution in society. If this was true, we concluded, then socio-cultural accounts of such inequalities must be seen as fundamentally obscuring structures of inequality and, at worst, justifying them.

3 The reference here is to what we, in our book called the class-culture paradigm of research. Its essential feature is a concentration on the way in which children are moulded by particular social and cultural contexts so that some can succeed at school while others fail. It represents what we felt was the dominant mode of analysis in this area of sociological enquiry. It was given considerable credibility in the late sixties by the research carried out for the Plowden Committee (see above note 1) and subsequently by A.H. Halsey *et al.* in their research

into so-called education priority areas. See A.H. Halsey (1972) *Educational Priority Vol 1*. EPA *Problems and Policies* London HMSO.

4 For excellent discussions of the political significance of these debates see D.C. Morton and D.R. Watson 'Compensatory education and contemporary liberalism in the United States; a sociological view' *International Review of Education* 17 1971, also D.R. Watson 'Urban and Cultural Competence' in *Education in the Cities of England* P. Raggett (ed) London Sage Publication 1973.

5 For an account of the significance of these arguments for how a capitalist society works see S. Bowles and H. Gintis (1976) *Schooling in Capitalist America* London, Routledge and Kegan Paul. For a discussion of the empirical and methodological difficulties see D. Pyle 'Models of Educational Attainment ... A Comment' *Urban Education* July 1975; D. Pyle 'Aspects of Resource Allocation by Local Education Authorities' Social and Economic Administration Vol 10, No. 2 1976. See also D. Hutchinson 'Areas of Difference. A Critique of the Work of Byrne and Williamson on Regional Inequalities in Educational Attainment' *Quality and Quantity* 9 1975. Some of these issues are also discussed in D.S. Byrne W. Williamson and B.G. Fletcher *op. cit. The Poverty of Education*.

6 It is technically very difficult to measure educational attainment. In our own work we have used the measure available until 1973 of staying at school beyond the ages of sixteen and seventeen. Clearly this does not tell us much about how clever people are or have become. But it does at least point to those groups who are using the educational system to give access to white collar employment. In this respect, although their attainment may not be in some sense educationally significant it is at least socially significant. For this reason we maintain that attainment measures are directly relevant to the discussions about social inequality in education.

7 ROBSON, B.T. *Urban Analysis: A Study of City Structure* (1969) Cambridge University Press.

8 As part of the national study we subjected our data to cluster analysis. The procedure resulted in the description of six main types of local authority. Cluster analysis is a statistical technique which allows a researcher to scan the data he has collected about different cases in a study, say, about local authorities or schools or even individuals and to analyse this data in such a way that those cases which most resemble one another can be grouped together and distinguished from other cases which they do not resemble. In short, the technique of cluster analysis is one way of producing typologies of cases from data descriptions of the cases being considered. It is not, as such, an

analytical technique; rather it is a form of data description. In *The Poverty of Education op. cit* the identified six main types were as follows: 1 working class authorities, predominantly labour controlled; low levels of attainment 2 middle class county boroughs; high attainment 3 mainly working-class urban boroughs; average attainment rates 4 mixed population, high levels of expenditure, high levels of attainment 5 mainly rural areas, below average attainment 6 mainly Welsh rural authorities. For a fuller description of these types and a listing of which local authority falls into which group see *The Poverty of Education* chapter 5.

9 ROBSON B.T. *op. cit.* p. 75.

10 *ibid* p. 85.

11 See DENNIS, N. (1972) *Public Participation and Planners Blight* London Faber and Faber.

12 The data upon which the remainder of this report deals comes, unless otherwise stated from questionnaires which were filled in by the Headteachers of the secondary schools in Sunderland. The questionnaire asked for data on schools resources, courses, course enrollments and examination successes, teachers and student careers in higher education.

13 The national average figure for all schools, excluding retirement, is 18.0 per cent. See DES *Report on Education* No. 79 1974.

14 The full list of variables employed in the correlation studies is set out in the Appendix. The data collected was subject to correlation analysis. This technique is used to measure how strongly two or more variables relate to one another. In itself it cannot prove anything; it merely shows the strength of an association between two variables. The strength of the relationship is given using the measuring range -1.0 to $+1.0$. A correlation of $+0.4$ or above is considered to be strong and significant, less than that weak and probably insignificant. Correlations with a negative value indicate that variables change in opposite directions to one another. The correlation coefficient must therefore always be interpreted according to the expectations of a particular theoretical perspective or proposition.

15 KING, R. (1974) 'Social Class and Educational Attainment: An LEA Case Study' *Policy and Politics* Vol. 3 No. 1.

16 For reasons of space we have not set out the tabular results of the cluster analysis. The results are available in the final report to the SSRC in which the main results of our research project are described. SSRC final reports are available from the National Lending Library. The report in question is *The Effect of Local Education Authority*

Resources and Policies on Educational Attainment D.S. Byrne and W. Williamson 1975.

17 There are seven schools in this cluster.

18 There are three schools in this cluster.

19 The techniques of cluster analysis allow a researcher to exclude some information about a given case from the analysis. This is called masking. In this study we masked some of the measures concerning sixth forms so that we could inspect the data for schools without sixth forms a little more closely.

20 ROBSON, B.T. *op. cit.* p.222.

21 *ibid* p.224.

22 *ibid* p.227.

23 *ibid* p.228.

24 In this respect Robson's work is a good example of a study conceived from within the class culture paradigm; his perspective makes him sensitive to cultural differences among pupils rather than to the structural inequalities of the educational system itself and their importance in predicting different educational careers. His perspective therefore delimits the range of questions he is prepared to ask.

2.5   The allocation of curricular resources

E.M. Byrne

The relationship of curricular aims, the allocation of curricular resources and administrative and education ideologies is at best difficult, not to say sensitive. The liberal-educationists eschew manpower planning, the social engineers seek relevance in education and neither seems conscious of the need to monitor and evaluate where the resources actually go and why.

Yet the discriminal patterns of allocating resources in the three survey areas, while predictable in their time, appeared to be based on widespread assumptions bearing little traceable relationship to assessed educational needs according to 'age, ability and aptitude' or to future social and industrial needs. What assumptions?

For example, only the top 12 per cent, 15 per cent or 25 per cent of the ability range respectively in the survey areas could cope with external examinations – until the late 1950s and mid-1960s proved the authorities wrong. But by then scores of schools had been designed and staffed for non-examination syllabuses without extended courses. Small schools are better than large schools for the less able whatever the educational product at 15 + ; but grammar school children need large, economic and viable schools offering a wider variety of subjects. The education of boys ought to be different from the education of girls. Secondary modern pupils don't want to stay on for a fifth year. Rural children and those in small schools don't need the full range of specialist subjects or resources. Less able pupils need less money, fewer staff, lower paid staff than the academically bright. Children in new schools need more money than those in old schools. Children in non-grammar schools don't need or can't profit from Nuffield science projects, Project Technology, audio-visual language courses. They shouldn't even learn modern languages. Girls don't want to do physics; boys don't want to do biology or to cook. Clever pupils don't

---

Source: *Planning and educational inequality* (1974), pp. 26–46

like or need technical crafts. And above all, teachers in post-war schools, especially non-grammar schools, can offer a full education in schools overcrowded by 10 per cent, 15 per cent or even 20 per cent.

But were any of these assumptions valid? For if they were not, they nevertheless underlay what actually happened to resources in the survey areas. It became evident from both records and from interviews with Council and Committee members, officers, heads and HMIS, that many assumptions were implicit, inherited and unexamined in current social terms. To question the basis of the assumptions caused almost universal surprise.

There may be general agreement that the main aim of education is to offer intellectual and creative educational development to each child to the highest degree of excellence for his age, ability and aptitude. This is a platitude, however, which begs the social question what the child is to do with the excellence once achieved? And excellence in what, if there is a choice, when resources are rationed – as accommodation and staff were for the whole twenty year period?

Opinions are, predictably enough, sharply divided on the further aims of secondary education, but most committee members, education officers and teachers interviewed by the writer in 1968–69 accepted that a second fundamental aim in the secondary years should be to equip a boy or girl for the most highly skilled employment, trade or profession of which they are capable. The findings of the report of the Schools Council in 1968 on young school-leavers give prominence indeed to the great importance which fifteen-year-old school-leavers attach to the school's role as instrumental in teaching them those things which would enable them 'to get as good jobs or careers as possible'. Eighty-six per cent of boys and 88 per cent of girls rated this as the most important school objective. About the same percentage of parents rated help towards good jobs or careers as a major school objective.[1]

About half of those involved in providing education interviewed by the writer, also accepted as a concurrent aim that the education system should be producing the skilled manpower needed by the country as a whole, by the region or by the locality. This is dangerous ground for an idealistic educationalist; but reform, innovation and development rarely wait upon a secure and uncontroversial path.

The desire of a schoolchild for the best job of which he or she is capable, is a form of explicit demand; as is the need of the country for trained labour. Are these two principles mutually exclusive? Should the needs of the individual outweigh the needs of industry, commerce and the public services for a steady flow of appropriately trained personnel? The *reductio ad absurdum* on the one hand might be a plethora of unemployable medieval linguists and social psychologists, while an equally unacceptable converse would be the 'direction' at 18 + of potential commercial managers or scientific research workers into sewage outfall engineering. Somewhere between the two extremes, decisions are in fact now already made by both central and local government agencies and by universities and polytechnics which are aimed at controlling resources for secondary, further and higher education, in an attempt to strike a balance of opportunity while eschewing the ultimate sanction of direction.

Floud and Halsey accepted at an early stage that an element of vocational bias and a responsibility to provide trained manpower, were valid educational aims, and concluded in 1956 that:

> Education affects the efficiency of the distribution of labour by its influence on both the "ability" and the "opportunity"; the skill of labour at various levels reflects the scale and nature of education provision, which exercises a decisive influence on vocational choice and on movement between occupations, i.e. on the adjustment of the supply to the demand of trained labour.[2]

Perhaps the most striking illustrations of the basic relationship were given by the 1968 (Swann) Committee on Manpower Resources for Science and Technology which concluded that:

> at present the pattern of supply of highly qualified manpower reflects in large measure the studies pursued by individuals at school and in higher education.[3]

and there is good reason to accept this view.

It is difficult to avoid the suggestion that in fact such negative factors as lack of rooms, teachers and examinations determines and limits the supply and distribution of skilled manpower quite as strongly as the positive guidance and related developments which many apparently eschew on philosophical or liberal grounds. For the less able moreover, manpower, employment and capacity on leaving school become an essentially local and not regional or national equation.

Curricular resources

For the purpose of the argument these are defined here as buildings, staff, books, equipment and money. The demand made by the curriculum on the pool of resources available to a local education authority, can be both implicit and explicit. The addition of extended courses to non-grammar schools carries, for example, an implicit assumption that extra money and staff will need to be provided. The addition of new subjects to a traditional course, means at the least, new staff, books and materials. Curricular innovation sponsored by, for example, the Schools Council or by local teachers' centres, creates further demand on the limited money for furniture, books and apparatus. Explicitly, staff make demands on a head teacher for more money or different equipment for their own department; for more periods on the timetable; even for more accommodation. Pupils and parents may specifically ask for new opportunities, for example a course in electronics or pre-nursing to match local employment outlets; or for a foreign language not hitherto taught.

Discriminal education by ability

In all three areas, as indeed elsewhere, two assumptions which might be questioned have been seen consistently to underly educational planning and the consequent resource-allocation for the more able children. First, that these necessarily need longer in school than the non-grammar pupils; and secondly, that they necessarily need more staff, more highly paid staff and more money for equipment and books. The questioning of these basic assumptions was regarded with considerable surprise in all three survey areas.

Authorities had built and staffed grammar schools (or streams) for five full years (plus an extended course to 18 years for about half of each grammar school age group). But local authorities, encouraged by the Ministry of Education, had planned and built schools for non-grammar children for four-year courses only. By the time that belatedly, Nottingham and Northumberland decided to build for a full fifth year, the Ministry then refused to allow the authorities to do so for a further ten years. But in practice in all three survey areas, secondary modern children stayed on after 15 + in defiance of the lack of accommodation with the result that over half of the schools surveyed in 1968–69 were still overcrowded. Effectively, accommodation had to be 'rationed'. Either all pupils were taught less specialist work, because appropriate rooms were not available; or some were not taught science or crafts at all. The Ministry considered, it appeared, that the regular economic crises meant that we could not afford to allow authorities to spend as much of their own money, as would provide fully for non-grammar pupils to remain at school until they were sixteen.

Secondly, it had been assumed by the educational administrators that for all courses and in all subjects, intelligent pupils need more money per capita for books and equipment than the less able. A similar assumption is made, that the curricular needs of all older pupils (over fifteen) necessarily involve more money than those of all younger pupils. All three authorities surveyed, in common with most at that period, operated a differential scheme of school allowances based on these principles. Head teachers of the schools surveyed were asked how they would have related a scheme of equipment and capitation allowances to the needs of their particular pupils; and whether they agreed with the differential rates for pupils in grammar schools and streams. Most of the heads of non-grammar schools produced realistic examples of curricular methods based on third and fourth year programmes, for remedial English, integrated studies in the humanities and basic modern languages costing up to twice the amount needed for a typical arts-based sixth form course. Four heads of grammar schools argued strongly for more favourable allowances for pupils in the remedial and duller streams of non-grammar schools. Five schools produced schemes for interdisciplinary or integrated studies costing substantially more than traditional history or geography – but could not obtain extra funds for the new courses because these were not (a) for examination candidates or (b) suitable to qualify for the Schools Council special projects allowances. Three-quarters of all heads (grammar and non-grammar) disapproved of a differential allowance for pupils under sixteen.

Curricular distinctions were widespread. In practice, the more able pupils tend to have been taught two or three separate sciences, while those in secondary modern schools have been assumed, for the most part on little real evidence, to be able to grasp only a diluted course of the simpler aspects of the three main sciences, presented as 'general science'. This was especially so in one-, two- and three-form entry schools in the survey areas which had only one multi-purpose laboratory. The deliberate design of 'general laboratories' has hindered the teaching of specialist sciences which in turn in four instances in schools surveyed, hindered pupils from transferring to grammar schools at 15 + or 16 + for lack of the right preparatory work. Conversely, however, one modern school in an area of high unemployment took a difficult decision to force physics on all boys (not girls) after the third year because the neighbouring grammar school would not accept sixth form entrants on transfer possessing 'general science' only, as a basis for advanced work. And the head could not tell at 14 + which boys might wish to transfer.

An analysis of the courses offered by the forty-two schools surveyed revealed that of the six schools doing Nuffield Science, three were grammar and two were technical schools. The only modern school involved in Nuffield work happened to have a head of science who was also the county organizer for Nuffield physics. All three schools involved in Project Technology, were also grammar schools heavily involved with Nuffield Science. The average annual allowance for Nuffield Science awarded to the seven schools from the special 'pool' controlled by the local authority inspectors, ranged from £300 – £500 per year per science subject. The secondary modern schools not able to afford to use the Nuffield approach, received from £50 to £80 per laboratory from the schools' allowance. At least one grammar and 12 non-grammar schools would have liked to use Nuffield programmes. But typical comments were 'the money goes to the grammar schools' and 'we would need £1,000 grant and about £300 a year to start each subject – and we haven't even the basic laboratories yet'. The special allowance for teaching science using Nuffield syllabuses were awarded to about 10 per cent of secondary schools in the survey areas. The national position is probably not dissimilar. Presumably one aim of the Schools Council in developing new approaches to learning such as these science-based courses is generally to improve our current methods of helping children to learn. There appeared to be widespread agreement however among teachers and inspectors in 1968 that to introduce the Nuffield approach to a school required about £1,000 initial grant and about £300 per annum maintenance allowance, for each science subject.

Since furniture, equipment, books, stationery and apparatus combined, accounted in the survey period for slightly less than 5 per cent of the total secondary education revenue budget, to have allocated so much money to two sciences out of nearly twenty subjects would be disproportionate and beyond the economic means of the authorities.

Similar extrapolations for the cost of applying more widely other new curricular approaches for different subjects, in turn make it seem most unlikely that the innovation which currently is supported in about 10 per cent of secondary schools with special project allowances, can be applied even to the majority of schools in the foreseeable future. This must put into question the principles on which the financing of the more expensive schemes of innovation are currently based.

The general position on revenue expenditure was not dissimilar in that the automatic grammar/non-grammar differential was equally marked. The Lincoln accounts were kept in such a way that it has been possible to isolate key sectors of expenditure for grammar and for non-grammar schools, and these figures are used. The Lincoln figures are used here therefore as an example which it is suspected would be mirrored elsewhere if comparable statistics could be isolated.

The following table shows the very substantial advantage enjoyed by grammar school pupils over a period of thirteen years.

The overall figures conceal further anomalies. Only rarely did the salaries of teachers of the 60 per cent or so pupils in modern schools exceed in total those of the teachers of the 40 per cent or so in grammar schools (42 per cent of all pupils on roll; 25 per cent of the age group).

Table 1 Annual gross revenue expenditure per pupil — maintained secondary schools

Year	Grammar £	Index	Modern £	Index
1949–50	46.57	100	32.7	100
1954–55	62.66	135	42.1	129
1958–59	83.44	179	57.46	175
1962–63	99.94	215	75.48	230

The differential was slightly less marked for educational equipment etc., although the cost per pupil of all educational furniture and equipment was still far higher in the grammar schools. Further analysis of the figures on which Table 1 is based shows that the grammar schools had proportionately far more money for books, but did less well on stationery and consumable stock.

Even less accountable is the difference which has been traced between expenditure on grammar and modern schools respectively in Lincoln, on other items. The figures per head annually for maintenance of buildings and grounds, for example could not be held necessarily to be linked directly with courses organized at each group of schools. Yet the grammar schools consistently obtained a larger proportion of the budget.

The other surprising fact is that the cost of maintenance rose so little over the years but there is some evidence from interviews that this element of the budget was especially vulnerable to cuts by Finance Committee seeking reductions in rateborne expenditure.

The secondary modern schools fared no better from the capital budget. Of £12,081 capital expenditure on secondary schools from 1946 to 1953 in Lincoln for example, only £1,279 was spent on the six county secondary modern schools, or one tenth; the remaining nine-tenths going to the four grammar schools. Yet from 1947 onwards there were consistently more pupils in the secondary modern schools than in the grammar schools.

This evidence supports the hypothesis that resources were not allocated in relation to demand, but according to (a) the philosophy of the Chief Education Officer and his Committee, (b) outside factors such as the Burnham agreements, and (c) inherited attitudes on the apparent need for preferential staffing and allowances for able pupils. For the secondary modern heads did fight for more resources, supported by their governors; but with no significant success. The grammar school heads appeared to exert no direct pressure in financial terms. The assumption was taken for granted by those in leadership, that the grammar schools should receive more and the educational reasons for the assumption do not appear to have been re-examined. It may be argued that this is now history. But generations of pupils educated in this twenty-year period are now competing with more fortunate peers in the adult employment market.

Breadth of curriculum – the less able

About two-thirds of heads and staffs in non-grammar schools in all three survey areas regretted the limited curriculm which they were constrained to offer. It was limited partly because of lack of appropriate staff, money and accommodation, and partly because of an inherited conception of what was 'suitable' for non-grammar children. In Nottingham and Northumberland in particular, where only 12 per cent to 15 per cent achieved entry to grammar schools until the late 1950s, the major curricular loss to the children which concerned the teachers, was the learning of modern languages.

One reason why the teaching of modern languages was mainly limited to the academically gifted in the survey period was the expressed aim of language teaching at the time. On the continent, and especially in countries like Holland whose very trade, not merely its tourism, depended on widespread competence in French, German and English, the aim was to teach pupils to speak and understand foreign languages fluently. So basic an aim has perhaps suffered in England from the pejorative connotation of 'usefulness', apparently alien to those concerned with a liberal (academic) education. Perhaps the dominant concept of the role of language teaching for much of the period from 1945 to the mid-1960s can be summarized by the following almost incredible quotation from a pamphlet issued by the Classical Association in 1967. Despite the provenance of the statement, it is one which some modern language teachers seem still to support and which the policy of many external examination Boards appear to have supported until relatively recently.

> Modern languages courses in schools are not designed solely, or even principally, to produce the ability to speak fluently the language concerned. A main object of these courses is precisely the same as that of classics courses, to stimulate an interest in the literature and civilization of another country.[4]

It can be seen that wherever this academic, literary attitude was held, the only resources regarded as necessary would be literary texts and a good teacher, and the subject as such would be regarded as inappropriate for non-academic children. And in the survey areas, very few non-grammar schools offered modern languages even when they admitted from 85 per cent to 88 per cent of the age group. None of the three authorities made serious efforts generally to staff and equip non-grammar schools for languages, until towards the end of the survey period. In the context of England's admission to the European Economic Community, this highlights an urgent need for resources to be specifically allocated for a special remedial adult education programme of modern language teaching, based on industry and commerce. It might well be argued again that resources have been allocated in accordance with inherited assumptions and not in direct relation to the pupils' or the country's needs.

Discriminal education by sex

A similar dichotomy is apparent in relation to the education of boys and the education of girls. If education according to the individual needs of 'age, ability and aptitude' is desirable, ought there necessarily to be any difference between the education of boys and of girls? Is there much objective psychological evidence that boys and girls have innately different needs or mental capabilities? But in the three survey areas this was the strongest inherited assumption underlying the design of schools and the allocation of resources. Boys' and girls' needs were held to be different.

The expectation of different educational goals was first translated into different accommodation standards. Girls' schools and boys' schools have different types and standards of accommodation. No metalwork in girls' and no housecraft in boys' schools – an inherited assumption of limited educational need and demand not matched by Sweden's practice of providing homecrafts and handicrafts for both.[5] Predictable differentiation, but not related to demand. Less defensible was the application of the Building Bulletin 2A which for 20 years specified a lower standard of scientific and technical facilities in girls' than in boys' schools.

But most schools in the survey areas were mixed – 88 out of 133. Since most of them were overcrowded during the survey period, however, accommodation had to be rationed (700 pupils into 520 places won't go; fewer periods per subject or some don't study it at all). It was by no means uncommon practice to give laboratory preference to boys (taking physics), teaching biology to girls in classrooms. The findings of the national science teachers' survey of 1960[6] were mirrored in the survey areas both in the period up to 1965 and during the schools' survey in 1968, except that by 1968 the sharp differential in science allowances for boys and for girls had been abolished. Science and technical studies were still female Cinderellas.

In many mixed schools visited in the three survey areas moreover even where laboratories were freely available in theory to both sexes, many heads created quite separate and differently biased courses and options for boys and for girls respectively at 13 + or 14 +. Even where CSE and not GCE was offered, heads tended to 'channel' girls to biology and boys to physics. Seventeen schools quite deliberately split boys and girls for science. But one mixed grammar school deliberately mixed its science groups – and had an advanced physics group of twenty two boys and seventeen girls. A bilateral school in Nottingham insisted on all girls doing a minimum of either chemistry or physics. Proportionately more girls a year from that school trained as laboratory technicians or entered technical industries on leaving school.

There were other tacit assumptions in the survey area, underlying 'technical' options in extended courses offered to boys or to girls at 13 + or 14 +, as 'interest based courses', in the words of one headmaster. For example, prenursing was offered only to girls – except at Hexham after the appointment of a male matron at the local hospital, when the boys developed an interest. Similarly, most of the schools surveyed, offering 'commerce', (which meant elementary shorthand and typing) organized it as a girls' option *cross-set* with technical studies or other 'boys' subjects on the timetable. And every mixed school organized its timetable so that needlework and homecraft were cross-set with woodwork and metalwork, with the result that pupils could not choose any two out of the four. Only two schools either allowed or encouraged boys to take homecrafts and girls to take handicrafts. Three child-care courses were designated for girls only. Even linked courses with local Colleges of Further Education were organized by sex of pupils – girls to the commerce and boys to the engineering departments.

Allocation of revenue resources also appeared to be consistently unequal. Again the illustrations are from Lincoln but there was some evidence in both other areas of patterns not dissimilar. Before the 1956–61 period, part of the difference can be accounted for by the lack of equal pay for women teachers but this does not by any means wholly account for the different costs per boy and per girl. Boys' schools appear to have had consistently more money (and better staffing) than girls' schools of comparable size and type, whether grammar or modern. As in Nottingham and Northumberland, schools with a head who has been a senior officer of a teachers' union appear to do consistently better than other schools. Four head teachers attributed this to their additional knowledge and experience of the system and their greater confidence in dealing with 'the administration'. Their explicit demands were more articulate.

An analysis of the detailed composition of the estimates for the two girls' and boys' county grammar schools reveals that consistently over twenty years the boys' school received more favourable treatment under the

Burnham reports, and a more favourable allocation of money for special equipment for science and technical subjects, including arrangements for laboratory assistance. The two voluntary aided grammar schools, comparable in type and size, show a similar pattern of apparently preferential treatment for the boys' school.

Extended courses and viable size of school

Here too discriminal assumptions were widespread. All three authorities deliberately planned, designed and built small non-grammar schools of three- or four-form entry for most of the period on the apparent grounds that the less able children needed more pastoral care, and that a school of 450 or 600 was large enough to be viable and small enough to meet the pastoral needs of the children. Viability becomes an important concept only when resources are limited, as they have been in all three areas and as they are likely to remain. In theory, there is no reason why the smallest school should not have a complete range of specialist rooms, specialist staff and equipment allowances. In practice, this would cost more money per pupil and per school than either the Ministry or local authorities have apparently felt able to justify on 'economic' grounds. This is another inherited value judgement since most one- or two-form entry grammar schools (200 or 360 pupils) were in fact provided with the full minimum range of facilities and staff, despite their small size, enabling them to offer a broadly based curriculum. Yet authorities felt 'they could not afford' an equivalent range of facilities for 300 secondary modern children. Some positive discriminations in their favour were awarded to small non-grammar schools in Northumberland but did not, in heads' views, meet fully even all basic needs though the county undoubtedly did a valiant best under the constraints of the Building Code and its limited revenue.

There is little evidence from the survey areas that conscious assessment of educational viability in relation to the staffing and curricular resources available, took place when the development plans were discussed and new schools were planned. The Ministry had however already declared in 1947 that:

> It is manifest that if a reasonable variety of courses to meet the differing aptitudes and abilities of the pupils is to be provided, there should normally be provision for at least two streams of each type of education that the school is intended to provide. Even where a technical school or side is based on a single branch of technical work (e.g. Engineering or Housecraft) it should have at least two streams.[7]

Clearly if new courses were to be based on modern (non-grammar) schools from 1945 onwards, the schools would need more specialist accommodation. Equally clearly other resources would need to be levelled up, since:

> Money provided for any one component in the capital cost of schools will be wasted unless adequate and balanced provision is made simultaneously for the others.[8]

The Ministry consistently refused to authorize capital building to enable authorities to build larger schools or extend existing ones at the rate that their Development plans to provide technical and extended courses, required. And in 1947, only a minority of schools were larger than 501 pupils.

The corollary of larger schools and more extended courses was more fifth-form accommodation, more specialist rooms and more staff. And these were not forthcoming in adequate measure. In practice, despite the Ministry's early statement, extended courses in non-grammar schools were actively discouraged by both the Ministry and its HMIs until the late 1950s and was not positively encouraged until the 1960s.[9] The Ministry controlled the teaching quotas of local authorities, allowing no extra staff for non-grammar courses. It also refused to allow some authorities to build and design for extended courses in the period 1948–58 when capital resources were restricted. Both Nottingham and Northumberland suffered in this way. Notwithstanding, many authorities did develop the principle of extended courses, in non-grammar schools.

Discussion of new approaches to housecraft and handicraft teaching would, of course, be purely academic to heads of schools where the subjects cannot be taught at all.

In 1956 the NUT made a special inquiry into the organization of bias courses, and discovered that in secondary modern schools GCE courses outstripped the rest, followed by commerce, rural science, technical and craft courses. 'In only two replies out of the hundreds we received in making our survey, was it suggested that definite decisions of the authority prevented specific courses in secondary modern schools.'[10]

In the three survey areas the position varied. Lincoln set its face firmly against the development of any bias courses or new developments in secondary modern schools beyond 15 + until 1964, and the promise in the early post-war years that:

> for the pupils in the secondary modern schools it is proposed to develop still further the practical side of the curriculum so that they may continue to make and strengthen their contribution to the needs

of industry and commerce and the future skilled craftsmen employed therein[11]

remained a dead letter in the absence of the provision of the secondary modern schools of workshops, classrooms for fifth-year pupils, extra teachers, head of department posts under the 1956 Burnham report or adequate equipment allowances to replace obsolete apparatus. Nottingham established commercial courses (mostly typing) at a girls' school as early as 1945–1946.

Northumberland tended to limit its intake to grammar schools to about 15 per cent of the relevant age group, and to plan for technical schools with some boarding provision. It built in fact very few technical schools before altering the basis of its development plan in 1959, by which time technical courses were being based at grammar schools, and not at separate technical schools. The county was on the whole tardy in developing any form of grouped course outside the selective schools, and the figures of fifth- and sixth-form stayers in the county have been well below the national average throughout, but are however consistent with the general trend in the North.

External examinations

If the argument for viability tends often to centre on the size of 'economic' teaching groups for pupils aiming at GCE or CSE, this is not necessarily to assume that these pupils and courses are more important. It is to acknowledge that if teachers and laboratories or equipment are being used (a) intensively for from five – seven periods a week per pupil subject and (b) uneconomically for teaching groups of less than eight or five, then the school is 'subsidizing' the GCE and CSE groups from its staffing quota and from its curricular allowances. This in turn may deprive the less able of some skilled teachers, small teaching groups and extra books and equipment unless compensating extra resources are awarded to the smaller schools to offset this. If the head of a small school does not offer external examinations to his more able pupils, he is depriving them in turn of their future opportunity to enter further and higher education or skilled employment. Viability should also be related to the ability of a school to offer adequate remedial education, a wide range of craft-based courses and education for the less able, relevant to their local situation on leaving school.

Many smaller schools could not offer GCE at all. Some could only offer CSE in two or three subjects. But almost all offered some external examination work and seven very small schools attempted to offer both GCE and CSE. Some offered bias courses based on 'interest-based' work, which as we have seen, led the head teachers to assume that girls would wish to take commerce or prenursing and boys engineering or craft courses.

As with accommodation, extended courses create demand for substantial staffing resources. A principle of 'weighting' for older pupils underlies the standard method of assessing the quota of teaching staff for a school. A school with substantial numbers of fifth- and sixth-form pupils will qualify for many more staff who are then available to help to teach the younger pupils. Schools of four-form entry or below, with only a small fifth-year and small GCE groups, will on this basis not be entitled to the extra staff who would automatically be available in a grammar school or a larger school.

In almost all secondary modern schools surveyed (some taking over 80 per cent of the age group) teaching groups for GCE or CSE were below eight. It was not uncommon for teachers to have a single pupil for CSE history, science, or maths. All schools of less than four-entry had had therefore to 'select' the limited subjects to be offered in external examinations. The selection would be based on an advance value judgement (that is by deciding to offer French or Biology and therefore advertising for and appointing a teacher) or on the existing accident of what the existing staff could teach. There are from fifteen to twenty subjects normally available in an averaged sized school. One two-form entry school surveyed, however, only qualified for thirteen full-time staff including the head and deputy head, if the normal staffing quota were followed. A one-form entry school surveyed had a staffing establishment of head + five full-time staff + four visiting teachers for housecraft, science, music and remedial work. Not only were subject options limited because of the need for economic groups; but these schools could only offer a third or a half of the total range of subjects to examination level, because they did not have the full range of staff.

A high correlation was found between lack of opportunity for external examination work in basic subjects in schools where the ability range included pupils potentially able to take GCE and CSE in small and in rural schools, and a higher proportion of leavers entering unskilled employment.

Schools below four-form entry in size made as strong a case for extra compensatory equipment allowances, as for extra staff. The award of a *per capita* allowance for educational visits for example, penalizes outlying small schools who may use almost a full year's allowance on one visit to an urban industrial area. Eight small schools (from one- to three-form entry) argued for a special 'pool' of money to be allocated by local authority inspectors, to bring resources in small schools up to a minimum standard of viability. All eight, and many other heads, considered that basic standards in smaller schools were 'pegged' to enable money to be allocated for Nuffield science, technical projects and experimental special programmes of innovation in grammar and larger schools. 'We are told it is uneconomic to give us a full range of major equipment for 170 pupils', one head of a small rural school commented, 'but it is economic to give £400 a year for fourteen boys to take Advanced level physics using the Nuffield syllabus.'

The pattern of inherent and correlated inequality begins to emerge. Less able children subjected to limited expectations, had less educational opportunity. Rural schools were at a basic disadvantage as were small schools. Girls' opportunities were more limited than boys'. Older schools suffered more. But a substantial proportion of pupils were either in small, non-grammar schools or small single-sex schools; or both. Many were in small, rural non-grammar schools. Short of substantial positive discrimination, the pattern of planning for distributing resources meant that these groups of pupils had a three- or four-fold chance of educational deprivation in the nature of things. We planned for a kind of educational inequality for nearly twenty years.

Notes

1 *Enquiry 1, The Young School Leavers* (Schools Council), London: HMSO 1968, pp.33–34.
2 FLOUD, J. and HALSEY, A. H. 'Education and Occupation: English Secondary Schools and the supply of labour', *The Year Book of Education*, 1956 p.519.
3 *The Flow into Employment of Scientists, Engineers and Technologists* CMND 3760, HMSO, 1968. Preface.
4 *Classics in the School Curriculum*, Council of the Classical Association, 1967, p.7. The Schools Council writing in *The Raising of the School Leaving Age* (HMSO 1968, para. 88) commented that 'there is of course relatively little experience of teaching a foreign language to the pupils who are the concern of this working paper'.
5 *The Status of Women*, report of Swedish Government to the United Nations, 1968.
6 *Provision and Maintenance of Laboratories in Grammar Schools*—a joint report by the Science Masters' Association, Association of Women Science Teachers, NUT and Joint Four, John Murray, 1960.
7 Ministry of Education, Circular 144 (16.6.47).
8 *School Building Resources and their Effective Use*, OECD, Paris 1966, p.87.

9 Interviews with HMIS in 1968 and 1969, and early published reports of the Ministry of Education.

10 Address by R. G. K. Hickman to the 1956 *Annual NUT Conference at Blackpool*, published by NUT, page 17. In addition to the more frequently offered courses in commerce and in crafts, the NUT survey lists Seamanship, Building, Catering, Distributive Trades and House Maintenance.

11 Lincoln, annual report 1946, p.4.

2.6 Virement and the alternative use of secondary school resources

E. Briault

The main purpose of this article is to describe the 'Alternative Use of the Resources (AUR)' Scheme which the Inner London Authority is introducing in its secondary schools from the start of the academic year 1973–4. In the first part of the article I shall sketch the main features of the scheme and contrast it with some other schemes of resource allocation, including virement. Then I shall try to set out the broad philosophy behind the scheme and some of the benefits which, it is hoped, will accrue from it. Finally, I shall want to see how the scheme might actually operate in practice in any particular school.

Broadly, I suppose, there are at least two familiar means of allocating non-capital resources to schools. The traditional method is for the local authority to distribute a sum of resources parcelled up under a number of headings and to require expenditure to take place only within those headings. Resources may not be transferred from one heading to another and money left unspent in one financial year cannot be carried over into the next. The resources allocated by the local authority may or may not be related, either in amount or kind, to the needs of that individual school as distinct from a type of school or its size. This system assumes that 'the local authority knows best' and does little to encourage responsibility or flexibility in the ways in which schools use their resources.

More recently the method known as virement has become familiar. The Study Group on the Government of Colleges of Education (the Weaver Committee, of which I was a member) defined virement as 'power to switch money from one head of estimates to another'. A particular benefit of virement is that it enables resource-allocation to follow more closely upon changes in needs and priorities which were unseen at the stage when

Source: *Secondary Education* (Spring 1973), Vol. 3 No 2.

the estimates were approved. The Authority's secondary schools have been able to exercise a measure of virement since September 1970. In particular they have been able to re-allocate up to 5 per cent of their total resources, although not all schools wish to do so. The Weaver Committee recommended that colleges should have power to allocate money within each of certain broad heads of estimates separately but not between these broad groups.

The 'Alternative Use of Resources Scheme' however adopts a different approach by distinguishing between resources which can be used in whatever way is desired. It can best be understood if we first examine the main categories of resources available to each school. These are set out in the following table.

Table 2.6

		assumes schools have common needs		assumes schools have differing needs
school cannot reallocate	1	basic teaching staff basic non-teaching staff	2	teaching and non-teaching staff for immigrants
school can reallocate	3	school allowance (capitation)	4	additional resources

No 1 includes basic allocations of staff. Teaching staff must be employed at the minimum rate of one teacher to every 17 pupils on the unweighted roll.

The District Inspector recommends how many of these can be on-quota. Non-teaching staff are employed in relation to the same estimated unweighted rolls: schools with a roll of 800 (or 600 with an annexe) for example will be entitled to a full-time librarian.

No 2 A pool of full-time teachers will be allocated (by the officer in charge of the Division of the Authority in which the school is situated) on the recommendation of the District Inspector, to schools with high immigrant numbers on roll. These teachers are additional to the basic 1:17 allocation. Extra general assistance on the nonteaching staff side will also be given to such schools.

No 3 comprises the School Allowance (Capitation). From September

1973 this will be calculated as a flat rate per pupil on estimated unweighted roll for January 1974, at £14 per boy and/or £15 per girl.

No 4 comprises additional resources. The mode of calculation is described below.

Schools will have been notified of the total amounts of resources allocated in February (1973). Heads should then decide, in full consultation with their staffs, how they wish to deploy the total resources available for re-allocation (i.e. Boxes 3 and 4). The decisons will have to be set out, on the form provided for the purpose, and sent to the Divisional Officer early in the summer term. The decisions will be reported to county school governing bodies later in the term. Heads may wish subsequently to vary their original allocation, perhaps because of an unexpected staff vacancy or because a post for which the school opted cannot be filled. The Divisional Officer will consider such variations although the minimum period for re-allocation is half a term and heads must decide in advance not to fill the vacancy for the period in question.

So much for the basic mechanics of the scheme. The main aims of the scheme are four-fold. The first aim is to enable resources to be more effectively allocated to schools with the greatest needs. Secondly, it is intended that schools should be free, as far as possible, to use their resources as they think best. This will also help to achieve a greater degree of coordination between the decisions which are made on resource allocation. Lastly, the methods of resources allocation are also simplified.

The additional staff in respect of high numbers of immigrants have already been mentioned. These positions are the subject of a specific grant and must therefore remain outside the AUR scheme. The other vehicle for help according to school need is the sum of additional resources (Box 4). This is allocated out of a global pool within the Authority, comprising four main elements: the money equivalent of off-quota teaching staff above the 1:17 basic (the largest element); the resources allocated to certain EPA secondary schools in 1972–3 for additional non-teaching staff; money previously allocated specifically for 'Newsom' activities and special curricular grants; and an additional sum of money to allow for an improvement in overall resources, relating to the raising of the school leaving age.

The allocation is made on the recommendation of the District Inspector, who takes into account the school's roll, its individual needs for specialist teaching, its position on the Secondary School Index and any other special factors or development within the school. The index is designed to do more than just pick out educational priority schools: it is intended to be a guide to the needs of all schools. It therefore includes the following criteria: social and intellectual background of pupils (percentage of 11-plus pupils in lowest ability bands; percentage of immigrants; percentage of pupils in attendance receiving free meals; percentage of children in families of four or more children: percentage of one parent families; percentage of pupils with semi-or unskilled guardians; percentage of pupils who have changed schools); school buildings (split sites; floor space/child; site area/child; age of building; height of building) and special factors (percentage of staff who are handicraft/housecraft/technical teachers; this factor materially affects the school staffing needs as these subjects are normally taught to half classes).

The second aim of the scheme is, as already mentioned, to give schools more freedom in their choice as to how resources should be used. One reason for this, the differing needs of schools, has already been touched upon: schools differ very widely in the curriculum they provide and in the ways in which they set about the task of providing learning opportunities for their pupils. In one school there may be a readiness to use non-personal learning resources of wide variety; in other there may be comparative reluctance.

The main reason, however, is to some extent managerial. It is an important principle of management that decisions should be taken by those having the most information relevant to that decison. The term 'the teacher as manager' is perhaps in danger of becoming a cliché. Nonetheless, management decisions are often, at root, decisions about resources. This means, therefore, that there should, in the school, be the opportunity to consider not only how the school should expend its capitation in terms of materials and equipment but also to consider that expenditure in relation to its expenditure on staff. The school itself should have to consider extensions of its curriculum or the provision of very small teaching groups at this or that level in the school against the demand that such arrangements make, not simply on teaching staff, but on the school's total resources. It should be put in a position to recognize and take decisions about its needs, for example, on the one hand for more teachers to provide greater variety in the curriculum, to staff new A level subjects or whatever it may be, and a desire on the other hand perhaps to improve its clerical and librarian support or its technicians support. It will be seen below how schools may do this under the Scheme. In my view the transfer of powers of choice and that of management responsibility in these matters is compatible with the safeguards which the Authority has arranged: the provision for a basic minimum teaching staff for example and of minimum standards of provision for non-teaching staff support.

This transfer of management responsibility will help also to achieve greater coordination of decisions about resource allocation. An authority (by which I mean committees) generally takes decisions about, say the level of the teaching force as an ad hoc decision in relation to the budget, the quota, the ability to recruit off-quota teachers and the existing pupil-teacher ratios and size of classes in schools. These decisions often bear little conscious relation to other decisions taken separately (and sometimes even in different committees) about the level of non-teaching staff. Yet the effectiveness of a nursery teacher relates importantly to the provision of an adequately trained nursery assistant; the successful teaching of science, at secondary level, depends not only upon the appointment of sufficient specialist and qualified teaching staff but on the adequacy, in terms of numbers and training, of laboratory technician staff. Again, the total amount of what we generally call capitation (school) allowances is decided by an authority for all its institutions of the same kind by one and the same decision. Even here the division between the expenditure on materials and equipment out of capitation and on equipment provided by an authority is an *ad hoc* one. An authority may decide on a certain level of audio-visual equipment for all its schools, for example, but that expenditure about which decisions are commonly taken separately, needs to have an effective relationship with expenditure on what is sometimes called the soft-ware which makes use of the hard-ware, and I suggest, also with expenditure on the non-teaching staff. Transfer of management responsibility may help to achieve a greater degree of coordination, at the level where it will be most immediately valid.

Lastly, the basis and methods of resource allocation are to be greatly simplified as far as we are concerned. This will mainly be achieved by ceasing to use the weighted roll and instead basing staffing allowances, and the allocation of other resources, on simple estimated rolls. The school allowance will now be made for the academic year, to bring it into line with the other resources, which are already made on this basis. School allowances will also be calculated as a flat rate per pupil rather than on a per capita basis with varying rates for different ages and allowances for certain specialist activities and accommodation. Moreover, schools will be enabled to carry forward balances from one year to the next. Finally, where vacancies in teaching or non-teaching staff arise, either in basic staff or in additional positions for which the school has opted, the unused resources can be redeployed (redeployment of this type must of course mean a positive decision on the part of the school not to fill the vacancy for the period in question).

The main options available to a secondary school under the scheme are off-quota teaching staff; non-teaching staff; cash allowance. In other words, resources available for reallocation by the school may be used by any combination of these 'goods': off-quota teaching staff which includes part-time qualified teachers; instructors and precollege students; and instrumental music teachers. Non-teaching staff includes librarians, media resources officers, technicians, storekeepers, shorthand typists, clerical staff and copy typists, ancillary and general assistants. These 'goods' are individually costed under the scheme on a notional basis: an instructor, for example, 'costs' £1,800, a junior technician £1,100. These are full-time equivalents: a school can opt to have such a person part-time. A term is the minimum period for this purpose and £100 the minimum value. Let us see how these options might be taken up in practice.

Firstly, let us see how an actual primary school has used its resources during the current session. (ILEA primary schools have been using this scheme since September last year.) This school's 'fixed' resources are:

15 full-time teachers notional cash value	£30,000
3 nursery assistants	£2,700
Woman helper (60 hours)	£1,500
Secretarial (30 hours)	£1,000

In addition, £6,200 is available for reallocation. This particular school has opted for the following:

	£
1.8 teachers	3,600
1 nursery assistant (for infants reception class)	900
Woman helper (12 hours)	300
Secretarial (6 hours)	200
Cash allowance	1,200
	£6,200

For a secondary school the choices to be made will be rather more complex. The wide range of options available, especially, has already been demonstrated. The fixed resources of a boys' secondary school with a roll of about 1,300 might be:

1 Basic teaching staff at 1:17 including head:
   70   on quota
   6.4   off quota

   76.4

2 Teaching staff for immigrants:
   2 full-time

Total teaching staff = 78.4

3   Basic non-teaching staff:
    3 full-time clerical
    $37^1/_2$ hours per week part-time clerical
    25 hours per week general assistant
    1 full-time media resources officer
    1 full-time librarian (Grade III)
    1 senior laboratory technician
    1 laboratory technician
    2 junior laboratory technicians
    1 workshop technician
    1 storekeeper II

4   Non-teaching staff for immigrants:
    12 hours general assistant

In addition resources available for re-allocation might be:

School allowance	£18,200
Additional resources	£14,300
	£32,500

Two alternative schemes of choice might be:

(a)	5.1 (FTE) part-time qualified teachers	£10,200
	1 laboratory technician	£1,900
	School allowance	£20,400
		£32,500

Nearly two-thirds of the variable resources will thus be used on non-personal learning resources – materials and equipment.

(b)   This assumes greater and perhaps disproportionate strengthening of the non-teaching staff side:

	£
4 (FTE) part-time qualified teachers	8,000
0.5 (FTE) part-time instructor	900
1 laboratory technician	1,900
1 AVA technician	1,900
1 shorthand typist	1,850
1 storekeeper	2,000
1 full-time clerical	1,650

1 ancillary assistant	1,200
school allowance	13,100
	£32,500

These are, of course, purely notional examples and might not be realised in any particular school. Reduction of these resources to a cash denominator means that the resource 'input' can be directly compared. As an example of the kind of managerial decison to which this scheme leads, let us imagine a school in which a choice was being made between providing 10 teaching sets in Maths to cover a total of eight classes in the second and third forms, and employing an extra half librarian. The former would involve .75 of a teacher, at a 'cost' of £1,500; the latter would cost £1,250 (these are average, notional figures). One group of staff no doubt favours the use of resources in the one way, another urges the values of the librarian. (In point of fact the cost of setting in Maths is appreciably greater than the cost of the extra half-time librarian). As things are commonly arranged that decision would not be made by the school. It would either get or not get enough staff to have 10 sets for the teaching of Maths; it would either get or not get the extra half-time librarian in relation to the size of the school. If, however, both of these advances lie within the scope of resources over and above the basic minimum, then the decision can effectively be taken in the place where it should be taken − namely, the school itself, which must judge its own priorities in relation to its total curricular needs.

Finally, it is perhaps worth mentioning some of the demand which the scheme will make upon the school itself. It is essential that heads should make decisions about resources re-allocation in full consultation with staff. Real opportunities will thus arise for staff to become involved in managerial decisions. If staff are not involved, the resulting decisions may be neither wise nor acceptable. Heads will hence be concerned in a major administrative task: the organization of effective participation. The corollary of giving the school itself greater responsibility in resource allocation should therefore be to increase the responsibility of the teacher in the organisation of the learning process. Moreover the terms of the scheme, and especially the facility to carry unspent resources over into the subsequent academic year, will both encourage and require planning on the school's part, whilst helping to promote and clarify discussion of the school's objectives. Finally, the scheme may enable administrators and inspectors, and all those not actually in schools on a day to day basis to perceive more clearly what teachers think their schools' needs really are.

3 Accounting to whom?

Introduction

Few countries permit the degree of freedom that teachers enjoy in Britain. Judgments about content and method have traditionally been left to the professionals. Increasingly this custom is being questioned. The conclusions of the public inquiry into the teacher organization and management of the William Tyndale Schools (3.1) make it clear that while the local education authority may delegate control to managers and heads, this does not remove their statutory obligation to provide an 'efficient education'. They are ultimately responsible.

Other ambiguities arise from shared responsibilities of managers and the head, particularly with regard to 'oversight' of the conduct and curriculum of the school. Corbett (3.2) argues that reformed governing bodies should have responsibility for approving the curriculum, the internal organization (for example the forms of grouping used) and for the broad division of resources. Furthermore, she argues, such a body 'would be a solution to the current demand for more accountability of teachers'.

In looking at the issue of accountability Kogan (3.3) notes the dichotomy between professional norms which claim freedom of judgment for each practitioner and public expectations of answerability to the public. Like Corbett, he argues that the head should be accountable to the governors. Ellis (3.4), in a direct reply to Kogan, states a case for accountability to peers.

Schools differ from each other in many ways. Their populations vary in their social, economic and racial characteristics and in the attitudes they bring to school. With such wide disparities of 'inputs' is it realistic to make schools accountable for their 'outputs'? This is the formidable task discussed in Dyer's article (3.5). His article takes us beyond an input − output model in generating a schools' effectiveness index.

Watts (3.6) develops the question of staff participation mentioned in earlier articles. In this model, the head is accountable *to* the staff for executing agreed policies and *for* the staff to external groups.

Levin's article (3.7) is informed by an emotional link with minority groups in the community. He argues that schools have been insensitive to their needs and inefficient, as measured by performance. He claims that community control is required to ensure responsiveness to need and to create more favourable attitudes towards education. For Levin, community control is a political as well as an educational matter. 'Community schools' would be a focus from which political and social structures would emerge.

Fein (3.8) presents the dualisms inherent in words such as community – for some it conjures the image of sturdy cohesiveness and mutual support, but for others it is the image of the oppressive, censorious, anti-libertarian small town. He forces the reader to recognize inconsistency in the rhetoric surrounding community participation, creating a community-oriented curriculum, for example, lies uneasily with responding to the diversity of the school population.

3.1 Summary and Conclusions of the Report on the William Tyndale Junior and Infants Schools

Robin Auld QC

The authority's policy and system in the provision of primary education through its county primary schools
The role of the authority
826. The Authority has three fundamental statutory obligations in relation to the provision of the statutory system of education within its area. They are:

(i)   to secure the availability of 'efficient education' to meet the needs of the population within its area;[1] and

(ii) to secure the availability in its area of sufficient schools to provide full-time education 'suitable to the requirements' of junior and senior pupils respectively,[2] and

(iii) so far as is compatible with the above obligations and the avoidance of unreasonable public expenditure, to exercise its powers and duties with regard to the general principle that pupils are to be educated in accordance with the wishes of their parents.[3]

The Authority does not and could not meet these fundamental obligations simply by providing or financing school premises and resources and employing teachers to man the schools. There is also a responsibility to control the conduct and curriculum of each school.[4]

827.   Subject to the above-mentioned fundamental obligations, the *1944 Act* gives the Authority a choice, in the case of a county primary

Source: Report of the Public Enquiry into *Teaching Organization and Management of William Tyndale Junior and Infants' Schools* pp. 268–74.

school, whether to control the conduct and curriculum of the school itself or to transfer such control in whole or in part to other persons under rules of management that it is obliged to make for the school.[5] As I have already indicated the Authority has made Rules of Management in common form by virtue of which it has exercised its statutory power to divest itself of the exercise of the control of the conduct and curriculum of each of its county primary schools. The effect of Rule 2 of such Rules is to vest the control in the headteacher subject to the 'oversight'[6] in consultation with him, of the managers. The Authority, however, has not divested itself of its power of control. I say that for two principal reasons:

(i) the Rules themselves, by Rule 1, expressly reserve to the Authority the power to intervene by giving directions;[7] and

(ii) the Authority has power to amend its Rules of Management generally or in the case of any particular school so as to re-vest in itself wholly or partly the exercise of the control of the conduct and curriculum of a county primary school.

828.   If one of the Authority's county primary schools is not providing 'efficient education' or education 'suitable to the requirements of' its pupils, or is failing to have appropriate regard for the wishes of its pupils' parents,[8] then, regardless of the person or persons in whom the exercise of the control of the conduct and curriculum of the school is vested for the time being, the Authority must intervene to ensure that it fulfils its fundamental obligations. If advice and persuasion by the Authority's Inspectorate fail to produce the desired effect, the Authority must take some effective action in relation to the school to remedy the situation. There are a number of ways by which it can do this, two of which I have already indicated in the preceding paragraph. Thus, it can give directions to the headteacher under Rule 1 of the Rules of Management; it can amend the Rules of Management so as to re-vest in itself in whole or in part the exercise of the control of the conduct and curriculum of the school; it can apply sanctions to the headteacher and staff of the school through its disciplinary procedures, possibly leading to termination of their employment with the Authority; it can close the school and provide its pupils with efficient and suitable education at another school; or it can reorganize the school so as to achieve the same result. The solution that the Authority chooses for such a problem in relation to any particular school would necessarily depend upon a number of practical considerations – not least of which is the regard that the Authority quite properly has for the views of the teachers' professional associations in such matters. Nevertheless, however, unpalatable and whatever the practical, policy or political difficulties in choosing a solution, if inefficient or unsuitable education is being provided at the school or insufficient regard is being paid to the wishes of parents of pupils at the school, the Authority must do something about it.

829. The problem is not just one of choosing the right method of treatment, it is in the first place a problem of diagnosis and prevention. The Authority must first judge whether it is fulfilling through the school in question its fundamental statutory obligations, and when, if necessary, and in what manner it should intervene. For such diagnosis and consequential intervention the Authority must rely principally upon its Inspectorate. However, the Inspectorate has no formal power to determine the way in which the teaching in a school should be conducted. Although supremely well qualified to 'oversee' the conduct and curriculum of a school, the Inspectorate does not have that power because the Authority has chosen not to exercise it. The Inspectorate's role is essentially to advise and to support the teaching staffs employed by the Authority, and, acting in conjunction with the Divisional Office structure, to act as an early warning system to the Authority of any potential troubles or difficulties in its schools.

830. The combined effect of the Rules of Management made by the Authority and its interpretation of its role as expressed by its witnesses at the Inquiry may impose upon the Inspectorate a formidable task in certain instances. That is because the Authority has no policy:

(i) as to the standards of attainment at which its primary schools should aim; or

(ii) as to the aims and objectives of the primary education being provided in its schools, save the very general aim of providing the best possible opportunities to be given to the children to acquire the basic skills and social attainments so that at the age of 11 they can transfer to secondary schools equipped to do so; or

(iii) as to the methods of teaching to be adopted in its schools.

My purpose in recording this lack of policy is not to criticize the Authority – whose approach, I understand, is typical of most local education authorities in the country – but to demonstrate the difficulties for its Inspectorate in the diagnostic and advisory function that it has. Thus if a headteacher is convinced that a particular educational policy or method is right for his school, and the District Inpsector is equally convinced that he is wrong, by what yardstick does the Inspector judge, and seek to advise the headteacher, that he is wrong? If the headteacher persists in ignoring the Inspector's strong advice, upon what basis can and should the Authority intervene in one of the ways that I have mentioned in paragraph 828 above? Is the headteacher to be left to go his own way until the Authority is satisfied that it is not fulfilling in the case of that school its fundamental statutory obligations and/or until there is sufficient evidence to justify disciplinary proceedings for inefficiency or misconduct? By that time the school may have deteriorated beyond recall.

831. The difficulties for the Inspectorate that I have described in the preceding paragraph may not arise very often in practice. In most cases, no doubt, the Inspectorate and the teaching staffs of the Authority's schools enjoy good relations, and a headteacher would not readily disregard advice expressed firmly to him by his District Inspector. Nevertheless, where there is an issue between a headteacher and the Inspector, the latter has no formal power to ensure that his professional advice is heeded.

The role of the managers

832. Rule 2 of the Rules of Management appears to give to managers – the majority of whom are political appointees with no professional teaching knowledge or experience – a responsibility that the Inspectorate does not have, namely, the exercise of the 'oversight' of the conduct and curriculum of the school in consultation with the headteacher. It is difficult to know in practice what this responsibility of 'oversight' by the unqualified over the qualified can amount to. As interested members of the local community, managers can undoubtedly make an important contribution to the life of a school. With their varied backgrounds and experience there may also be great value in managers discussing with the headteacher and his colleagues their teaching policies and methods. In such discussions, managers may make suggestions about the teaching and work of the school which are accepted and adopted by the teachers. This function of consultation is, however, different from that of 'oversight', which purports to give managers, albeit 'in consultation with the headteacher', a responsibility to supervise the conduct and curriculum of a school.

833. In most cases, I imagine that there is little difficulty for managers arising out of the wording of Rule 2 of the Rules of Management. Both the managers and the headteacher apply it principally as if it referred to 'consultation' only and not to 'oversight'. The headteacher keeps the managers informed about what is going on in the school, and the interested managers keep themselves informed by visits to the school and discussion with the headteacher and staff and parents of children at the school. However, where managers are concerned about the quality of the teaching being provided, then – qualified or not – the Rule imposes upon them a responsibility to do something about it. The way in which this responsibility is exercised will depend largely upon the relations between the headteacher and his fellow managers and the extent to which the headteacher is inclined to take notice of their views. If the managers are justified in their anxieties, and relations between them and the headteacher are good, a word from the chairman of the managing body to the headteacher may suffice.

834. However, if the managers and the headteacher disagree about the managers' anxiety, or relations between them generally are bad, then a number of considerations have to be taken into account. They are as follows:

(i) The managers should act corporately. This is particularly important now that the headteacher and one of his staff are members of the managing body. Whatever the managers decide to do, they should decide together, and by vote if necessary, at a properly constituted managers' meeting. There should be no decision taken by factions of the managing body. Nor should there be meetings between members of the managing body with the Authority's representatives to discuss the problem in the absence and without the knowledge of the chairman of the managers, or of the headteacher or the teacher-manager.

(ii) Managerial oversight can only be exercised under Rule 2 of the Rules of Management in consultation with the headteacher. If he disagrees with the managers on a point of importance relating to the conduct and curriculum of the school, it would be wrong, and totally counter-productive, for the managers, to force their 'oversight' upon the school in the form of managerial visits which are really lay 'inspections'. Such visits would be wrong whether decided upon collectively and by vote at a managers' meeting or individually by certain managers. Pending the action to which I refer in the next sub-paragraph, managers should be sparing in the managerial visits that they make. They should also be scrupulous to visit only by appointment and to avoid, so far as possible, any behaviour of an 'inspectorial' nature. I use the words, 'so far as possible', because I appreciate that the dividing line between a managerial visit and an 'inspectorial' visit by a critical manager may not always be easy to draw.

(iii)   If the headteacher is adamant in his refusal to accept that there is any justification for the managers' concern, the managers should draw the matter to the attention of the Authority by means of a resolution voted upon at a properly constituted managers' meeting. Such a resolution could call upon the Authority to institute a full Inspection, or it could simply express in general terms the managers' concern about the school. As a result of such a resolution the Authority would almost certainly take some action. At the very least, it would ask the District Inspector to visit the school in order to determine if he can whether there is any justification for the managers' anxiety.

(iv)   Following the intervention by the Authority in the form of the District Inspector's visit to the school, there are a number of possibilities that the managers may have to consider. First, the District Inspector and/or other representatives of the Authority may form the view that the managers' concern is justified, and may take steps which result in the headteacher remedying the position. Alternatively, the District Inpsector and/or other representatives of the Authority may take the view that the managers are not justified in the concern that they have expressed, or, whilst accepting the justification for that concern, do insufficient to require the headteacher to remedy the position. In either of the latter two cases the managers have only two courses of action properly open to them if they feel strongly about the matter. They are:

(a)   to make a complaint against the headteacher and/or members of his staff for inefficiency, misconduct or indiscipline under the Authority's Disciplinary Procedures;

(b)   to invite the intervention of the Secretary of State, by requesting him to direct a local inquiry under Section 93 of the *1944 Act* and/or to refer the matter to the Secretary of State under Section 67 of the *1944 Act* for determination by him.

835.   If managers are justified in their concern, and it is a matter of importance, the Authority would be gravely lacking in its duty if the managers were obliged to give expression to their responsibilities as managers by the institution of disciplinary proceedings or by referring the matter to the Secretary of State. Nevertheless, those are the steps which responsible managers should take in the interests of the school and the children in it if they feel strongly enough that some action should be taken.

The role of the headteacher

836. The system adopted by the Authority depends largely for its success upon the ability and good judgement of the headteacher whom it apoints. Subject to such powers and responsibilities as are conferred and imposed by Statute and the Rules of Management upon the Authority and the managers respectively, the headteacher is in effective control of the school, its aims, policies, and methods of teaching. A system that reposes such trust and control in one man also demands that he should act with great care and responsibility in the exercise of his functions. Although the Authority encourages the headteacher to consult with his staff in the formulation of the schools' teaching policies and methods, it is the headteacher who, under the present system, is ultimately responsible for the conduct of the school and hence its success or failure.

837. Whatever system of consultation or collective decision-making among the staff a headteacher introduces to his school, it is his responsibility to see that it works to the advantage of the school. This may require a great deal of skill and diplomacy on his part. He also needs that skill and diplomacy in his relations with managers, with whom he has an ill-defined shared responsibility for the conduct and curriculum of the school, and with the parents of the children for whose education he is responsible.

Notes

1 The *1944 Act*, S.7.
2 The *1944 Act*, S.8(1).
3 The *1944 Act*, S.76.
4 The *1944 Act*, S.23(1).
5 The *1944 Act*, S.17(3)(a).
6 i.e. the first meaning of the word in the Shorter Oxford Dictionary, namely, 'supervision, superintendence; charge, care, management'.
7 The material parts of Rule 1 of the Rules of Management: 'The County Primary School shall be conducted in accordance with the provisions of the *Education Act 1944* as amended ... with the provisions of any regulations made by the Secretary of State ... with any directions of the Authority and with these rules'.
8 The *1944 Act*, S.23(1).

3.2 Whose schools?

Anne Corbett

What we have now and how we got there

The present system of school government and management dates from the *Education Act, 1944*. It is a result of a compromise between the government, the local education authorities and the churches.

In the White Paper preceding the *1944 Act* (Educational Reconstruction, 1943) the Government said: 'There is ample room for the exercise of powers by governors, particularly in the case of aided schools, over the general conduct of the school, including the appointment of teachers and the organization and curriculum'.

They followed this up in the Act by requiring all schools maintained from public funds to have a body of governors or managers, and to be run in accordance with rules approved by the Secretary of State for Education and Science. The powers of governors and managers were to be defined in articles which also needed the Secretary of State's approval.

These vary between county and voluntary, primary and secondary schools and between local education authorities. But most follow model articles as issued by the ministry in 1945 (Administrative Memorandum 25). These give governors a part in appointing the headteacher and the responsibility for appointing other teachers. They require them to approve the school finances and to make suggestions for the local education authority (LEA) expenditure. They also give them the general oversight of 'the curriculum and conduct of the school'. The usual form of words is that 'the headteacher shall be responsible for the day to day running of the school and the governors shall be responsible for the general conduct and curriculum'. The only apparent difference between county and voluntary schools is that voluntary aided schools control their own admissions whereas voluntary controlled and county schools have to conform to the local education authority scheme.

Source: *Whose Schools?* Fabian evidence to the Taylor Committee. (1976) pp. 3–16.

But things are not what they seem. The principle of a local body with some decision making function in relation to each school is vitiated in practice by two facts.

First, local education authorities are not required to set up individual governing and managing bodies for each school. Curiously, it is not known how many group several schools together, or even group all their schools under the schools sub-committee, which becomes the authority's governing or managing body. But authorities with individual managing bodies are thought to be exceptional; and some of the largest authorities do not have individual governing bodies.

Second, even where LEAs do have separate bodies, for each school, the practice has been for all but the governing bodies' own cooptions to be appointed through the local political parties, in proportion to their strength on the local council. Thus the governing bodies of these schools have been in practice front organizations for the local education authority, while the voluntary aided schools, with their crucial control of admissions and a majority of independent members have been able to operate like medieval barons. It has been only too easy for the voluntary grammar schools among them to hold out against local authority comprehensive plans and wreck them by continuing to cream the brightest pupils.

The presence of robber barons is of course intolerable for the local authorities, but covert control and manipulation – the wolf in sheep's clothing – is just as intolerable for the school's own community. Since it is essential that Taylor untwists these strands, it is worth tracing the history of school government and management.

Baron and Howell, the most assiduous of the authorities and authors of the standard work[1] see the school governing body's origins in the Middle Ages. Then, the first grammar schools, like the hospitals and other charitable institutions, needed to have their wealth safeguarded. Trustees were formed to guarantee an institution's future. By mid nineteenth century, governors were not merely the guarantors of finances, they had become entrenched as the representatives of the public interest against an absolute control by head teachers. The Public Schools Commission report of 1864, one of the pioneering educational reports, put it thus: 'The introduction of a new branch of study, or the suppression of one already established, and the relative degrees of weight to be assigned to different branches, are matters respecting which a better judgement is likely to be formed by men conversant with the general requirements of public and professional life and acquainted with the general progress of science and literature, than by a single person, however able and accomplished, whose views may be more circumscribed and whose mind is liable to be unduly pressed by difficulties of detail. What should be taught and what importance should be given to each subject are therefore questions for the governing body: how to teach is a question for the headmaster.'

This principle of a counterweight to the head was reiterated when the state moved directly into providing education following the *Education Act, 1870*. Managers were established for the elementary schools (this is the basis of the historical distinction begun between governors and managers). They were required to both manage the funds and conduct the general policy of the school.

It was probably a satisfactory solution while schooling was independent or a matter for school boards. But the perspective changed with the establishment of local education authorities in 1902.

Managing bodies for the elementary schools were to continue to exist and voluntary grammar schools retained their governing bodies. But Parliament in the *1902 Act* had intended local education authorities to have a free hand to manage their own schools in accordance with local requirements, argued a John Hampden of the time, Sir James Graham, the director of education for Leeds. There was no place for governors. He defied the ministry, refusing to set them up; and he won. The government did not insist that Leeds appointed governors or managers for its own schools.

Thus the first important confusion was created; on one hand the government claimed that governors and managers were vital; on the other it did not insist that they should be established. By 1944 the so called system of governors and managers was a patchwork. The voluntary schools had them. The county (shire) authorities had them for their secondary schools (grammar schools). Many of the borough authorities followed the Graham line.

Some of the established (voluntary) schools recognized that governors could both protect them from bureaucratic pressure, and safeguard the public interest against the head. By the 1920s governors and managers were promoted as positive links with their community by Henry Morris, the famous chief education officer of Cambridgeshire. They were not managers in his view. But they were the ideal channels to represent local interests. Then the Hadow report of 1926, which proposed the introduction of secondary modern schools, said managers 'might fulfil a very useful function, as they often do at present, by explaining and interpreting to parents, local employers and the community generally the special province, function and aim of modern schools and senior classes.'

These were three very different interpretations of the governors' job: managers for the local authority, a pressure group against the authority, or a body to oil the neighbourhood wheels. They were bound to be in tension. But these were not resolved by the *Education Act 1944*. For by then the government was in difficulties on its new policy of universal secondary schools. It needed help from the voluntary church schools. What deal could it offer which would bring them in, with local education authorities newly strengthened by their additional responsibilities?

School governors' powers turned out to be a key issue. The government wanted to appease those whom Baron and Howell quote as saying that there should be 'no handing over the local education authorities of secondary schools whose individuality had been handed down by successive headmasters'. Equally they had to meet a new version of the Graham argument, that to back governors would be to remove publicly provided education from public control. The strength of that argument was clearly indicated by the fact, as Baron and Howell point out, that in the end the government was helped by independent school supporters, who found it expedient to stress not the school's distinctiveness but the possibility of their most desirable features being more widely diffused. As after 1902 there was a compromise. The government approved the principle strongly enough to make governing and managing bodies compulsory for all schools, but would not legislate for each school to have one.

It has been an unsure basis on which to build. Yet building there has been. The search for ways to give institutional shape to some of the political beliefs of the last ten years brings governors and managers constantly into the spotlight. The desirability of public participation in decision making, the suggestion of some community control to balance more powerful local authorities, the stress on parental involvement, and even worker participation in management; all these have combined to suggest a modern role for governors and managers.

Beginnings of reform

The Plowden report[2] provided the first authoritative backing for rescuing governors and managers from gentle irrelevance. Out of the committee's concern to link parents more closely with the process of their children's education, came a view that managers could play a key part in deciding and explaining the way the school worked. The Public Schools Commission report[3] on direct grant schools made many of the same points. Evidence to the Royal Commission on Local Government also stressed their potential.

Since then reform has been stimulated by the pressure groups, such as the Confederation for the Advancement of State Education and the National Association of Governors and Managers which was founded in 1970. NAGM has effectively monitored progress and publicized the results, campaigned for individual governing bodies and for the representation of all those with an interest in the school – parents, pupils, teachers and the local education authority. It has devised training schemes for governors and managers and encouraged authorities to run courses.

That is what pressure groups exists for. But the change from within has been striking too. All the teachers associations are tolerant of reformed governors and managers except the National Association of Schoolmasters which would like to see them abolished. But it is the biggest association, the National Union of Teachers which has responded most fully to changing views about the part that assistant teachers can play in running schools, and the extent to which a headteacher ought to have to take account of the views of staff and parents in running the schools. In 1944, the NUT had been openly hostile to governing and managing bodies.

It retained its reservations up to the end of the 1960s. Then in 1970 its conference voted for mandatory teacher membership of governing bodies, as part of the strategy for more ordinary teacher participation in running schools. In its evidence to Taylor the NUT argues strongly for individual governing bodies respresenting teachers, parents, and those with local knowledge as well as the local authority. It is against grouped governing bodies which cannot give proper attention to individual schools.

Reform in the local education authorities

As for the local education authorities, there Taylor can look to practical experience. Sheffield, which had had all the characteristics of a tightly controlled borough, was the first authority to introduce reform. In 1970 it set up individual governing bodies for all its secondary schools, instituted managing bodies for its primary schools, and abolished party political control.

'The governing body should represent a wide cross section of the friends that every school has', says the booklet issued to all its governors and managers. And these turn out to be a wide ranging group. Since 1970, governing bodies have consisted of between eight and fourteen members, two of whom are coopted. The representative governors appointed by the local education authority must include the headteacher, an assistant teacher and at least one representative of the parents of pupils at the school. Beyond this, the representative governors need not be (and in practice almost always are not) members of the appointing body. As the instruments put it: 'in making its appointments, the authority will have regard to the desirability of including representatives of industry and commerce, of universities, polytechnics and colleges of education and of primary schools'; in the case of primary schools, links with secondary schools and with teacher training are stressed.

The achievements are notable. Michael Harrison, chief education officer of Sheffield described it 'as a great weight of concerned manpower working for the schools'. The chairman of Sheffield Education Committee, Peter Horton, adds that the increased expenditure for the authority, which is chiefly accounted for by clerking, 'is largely offset by the much better contact with schools that the routine of governors and managers meetings brings. Primary and special schools, originally nervous of the change, are now enthusiastic of their managers support.'[4]

Membership of governing bodies

By 1975, according to NAGM, 85 per cent of authorities in England and Wales had parents represented in their own right on governing or managing bodies and 74 per cent (sixty-one authorities) had teachers. Around 25 per cent have a pupil present, though not necessarily as a full governor. Over thirty authorities were reviewing their procedures.

However, changing the membership of governing bodies is only a beginning. The governing body may immediately become a more informed body because some members know the school well. But then it also becomes necessary to clarify their responsibilities. There has been very little attempt by most authorities to do this and, until the appointment of the Taylor Committee, no attempt at all by the Department of Education and Science.

One of the most positive steps to clarify procedure was taken by the Inner London Education Authority in 1972 when it reversed the usual conventions about confidentiality and said that in future nothing should be regarded as confidential unless the chairman of the governing body ruled it so – a recognition that the governing body has responsibilities to different interest groups.

York in 1974 had probably gone furthest in the redefinition of governors' powers. Its governors are empowered to receive from parents, local employers and others 'ideas and suggestions relating to the school and to submit to the authority suggestions on any matter relating to the conduct of the school which would be to the advantage of the school'. They also 'have the right and duty to acquaint themselves with matters concerning the curriculum and organization of the school and where appropriate to pass on such facts'.

An individual initiative

Otherwise it has been a question of individual governing bodies taking an initiative, and nobody knows how many of them have done that. Many things are possible, given initiative, as I know from first hand experience of what had happened in a Haringey school sometime before I joined its board. At that time (1970) Haringey's policy had been typical of small politicized boroughs. All appointments were made through the political

K

parties. Even the coopted places, supposed to be reserved for people who could make a particularly useful educational or local contribution, were carved up between the political parties. In the 1970 elections the Labour party, which had previously brought in a few non-party members, had a manifesto commitment to make 50 per cent of the places available to parents, pupils and teachers, and also to set up individual managing bodies.

But when it came to the point the new labour council would do no more than encourage governing bodies to use one of their co-opted places for an elected parent, teachers being excluded by the (very common) instruments which do not allow a council employee to serve on a school governing body.

Yet it was still possible for an individual governing body, even with 100 per cent political control, to take the first steps to becoming much more representative than council policy specified. At that time one school, Drayton, brought in parents, teachers and pupils by the device of calling a committee meeting of the governors with representatives of the school; and organizing that meeting to take place immediately after the main business of the governors. After that all but confidential business was transferred to the 'committee' meeting. Eventually, the 'committee' meeting preceded the governing body meeting. The coopted places were made over to elected parents and an elected pupil (the governing body failed to get the council to change its policy and allow the appointment of teachers).

Other schools in the borough then started to work their way round the local policy, convinced of the need for first hand contact with parents and teachers. In two cases they followed the same device to get teachers present. This last was in the face of opposition to teacher membership of governing bodies from the local NUT which thought that governing bodies were 'moribund bodies and ought to be left to die'.

Continued opposition and future uncertainties

Some authorities claim to be introducing reforms by bringing in parents and teachers. Yet at the same time they strengthen the political grip. Sometimes they even reduce the governors' existing powers. Huntingdon and Peterborough had the most notable success when they extracted approval from the Secretary of State, for handing over the general responsibility for the curriculum to the headteacher. But there is some evidence that the Department of Education was anxious about that.

A more common worry for those who want reform is the outright opposition of some of the largest authorities to individual governing and managing bodies. At a conference in Windsor in 1975, the chairman of the Manchester education authority, Sally Shaw, justified her authority's use of a single 'governing body' for all schools by saying that, particularly in authorities with many deprived areas, 'the LEA must retain a very great deal of power. There is simply no room for governing bodies'. She argues that the authority needs to some extent to supervise the curriculum: 'We have a strong inspectorate in Manchester to do this'.

In Birmingham the schools have grouped governing bodies. And why? According to Sheila Wright, the chairman of Birmingham education committee: 'because a local education authority could not tolerate much difference between its schools'.

A number of the chief officers of the local education authorities are also against governing bodies with decision making powers. The evidence to Taylor from the Society of Education Officers is split between those who want reform and those who want merely advisory bodies.

It is less surprising that teachers' organisations should be hostile to governors and managers being able to exercise effective powers. For the most difficult questions concern them much more than the local education authorities: the boundaries on curriculum and the related questions of whether the head alone should exercise the authority or whether the head should have to act in conjunction with the staff. The National Union of Teachers and the Assistant Masters Association, for example, in their evidence to Taylor, both take their stand on the view that decisions on the curriculum should be taken by the head in conjunction with the staff.

In all this the Secretaries of State, through the Department of Education and Science if not hostile, have not been positively enthusiastic. Although not required to approve instruments of government defining the membership, they considered Sheffield's new instruments for two years. Then without so much as a public word they approved in Huntingdon's and Peterborough's articles a dramatic change of policy. But on the other hand they refused to approve Liverpool's identical draft articles. Reg Prentice's appointment of the Taylor committee in April 1975 was, however, a recognition that some national stocktaking was needed. The next chapter takes up the questions as to why it is vital, in the interests of all children, not to be diverted by the idea of advisory councils, and to evolve instead a modern form of governing body.

The curriculum

Not long ago a senior French civil servant explained how the French government was now encouraging public participation in the management of schools. Secondary schools could now have boards representing parents, pupils, teachers and the local community, he said, to draw up regulations for the internal conduct of the school and to approve the school's finances and to plan extra-curricular activities. But he said 'very reasonably' the public authorities 'have debarred the boards from deliberation on the curriculum in order to ensure that the educational system applies to all alike and prevents any rash experimentation from being conducted unchecked, with children whose critical faculties still require the sharpening of age'.[5]

It is a fair guess that that view attracts a far more sympathetic audience in England than would have been conceivable even five or ten years ago. At least until then there had been widespread support for the view that the National Union of Teachers and the Assistant Masters Association have put forward in its evidence to the Taylor committee: that the responsibility for the curriculum 'is properly the preserve of those who have been professionally trained to design curriculum and to teach'. But a few well publicized examples of a mindness adoption of 'modern' methods, especially when used on children who will have the fewest opportunities to get help from home, have a powerful effect on public opinion. The seeds that the Black Papers have been sowing since 1969 bloom with William Tyndale. Because so many of the familiar educational landmarks have gone, and because teachers have not encouraged new forms of accountability in their place, even moderate opinion is influenced. With new school examinations like the Certificate of Secondary Education and the Certificate of Extended Education, the end in sight for GCE O level, new curricula in all shapes and sizes, most outsiders are lost. A national curriculum, expressed as 'minimum standards for all', or 'giving all children their educational rights', begins to have a progressive as well as a right wing appeal. There was once a prescribed curriculum in England, consisting of the three RS. In 1862, the reading standards included the following: 'reading standard one: narrative in monosyllables. Standard two: one of the narratives next in order after monosyllables in an elementary reading book used in the school. Standard five: a few lines of poetry from a reading book used in the first class of the school. Standard six: a short ordinary paragraph in a newspaper or other modern narrative'.

That was an unhappy experience because it made teachers' pay dependent on their results. The poet, Matthew Arnold, who was also an HM Inspector, reported in 1867, five years after the code was introduced: 'The mode of teaching in the primary schools has certainly fallen off in intelligence, spirit and inventiveness during the four or five years which have elapsed since my last report. It could not well be otherwise. In a country where everyone is prone to rely too much on mechanical processes and too little on intelligence, a change in the Education Department's regulations, which, by making two thirds of the government's grant depend upon a mechanical examination, inevitably gives a mechanical turn to the inspection, is and must be trying to the intellectual life of the school'.[6]

After 1926 the idea of a centrally defined curriculum was, in effect, abolished. Lord Eustace Percy, the then President of the Board of Education had the elementary school code made much more general. John White has suggested that this was due to a Conservative government fear that an incoming Labour government would use the curriculum for political ends. Whether or not this was true it leaves the curious situation that religious education is now the only subject prescribed by law: and that was the outcome of the religious settlement of the *1944 Act*. There is now, as suggested earlier, some swing back in favour of minimum prescriptions. In the Labour party itself there is some talk of the arguments in terms of a children's charter. It is a move I would support. But it does not get round the fact that in practice curricular policy is largely, if implicitly, made at the level of the school. Taylor will have to consider whether this policy should be more explicit, and whether it should be sanctioned by the governors, by the headteacher or by the headteacher in consultation with the governors or with the staff.

So I want to pick up again the theme that reformed governors and managers should have to give final approval to curricular policy; and again take issue with a fashionable view that the curriculum should be determined by a participative body of teachers. This is not to oppose academic boards (rather as the Weaver report in 1966 advocated for further education). Indeed it seems a very necessary reform, particularly in secondary schools. But governors and managers have a sanctioning role which is rather different, since in practice the definition of curiculum policy is so diffuse and it cannot be easily defined in relation to one set of interests only.

Interestingly enough, this case has been made recently by the Schools Council, a body on which the teachers' organizations are in the majority. A recent report from one of its working parties argued that the individual school's curriculum must be seen as a 'convenant'.[7] The general pattern should be debated and agreed by all those with an interest in the school: the pupils, parents, the teachers, the governors and the local education authority.

'The school's aims should start from an acknowledgement of the legitimate expectations of the various groups of people who are involved ... The covenant defines the reasonable expectations and mutual responsibilities of the pupils for whose welfare the school exists, the parents, teachers and such agencies as boards of governors, the local education authorities, and the Department of Education and Science ... The covenant must derive its authority from the basic willingness of the parties to assent to its principles and to be governed by its terms, but this they can only be expected to do if the terms are seen to be fair and reasonable. This covenant will be strengthened if the principles upon which it is based are shared, rather than simply reflecting the beliefs and attitudes of a single group'.

Some commentators have seen all this as hopelessly vague. On the contrary, I would argue the Schools Council has taken a practical step forward from some of its earliest work: the research survey *Enquiry One*[8] which showed in embarassing fullness just how different are the educational priorities of pupils and parents on the one hand, and teachers on the other. The new report recognizes that some of those differences need to be tackled openly in a way which gives standing to all the various different interests.

One can see more clearly the way a governing body could be involved by taking three examples which may be diverse, but are not untypical.

In 1971, a storm blew up in Cheshire as to whether *Kes* and *Billy Liar* were dirty books, unfit to be read in schools. In 1975, Bradford education authority failed in its attempt to get a Moslem parent to send his daughter to a mixed secondary school. Almost any day a school decides on subject options or how pupils should be grouped. Take for example how one school decided to retain Latin.

The Cheshire dirty books row began with a letter to the local paper from a parent complaining about the 'use of kitchen sink books masquerading as classics' in schools. Her case was taken up by the local MP and, due to a quiescent governing body, the local parish council. It blew over and when the secretary of the local Certificate of Secondary Education examinations board and some of the chief education officer's staff had convinced parish council, MP and governors that pornography was not being prescribed, and they ended up grateful for the public education.

The point of the incident is twofold: it was widely recognized that the general shape of the curriculum was not a matter for the teachers alone. Second, that a forum was needed.

The Bradford case, likely to be paralleled elsewhere as cultural diversities become more deeply rooted, is potentially more explosive. Here, part of the problem was the authority's rigid policy of 100 per cent mixed secondary schoolings. Only late in the day was this recognized as likely to cause conflict with traditional Moslem beliefs that after puberty a girl should not have any contact with boys until married. The authority, which in many ways has done a great deal to try and help its non-English speaking population, tried to play this particular case as an isolated incident involving one troublesome parent. But it was never that. It was estimated at the time that only ten or twenty teenage Moslem girls out of a potential 200 were in the mixed schools of Bradford. Inevitably part of the solution lay with the local education authority (and Bradford did eventually agree to ask schools not to force Moslem girls to do the mixed PE or swimming which so offended parents). But it was clear that there was a need for a body to work out what individual schools could do to balance their general philosophy with the particular sensitivities of large numbers of parents.[9]

The Latin case, on the other hand, illustrates at a less contentious level how ideally placed the governors could be. Who should take the decision about whether to offer a particular subject on the curriculum and to divert resources accordingly: the authority, the governors or the teachers? It is clear that within its framework of a comprehensive policy, it must actually suit the authority to leave that decision to the school. It neither wants to say that all schools should provide Latin, sometimes at great cost. Nor does it want to forbid the teaching of a subject with such prestige connotations. In practice the decision was taken by the headteacher as so often. For in every school in the country there are likely to be dozens of examples of the same point. One headteacher presents the summer term meeting of the governors with a printed brochure of a quite different style of fourth-year courses to start in the autumn. A second announces that pupils will now take the Certificate of Secondary Education exams rather than the General Certificate of Education. A third puts forward a common curriculum for all. A fourth buys all the technological gadgetary to support individual learning. A fifth reimposes streaming in the primary school. A sixth brings back corporal punishment.

And why? Because of a fiction. Because of a view that since the day to day running of the school must be in professional hands, everything concerning the curriculum must go unchallenged. No industry works with so little accountability. Is bringing up children less important than making money?

Who should be governors?

It has been argued earlier that governors or managers should in future be the forum for discussing and agreeing the policy that a school adopts within the framework of local policy. It follows that they must represent all those groups with an interest in the particular school, and should not be dominated by any one group: pupils where appropriate, parents, teachers, and non-teaching staff and the local authority. It should include some people living locally and having a particular knowledge of the area surrounding the school. This implies that the present common place pattern of political control and even majority party political control would vanish. It is right that it should. Problems that are so politically controversial or related to an authority's general policy as, for example, whether a school is single sex or whether it should take a particular age range, should unambiguously be the responsibility of the local education authority.

But that is not to say there should be no political links. Experience of reform indicates the advantages of representation from the local council or (where there are not enough to go round) from political party activists. It adds to the power and credibility of governing and managing bodies that they should be in touch with local policy and it is an advantage for the schools that there should be councillors aware of them. It is significant that Sheffield, in assessing the effectiveness of its 1970 reform, felt it had lost more politicians than was useful for the schools.

As for teachers, they, like other workers, should be represented on bodies which take decisions affecting their working life. They also have a great deal to contribute. For if governing bodies are to approve policies which are forward looking educationally, rather than harking back to what they remember of their youth, they are going to have to be persuaded by the teachers doing the job. This applies to headteachers and elected teacher representatives. It has been argued that there are legal difficulties for headteachers – 'the servant of the governors' – being full members. This has less relevance if governing bodies are to be the sort of forums advocated here. As for teacher representatives, it seems reasonable to argue that the elected teachers should also be full members of the governing body, and should exercise their judgement, in the light of their professional code of conduct, as to whether they withdraw or refrain from voting.

Parents, too, should be elected by all parents, and not merely by members of a parents association. One would hope indeed, as with teachers, that requirements of election would stimulate the creation of their own bodies (academic bodies and parents' associations) to give some reality to the idea of representatives and to put an end to the view that the best representative is the person that the headteacher nominates: a not uncommon practice at present.

Pupils and students should also be represented in secondary schools. It is one practical way of taking part in democratic decision making. Again they should be elected. In their case it is suggested that they are excluded from some sensitive discussions such as staff promotions. One established practice should remain: the provision for the governing body itself to co-opt members. It should perhaps be limited to no more than a quarter of the total. But it gives useful flexibility. One thinks of its benefits for example when large numbers of children from overseas arrive in a school; or the occasions when the governing body itself is keen to promote some new venture like the establishment of a community association, and where there may be outsiders who could be particularly useful.

There is also the matter of the voluntary schools. They are just as much part of the local community as the county schools. Nearly all their resources come from public funds (the voluntary aided schools paying only 15 per cent of their new building costs). Taylor must surely urge a similar pattern of parent and teacher representation on voluntary school governing bodies, even though the terms of reference do not specifically refer to the voluntary schools.

There remains the question of whether governing and managing bodies might attract local people other than through the nomination of political parties. It is not so much a question of rights, as desirability: how might members of local tenants associations benefit a school governing body? Taylor could usefully recommend that coopted places were kept open for nominees of local organizations and those who say they are interested and have some time to give. Certainly there seems no problem of availability. Authorities including Hertfordshire, Sheffield and Southampton searching for non-political governors filled their places. Inner London needing political appointees for its managing bodies found difficulties. The more difficult issue lies in convincing outsiders that school governors and managers have a worthwhile job to do.

What else should they do?

Once one accepts that governors have a realistic, decision making job to do on curriculum, a job which urgently needs doing, other functions follow. Firstly, finance, where at present governors' responsibilities are nominal. The reformed governing body should have to approve positively the school's resource policy: its curricular decisions, of course, have resource implications. It should have the information in time to be able to ask for modifications. Taylor should surely, too, recommend the practice of Hertfordshire and the ILEA and possibly other authorities and give the schools some degree of real control. These authorities allow the schools to decide how to spend 5 per cent of their budgets.

Governors and managers should not however, have the power to raise additional funds for the basic running of the school. The argument of this pamphlet has been that governors and managers must operate within the framework of local policy. Nowhere is this more crucial than in finance. It has taken 100 years of public education to translate into public policy the necessity to give favourable treatment to schools in the poorest circumstances. To allow governors to raise funds would be to reverse such a policy overnight. It would be a charter for the schools drawing on the most prosperous areas.

Governors and managers, currently have important responsibilities for the appointment of senior staff, including a share in the appointment of the headteacher. The headteacher is usually responsible for making all other appointments. Governors have often been criticized for their inadequacies. And control of appointments, like the control of the curriculum, is an area where much progressive opinion favours giving the power to a participative body of teachers.

Two points need to be made. There are dangers of parochialism if even senior appointments are internal. And, there are ways in which present procedures can be improved. The presence of elected teachers on reformed governing bodies would immediately make the governing body more informed. But it also seems worth examining the higher education practice of calling in an external assessor — as PRISE(The Programme for Reform in Secondary Education) has suggested in its evidence to Taylor: 'a well respected teacher from outside the authority's employment'. The governing body should continue to consider problems and complaints to the conduct and tenure of teachers. It should have to approve the suspension or exclusion of pupils.

With reform one would expect governing bodies to be much more involved non-managerially. They should be much more visible. They need to do the explaining and interpreting to the local community that Hadow had talked about back in 1926. Today that includes using local radio and the local press. They should be known as a channel which parents and local residents can use. They have an especially important part to play in the case of those schools whose reputation suffers regardless of the work being done because, for instance, the school has an old building, or a large number of coloured children. Taylor should look carefully at the York experience in terms of whether governors and managers have been able to fulfil their job as community link people. It should also look at the areas, like Manchester, where the local councils have refused to have individual governing and managing bodies to see whether their schools are not particularly the preserve of the professionals. Here then is a framework for reformed governors and managers. The challenge is to make it work.

Making reform work

So far this article has taken issue with the view that schools run best on 'delicate balances' and has argued for a greater definition of membership and function of governing bodies. This chapter looks at ways to translate reform into practice. Reform requires changes in the law, changes in the way local education authorities themselves define the function and membership of governors and managers, and some major changes in practice. But it is all within the range of the possible.

The law and the DES

There are some strong arguments against changing the law: that is, there are arguments which tend to weigh strongly with secretaries of state and many reformers. The law takes a long time to change. Much of the reform being argued for is possible within the present framework. But the answer, of course, is that within the present framework it has not happened. For every school governing body like the one quoted on page 280, there must be hundreds if not thousands who have not had some innovator working on their behalf. So if a kind of forum is to become the norm, three changes in the law are necessary.

First, to provide for the statutory establishment of individual governing and managing bodies. This means an end to section 20 of the *1944 Act*, which allows authorities to retain for themselves the powers and responsibilities of governors and managers.

Second, to provide statutory backing for the principle of a forum of all those most closely interested in the school. It needs to be stated that governing bodies should be required to represent parents, teachers, the local education authority and the local community and, in the case of secondary schools, pupils. They should also still be allowed to coopt. The law should also state that the composition of governing bodies should be such that no one group has a majority (the amendment of sections 18 and 19). It should then be up to the local education authorities to define the membership (as they do at the moment). The different ages of pupils catered for, the different sizes of schools, the extent to which they are open for community use, even their site, be it rural or urban, should influence the precise shape of the governing body.

The third change is the most important. The law now ought to define governors' and managers' powers and their status in relation to the local education authority. It is now a very curious anomaly that the law (section 17) says schools must have governors or managers and must be conducted in accordance with rules or articles, but that at no point does it say what they should do. In 1944 when some schools with centuries of tradition were being brought into the publicly maintained system, and thousands of totally new secondary schools were being created, it was perhaps reasonable to leave the Secretary of State to approve a school's articles. (It is still widely but erroneously believed that governors have far greater control over the ex-secondary modern school than the local grammar school in the same authority.)

But today it is much easier to define a set of principles of government and management appropriate to all schools. It is entirely possible to say that governing bodies should have responsibilities for the general conduct and curriculum of the school, for its finances and for its staffing within the framework of local education authority. The voluntary schools with still be the stumbling block for many. But even if they are excluded at this point, there is no legislative problem. The act could refer to county schools only.

It would still seem appropriate for the Secretary of State to issue some guidance to local education authorities. For however much one wants to leave to local education authorities to fit with local circumstances, as with membership, there are still some issues of principle which do not fit comfortably within an act, but still need to be given a firm base in authority.

After the *1944 Act*, the minister of the day issued a white paper.[10] Model articles and instruments were also drawn up. In one or other form, the Secretary of State needs to do the same today. For example, the fact that the governors have a collective responsibility needs to be clearly stated at a national level. (It was the fact that they did not exercise their responsibilities collectively that was part of the trouble in the Tyndale case.) But clearly there must be some procedural safeguards to protect teachers from spontaneous investigations by individuals, and to safeguard the governing body itself.

It also needs to be recognized by local education authorities and teachers, that one consequence of making the governing body a forum, must be to end the usual convention of confidentiality. There are difficulties. Some will no doubt use the arguments to say that it is now more important than ever to prevent anything important coming to the governing body. My interpretation would be quite the opposite – that it seldom has in the past. Confidentiality is much more likely to be a device to boost the self importance of the governors and at the same time prevents them asking questions and getting outside opinions. A local education authority should not be bringing business to a governing body, which it is not in the public interest to have known publicly.

Another principle, which requires backing from the centre is that governing and managing bodies should have access to information independently of the headteachers (and the clerk to the governing body, should the clerk be on the staff of the local education authority). Undoubtedly one of the factors most handicapping the effective operation of governing and managing bodies at present is that they have nobody who is primarily concerned to help them.

There could usefully be central guidance on standards of reporting: the head to the governing body, the governors to their interest groups. Another factor which needs elucidation is whether governing bodies should have their own clerk. It has been the practice of voluntary bodies. The old North Riding of Yorkshire imported the practice into its county schools. York did the same when it introduced its community conscious governors.

In practice: the local education authorities; the inner cities

The effectiveness of reform would still, however, depend quite largely on the local education authorities: whether their conflict procedures were clear, and whether they were willing to use them; whether they informed governors routinely of local education committee decisions or relevant national policy; what efforts their staff (including the advisers) made to attend governing body meetings.

But effectiveness depends too on what governors can learn on the job. Much of the evidence to Taylor has stressed the importance of training. While it is difficult to see authorities currently running ambitious training courses for governors, or laying on regular conferences, there is undoubtedly much that they can do. They can get some courses laid on at local adult education institutes. They can ensure that they circulate relevant education committee decisions with the papers for governors meetings. They can issue helpful booklets. They will be immensely helped in all this by the fact that a governing body with teachers and parents on it becomes immediately a more informed and demanding body. It is no longer so dependent for its information on the headteacher or the local education authority clerk, both of whom have an interest in gliding over some matters.

It may still be that governing bodies need extra help, though Taylor needs to examine the evidence sceptically. Suggestions have been put forward for local conferences, or standing committees of parent governors. It is also being suggested that some education body analagous to the community health councils should be set up. For it is being widely said that reform is all very well for the middle class, but irrelevant for most of the working class and pointless in areas of deprivation.

Such remarks should be seen as a warning light to ask what sort of school government is being thought of. Reform of a slightly mysterious but nonetheless important kind which 'good chaps' will understand and take part in? Or a reform whose point is obvious and whose institutional base is clear? Taylor should indeed examine the work being done by the secretaries to the community health councils or other officials whose prime responsibility is to the community. There are plenty of examples of community development officers working both with and against the local authority. But it should also examine whether such people have been needed just because responsibilities and procedures are not clear.

For the effectiveness of any reform that Taylor suggests in the end will hinge on that one point: will Taylor take governors and managers seriously enough to define their responsibilities and give them a public function. If it does, reformed governors and managers ought to work as well as tenants associations and a host of different forms of neighbourhood councils, already operating effectively in hundreds of working class areas, and dozens of deprived ones. And Taylor would have brought to education a reform as important as any in the last 100 years. For it would have established a new and relevant way of showing that the public institutions were in public hands.

Notes

1 BARON, G. and HOWELL, D. (1974) *Government and Management of Schools* Athlone Press.
2 *Children and their Primary Schools* HMSO, 1967.
3 The Public Schools Commission Report on Direct Grant Schools, HMSO, 1970.
4 *Times Educational Supplement*, 4th December 1974.
5 PRADERIE, M. (1974) *Participatory Planning in Education*, OECD.
6 Quoted by MACLURE, S. (1975) *Educational Documents, England and Wales, 1816 to the Present* Methuen.
7 School Council Working Paper No. 53, *The Whole Curriculum 13–16*, Evans Methuen (1975).
8 *Enquiry One*, HMSO 1968.
9 *Times Education Supplement*, January 25th 1974.
10 Principles of Government in Maintained Secondary Schools, Cmnd 6523, 1944.

3.3a Institutional autonomy and public accountability

M. Kogan

As with most important issues, the question of accountability for education has journeyed across the Atlantic. Yet there are differences in the problems as perceived by the Americans and by the British. In the late 1960s the problem for Americans was how the school system might become more open to the community, parental participation, and control. That issue is certainly alive in the UK today and we all wait to hear the truths enunciated by the Taylor Committee. There is, however, an important difference in that American liberals were attacking highly formalized and impervious school systems in which administrators and teachers alike, it was maintained, were opaquely defensive to the wishes of the people. Here there is, of course, criticism of local authorities, and of central government but the emphasis is more on the question of how teachers are and should be accountable to publicly elected authorities who are granted a reasonable degree of moral legitimacy and the right to administer. The heat is, in fact, on the teaching profession rather than on the larger governing system.

These issues have not, thus far, been subject to much research, and certainly not by the author of this paper, even of an historical or impressionistic nature. The comments here are, therefore, based largely on informal conjecture rather than on detailed study.

The concept of accountability and autonomy
The dichotomy expressed in the title of this talk is classic. Accountability or answerability relies on the assumption that public institutions and those who work in them should respond to community and social prescriptions. The underlying premise is collectivist. Institutional or professional autonomy (and I shall argue that these are not necessarily the same thing) responds instead to individualist, or atomistic, assumptions which would confer initiative and freedom on the smallest possible units, preferably

Source: *Autonomy and Accountability in Educational Administration* (1975), pp. 19–28.

individual people. This antimony underlies the whole body of social policies[1] and, I have maintained elsewhere,[2] the range of human desires and propensities as well. The duality is echoed in virtually every social setting where people have to do their own thing, but do it with regard to other people as well. It permeates all individual roles so that, for example, an effective teacher or educational administrator is forever changing gear: at some times the role demands collaboration and mutual service giving and attempts to relate collaterally to others within an institution, whilst at other times the role demands taking on a sanctioned and necessary role of monitor, adversary or advocate of some outside or dependent or stigmatized group.

The units of discussion

If, then, we must observe these quiddities of accountability and autonomy in tension with each other within institutions, we must next determine what unit is appropriate for study within the educational system. It would be tempting to assume that professionalism and the discretion that surrounds it make autonomy essentially that of the individual practitioner. And we tend to mix two assumptions that do not easily relate to each other. The first assumption is that individual teachers have, or should have, professional autonomy and freedom. The second is a leading assumption of British educational governance that the prime unit of control and of work is and should be the school, the college or the university which also has autonomy and freedom.

In fact, however, we need at least three levels of analysis. The first is that of the individual practitioner and role holder. Secondly there is the level of what I will call the prime institution (to be defined later). Thirdly, there is the level of the total governing system or organization. And they interfold with each other like one of those wooden Russian dolls. A large number of roles within education are both managers of subordinates and subordinates of managers.

Individual teacher autonomy, accountability and professionalism

The first unit for analysis is, therefore, that of the individual teacher. To refer to a point mentioned earlier, professionalism does indeed come in individual packets. Inasmuch as the term means anything at all (and I personally find some of the classic statements too full of overlapping categories to be at all certain about their usefulness) it is the freedom of the individual practitioner to assert professional standards and norms of discretion on individual problems or cases or people. He may work by himself, as does a medical general practitioner, or a solicitor, or a barrister, or in a federal practice relationship. If he works in a federal relationship, by definition he is really a solo performer sharing resources, institutional reputation, and so on. If, however, he works in a hierarchy, as teachers in schools do, the professionalism does not lie so much in the institutional oneness of the role, for prescriptions certainly are laid down by the total institution, but in what I think is really meant by professionalism anyway – the maximum of discretion to make individual judgements over the core activity of the institution – teaching and learning in schools, prescribing treatments in hospitals, determining social work procedures for individuals and so on. And the public service has a wide range of such discretionary arrangements. The clearest example of the free practitioner working within an otherwise strongly hierarchical system is that of the hospital consultant within the National Health Service. He is, in effect, a free entity, some would say autonomous, who runs his firm or department and expects from the hospital authority only the most general of organizational prescriptions which are embodied in the allocation of resources or the assumption that he will not be negligent rather than on the detailed allocation and surveyance of task performance.[3]

My starting generalization is, therefore, that teachers in educational institutions, including schools, FE colleges, and universities, are within the British ethos expected to work within broad prescriptive limits, with wide discretion or with what some would call differing degrees of autonomy.

Prime institutions

Now I must not go much further in analysing the role of the individual teacher if I am to keep to the terms of reference set me. But I need to examine this a bit further because, thus far, there has been no answer given to the question of 'What is the prime institution in education?' By prime institution I mean that role or collection of roles that has sufficient authority in terms of resources, legitimacy, public acceptance and so on, to perform the core activities without recourse to the total system except for the most general prescriptions. So a primary school is very likely a prime institution by this definition. Whilst teachers certainly have strong discretion over the way they perform their tasks in the classroom, if only because relationships between pupils and teachers are virtually impervious to outside scrutiny, the primary school must have a unitary philosophy, integration of curriculum and use of time. This requires submission to collective decision making (either by the Head or by the whole body of teachers). The clientele think of the whole school as the place where their child is being educated, rather than the class of the individual teacher. The school has, in fact, a public personality. In secondary schools, too, the same is true but many would now begin to ask whether for purposes of curriculum development, the exploitation of full teaching knowledge and skills, as well as democratic purposes of participation, a secondary school should not be regarded more as a federation of prime institutions which might be the departments or the houses or the years or whatever is the place where the core activities are worked out.[4] For the most part, the secondary school as a whole remains as the prime institution. Is is not, as it were, a holding company for a federation of colleges. The individual teacher responds to prescriptions laid down by heads of departments but all, for the most part, have recourse to decisions made by the headmaster, very likely in consultation with his senior colleagues, and with consultative machinery within the school, for the various components of the key tasks of the school. The allocation of time (through timetabling), of accommodation, of equipment, and of the more intangible but equally potent dimensions of his work such as expectations of curriculum, internal organization, educational style and aspiration, would, in the traditional model emanate from the head. No study so far[5],[6] has really derogated from the role of the head as manager or as chief executive.[7]

Developments from this position are being quite cogently argued. The demand is for a collegiate in place of a management or chief executive structure. As I understand it, those were the arguments originally proposed for Countesthorpe[8] and now by those secondary school teachers who argue that the whole school is too large for decisions on the main tasks and that, in effect, the department or if possible the individual should be the prime institution. It is true, of course, that the individual teacher is the provider of teaching and learning for his pupils but in a secondary school so many teachers have contacts with an individual pupil and the tasks of the school go well beyond what an individual teacher can provide, that we cannot say that he alone has enough authority or performs enough of the principal tasks to meet this definition. As a matter of fact, therefore, I conclude that in secondary education the prime institution is the school, although developments might change this position in some cases.

In further and higher education the position is somewhat different, in the universities and polytechnics of which the author has knowledge, the arrangement is predominantly collegiate. A university is essentially a federation of departments. The departments generate and authorize the curriculum although within the overall procedural structure laid down by the university and with monitoring by external examiners or, in some cases, professional bodies such as the Law Society or the British Psychological Society. But the department (or is it the individual teacher within it) is much like a medical firm within a hospital. It looks to the university for general sanction for its existence and for resources. It responds to general prescription about numbers of students to be admitted and the overall shape of degree courses. Where universities attempt to control or to colour the performance of departments' main tasks of teaching, learning and research, they become somehow unreal as universities. Thus the strongly denominational university of the USA or even the technological university in this country either sheds that distinctive orientation or is thought to be a bit funny. The university is, in fact, primarily an institution for allowing individual practitioners to do their work. And, as far as I can see, this is often true of polytechnics as well.

It is not clear, however, whether a university is a federation of individual teachers or of departments. The department can impose consistency in the curriculum it offers for its teaching and can also do something about teaching standards (but not too much) through the promotion power of its head, through collective policies about the admission of students and the classes awarded students. In some cases, I am told, but it is quite beyond my experience, the Head of Department may prescribe the teaching content of individual teachers. But, then, it is a matter of individual departmental preference as to whether those collective prescriptions are made collegiately by all members of the department or whether the Head of Department imposes them.

Thus far, the argument has been, therefore, that professionalism, an uncertain entity, might best be thought of in terms not of autonomy as much as degrees of discretion which individual teachers hold. At one extreme, the individual teacher might be, in effect, a prime institution all of his own. To examine this properly, we should have to look at the role of, say, a Fellow of All Souls' College, Oxford. In between, the units which are both free and accountable, in differing degrees, might well be the individual teacher, the department within the institution, the total school or college, or, perhaps, the whole system. My feeling is, however, that in primary and secondary education the prime institution is now the school. Within the 'freer' part of higher and further education, the department looks very much like being the prime institution. Reputations tend to be departmental rather than university as a whole, and that is where much of the academic freedom is exercised.

Institutions and the total system

We must now turn back to the main theme of how far the prime institutions within the system are both autonomous, or free, and accountable. In the literal sense of the word, it seems likely that the only autonomous institutions are private schools and University College, Buckingham. But this turns, perhaps, on the pedantic question of whether there are degrees of autonomy.

The generalization to be made is that there is no educational institution receiving public monies which is fully autonomous and which does not respond to one form or the other of prescription from one superior or otherwise controlling body.

Again, let us take the always ambiguous case of higher education. Relationships have changed radically since the 1972 White Paper merely decelerated the rate of expansion.[9] The standard description[10] of universities' relationships with the state was that they were given discretion in five-year lumps, so that the prescriptions were concerned fundamentally with the balance between different course offerings and research, and the number of students accepted, within generalized cost limits, but that the core activities, teaching, learning and research, could be conducted in a way in which the universities thought fit. On those core activities there were, and still are, the external controlling influences such as those exerted by external examiners, the academic peer groups who so relentlessly review what is written, as well as the professional bodies that impose their own requirements.

In a formal sense, nothing has changed on the balance between prescription and discretion. The prescriptive limits are always expressed in terms of resources and both the resource margins and the time span over which discretion is accorded institutions have tightened up considerably. Indeed, if, as A. V. Dicey says somewhere, the essence of the Rule of Law is predictability, the DES and the UGC are quite near to taking on the characteristics of the Mafia.

Yet resource controls over universities have always been there and the manpower planning component has always been there as well. But it becomes far more explicit in the UGC letters allocating resources for the quinquennium beginning in 1967 when UGC 'guidance' and expectations as to the balance between different types of courses and student numbers were overtly expressed.

But there is an important point raised at a previous conference by Dr Eric Briault. He made the point that control over resources and control over the curriculum operate at two different levels within the school system. And he argued that there is no true control over the educational process if control over resources is separate. It is not completely certain that this must be so: it would be possible to argue, for example, that mutual vetoing – of the resource controllers who will only grant resources for the education which they want, and of the curriculum controllers who will only provide education in return for the resources they need – is a reasonable and natural way of proceeding in a complex political structure.

But Eric Briault illuminates an important point about universities' discretion. For there must come a point where resource decisions bite into the essential discretion over the core activities of the universities and the polytechnics. For example, teaching in British higher education is thought to be strongly related to the research being undertaken by teachers. Whilst basic undergraduate courses might be taught from the main texts, no honours course is complete if at least some of it is not taught by specialists in their areas of expertise. If the UGC cuts our present quite liberal staffing ratios, and if teachers have to broaden the range of their work to meet the needs of a far wider student population, undergraduate teaching will inevitably be of a different kind because teachers will not have free time for research. Again, if the main resource for researchers will be that of public contracts, the nature of their other activities will be affected. I hasten to say that they may not be affected for the worst. But they will change.

So discretion over teaching and learning and research is there and is embodied in the teacher's free use of time. But inasmuch as that free use of time is limited, and the physical setting within which teaching is undertaken is cut down, curriculum will be affected.

Much the same will be true of the rest of higher and further education. But there are three important differences that affect the institutional discretion of the public sector. First, the governing mechanisms, namely, the local authorities have a direct control over resources so that the polytechnic or FE college is simply not free to determine how it might deploy them. Secondly, though the Departments in polytechnics, to take the strongest case, are often indistinguishable in style, expectation and assumed freedom from the universities, they have three quality controls in place of the university's one. Both types of institution have external examiners. The polytechnics have to face the CNAA and also the staff inspectors with the regional advisory councils who make quality judgements determining whether advance courses should run and qualifications be given for them. And by the time we get to the national certificate and diploma system with their joint committees the same is true, but even more so.

As far as the schools are concerned we ought, once again, to recall the peculiarities of the British system. For where education is seen to be strongly instrumental and capable of being programmed to produce distinct results, a strict hierarchical structure with strong management and inspection roles and with small discretion at the school level follows logically. But where it is assumed that teaching and learning processes rely on interaction between individual teachers and pupils within a wide knowledge framework, the strong management systems do not disappear but there is more of a premium on discretion within increasingly wide prescriptive limits.

Most school systems have a hierarchical structure in which the providing or governing authority are in a position analogous to that of a manager to the subordinate head of institution. And central government prescriptions also have a place although there is certainly not a 'managerial' relationship between central government and local authorities in the schools. If we look at the main tasks of the school it is clear that they are not autonomous. They have freedom and discretion but within prescriptive limits. The British school has wide discretion over the content and organization of teaching and learning which is its main task. The limits are those of finance, whether embodied in a general grant or specific grants to institutions, physical resources made available to schools, the number and types of teachers, the law of education which determines the number of sessions taught each year. The secondary school examination system and major issues such as the age of admission and type of subject structure in exams are decided by central government.

Moreover, and increasingly, governing bodies are beginning to take up a strong role. Professor Baron and Mr. Howell's researches[11] show a widely varying pattern throughout the country. In the larger cities, at least, demands are being made by parents and local pressure groups that the governing bodies, on which they get representation, will have a larger say in the appointment of staff, and will not shirk discussion of the curriculum, although that is where active pressure from outside meets active resistance from many teachers.

Policies for accountability

So far, the argument has been almost totally in terms of autonomy, freedom and discretion. In what sense are teachers accountable?

First of all as far as school teachers are concerned there are components of accountability which can be stated. It is the teacher who establishes the content of the curriculum in terms of his and the school's perception of children's development, and cognitive and affective skill needs. Secondly, he establishes curriculum in response to social expectations of what children need and what society wants children to have. Thirdly, he cannot do everything that society wants because society itself produces conflicts as to what the school should do, so choices have to be made. But then, fourthly, he ought to be accountable, but rarely is, for making clear the values being promulgated or, more often, insinuated into teaching, and what are the expected outcomes of teaching.[12]

Who is going to ensure that this accountability is discharged? The school will remain hierarchical and managerial, I assume, and the head, acting far more than is now common with an academic board of the school and with a strongly participative departmental academic system, will be accountable to the governing body for declaring the aims of curriculum and internal organization as the school sees them. I do not suggest that the governing body should attempt to interfere in detail or even substantially with the curriculum. But they should be a point to which public declarations of intent should be made. And their role will be all the more essential as secondary education rids itself of selection, moves through a decade of uncertainty on to a genuine comprehensive system in which pluralism, which means everybody getting what they need, predominates.

Beyond the governing bodies are local authorities who should not shirk their accountability to the public to provide good schools. That must mean that they do not pretend that all teachers respond to advice and guidance and that some do not need inspection and sanctions. I have argued elsewhere that the tenure system ought now to go[13] although teachers might be *de facto* in tenure unless good cause is shown. And I should like to see the local government ombudsman turned into a real instrument of review so that parents who do not get a square deal from the local authority or the schools can go right outside the system to make their case.

What does this do to professionalism? It will strengthen it. Judges are quite strong people but are subject to meticulous appeal and review. Doctors can be sued for negligence. Academics can be hacked to pieces when they produce a bad book. These are the toning up processes which teachers do not have to face. True they have to face many other difficult situations not encountered by other professions.

It is far more difficult to specify the accountability of the university academic, or of the other academics, or of the other academics outside the compulsory ages and zones of education. Children have to attend schools. Nobody has to attend higher education and I hope it will not be thought special pleading to suggest that accountability of, say, university teachers might be exacted in two ways. First, higher education has been seen to be far more vulnerable to government decisions than is the school system. The schools have to go on, and with their continuing flow of pupils the reward system of promotion and so on are also continuous. Higher education is subject to opportunity waves and to far more manipulation by public policy. This should not be a cause for complaint. Society will be exceedingly stupid if it does not continue to value higher education but, ultimately, the intensity of that valuation is a social decision in which university academics should have the last and not the first say. If higher education is thought not to be responsive enough to social needs, the government can withhold resources and impose conditions on everything except the content of teaching. The present complaint of the universities should not be about the government's right to make decisions but that the government has no policy whatsoever for the universities, that judgments are being made which simply do not accord to the facts – some university teachers work far harder, for better causes, and for less money, than do some civil servants – and that uncertainty has been allowed to cloud the relationships between the universities and government. Secondly, there is accountability to the market. The word soon gets round if a higher education course is no good. And universities, polytechnics and further education have been quick to respond to market pressures on them. Again, however, the tenure system needs a thorough review.

But having said this it seems to me that the case for the widest possible discretion is insuperable. At the conceptual level, we have the powerful claim for poly-centralism put up by Lindblom and Braybrooke.[14] By assuming that institutions will be free, we are pursuing ends by choosing the best available means and giving them authority to get on with the job. In countries where the schools is neatly tied up by the central ministry they have been no more successful than ours in inducing high skill training or in keeping delinquency at bay. As long as the accountability rules become strong, there is every reason for school to become stronger and for institutions within schools to begin to be powerful. If the collegiate structure is not accepted yet in this country, at least schools can recognize that they are complex institutions in which collegiate sub-structures should be encouraged.

This leaves over, of course, the question of super-institutional objectives and how they might be achieved. Given discretion to each school or university or polytechnic the local authority or central government administrator has some real problems. For he, too, is accountable for the use of money and resources and for ensuring that people get what they want. This brings us into the touchy question of evaluation which is not part of my present subject. And it brings us into the more general problem facing officers of the larger local authorities and central government. How do they aggregate and disaggregate the work of a large number of free institutions ?

This paper has necessarily been diffuse in its discussion and uncertain of its empirical base. The duality with which it began, of autonomy and accountability, is a good one. Indeed, it is difficult to conceive of anybody in any social system who does not benefit from a measure of accountability. It tones up the freedoms which are enjoyed and sets purposes. Those purposes need not be exclusively external or immutable. Indeed, accountability within a publicly paid for system should include the duty to propose change in that for which one is accountable. Pushing out the limits of discretion, changing the prescriptive framework, and thus responding to the social environment which teachers should serve are part of the freedom and accountability which I have been describing.

Notes

1 PINKER, R. 'Social Theory and Social Policy'.
2 KOGAN, M. 'Social Policy and Public Organizational Values', *Journal of Social Policy*, Vol. III, Part II.
3 Report of a Committee on Hospital Complaints Procedure (Davies Committee), 1974.
4 Unpublished notes prepared for the Progress Reform in Secondary Education by Pat Fitton.
5 For example RICHARDSON, R. *The Teacher, the School and the Task of Management.*
6 COOK, A. and MACK, H. *The Role of the Head Teacher.*
7 HUGHES M. G., 'The Professional as an Administrator: The Case of the Secondary School Head', *Educational Administration Bulletin*, 2(1) and 2(2).
8 McMULLEN, T. 'Internal Organization and Social Relationships in the School', paper given at 'Creativity of the School' workshop, OECD, Portugal, 1972.
9 KOGAN, M. *Educational Policy Making*, Chapter X.
10 MORRIS, A. Background papers, University Planning and Organization, University of Sussex, 1974.
11 BARON, G. and HOWELL, D. A., (1974) *Government and Management of Schools* Athlone Press.
12 KOGAN, M. 'How Free Should Teachers Be?', *Times Educational Supplement*, 5 September 1975.
13 See 12.
14 LINDBLOM, C. E. and BRAYBROOKE, D., *A Strategy for Decision Making.*

3.3b A response

Anita Ellis

In responding to Professor Kogan's paper, I speak from the standpoint of one whose professional experience is – and always has been – based in secondary education. I shall address myself particularly to the word 'accountability' although, without a certain measure of autonomy, it would be a word of little significance.

Accountability is for heads and their staffs both a crucial and painful word. It is my belief that in this country, secondary heads and their staff have a degree of autonomy which is considerable when one compares their situation with that of, for example, their American or French counterparts. However, there is very frequently an unwillingness to acknowledge fully the degree of autonomy which they possess, so as to protect themselves from the thorny responsibility of being accountable: for the type, content and organization of their curriculum; for the spending of their capitation; for the appointment and distribution of staff and their promotion; for the values and priorities which the daily organization of the school embodies, etc. They are nevertheless accountable to their pupils, to their pupils' parents, to the society both of the present and of the future, to the LEA and in a particular way to their colleagues within their own institution. It is perhaps worth reflecting on the fact that a teacher's and a school's accountability has for a long time been exclusively based upon his/their examination results. In my first school, the unfortunate teacher whose examination results were poor, two years in succession, was handed a copy of the *Times Educational Supplement* as a strong hint that she should move on! The whole question of evaluation is in the melting pot – certain of the new curricula are far less easy to evaluate in the traditional method, not all pupils have the same awesome respect for public examinations held by some schools and teachers; the whole question is far more sophisticated and complex than was previously thought.

Source: *Autonomy and Accountability in Educational Administration* (1975), pp. 29–31.

Before developing these points further, I should like to extend Professor Kogan's definition of professionalism – which underlies and informs what I wish to say. I believe professionalism further involves an absolute loyalty to the prime task. It requires an ability so to protect the boundaries of the task, that it is well and fully carried out; implicit within this is a respect for the integrity and work of one's colleagues, because the task in which everyone is engaged commands one's loyalty above all else. In that sense one's loyalty ultimately is to the task, rather than to persons. In the case of secondary education, the task is unequivocally about pupils' learning: intellectual, social, emotional and physical.

Schools are increasingly caught in a very painful dilemma as to the nature, both of the teacher-parent contract, and of the contract between the teacher and society – in respect of the present, as well as of future generations of adults. The parent-child relationship is, in my judgment, paramount. In exercising his professional skills and judgment, the teacher can find that he is in direct conflict with the wishes of a parent. The fine line which divides, in certain circumstances, his professional responsibility to his pupil, from the parents' rightful position (and his respect for that position) can be hard to maintain when he feels the parent to be in error. However, schools, especially in the state sector, have traditionally often paid only scant lip-service to the fact that their pupils *actually have parents* and that formal education up to the mid-adolescent phase is a three-cornered affair: pupil, school, parents. There are often cases of enormous arrogance on the part of a head and his/her staff in relating with parents. We are undeniably accountable to each parent who, either through choice or not – entrusts his child to us for the duration of the child's formal education. We must make clear our aims, our values and our priorities; inform parents about the thinking behind changes of curriculum and organization and expect to be challenged by them as we work. We are, after all, working with their children. In my experience, there are very few parents who do not care about their children.

Parents often do not receive the respect due to them by schools; schools are often trapped by knowing that the necessary innovations are difficult for parents to appreciate, as they are quite outside their own former experience of school. How does the school handle the parents' understandable anxiety and apprehension that their child is the guinea-pig, without compromising their professional integrity? In the case of the breakdown, albeit temporarily, of parent-child relationship, the school must put its weight behind trying to support the healing of that relationship, without compromising either the child's future or the teacher's professional integrity. This is what accountability is about in this context – it is hard and painful, but it is of the very essence of one's professionalism as a teacher.

We are, at present, those of us working in comprehensive schools, struggling along a very difficult pathway. For the first time ever, the whole of the population is required by law to remain in formal education institutions well into the mid-phase of adolescence. The only curriculum models which we have, are those worked out by our predecessors (and still largely in use everywhere) at the turn of the century, for the formal education of the sons (rather than daughters even) of the middle and upper middle classes, whose children were destined for the various professional and leadership roles in society. Furthermore, we are right in the midst of a technological and, one might argue, social revolution – such that none of us has any conception of what the adult lives of our present-day pupils will be like. What, then, is an appropriate and relevant secondary school curriculum to be, and how should it be ordered? Those of us working in schools whose staff have the intellectual competence and self-confidence as well as social commitment to struggle with these questions, are working in virgin territory. We are, nevertheless, still undeniably accountable to our pupils, to their parents, to present-day society and to the next generation for what we do. This is hard, but we must fully accept the responsibility and load of this accountability, as well as finding the courage to proceed further with our pupils into these unchartered forests. The manpower forecasts of the next thirty to fifty years tell us that the need for hewers of wood and the drawers of water will decrease drastically, but that society must have many more young adults trained to higher levels of technical skill than at present, and able to cope with a number of fundamental job changes during their lives; they must be able to cope with the uncertainty of much more mobile living and working situations, be able to cope with a reduced working week of perhaps 20–25 hours and the remaining so-called leisure time. Consequently, being realistic, we should be working within a time span of forty to fifty years when we work with our pupils now.

Society is currently highly critical of many of those coming out of schools and demanding a much improved product. Theirs is the right to demand – when they place an every increasingly large slice of the economic cake into education. Notwithstanding that, schools cannot be the panacea of all social problems, we must necessarily struggle with the issues of the future as we identify them, if we are not to sell our pupils, the next adult generation, down the river, and if we are to justify our existences to those who foot the heavy bills of education.

Finally, I want briefly to consider the problem of autonomy and accountability within the actual institution. I do not agree that bodies, including governors, external to a school should have any particular rights in the appointment of staff (other than of the head and senior staff such as deputies) or in the allocation of resources, or in developing and planning the curriculum. They should have the right to establish and require that those professionally skilled to work in a school are appropriately competent and professionally and morally sound. Thereafter 'the maximum of discretion to make individual judgments over the core activity of the institution' (Kogan) belongs to those who work within the school.

Traditionally each teacher has been fairly autonomous within his own classroom, accountable to the head, but otherwise safe unless he infringes the criminal law, because of the security of tenure which he enjoys. In my own experience, this is, in part, changing: the concept of group-teaching, and a corporate management approach born out of the federation of faculty and pastoral units, in which each faculty chairman or year head is accountable to his staff for representing them and acting on their behalf at senior management level, demand a degree of accountability amongst colleagues that is probably new and painful, but certainly invigorating and strengthening of professionalism. The concept that each member of staff whether he be head or probationer, is acting on behalf of his colleagues in everything which he contributes to the whole enterprise, is difficult for many initially to grasp, but staff development along these lines demands greater public accountability amongst colleagues and less protective covering up of the weaker members of staff. In such circumstances the head must be as accountable to his staff as they are to him for his decisions, behaviour etc. Unfortunately some staff prefer to choose the quieter life in which the paternalistic 'he's paid to take the decisions and carry the can' – philosophy obtains. In my judgment pupils deserve a better model of adults working together than that.

In conclusion, I should like strongly to support Professor Kogan's statement: 'that the tenure system ought now to go although teachers might be *de facto* in tenure unless good cause is shown'. The poor self image and low level of real professionalism which has persisted amongst teachers since the last century has allowed them to defend themselves within a fortress of multi-union armour, whereby the incompetent, the idle and the inadequate who do not break the criminal law have an almost solid security of tenure, regardless of the fact that generations of pupils and colleagues have a 'raw deal' in being obliged to work with them. This is the antithesis of professionalism, and ultimately blocks the rightful demands for accountability from government, the LEA, parents, pupils, governors and colleagues alike.

Like Professor Kogan, I am utterly convinced that public accountability with institutional autonomy strengthens the school, the teachers and their professionalism: it thereby offers their pupils and society a superior education service.

3.4 Toward objective criteria of professional accountability in the schools of New York City

H. S. Dyer

The concept of professional accountability

The concept of accountability can have many levels of meaning, depending upon where one focuses attention in the structure of the school system. Throughout this paper I shall be using the term in a restricted sense as it applies to the individual school as a unit. At this level I think of the concept as embracing three general principles:

1 The professional staff of a school is to be held collectively responsible for knowing as much as it can (a) about the intellectual and personal-social development of the pupils in its charge and (b) about the conditions and educational services that may be facilitating or impeding the pupils' development.

2 The professional staff of a school is to be held collectively responsible for using this knowledge as best it can to maximize the development of its pupils toward certain defined and agreed-upon pupil performance objectives.

3 The board of education has a corresponding responsibility to provide the means and technical assistance whereby the staff of each school can acquire, interpret, and use the information necessary for carrying out the two foregoing functions.

I emphasize the notion of joint accountability of the entire school staff in the aggregate – principal, teachers, specialists – because it seems obvious that what happens to any child in a school is determined by the multitude of transactions he has with many different people on the staff who perform

Source: *Phi Delta Kappan* (December 1970) pp. 196–205.

differing roles and presumably have differing impacts on his learng, which cannot readily, if ever, be disentangled. I emphasize the notion that staff members are to be held accountable for keeping themselves informed about the diverse needs of their pupils and for doing the best they can to meet those needs. In the light of what we still don't know about the teaching-learning process, this is the most one may reasonably expect. To hold teachers, or anybody else, accountable for delivering some sort of 'guaranteed pupil performance' is likely to do more harm than good in the lives of the children. Finally, I emphasize that professional accountability should be seen as a two-way street, wherein a school staff is to be held accountable to higher authority for its own operations while the higher authorities in turn are to be held accountable for supplying the appropriate information and facilities each school staff requires to operate effectively.

An important implication in the three principles set forth above is that there shall be developed a district-wide educational accounting system optimally adaptable to the information needs of each school in the district. Later in this paper I shall describe the salient features of such a system and shall suggest the procedures by which it might be developed and put to use. In this connection it should be noted that the type of educational accounting system here contemplated is to be distinguished from a fiscal accounting system. The kind of information provided by the former should not be confused with the kind provided by the latter. At all levels, the two types should complement each other in an overall management information system capable of relating benefits to costs. At the individual school level, however, educational accounting per se is of prime importance and is not usefully related to fiscal accounting, since the staff in a single school does not have and, in ordinary circumstances, cannot have much if any latitude in the raising and expanding of funds for its local operations.

The next section of this paper outlines what a fully functioning educational accounting system might be like and how it could operate as a means for holding a school staff accountable within certain constraints, for continually improving the effectiveness of its work. The last section briefly sketches plans by which the system might be brought into being and contains some cautions that should be heeded along the way.

Characteristics of an educational accounting system
Pupil-change model of a school
The theory behind the first of the three principles stated in the preceding section is that if a school staff is to fulfill its professional obligations it must have extensive knowledge of the pupils it is expected to serve. This theory is based on the notion of a school as a social system that effects changes of

various kinds in both the children who pass through it and in the professional personnel responsible for maintaining the school. The school as a social system becomes an educational system when its constituents are trying to ensure that all such changes shall be for the better. That is, the school as a social system becomes an educational system when its constituents – pupils, teachers, principal – are working toward some clearly defined pupil performance objectives.

There are four groups of variables in the school as a social system that must be recognized and measured if one is to develop acceptable criteria of staff accountability. These four groups of variables I call input, educational process, surrounding conditions, and output. Taken together, they form the pupil-change model of a school.

The input to any school at any given level consists of the characteristics of the pupils as they enter that level of their schooling: their health and physical condition, their skill in the three R's, their feelings about themselves and others, their aspirations, and so on. The output of any school consists of the same characteristics of the pupils as they emerge from that particular phase of their schooling some years later.

According to this conception, the input to any school consists of the output from the next lower level. Thus, the output of an elementary school becomes the input for junior high, and the output of junior high becomes the input for senior high. It is important to note that the staff of an individual school which is not in a position to select the pupils who come to it has no control over the level or quality of its input. In such a case, the pupil input represents a fixed condition with which the school staff must cope. The pupil output, however, is a variable that depends to some extent on the quality of service the school provides.

The third group of variables in the pupil-change model consists of the surrounding conditions within which the school operates. These are the factors in the school environment that may influence for better or for worse how teachers teach and pupils learn. The surrounding conditions fall into three categories: home conditions, community conditions, and school conditions. Home conditions include such matters as the level of education of the pupils' parents, the level of family income, the family pressures, and the physical condition of the home. Community conditions include the density of population in the enrollment area, the ethnic character of the population, the number and quality of available social agencies, the degree of industrialization, and so on. School conditions include the quality of the school plant, pupil-teacher ratio, classroom and playground footage per pupil, the esprit de corps of the staff, and the like.

In respect to all three types of surrounding conditions, one can distinguish those that the staff of a school finds easy to change from those that it finds hard to change. For example, in respect to home conditions, the school staff is hardly in a position to change the socioeconomic level of pupils' parents, but it may well be in a position to change the parents' attitudes toward education through programmes that involve them in the work of the school. Similarly, in respect to school conditions, it might not be able to effect much change in the classroom footage per pupil, but it could probably develop programmes that might influence the esprit de corps of the staff through in-service training. The identification of hard-to-change as contrasted with easy-to-change surrounding conditions is of the utmost importance in working toward objective criteria of professional accountability, since the staff of a school can hardly be held accountable for changing those factors in its situation over which it has little or no control.

The final set of variables in the pupil-change model are those that make up the educational process; that is, all the activities in the school expressly designed to bring about changes for the better in pupils: lessons in arithmetic, recreational activities, consultation with parents, vocational counselling, etc. Three principal questions are to be asked about the educational processes in any school: (a) Are they adapted to the individual needs of the children in the school? (b) Do they work, that is, do they tend to change pupils in desirable ways? (c) What, if any, negative side effects may they be having on the growth of the children?

The four sets of variables just described – input, output, surrounding conditions, and educational process – interact with one another in complex ways. That is, the pupil output variables are affected by all the other variables. Similarly, the educational process variables are influenced by both the pupil input and the surrounding conditions. And certain of the surrounding conditions may be influenced by certain of the educational processes. This last could happen, for instance, if a school embarked on a cooperative work-study programme with businesses in its enrollment area.

From the foregoing considerations, it is clear that if a school staff is to maximize pupil output in any particular way, it must be aware of the nature of the interactions among the variables in the system and be given sufficient information to cope with them in its work. This in turn means that, insofar as possible, all variables in the system must be measured and appropriately interrelated and combined to produce readily interpretable indices by which the staff can know how much its own efforts are producing hoped-for changes in pupils, after making due allowance for those variables over which it has little or no control. I call such indices school effectiveness indices (SEIS). They are the means whereby a school staff may be held responsible for knowing how well it is doing.

3 Accounting to whom?

Nature of the SEI

The functioning of a school can be described by a profile of school effectiveness indices, so that each school staff can readily locate the points at which its educational programme is strong or weak. Such a profile is fundamentally different from the traditional test-score profile, which is ordinarily generated from the grade equivalencies attached to the general run of standardized achievement tests. The underlying rationale of an SEI profile rejects grade equivalencies as essentially meaningless numbers that tend to be grossly misleading as indicators of a school's effectiveness. Appropriate indices in the SEI profile of any given school at any given level can be derived only through a procedure involving all the schools at the same level in the district. The procedure consists of a series of regression analyses which I shall touch upon presently.

Two features of an SEI profile differentiate it from the usual test-score profile. First, each index summarizes how effective the school has been in promoting one type of pupil development over a definite span of years; for example, the three years from the beginning of grade four to the end of grade six. Second, the profile has two distinctions: a pupil development dimension comprehending different areas of pupil growth (e.g. growth in self-esteem, growth in the basic skills, growth in social behaviour) and a level-of-pupil-input dimension which might encompass three categories of children in accordance with their varying levels of development in any area at the time they entered grade four.

With this sort of profile it should be possible to discern in which areas of pupil development a school is more or less effective with different groups of pupils. Thus, SEI profile for a grade four to six school should be capable of answering questions like the following: in its teaching of reading over the three-year period, has the school done a better or worse job with pupils who entered grade four with a low level of reading performance as compared with those who entered with a high level of reading performance? During the three-year period, has the school been more or less effective in developing children's number skills than in developing their sense of self-esteem, or their social behavior, or their health habits?

The areas of pupil development to be incorporated in the educational accounting system for any district must grow out of an earnest effort to reach agreement among all the parties involved (teachers, administrators, board members, parents, pupils) concerning the pupil performance objectives that are sought. Such objectives will vary for schools encompassing different grade levels, and they will also vary, in accordance with local needs, among schools serving any given grade levels.

Securing agreement on the objectives is no mean enterprise, but it is obviously fundamental to a meaningful approach to the establishment of

314

any basis for holding professional educators accountable for their own performance in the schools.

Derivation of the SEI

One important point to keep in mind about any social effectiveness index is that it is a measure that must be derived from a large number of more fundamental measures. These more fundamental measures consist of three of the sets of variables suggested earlier in the discussion of the pupil-change model of a school as a social system, namely: (a) the pupil input variables, (b) the hard-to-change surrounding conditions, and (c) the pupil output variables. Measures of easy-to-change surrounding condition variables and of the educational process variables do not enter into the derivation of SEIS. They become of central importance subsequently in identifying the specific actions a school staff should take to improve the effectiveness of its operations.

The fundamental measures from which the indices are to be derived can take many different forms: academic achievement tests, questionnaires to get at matters like pupil self-esteem; physical examinations to assess health and health habits, a wide range of sociological measures to assess community conditions; and measures of various aspects of the school plant, equipment and personnel. Techniques for securing many of these measures are already available, but new and more refined ones will be required before a reasonably equitable educational accounting system can be fully operable.

Given the total array of measures required for the derivation of the SEIS, the first step in the derivation will be to apply such measures in all schools in the system at any given level − e.g., all the elementary schools, all the senior high schools − to secure the necessary information on pupil input and on the hard-to-change surrounding conditions.

The second step, to be taken perhaps two or three years later, will be to obtain output measures on the same pupils, i.e. those pupils who have remained in the same schools during the period in question.

The third step will be to distribute the pupils within each school into three groups − high, middle, and low − on each of the input measures. Two points are to be especially noted about this step. First, the distribution of input measures must be 'within school' distributions, with the consequence that the pupils constituting the 'high' group in one school could conceivably be in the 'low' group at another school where the input levels run higher with respect to any particular 'area of development'. Secondly, within any school, a pupil's input level could be high in one area of development (e.g. basic skills) and middle or low in another area of development (e.g. health).

The fourth step in deriving the SEIS is to compute, for each school, the averages of the hard-to-change condition variables that characterize the environment within which the school has had to operate.

Figure 1 Illustration of method of deriving school effectiveness indices in the teaching of reading

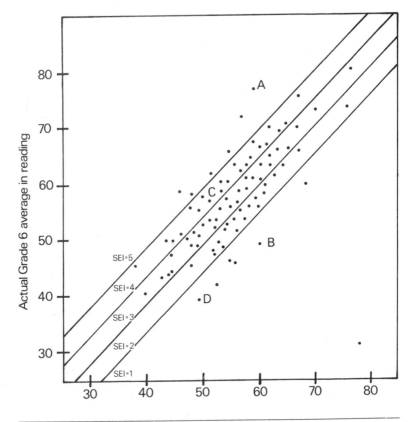

Grade 6 Predictions based on Grade 4 input and environmental variables

The fifth step is to get, again for each school, the average values of all the output measures for each of the three groups of pupils as identified by the input measures.

When all these data are in hand it becomes possible, by means of a series of regression analyses, to compute the SEIS that form the profile of each school.

A rough impression of how this process works may be obtained from an examination of the chart in Figure 1, which was developed from reading test scores obtained on pupils in ninety-one schools. The measures of input in reading were taken at the beginning of grade four, and the measures of output at the end of grade six. The numbers along the horizontal axis of the chart summarize the level of grade four reading input and hard-to-change conditions with which each school has had to contend. This summarization is expressed in terms of the grade six predicted average reading levels as determined by the regression analysis.

The numbers along the vertical axis show the actual average reading levels for each school at the end of grade six. For each school, the discrepancy between its predicted grade six reading level and its actual grade six average reading level is used as the measure of the effectiveness with which it has been teaching reading over the three-year period. It is the discrepancy between predicted and actual level of performance that is used to determine the SEI in reading for any school. In this case the SEI's have been assigned arbitrary values ranging from one to five.

Consider the two schools A and B. They both have predicted grade six reading averages of about 60. This indicates that they can be deemed to have been operating in situations that are equivalent in respect to their levels of input at grade four and the hard-to-change conditions that have obtained over the three-year period during which their pupils have gone from grades four through six.

The actual reading output levels at grade six for schools A and B are considerably different. A's actual level is about 73: B's actual level is about 48. As a consequence, school A gets an effectiveness index for the teaching of reading of five, while school B gets an effectiveness index of only one.

Schools C and D present a similar picture, but at a lower level of pupil input and hard-to-change conditions. Both have predicted averages of about 50, but C's actual average is about 56, while D's is only 38. Therefore C gets an SEI of four, and D gets an SEI of only one.

From these two pairs of illustrations, it should be noted that the proposed method of computing school effectiveness indices automatically adjusts for the differing circumstances in which schools must operate. This feature of the index is a sine qua non of any system by which school staffs are to be held professionally accountable.

Uses of the SEI

It was suggested at the beginning of this paper than one of the general principles underlying the concept of professional accountability is that the staff of a school is to be held responsible for using its knowledge of where the school stands with respect to the intellectual and personal-social development of its pupils. This is to say that it is not sufficient for a school to 'render an accounting' of its educational effectiveness. If the accounting is to have any educational payoff for the pupils whom the school is supposed to serve, the indices should point to some specific corrective actions designed to increase the school's effectiveness.

Many of such actions will perforce be outside the scope of the school itself, and responsibility for taking them must rest with the central administration. In most cases, however, a considerable number of such corrective actions should be well within the competence of the professional staff of the individual school. Responsibility for carrying them out can and should rest with that staff.

The function of school effectiveness indices in this connection is to indicate where a school staff might turn to find ways of improving its performance.

To illustrate how the SEIS might serve this purpose, let us speculate further about the relative positions of schools A and B in Figure 1. Since both schools show the same predicted output in reading for such pupils, it can be presumed that both schools are operating under equivalent advantages and handicaps in respect to the conditions that affect the reading ability of those pupils. Therefore, it is entirely legitimate to raise the questions: Why is school A doing so much better than school B in the teaching of reading? and What specifically is school A doing for its pupils that school B is not now doing, but presumably could be doing and ought to be doing to close the gap?

The reasons for the discrepancy between the two schools on this particular SEI are to be sought among the two sets of variables that did not enter into the derivation of the SEIS: namely, those variables that were designated 'educational process' and those designated 'easy-to-change surrounding conditions'. A systematic comparison of how the two schools stand with respect to these variables should provide the professional staff of school B with useful clues for actions that might be taken to increase its effectiveness in the teaching of reading.

The outcome of this exercise might turn up something like this:

1   School A conducts an intensive summer programme in reading; school B does not.
2   School A has a tutorial programme conducted by high school students for any pupil who wishes to improve his reading; school B has no such programme.
3   School A conducts parent-teacher study groups to stimulate more reading in the home; school B has little contact of any kind with the parents of its pupils.

There is, of course, no absolute guarantee that if school B were to initiate such programs it would automatically raise its SEI in reading from one to five. The factors involved in the life and workings of a school are not all that certain and clear-cut. Nevertheless, there should be a plain obligation on the staff of school B to at least try the procedures that appear to be working for school A and to monitor such efforts over a sufficient period to see whether they are having the desired effects. This particularization of staff effort contains the essence of what must be involved in any attempt to guarantee the professional accountability of a school staff.

The approach to accountability through a system of SEIS, if it is well understood and accepted throughout the schools of the district, should provide a mechanism for stimulating directed professional efforts toward the continuous improvement of educational practice on many fronts in all the schools.

Plans and cautions
Short-range and long-range plans
Clearly a full-scale educational accounting system of the sort here envisaged is hardly one that can be designed and installed full-blown in a year or two. It is one that would have to be worked out, piece by piece, over a considerable period of years. It contains technical problems many of which cannot be forseen in advance and can only be tackled as the accounting system comes into actual operation. More importantly, it would require a massive effort to secure the necessary understanding and cooperation from all the professional and community groups to be affected by it.

Nevertheless, because of the urgency of the situation in urban education and because no adequate and equitable educational accounting system can ever eventuate until some practical action is taken to get it under way, it is strongly suggested that a beginning should be made forthwith by means of a two-pronged approach. One approach would look to the carrying out of a partial short-range plan over the next two years; the other to the laying out of a long-range plan for the full-scale operation of the system to be achieved in, say, six years.

The short-range plan could begin with the reasonable assumption that there are two areas of pupil development that are of universal concern, especially as they touch the lives of minority group children in the early years of their schooling. These areas are reading and health. Acting on this assumption, one might, from currently available data, obtain input measures of these two variables on all children entering grades one and three with a view to getting output measures on the same children two years later. During the two intervening years a number of the more readily available measures of the hard-to-change conditions affecting each of the elementary schools in the system could conceivably be obtained – e.g. socio-economic status of pupils' parents, population density and ethnicity of each enrollment area, pupil-teacher ratio, classroom and playground footage per pupil, rate of pupil mobility, and the like. Thus, by the end of the second year, one would be in a position to compute tentative school effectiveness indices and prepare two SEI profiles for each elementary school in the system – one covering grades one and two, the other covering grades three and four. These profiles could then be used as bases for local discussions concerning their meaning and utility as measures of professional accountability.

The purpose of a short-range programme of this sort would be twofold: (1) to provide a first approximation of two important and practically useful objective criteria of professional accountability, and (2) to provide a concrete basis for bringing about a genuine understanding of what an educational accounting system is and how it can work for the benefit of the schools and the children who attend them.

Concurrently with the foregoing short-range effort, the development of a long-range plan should get under way. The first step in this planning process would be to initiate parent-teacher discussions to try (1) to reach a consensus on educational objectives in terms of the areas of pupil development that should be involved in an overall annual system for professional accounting, and (2) to agree on the priorities among such objectives as they might most appropriately apply to the educational needs of the pupils in each school. The second step in the long-range plan would be to assemble instruments for measuring input and output which would be appropriate and compatible with the objectives for each level of schooling. The third step would be to work out the means for collecting and analyzing the necessary data for measuring the conditions within which each school is operating and the specific processes that characterize its operations.

Avoiding false starts
One reason for initiating long-range planning concurrently with working through a partial short-range programme is to try to ensure that the ultimate goal of the full-scale system will not be lost from sight while major attention is necessarily focused on the detailed problems of getting a partial operating system under way quickly. In the search for ways around the short-range problems, it is altogether probable that a number of compromises will have to be made. The danger is that, unless the final end is kept in full view, some of these compromises will be such as to preclude attainment of a viable total system.

One mistake, for instance, that could be made at the outset of the short-range programme would be to yield to demands to use the input or output measures as if they were themselves measures of school effectiveness. The whole point of this paper is that a meaningful and equitable accounting of school effectiveness is possible only under two stringent conditions: (1) it must rest on at least two measures of pupil performance with a sufficient interval between them – probably not less than two years – to permit the school to have an effect on pupil learning which is large enough to be observable; and (ii) any output measure of pupil performance must be read in light of the level of pupil input and also in light of the conditions in which the school has been forced to operate during the period for which its effectiveness in the several areas of pupil development is being indexed. This point cannot be too strongly stressed. To compromise with this basic principle would wreck the entire enterprise.

A second mistake that could seriously damage the development of the system would be to introduce into it measures of IQ, as though they were measures of pupil input available simultaneously with measures of pupil output. This type of misuse of test scores has had a disastrous effect on the interpretation of educational measurements for at least fifty years. It should not be prolonged.

A third type of mistake to be avoided is that of concentrating the effort to develop SEIS on a certain selected group of schools (e.g. those in poverty areas) but not on others. If this is done the SEIS simply will not mean anything. A basic requirement in their derivation and use is that the essential measures must be obtained on all schools in the system so as to determine which schools are indeed comparable.

One other type of mistake that could be made in embarking on the short-range project would be to concentrate all the effort on a single area of pupil development, namely, the 'basic skills'. The danger here – and it is one by which schools have all too frequently been trapped – is threefold. First, it encourages the notion that, as far as the school is concerned, training in the basic skills is all that matters in a society where so many other human characteristics also matter. Secondly, it tends toward neglect of the fact that if a school gives exclusive attention to this one area of pupil development, it may purchase success in this area at the expense of failure in other areas – social behaviour, for instance. Thirdly, it tends to blind people to the interrelatedness of educational objectives, that is, to the fact that pupil development in one area may be heavily dependent on development in other areas. Learning to read, for example, may be dependent on the pupil's maintaining good health. And the pupil's sense of his worth as a human being may be dependent on his ability to read. It is for these reasons that the short-range programme suggested above includes at a minimum two widely different areas of pupil development.

Avoiding false analogies

The term educational accountability, as used most recently by certain economists, systems analysts, and the like, has frequently been based on a conceptualization that tends, by analogy, to equate the educational process with the type of engineering process that applies to industrial production. It is this sort of analogy, for instance, that appears to underlie proposals for 'guaranteed performance contracting' as exemplified in the much-publicized Texarkana project. But there is also a point beyond which it can be so seriously misleading as to undermine any sensible efforts to develop objective criteria of professional accountability.

It must be constantly kept in mind that the educational process is not on all fours with an industrial process; it is a social process in which human beings are continually interacting with other human beings in ways that are imperfectly measurable or predictable. Education does not deal with inert raw materials, but with living minds that are instinctively concerned first with preserving their own integrity and second with reaching a meaningful accommodation with the world around them. The output of the educational process is never a 'finished product' whose characteristics can be rigorously specified in advance; it is an individual who is sufficiently aware of his own incompleteness to make him want to keep on growing and learning and trying to solve the riddle of his own existence in a world that neither he nor anyone else can fully understand or predict.

It is for this reason that the problems involved in developing objective criteria of professional accountability will always be hard problems. They are problems, however, that must be tackled with all the human insight and good will that can be mustered if the schools of this urban society are to meet the large challenges that now confront them.

3.5 Participatory government – the place of the head

J. Watts

Any head must delegate or disintegrate.

However, delegation may be executed in such a way that no real authority, only workload, is passed out by the head. The crucial questions concern where the decisions are made and to whom decision-makers are accountable. Probably most heads today claim that their decisions are made in consultation, either with their deputies, some form of cabinet of faculty or pastoral heads, or even with their whole staff. Yet none of this consultation constitutes participatory government in the sense in which I wish to speak of it, and which has been practised at Countesthorpe since it opened in 1970.

At that time of opening, the question was asked, 'How may we maintain an innovatory approach once we have embarked upon it?' It was not enough to have instituted a school with a number of radically new features; change was envisaged as a continuous process. Hierarchical organizations are relatively impervious to change. How were we to remain open to change? More particularly, whence would come the initiative and the inventiveness for change? If it were to come only from the top, how could it be adequate? However experienced a head and his senior staff might be, however reliable their judgement, what likelihood was there of their imaginations being fertile? Younger teachers are more likely to have ideas and propose innovations than their elders. The ideas may need the riddling of experience, expertise and judgment, but they must keep coming.

My experience with graduate teacher training left me worried about the number of young men and women, ones with initiative and a sense of service, who changed their minds about becoming teachers after the experience of school practice had revealed to them the extent to which the hierarchy in staff would stifle their ambition. 'Keep quiet and conform'

Source: *The Countesthorpe Experience* (1976) pp.123–31.

was the message. They traded the securities of teaching for work with more risk, but a high demand for showing within a year or two what they could do with some opportunity for enterprise.

So the need to attract young teachers who want to get something done argues for their being given increased opportunity and responsibility. New developments in school place increased demands upon the teacher, and in particular he is required to forego much of the autonomy he formerly enjoyed in the classroom in order to plan and execute work jointly with groups of colleagues. What may have been acceptable in the closed classroom must be modified to balance the working of a team. With the general growth in the size of schools there is danger that the teacher may come to feel depersonalized and alienated. It is reasonable for him to expect, in return for meeting new demands, a new degree of control in determining the conditions under which he works (particularly concerning the distribution of available resources), whom he works with, and in what sort of atmosphere. Control of, and responsibility for, these conditions may be expected to produce increased satisfaction and dignity.

There are of course other arguments for reducing the powers normally invested in the head. Although a newly appointed head may be the most effective agent for rapid change in a school, his impetus will be lost within five years. The school may then have to wait for one or two decades to make another lurch forward.

Public demands for changes in the school may lead increasingly to ways being found to by-pass the head and introduce change-agents from outside. These may prove to be less gentle than the advisers and Schools Council project officers encountered up till now.

The school needs equally well to be protected from the destructive wake that may be left by the progressive reforming head who has failed to win a consensus of support from the staff, students and parents. An authoritarian progressive will usually come unstuck when outside agencies can exploit the division he has created among his staff. When this happens the reform aimed for by the head is thwarted, the power passes out of the school even to the point of its closing down and, more to the point, children suffer.

We are thus faced with the question of which way the head's powers will be redeployed. Will they spread to external authority, or will they be shared within school? In depicting what happens when shared internally at Countesthorpe, I wish first to outline the powers in question, then to consider the reshaped role of the head, then to look at the problems I have encountered in the process, and finally, to venture a forecast of further development.

Within normal terms of appointment, a head has usually enjoyed powers that can be considered under six broad headings. There is some variation in the extent to which governing bodies have retained control in any of these areas, and there are worrying current tendencies which threaten to take back powers from governors to local councils that I shall refer to later, but whoever holds these six cards is running the school and where governors have trusted the head whom they have appointed, these are the cards that he has been dealt.

First, the head has defined the objectives and the values for his school. He will operate within the limits of what the governors and parents expect, but this is seldom a problem if they have chosen the head they want. (In other words, the constraints will not need to be spelt out as the chosen head will be presumed to have internalized them.) The head seldom needs to make his objectives and values explicit. In fact, part of his power lies in leaving them implicit, or expressed only in ritual, so that they are not exposed to rational cross-examination and consequent modification. They can nevertheless be clearly understood and thus effectively govern the school. Wherever the objectives and values are explicit, the head still wins as he is the mouthpiece of the school in all public statement.

Second, the head determines curriculum, what is taught.

Third, distinguished but related, is control of the internal organization by which the head has power over access to the courses of learning within the general curriculum. He decides who has opportunity to learn what, who can study German and who has extra woodwork. He controls the timetable. He decides how the pupils are grouped, who teaches them and, within the statutory requirements, how long they stay at school.

Fourth, the head distributes the available money. Therein lies one of his greatest sources of power. He decides how capitation allowances from the local authority are used; he can starve one department to build up another. He virtually controls the distribution of special allowances to the staff, thus having authority over teachers' income outside their basic salaries. In some authorities this distribution of additional payments is made by the governors, but the head's recommendations to them remain crucial. This particular power can become, almost invariably does become, the most resented of all, especially when his distribution of favours remains secret. Through it the head can control staff by promises, threats and bargains. At the same time, he is laid open to promises, threats and bargaining from the lobbying of his staff. It becomes very difficult for a head to be sure when a teacher is being completely honest and frank with him, not saying what he thinks the head wants to hear, and it becomes difficult for the teacher behaving in that way to retain self-respect – which is the main reason for the isolation of the head; staff find it easier not to speak to him too often. Fifth, the head chooses his own staff. The extent to which the local authority qualifies this varies considerably but the head can usually make his pick. In contrast with employees in industry, he cannot dismiss the staff. But my main point is that it is the head who decides for his teachers whom they have to work with. They like his choice or lump it. This was all very well when we only had to tolerate each other in the staff-room and could retreat to the idiosyncrasies of our classrooms, but increasingly now we have to plan and work in close conjunction with these colleagues and feel a growing right to share also in their selection.

Finally, less obvious, but significant, is the degree of power that a head exercises through control of the media of communication. Quite apart from being the spokesman through the external media, via statements to the press, letters to parents, and so on, the head can assert his authority internally by such means as (a) control of paper and print for circulating notices, (b) convening and chairing staff meetings, (c) conducting assemblies, (d) access to public address equipment, (e) installation and distribution of telephones, (f) preparation of policy statements and reports. All of this amounts to a one-way system of regulative communications, with negligible means of feed-back for assistant staff or students.

At Countesthorpe we have changed all that. The major policy decisions that have shaped the curriculum and discipline of the school have been made by the consensus of the staff. Increasingly, students have contributed to this consensus, and in some instances parents and governors have participated. I accepted the headship in 1972 because I found the policies and the means of determining them attractive, and was prepared to answer for them externally while being accountable internally to the College. I remain as long as those two zones of accountability are compatible. Within the College we have varied executive roles, many of them held interchangeably by staff other than myself and deputies, but without the conventional chain of authority. Our chain of authority links decision-making groups whose composition is not fixed. The body that establishes any ruling consensus is a general meeting, the moot, which is open to all, including non-teaching staff and students. The moot establishes its own constitution, procedures and chairmanship. It meets as necessary, about once in six weeks. Other decision-making groups are responsible directly or indirectly to the moot and any individual may challenge their decisions through the moot.

The sub-groups may be standing or *ad hoc*. The principal standing committee consists of one quarter of the staff with student representation and it holds office for one quarter of the year. Thus every member of staff has a period on committee. Standing committee meets every Monday after school to receive reports and take intermediary decisions. It issues minutes the following day. Other committees include finance committee which is elected annually to make and apply the budget, and *ad hoc* appointment committees set up with each vacancy to select whoever is finally recommended to the authority for appointment to staff. All meetings are advertised and open.

Stated this way, structures appear to dominate. In operation, all depends on the attitudes of the participants, their readiness to use and, if necessary, to modify the structures in order to exercise and take responsibility for powers placed in their hands through them. All six areas of power that I have listed become shared by these means. The moot may finally decide major policy and organization, but in the preparatory ferment the ideas may spring from any source. Working parties, which eventually formulate proposals for development, are open to all. Anyone may put forward a scheme. It will be tested for its desirability and practicality under the constraints of resources, staffing, space and money. A final proposal will be the work of many hands, a modification of many ideas. Once it is ratified, though, everyone is committed to making it work, because no one has had it imposed from above without opportunity to shape it.

Far from becoming a lift-attendant in a bungalow, the head has much remaining to him. When Countesthorpe opened in 1970, Tim McMullen, its first head, intended to make himself redundant. There are still those who would like to see the head phased out while accepting him as an unfortunate necessity for the time being. I do not share this view and will consider it further in my concluding section. Anyway, what do I do at present?

What I do not do is to allow myself to become the administrator. Except in small schools, where the head may still be a general factotum, heads who allow themselves to become administrators must have a liking for admin. Otherwise they could perfectly well delegate all that square-footage. Most local authorities will appoint someone for that function, responsible to the head. I find that a reliable bursar is indispensable.

For a start, it enables me to remain a teacher (at present I teach a 25 per cent timetable) and a teacher-trainer, in the sense of having an influence upon the practice of less experienced staff. However, this is a role played quite as effectively by a senior teacher, and there is more to my headship than that.

As head, I carry a particular responsibility for continuity. Where the curriculum and organization unrolls steadily, I need to maintain the diary of events to ensure that the flow is not checked for want of forward planning. I and the deputies (always called 'the executive' for want of a better term by staff) between us attend all meetings. We warn various chairmen of deadlines, such as dates for appointments to be made, and initiate working parties before decisions have to be rushed or overtaken by events.

327

3 Accounting to whom?

At any meeting, the head's influence is quite unrelated to his voting power. Some critics have expressed disquiet over my having one vote along with any probationer or fifth former. This is beside the point; what one has to consider is what happens before any vote is taken. In that period, the head's influence may take various forms excepting only that it cannot be authoritarian, though it may be authoritative. That is to say, nobody has to accept the wisdom of my view on my say-so: nobody has to do or think what I tell them to because of my position. On the other hand, I do have the authority to give information available to me by right of position, such as rulings from local authorities and legal obligations. And there still remains the possibility of an authoritative (not authoritarian) voice allowed to me by virtue of accorded authority, that is, whatever the others may want to take from me simply because I am me. That authority is a trust that has to be won, can fluctuate and could be lost altogether, but it is real.

If that trust holds, then as head, I have a crucial function as two-way transmitter of pressures. Whether staff want it that way or not, I am the one to whom external authorities refer. Their approaches differ hardly at all from the normal. If the director of education, or any of his many officers or political superiors, want to extract information or commitment from the school, or to communicate either to it, they get on to me. If a parent is unhappy about the school, he identifies it through me. If the press wants a comment, they ring up me. If the chairman of governors wants to pass on a comment, or sound out some proposed move, he buttonholes me. The transmission of pressure is through my bloodstream and I feel no guilt over being paid danger-money.

Perhaps the most important aspect of this osmotic role, is the extent to which I modify actions and decisions in school by sensitizing all the participants to outside reaction. There is a regard for my situation, and what might render it an impossible one, going beyond personal consideration (warming though that is when it emerges) to an appreciation of what is possible within the tolerance of public opinion and those in political power. Teachers can remain unusually innocent over political realities lacking, as they do, any continuous face-to-face contact with the adult world. They can usually leave that sort of thing to the head and then denounce his worldliness. At Countesthorpe, though we are not without our Utopians, everyone has been forced to face realities. Their own idealism has been observed in practice (with wildly conflicting reactions), whilst the demands of outside forces have led them to make working compromises in order to survive and prosper.

In so far as this has succeeded – and after every kind of local hostility, we have survived and prospered – and it has afforded me a changed kind of satisfaction. Instead of experiencing the gratification of seeing my own educational will take on flesh, as I had done in previous headships, I now feel that I have made possible, and participated in, a form of school in which teachers and school students have been able to enjoy an increase in dignity which results from their sense of determining, to a large extent, the conditions under which they work and grow.

Problems abound. You solve one set only to encounter, and even create, new ones. Some can be surmounted while others remain as permanent constraints. Some I can identify as arising from the role of the head in a participatory government. The problem that most often is raised for me by others is that of possible conflict between head and moot. This is an obvious one only because conflict between head and staff is normal: even under a liberal headship they advise and consent, while he consults and decides. But the participatory system depends upon an initial agreement of aims. That is why it is very doubtful whether an existing school could go over to a participatory approach – I wouldn't recommend it. Countesthorpe was made possible by the first head's clear announcement of intention which enabled him to recruit a staff who wanted to work in that way. With head and staff agreed on basics, then conflicts can be resolved by open discussion in reference to them, provided all parties learn to tolerate conflict, use it to identify issues and make compromises in order to reach consensus. Conflict – compromise – consensus – commitment. Real difficulty arises if we neglect to get together regularly for talk. If this should ever lead to insoluble conflict between me and moot, either I should have to go, or the participatory system would.

A head gets used to just so much talk before he has to make his mind up. Here, the decisions take longer to emerge. This puts a strain upon my tolerance that has made for occasional impatience. In my case the novel situation was made possible by a transitional period between headships as a lecturer at the London Institute of Education. There I learnt to tolerate ambiguity and delayed decision in growing to appreciate the strength of consensus. (I took up smoking, otherwise I think it did me good.) Others it might drive to apoplexy: participatory democracy would not be for them.

Another strain upon my psyche arises from the need to balance the self-effacement of participation with the firmness and fight so often needed on the school's behalf in outside dealings. This alternation of humility with aggressiveness has often required rapid changes of role and I am sure that they have often been confused. Though more obvious in critical times, this probably abides to some degree. One just has to let the problem be known to those who wonder why they have undeservedly been snapped at, and hope they will be understanding.

Of course, some teachers need an authority figure in order to rebel against him. The more mature will have learnt to internalise their enemy, but I have not entirely escaped those who will push one into an authoritarian role apparently in order to object to it. We did have one teacher who boasted that he had taught children to stick pins into headmaster dolls, but he left when the rest of the staff discovered his inflexibility. So we do our best to appoint people who seem to be ready to carry their joint responsibilities.

Turning from the psychological problems to a sociological one, public opinion has a long way to go to catch up with the idea of a head who is anything but autocratic. More than in any other field, people's attitudes to schools are conditioned by the intensive experience of them in the formative period of their earlier years. The head as a stock figure is inevitably anachronistic. Men who have had to learn that negotiation between employer and employee is inescapable have yet to accept that, even if he should want to be autocratic, the head can no longer wield absolute authority, and in the long run will only make himself look ridiculous if he tries to. County councillors who would never risk sacking any of their own employees because they had been on strike may be the very ones who will still demand of a head that he should instruct his staff not to strike. Everyone, from the RSPCA to the anti-abortionists, assumes that if only the head has a word with the pupils in assembly, they will stop it, whatever it is. The only strategy in face of these pious hopes seems to be one of persistence, declaration, and publishing articles like this one.

Of course, power is enjoyable: it enables one to get things done. Even discounting the unreasonable expectations of those who ask for magic from a head, much remains for heads who do not want to relinquish power. I have argued for a spreading of this power, for sharing it with teachers before it is taken into the hands of non-educationists. Nevertheless, it is not a popular argument with heads, and I run a severe risk of antagonizing colleagues who see it as undermining their position. I need to reassure them that I do not perceive them all as power-drunk ogres who need to be told their job and deflated into the bargain. Indeed, if they will examine the foregoing they will see that in their own positions, I would be extremely cautious about relinquishing power into dubious hands. How is this paradox going to be resolved?

I do not at present see any maintaining authority entering into contract with a body of teachers on a collegiate basis. Their need to have the accountability of one person ensures the continued existence of the head for some time to come. Given examples of satisfactory stewardship by a head within a participatory system, the most we can hope for is a partnership between LEA and the staff of a school in selection of any new head. A rotating headship is therefore not on, except in non-maintained schools such as those of the Rudolph Steiner foundations.

Parents and teachers should be much less worried over the shift of a head's powers towards his school than over the more sinister threat at the moment of its removal into the hands of non-educationists. His power has at least been checked and balanced up till now by governors, officers and councillors with a special concern for education. With the establishment of the new enlarged authorities of local government, there has been a detectable pull of power towards their centres. Politicians claiming to act for their electorate have questioned the powers residing with heads and governors, even with education committees, and, in the name of efficient management, have sought to by-pass them. Heads could become accountable direct to councils, and education officers give place to chief executives, civil servants with who knows what notions on education.

Not only does this situation call for vigilance, but it should be borne in mind by those of us trying to spread participatory school government. Any suspicion of irresponsibility on the part of teachers will strengthen the hand of those advocating central authority. Any attempt by teachers to dispense with the head and go it alone would gain no union support at present, and would have no legal basis. The result would only be confrontations, that would be destructive to school staffs and damaging to school students. The critical issues therefore are these. Will heads prepare their staffs, students and parents to share more power with them, or will it be removed to the centre? My own guess is that unless heads and teachers work together on this, they will all lose power that will be gathered in to County Hall where the old autocratic head will then sit in all his remoteness under the new guise of efficient corporate management.

3.6　The case for the community control of schools

H.M. Levin

Among all the major social movements of our time, demands for community control of the schools must certainly be one of the least understood. Perhaps this is the case for most complex issues, but it would seem that a major share of the confusion is due to the sensational, but relatively superficial, reporting of the news media. The press has tended to present this phenomenon in the context of a temporary racial crisis, giving greater emphasis to implications for 'law and order' than to the education of minority-group students. An analogy might be made to the journalists who, in reporting the causes for the outbreak of World War I, intensely explored events surrounding the assassination of Archduke Ferdinand, while ignoring the more complex set of economic and political relationships that led to the extensive international conflagration.

In an attempt to provide greater depth and balance to discussion of this issue, this essay focuses on the rationale or justification for the community control movement. Indeed, demands for community control cannot be fully understood without first recognizing the situation that presently confronts racial minorities in their quests for equality and dignity. Though two hundred years of slavery have been followed by one hundred years of 'freedom', the black American still remains outside the mainstream of American life. By almost all standard measures, his welfare is substantially below that of the American majority; statistics on income, employment, life expectancy, housing, and infant mortality all reflect his unenviable position.

He has migrated from rural to urban areas seeking opportunity, and he has worked hard at the jobs that were available. However, the rapid upward mobility that greeted immigrants from other lands has eluded the black American. In part this is due to his arriving in the cities at a time

Source: *Schooling in a Corporate Society* (1972) pp.193–210.

when opportunities for unskilled labour were fast diminishing and when the large-city political systems had already established themselves without his participation. Thus, he found himself caged by the walls of the urban ghetto with housing and job discrimination handicapping his chances of substantially improving his status. Massive discrimination and racism in both the government and private sectors have prevented any semblance of equal human rights for the black man, and while our society has recently begun to attempt to redress these inequalities, progress has been pitifully slow.

Of all the conditions facing the American black, the worst probably has been his feeling of powerlessness. Given the same high aspirations as his fellow citizens, the black is unable to fulfil them because of discriminatory barriers placed in his path. He is imprisoned in substandard, overpriced ghetto housing, and his choice of jobs is limited. He has neither the occupational nor residential mobility, nor the political power to counter these disabling conditions. Compounding this feeling of impotence is the fact that the very social institutions which were designed to improve his prospects have not been able to do so. It is this frustrating lack of control over his life's circumstances that may well be the most bitter pill to swallow. Without some measure of control over his destiny, his aspirations can never be more than pipedreams.

Thus, the basic problem of the black American is that of gaining control over his destiny, and in recent years a prospective solution to this problem has come into focus. Through racial cohesiveness and self-development, many black men intend to liberate themselves from racism and to gain equality and dignity. Foremost in this drive is the quest to redirect and reform those institutions that seem to have failed black Americans or, worse yet, have inflicted injury and further disadvantages on racial minorities. In the black neighbourhoods of large cities, schools have become among the first of these institutions to be challenged.

One point that is not at issue is the fact acknowledged by urban educators and informed laymen alike that city schools have failed to help the black American to improve his status. The indictment of the schools is an especially serious one because formal education has represented the primary social device for more nearly equalizing opportunity among children of different races or social groupings. Yet, while about three-quarters of white males in their latter twenties have completed high school, only about half of non-white males in this age bracket have fulfilled a high school education. These data provide only a portion of the picture. Even among those students who do reach the twelfth grade, the average Negro is about three years in standardized achievement units behind the average twelfth-grade white.

The black American, then, enters his adult life with severe educational deficiencies, and the nature of the schooling experience which is provided for him must share some of the blame for this condition. The average black in the large cities attends a school which is less well endowed than that attended by whites. For example, teachers in Negro schools have less experience and lower verbal ability than their counterparts in schools attended by whites. In addition, schools with black enrollments are more likely to be crowded and to experience shortages of supplies and other materials; and historically they have been characterized by lower expenditures.

But inferior resources are only one way in which schools handicap the ghetto child in preparing him for life. Even more destructive to his self-concept and growth is the cultural intolerance reflected by his schooling experience. The materials, curriculum, and teaching methods were developed for children of the white middle class, and they have been largely irrelevant to the experiences and special educational requirements of the black child. Thus, the present schools situated in Negro neighbourhoods tend to undermine the black student's identity by ignoring his cultural heritage. That is, in their effort to be 'colour blind', many schools have ignored colour; they demand that the ghetto child reflect the language patterns, experience, and cultural traits of the white middle class. In this sense, city schools have been guilty of massive institutional racism by forcing black students to be captive audiences in a hostile environment, an environment that just did not have their needs in mind. In this respect, city schools tend not to reflect the pluralism that is claimed for our society.

Given the intention by blacks to take responsibility for those institutions which mould their lives and the lives of their children, it is no accident that the schools represent an initial focal point. As one spokesman noted:

> The schools are rather natural and logical vehicles for the first thrust because they represent the white underbelly of society. They are present. They are constant. They are not something that is hidden in a back room in city hall which you can't reach. The principal of the school is at hand. The teachers are there. So there is a very tangible instrument around which action could focus.

In addition to the visibility of schools, there is a widespread notion that in the long run education is a potent power in society, and that those who control schools, control something that is extremely meaningful.

An additional factor in favour of decentralizing control of the schools has been the fact that the black community frequently has the sympathy of a large segment of the white middle class who are also frustrated with the empty promises, administrative rigidities, unresponsiveness, and red tape that seem to characterize many city school bureaucracies. Yet another powerful element underlying the crusade for radical changes in school governance is the fact that the palliatives suggested by educational professionals for improving the ghetto schools have frequently been shown to be difficult to implement at best, and totally ineffective at worst.

Conventional wisdom of the late 1950s and early 1960s suggested that, through racially integrating the schools, educational problems of blacks and other minorities could be solved. In most cities, promises of integration were never fulfilled. Inaction on the issue or, worse yet, gerrymandering of local attendance districts to prevent meaningful integration, created great bitterness among many blacks whose top priority was racially integrated education. The fact that many city school boards could not deliver what they had promised led to much of the present minority distrust of centralized school boards. Where integration did take place, it tended to be token in nature, with black students placed in different 'ability' groups or curricula than white students. Indeed, the US Commission on Civil Rights found in 1966 that 'many Negro students who attend majority-white schools in fact are in majority-Negro classrooms'.

Today, white middle-class outflow from cities in combination with black in-migration and political opposition to busing and other methods of alleviating de facto school segregation have made large-scale integration an improbable event. Of the twenty cities in the largest metropolitan areas in 1966, nine had Negro majorities among their elementary school enrollments, and fifteen had enrollments that were over 30 per cent Negro. Thus, true school integration implies transgressing traditional political boundaries and incorporating metropolitan school districts that would encompass city and suburbs. Substantial opposition to this proposal by suburbanites will probably prevent such a development for the foreseeable future. In the meantime, inability of large city schools to adapt to the special needs of 'minority' students will become increasingly a failure to adapt to the needs of a majority of students, most of these students obtaining their schooling in segregated environments. Among seventy-five cities surveyed by the Civil Rights Commission in 1966, three-quarters of the Negro students in elementary schools were already attending schools whose enrollments were 90 per cent or more Negro.

Indeed many blacks reject integration as a solution not only because it is a phrase that is replete with false promises, but also because it had ideological overtones that are an affront to their dignity. As Floyd McKissick has suggested, the view that quality education can only take place in an integrated school seems to be based upon the degrading proposition: 'Mix Negroes with Negroes and you get stupidity'.

A second approach to improving schools in the black ghetto has been that of compensatory education. During the early 1960s it became increasingly in vogue among educators to refer to the 'educationally deprived' or 'disadvantaged' child. In particular, most urban black children were considered to be disadvantaged, because it was said they lacked the home and community environment that stimulated educational motivation, achievement, and the derivation of middle-class attributes. Therefore, additional school resources were to be provided to the disadvantaged child in order to compensate for his middle-class deficiencies.

Unfortunately, the record to date for compensatory education is unimpressive. Most compensatory efforts have focused on smaller class size and additional personnel. The types of teachers, curriculum, school organization, and educational methods that have consistently failed the ghetto child have been largely retained, and little educational progress has been demonstrated. Some school spokesmen have excused compensatory programme failures by asserting that most of these attempts have been underfinanced. Perhaps this is true, but one can certainly question how spending more money on such traditional panaceas as the reduction of class size is going to change the qualitative nature of basic schooling processes that did not have the urban black youngsters in mind to begin with.

It is clear that schools as presently constituted have shown little evidence of being able to fulfil the educational needs of the disadvantaged child and particularly the black disadvantaged child. Both compensatory education and school integration have witnessed more failures than successes (with the possible exception of preschool programmes), and most future plans for improving the education of black children revolve about these two approaches. In a sense, representatives of the black communities are saying 'You've been given your chance, and our schools have not improved'. Now blacks want a chance to show professionals have not been able to counter these demands with genuine alternatives. Instead, the rather tired response has been something to the effect: 'Just give us a chance to provide really racially integrated, quality education'. In the eyes of the black community, this reply has not only come too late, but it smacks of the same stale remedies that have failed to change the picture in the past. The surge for self-determination in combination with the failure of the professionals to prove themselves has made schools particularly vulnerable. This vulnerability has manifested itself in the increasingly voiced sentiment that the education of blacks can no longer be considered to be the 'white man's burden'. The black community has rejected this paternalistic approach and wishes to take responsibility for the schooling of its own.

Making schools work for minority children

Before embarking on a description of how community-controlled schools might improve the schooling experiences of minority children, it is useful to offer a more precise analysis of why the present approach to compensatory education must inevitably fail the culturally different child. Inherent in compensatory education programmes is the condescending view that the urban minority child is somehow inferior to the middle-class child. Relative to the white middle-class child, he is 'deprived' and 'disadvantaged'. Therefore, he needs remedial work and compensatory resources to improve his prospects. That is, remediation is considered to be the key to the minority-child's emancipation.

That the minority child is different from the middle-class white child is a mere tautology. Yet, in this case the schools assume that the child's cultural differences represent inferiorities that must be eliminated. Inherent in this approach is a total disrespect for the cultures and experiences of black and other minority children. Yet, to a black youngster, his experience is certainly as valid as that of his white counterpart.

There is no reason that a minority child must deny or deprecate his background in order to 'learn'. Indeed, such forced self-denunciation can only guarantee the development of a serious and widening breach between the school and the child. 'Quite the opposite, the schools must capitalize on the cultural strengths of minority children in order to build cultural bridges between the experiences of those children and the goals of the larger society.'[1]

But this goal requires taking a specialized approach to educating minority students, one that violates the underpinnings of the present universalistic model. The present method tacitly assumes that the same approach is universally applicable to all children despite the pious rhetoric often espoused about 'individualized' instruction. Unfortunately, large urban school systems have shown themselves to be incapable of building educational programmes that capitalize on the cultural attributes of minority children. This fact becomes quite clear when one examines the way in which so-called compensatory education programmes have been formulated. Most money has been spent on such traditional methods as reducing class size, increasing the number of counsellors and remedial specialists, and buying more library volumes. That is, more money has been spent on the same remedies that have not worked well in the past. The inevitable result is a larger version of the same dismal cake. There must be qualitative changes in the recipe in order to improve the quality of education for minority children.

The fact that such qualitative changes have not generally taken place has meant that dollar resources have been misspent. The US Office of Education in evaluating the effect of Title I monies on reading scores found that ' ... a child who participated in a Title I project had only a 19 per cent chance of a significant achievement gain, a 13 per cent chance of a significant achievement loss, and a 68 per cent chance of no change at all relative to the national norms.'[2] Further, projects that were investigated were ' ... most likely to be representative of projects in which there was a higher than average investment in resources. Therefore more significant achievement gains should be found here than in a more representative sample of Title I projects.'[3]

In fact, comparing dollar inputs between schools attended by minority students and those attended by middle-class whites is an erroneous way of measuring school resource endowments between races. To the degree that money is spent in both cases on teachers, curriculum, and other inputs that are more effective for white children than for black or Spanish-speaking students, dollar expenditures tend to overstate vastly the relative resources available to the latter group. Rather, nominal resources devoted to the two groups of schools must be weighted by their effectiveness to ascertain their true values.

The ludicrous nature of comparing schools attended by majority and minority students on the basis of checklists of physical characteristics or on dollar expenditures is reflected in the following illustration. If black schools and white schools have the same number of teachers with the same preparation and experience, the two sets of schools are considered to be equal according to conventional criteria. Now what if all the teachers have white racist views? Clearly, if black schools and white schools have equal numbers of white racist teachers, the two sets of schools are not equal even though the physical quantities of teachers are. This example raises additional questions about the present definition of remediation and compensatory education. If we double the number of white racist teachers in black schools, class size will be reduced by 50 per cent; yet it is difficult to argue that healthy increases in educational output will take place. Such a situation is perfectly consistent with the conventional arithmetic of spending on compensatory education. Attention is heavily focused on the amount of traditional resources available to minority children with almost no consideration of the appropriateness or the efficacy of those resources.

Making urban schools more responsive
For many blacks and members of other racial minorities, community

control of the schools is seen as the only path that will succeed in making schools more responsive generally to the needs of the populations they serve. Under existing centrally administered systems, principals, teachers, and parents have found attempts to improve their schools frustrated by cumbersome procedures and regulations which protect the status quo. The school systems are so large that they cannot view themselves as being accountable to particular schools or parents, especially if those schools serve children whose parents lack political muscle. Since departures from tradition must usually be approved in the offices of the central school administration, bold and imaginative proposals for change are throttled by the lack of decision-making power in individual schools and classrooms. In fact, the central school board's obsession for procedural order above other considerations has encrusted schools with a drab and uniform educational approach despite the large variety of educational situations and student needs that are actually present in large cities. To the degree that many of the methods, curricula, and personnel have not been appropriate and have failed to give minority children in particular, the skills and healthy attitudes that the schools claim as objectives, the failure has become institutionalized and systematic.

The massive inefficiencies and rigidities evident in the existing approach have been documented by so many novelists and journalists that many members of the public simply take them for granted. In one city, schools have waited for two years for textbooks that could have been received within two weeks had they been ordered directly from publishers. Many city schools have reported storerooms full of unused scientific equipment and library books without having the programmes, laboratories, and libraries to make use of these materials. Other schools have the programmes and physical facilities but lack equipment. In schools of some cities, a simple request for stationery or paper clips must be approved by a dozen different signatories before the request can be filled.

Further, the choice of textbooks and curriculum can rarely be modified by a teacher, no matter how useless or deleterious they may be to his or her pupils. One of the better publicized incidents that illustrates the administrative callousness of large city schools took place recently in a black junior high school. A young white teacher was harassed by her principal, who received support from the office of the central school board, for daring to introduce the Negro play *Raisin in the Sun* into her English class and for encouraging and supporting her pupils' efforts to produce a student newspaper. Her creative attempts to introduce relevant activities were criticized as violations of the 'required' curriculum. That she had succeeded in getting her students excited about their English classes was ignored in favour of administrative uniformity. There is evidence that many of our better teachers leave the schools in part because of these same frustrations. In fact, the general failure of compensatory education programmes is a monumental tribute to the inability of large-city school bureaucracies to adapt themselves to the needs of the sizeable group of black children.

Thus, a major objective of school decentralization is that of making schools more responsive to the particular populations they serve, by making them accountable to the communities from which they draw their enrollments. The unwieldiness of the present highly centralized administrative structure prevents this type of accountability. It is expected that by being answerable to a local rather than city-wide governing board, schools will improve the learning environment for the children involved.

The direct impact of decentralization on schools would be derived from the ability of each community to select the curricula, materials, programmes, and personnel that were most appropriate to the specific needs of its students. Experimentation and innovation, then, might lead to school environments that were more receptive to students and more successful in stimulating intellectual and emotional growth than are the present schools. In addition, decentralization would enable schools to handle logistical problems more efficiently by obtaining textbooks and other supplies in appropriate quantities at times when they are needed. Decentralization could also enable schools to obtain outside consulting on specific problems, utilize new types of personnel, such as artists and writers, and contract certain services that might be supplied more efficiently by private firms.

But, in addition to these direct effects, it is possible that the learning process will be enhanced indirectly by a healthy metamorphosis of community education attitudes. That is, the participation of parents and other members of the community in the operation of schools will lead to a more total involvement between the school and its constituency than is possible under the present bureaucratic structure. It appears that parental involvement in schools leads to more favourable attitudes toward education among the children: however, under the present system of highly centralized control, the school appears to be an impenetrable and alien fortress to the community and its parents. The inability of parents to have any meaningful influence in modifying rigid and anachronistic school policies has certainly led to parental frustrations and hostile attitudes that are easily transmitted to their children. It is believed that if the school were accountable to the community by being truly responsive to its educational needs, parents would show greater respect for schools and more favorable attitudes toward education. These attitudes would filter down to their children and would be reflected in the attitudes and performances of the students in those schools.

Decentralization and the black community

To the black community, the educational rationale for community governance is equally compelling, but the need for change is far more urgent than that suggested in the general case. Not only is the present highly centralized system considered to be educationally inadequate, but also it is viewed as one which must inevitably have racist consequences. That is, the school system can afford to favour middle-class white children at the expense of black children because black citizens simply lack the political power to do anything about it. In this respect, the schools reflect a type of racism which is ignored by the average white American. Kenneth Haskins, the principal who initially led the Morgan Community School in the District of Columbia, suggested that racism in this sense means ' ... that a public school system that fails black children can be tolerated, while a public school system that fails white middle-class children cannot'.[4]

There is a stong belief that this dereliction might be reversed if the administration of those schools in black neighbourhoods was responsive to the needs of large groups of black parents who were deeply concerned and involved in the process of education. In this regard, it is interesting to note that the Morgan Community School showed gains in the reading proficiencies of students in its very first year of community control. Only a handful of other public schools in the entire district exhibited such improvement over this period, while most schools showed declines.

Many black Americans also see a new and important educational focus emerging from community governance. They suggest that schools should be responsible for helping to fulfill the ideals and aspirations of the people served. The constituency of the school must necessarily include all the people of the community since the needs of the students cannot be divorced from the context in which they live. The school should be expected to promote the sense of self-worth and identity of the students served while imparting to those youngsters the ability to influence what happens to their lives. That is, the often noted observation that schools and the larger society tend to destroy the self-worth and identity of black children is considered to be as reprehensible as the academic failures of the schools.

In order to carry out these responsibilities, the community school must address itself not only to transmitting academic or cognitive skills, but also to affective skills, with particular attention given to the formation of positive attitudes. Indeed, community schools must be designed to compensate for the second-class treatment of black citizens in other sectors of society by building educational programmes that will help black children to succeed.

But, even beyond that, many black Americans view community control of those schools in black neighbourhoods as the beginning of a significant

341

drive toward full equality. This approach springs from the widely held concept that as long as black Americans lack political and economic power, they will not be able substantially to improve their lot. Accordingly, community control of the schools represents the thin edge of a political wedge which would begin to redistribute decision-making power to those whose lives are affected by the decisions, in this case, the black community. Control of the schools is viewed as the first step in effecting a more just distribution of political power and a greater degree of self-determination for black citizens.

As one spokesman explained: 'Improving the schools attended by black children is an urgent priority, but it seems to me that the bigger issue is one of how large numbers of people who have been effectively disenfranchised begin to find their way toward being a part of the society'. It is interesting to ask, then, if large numbers of black communities did indeed obtain control of their school systems how meaningful would that phenomenon be in securing complete liberation from the powerlessness that has hindered black advancement? His answer is that it could be very meaningful:

While the answers are not in, it seems very clear that this could be an initial step toward more effective control of other institutions in the community, for it is the success patterns of communities which give those communities a sense of better future instead of futility. Given control of the schools, the community could sense a beginning of political potency. It is this factor which would enhance the community's ability to deal more effectively with other problems such as jobs and housing and which would construct the groundwork for full equality.

In this respect community schools represent a focus around which political and social structures would emerge for black Americans where such structures are presently lacking. The factors that link black men today are the largely negative ones of enduring racial discrimination at the hands of white society. While there is a recent emphasis on black culture, the school represents a tangible institution about which a sense of community involvement and black pride might develop. Responsibility for the schools represents a positive experience which can be shared by all blacks as opposed to the negative one of white racism.

The importance of the school in developing the communal ties that black Americans and perhaps most Americans, desire so passionately cannot be overemphasized. As Robert Maynard has suggested: 'An issue has been raised around which many residents can rally as never before and one in which their mutual, or community, interest is most clearly defined.'

In this sense it seems that the often cited term, 'black community', in fact, reflects the common attributes which blacks wish to develop and share with each other. Control of schools represents a setting within which these latent and somewhat mystical ties might emerge to form a true sense of community, a sense of a common purpose and destiny.

Thus, the black American views community control as a way of improving and broadening the educational performance of ghetto schools as well as more generally improving the status of black citizens. This would be done by breaking down many of the rigidities that characterize these schools, as well as by introducing programmes, personnel, and materials that are specifically designed to transform black children into capable young adults. The historical evidence suggests that presently structured school bureaucracies are incapable of carrying out such changes. Therefore, community control becomes a logical alternative for educational reform.

In addition, many blacks feel that community support for operating schools will provide the nucleus for a community power base; and it is believed that strong and cohesive black communities represent the most effective strategy for obtaining a more equitable share of power in the larger society. While few critics might deny the importance of the immediate educational goals of the community schools, many have reacted strongly to these political implications.

Political implications of community schools
The main criticism against community control of schools seems to be that the search for political 'liberation' of black Americans has no place in the schools. One wonders whether it is not the ends of obtaining power rather than the means that are being questioned, for the schools have traditionally claimed the goal of preparing students for a participatory democracy. Courses given throughout the standard curriculum are designed to give students the requisite literacy, knowledge, and common set of values that enable them to understand and participate in the political life of our society. But blacks and other racial minorities have been excluded from the power structure. They have been unable to form a coalition or find any other group that will represent their needs and the present objectives of the schools have not served them well. Indeed, present values reflected in the school curriculum are necessary for perpetuating the present distribution of political power; they do not encourage opening the game to players who have not been dealt a hand.

Since a significant portion of the black community feels that only self-development will invest it with the strength to reinforce its demands for a fairer representation in the larger society, it appears consistent that schools in the black community emphasize political goals of black cohesion rather than those of the beneficent democracy. Democratic trappings presently reflected by schools are clearly deceptive to black Americans who still lack political equality and meaningful representation. Thus, from the black point of view, there is necessarily an important educational precedent for relating its educational goals to its political ones.

Socialization and racial separation

A second and related major objection to decentralization is that it would institutionalize racial separation. Presumably neighbourhoods would represent the initial basis of community, so that blacks would continue to attend schools that were predominantly black and whites would attend schools with white enrollments. Yet a major objective of the schools in a democratic society is that of exposing children to fellow students who are drawn from a variety of social, economic, and racial backgrounds. This goal is considered to be part of the socialization function of the schools, whereby individuals are being prepared to fulfil their interpersonal or social obligations in a multicultural setting. It is believed that exposure to a heterogeneity of cultures, races, and social classes improves understanding and interactions among the various groups and increases social mobility. These end products are considered to be prerequisites for an effectively functioning democratic society.

In this respect the community school appears to be both socially divisive and antidemocratic. But blacks are frequently among the first to point out that the concept of the 'melting pot' has been a historical myth as far as black Americans are concerned. The fact is that blacks presently live in a separate society, and neither legal remedies nor the putative good will of the white community have been able to give them housing, education, and other social activities in an integrated setting. In the particular case of city schools, it was not blacks who rejected integration; it was the large-city school boards representing a sizable component of the white community. The vast majority of black Americans have always lived in a separate society, and past efforts to integrate them have not been successful.

But if we assume that a healthy America requires the full economic, political, and social integration of blacks and whites, the real question is how to achieve such a goal. Paradoxically, black cohesiveness appears to be a more effective strategy than any other existing alternative. The reason for its promise is a simple one. This society responds much more quickly to demands from powerful constituencies than it does to requests from weak ones, and black community is the basis for black political potency.

The effects of black separation in getting a larger piece of action are noticeable on the university campuses. The demands of newly formed black student unions for increases in black enrollments, black faculty members and administrators, and courses in Afro-American culture have been met with positive responses at many institutions. In addition these demands have spurred substantial increases in the recruitment of blacks by professional and graduate schools as well as greater provisions of financial aid and counselling services for such students. These gains are particularly relevant because they represent the traditional paths of access to the middle class that have been heavily trodden by whites, but, until very recently at least, have been largely inaccessible to minorities. What the issue comes to in the final analysis is the view by community control advocates that integration and equality will never come until blacks have the power to pursue such objectives meaningfully, and the requisite power cannot develop without black unity.

Community schools and white Americans

Is political decentralization of the schools an equally valid response to the educational problems of whites? One of the most serious flaws that characterizes city schools, as well as many other American institutions, is the fallacious assumption that identical treatment of different groups yields the same outcomes for all groups. The fact is that, given the different cultural attributes of racial and social groupings, application of the same educational approach yields highly unequal results. In particular, evidence suggests that the traditional schooling approach has been far less effective for black children and those of some other racial minorities than it has been for children of the white middle class. If this is so, then the same logic must be applied to the choice of remedy. That is, organizational reforms that are drastically needed to improve the status of minority students are not necessarily the most appropriate remedies for curing the educational infirmities of those schools serving white populations.

In this respect, community control of the schools is far more urgently needed by minority Americans than it is by whites. Blacks (and other racial minorities) are a special educational case because their exigencies are not represented by the power structure or by traditional institutional arrangements. The result of their lack of representation is that blacks have been shortchanged in the allocation of school resources, and their needs have been ignored in determining the nature of the schooling experience that is provided for their children. As a consequence, there exists an enormous breach between the context in which the black child lives and the schooling that is imposed upon him. In addition, the central school authorities have shown themselves to be insensitive to other major concerns of the black population. Sites have been selected for new schools that are to be built in black neighbourhoods without consulting inhabitants

M

of the local areas. As a result, black residents and businesses have been uprooted despite the availability of suitable alternative sites that would leave housing and other neighbourhood buildings intact.

On the other hand, no major contradiction is found between the values represented in the school and those embodied in the white community at large, and whites already have the political power to protect their major school interests. The central school authority is politically sensitive to both school-resource demands and site-selection preferences of residents in white neighborhoods. In fact, in these as well as other major respects, whites already send their children to community-controlled schools. The very failure of policies to reduce de facto school segregation is a tribute to the power of white neighbourhoods to keep black students out of their schools.

To be sure, particular whites might not be altogether happy with their schools, but most white Americans can express their dissatisfactions through political channels or through moving to another neighbourhood or school district, and many white Americans have the financial ability to send their children to private institutions. The minority American has neither the luxury of obtaining political responsiveness, the income necessary to seek private alternatives, nor the choice of a large number of neighbourhoods or communities in which he can obtain housing and better schools for his children. Locked-in to his community, and locked-out of city hall, the minority American's only hope for improving his schools appears to be through their immediate and direct governance. Therein lies the case for community control of the school.

Notes

1 This approach is well documented and illustrated in Sylvia Ashton-Warner, *Teacher* New York: Simon and Schuster, 1963.
2 Harry Piccariello, 'Evaluation of Title I' mimeographed (1969) p.1. To be published in Joseph Fromkin and Dennis J Dugan, eds., *Inequality, Studies in Elementary and Secondary Education*, US Office of Education Planning Paper 69–72.
3 *Ibid.*
4 Kenneth W Haskins, 'The Case for Local Control', *Saturday Review* (11 January 1969): 52.

3.7 Community control and political theory

L. Fein

Community and neighbourhood

Community control seems a plausible response to the present need of the educational system to restore its legitimacy in the eyes of its constituents – particularly its black constituents – and to endorse institutionally the enduring sense of community which many Americans appear to share. But neither derivative speaks clearly to the question of boundaries. At first blush, it might seem that each school, or group of schools, should, at least for some purposes, have its own mechanism of control, drawing upon the people who live near it, or the parents whose children are enrolled in it. But before accepting such a conclusion, we are required to distinguish between the neighbourhood and the community. Community, at least as we have been using the term, suggests organic connection, a sense of shared destiny. As Nisbet points out:

> Community is founded on man conceived in his wholeness, rather than in one or another of the roles, taken separately, that he may hold in a social order. It draws its psychological strength from levels of motivation deeper than those of mere volition or interest .... [It] is a fusion of feeling and thought, of tradition and commitment, of membership and volition. It may be found in, or be given symbolic expression by, locality, religion, nation, race, occupation, or crusade. Fundamental to the strength of the bond of community is the real or imagined antithesis formed in the same social setting by the non-communal relations of competition or conflict, utility or contractual assent.[1]

Source: *The Ecology of the Public Schools: An Enquiry into Community Control* (1971) pp. 74–93.

Now it may be that this meaning of community should not be given offical and institutional sanction in America. Ethnicity, to take one example, is a powerful social fact, but that does not necessarily mean that it should become a political fact as well. Clearly, to give political sanction to ethnicity would be very different from merely providing some measure of autonomy to people who live near each other. For physical proximity is only sometimes coterminous with the boundaries of the organic community.

Here again, we encounter some theoretical ambivalence, most recently and comprehensively dealt with in litigation on legislative apportionment. The effect of Supreme Court decisions since *Baker v. Carr* (1962) has been to disallow, in legislative bodies at the state and lower levels, representation of any organized interest. The only allowable basis for apportionment today is population – i.e. one man, one vote. This seems a manifestly fair principle, and has been widely endorsed by liberal organizations. In addition to the fact that it sounds fair, it raises some hope that the long-standing rural bias of many state legislatures may be repaired. Taken literally, however, as the doctrine of 'one man, one vote' has been taken by a number of state courts, as well as by the Supreme Court itself in subsequent decisions, it has interesting ramifications. The Supreme Court did not insist that all legislative districts within a given political jurisdiction be of exactly equal population; clearly, such a standard would have been impracticable. Instead, the Court held that districts must be as nearly equal in population as possible. In practice, this has meant that there might be, say, 5 per cent deviation from the mean size in any given district.

A recent reapportionment proposal of the Missouri legislature was invalidated by the United States Supreme Court. That proposal would have created districts with a maximum variance of only 3.13 per cent from the mean size. While the variance was well within limits which had been found acceptable elsewhere, the Court held the proposal invalid on the grounds that standards other than numbers alone had been used in drawing the boundaries. Specifically, the proposed reapportionment sought to avoid fragmenting areas with distinct social and economic interests, on the theory that such fragmentation would dilute the effective representation of historic interests. The Court, in striking down the plan, held that 'to accept population variances, large or small, in order to create districts with specific interest orientations is antithetical to the basic premise of the constitutional command to provide equal representation for equal numbers of people'. The objection, in other words, was not that the deviation was 'too' great, according to some arbitrary standard, but rather that it was greater than it would have been had numbers alone guided the process. And the reason that it was greater than it need have been was that the legislature sought to preserve the political identity of certain historic interests in Missouri. Only if there were a fortuitous match between raw numbers and historical communities could the boundaries have been drawn around communities.

The interests in question in Missouri were largely economic. But one can easily imagine noneconomic interests which might form the basis for an apportionment plan. Race and religion are only two examples among many. The theoretical objection to any such recognition derives directly from that view of the polity which holds the basic building block of the political system to be the individual, rather than, say, the caste, or the family, or the economic interest. In addition to the theoretical objection, there is also a powerful practical consideration: if the system gives official recognition to communities of interest, where does the process begin, and where does it end? People group together with others in diverse formations; our economic mates are not necessarily, or frequently, our coreligionists, or our brothers, or our ideological bedfellows. Yesterday, women had only limited political interests as women; today, women are coming increasingly to share a political agenda with each other. How can the system know when an interest deserves to be recognized, and how can it deal with the problem of multiple memberships?

There are, perhaps, answers to these questions, but the answers are frightfully complicated, and the theoretical argument in favour of strict numerical equality is sufficiently persuasive so as to diminish, if not eliminate, interest in the practicability of alternative proposals. The net result is that, with the exception of the special status accorded the several states, in both the Electoral College and the United States Senate, the political system is forbidden, in apportioning legislative districts, from taking explicit account of communities of interest.

This line of reasoning does not necessarily apply to all the component parts of the system, since, if it can be shown that there are substantive reasons for recognizing interest-based groupings, the courts might permit exceptions to the general rule. Constitutional doctrine on such matters is far from settled, and the creation of school districts of different size, based on things other than numbers and geographic propinquity, or both, does not automatically dilute the quality pursued in the apportionment decisions. No analogy is intended; instead, the important point is that were schools organized around communities of interest, community control would be a dramatic exception to the basic, and general, governmental formula which informs almost all government structures.

Insofar as the thrust for their organization is an effort to assert the validity of the organic community, and inasmuch as the organic community is not identical with the neighbourhood, we are faced with a dilemma. Shall we except the schools from the conventional rules, permitting them to be tied to communities rather than neighbourhoods, or, tying them to the neighbourhood, shall we sacrifice a major justification for community control?

To tie the schools to the organic community rather than the neighbourhood would raise the same practical problems that we alluded to in connection with legislative apportionment, albeit in less complicated fashion. For, unlike legislative apportionment, there is no intrinsic reason why the delineation of communities of interest would have to be undertaken by a higher political authority. Instead, it would be perfectly possible for communities to define themselves, something which school-communities now do in the case of private and parochial schools. If such a procedure were generally adopted, there is every reason to believe that some communities would be based on neighbourhood, some would be based on ethnicity, some, perhaps, on educational or political ideology. Unhappily, there is also every reason to believe that a large number would be based on race. It is one thing for blacks freely to choose other blacks as their brothers; it is quite another to have such a choice forced on them by white bigotry. Ethnic communities can only be benign where they are not an inescapable assignment. For white ethnics, there are sufficient polyethnic communities to satisfy this need for options. But for blacks, the absence of multi-racial communities changes the nature and severity of the problem markedly. If people were entirely free to choose their community of interest for purposes of school selection, large numbers of whites, in the current climate, would adopt a negative principle of selection, defining their community as one excluding blacks. Some Negroes might choose to associate with predominantly white schools, but the provision of complete freedom to define the boundaries of the community would, in effect, provide whites with veto power over the entry of black students, a veto it seems likely they would exercise. And this seems a fatal flaw in such a system.

What, then, if the neighbourhood were used as the basis for the community school? Even if most neighbourhoods are not significant organic communities — and a substantial number are — neighbours do share certain interests, as neighbours. These are primarily instrumental interests; they deal with such matters as the adequacy of municipal services, public morality, recreation, and, of course, the schools. In fact, the school is the central tie in many neighbourhoods; to deprive the neighbourhood of the school as a focus might well lead to a serious diminution of the sense of relationship which makes of some neighbourhoods more than a random group of people. At the same time, by providing the neighbourhood with genuinely significant responsibilities, we help to increase the sense of community. Moreover, if we rank American neighbourhoods according to the degree to which they are also organic communities, we find that the demand for community control of the schools arises primarily from the most community-oriented neighbourhoods. Space becomes an increasingly signficant social variable as one moves nearer the bottom of the economic ladder; for blacks, whose spatial mobility is limited both by income and by race, the neighbourhood boundary is often nearly identical with the communal boundary. That, after all, is why the term 'ghetto' is useful. It suggests both a physical border and a community of interest.

On balance, then, it would appear that the neighbourhood is a somewhat less problematic base for the community school than the organic community. Still, it is not without problems. Local areas in American cities, if they are communities at all, are, for the most part, communities of limited liability. Geographic mobility in America is significantly encouraged by the knowledge that to move to a new neighbourhood does not require formal or informal induction ceremonies of serious quality. Controlling for class, one neighbourhood is pretty much like another; even the neighbours themselves become interchangeable. Our neighbours do not expect much of us, save rudimentary courtesy, nor we of them. While such a lack of serious sentiment significantly undermines the possibility of genuine fraternity, it simultaneously increases the possibility for personal freedom.

Were the neighbourhood provided with a serious shared responsibility, the liability would be increased. As an antidote to urban anonymity, as a spur to genuine participation, the prescription seems useful. But we ought not underestimate the degree to which communities of limited liability have come to be valued as a core feature of the American way of life. Those who have special needs for the geographic expression of organic ties may, of course, seek out the like-minded, and together create as intimate a community as they wish, but others either have long since left behind the organic community, or see no need to define it spatially. Were the system to shift dramatically away from the community of limited liability and towards relatively isolated fraternities, many people would be totally confused; so long accustomed to the suppression of fraternity, they are by now incapable of it.

Finally, the facts of residential segregation make the neighbourhood nearly as exclusive (racially) a base as the organic community would likely be. While the neighbourhood may, for several reasons, be less problematic than the organic community, it is, therefore, far from ideal; if our concern is with maximizing choice, external inducements and guarantees are required in order to ensure the development of multi-racial neighbourhoods.

The *caveats* need not deter us for long just yet. The community school will not suddenly transform a neighbourhood of isolates into a community of meaning; the more likely prognosis is for a marginal increase in neighbourhood sentiment, and marginal increases are hardly a threat to the established culture. Moreover, it is important to recall that the community of limited liability is, in most respects, a middle-class phenomenon. It is intimately related to geographic mobility, and such mobility is of concern primarily to the more affluent. Indeed, such people may participate in meaningful communities, but their communities, as distinguished from those of the less mobile, are tied together by a more diverse array of media – professional conventions, journals, telephones. It is not necessarily that community has ceased to matter to them, but rather that space has ceased to matter. Whether it is necessary, or even desirable, to 'free' others from the constrictions of space, or whether the urge to do so is merely a liberal conceit, are moot questions. Those who would object to endorsing the neighbourhood as a politically relevant unit, at least with respect to the schools, on the grounds that neighbourhoods should be treated as more incidental categories of classification, should remember that the affluent, both by virtue of their social status and by virtue of their ability and propensity to live in smaller suburbs, already have the opportunity to intervene in school politics. Indeed, a foremost argument of the proponents of community control of the schools is precisely that they seek no more than many Americans already enjoy.

Scale
There is, in fact, a more perplexing element in choosing between the geographic neighbourhood and the organic community as the basis for the school system, and it becomes apparent as we confront the question of scale, a question we cannot avoid if the neighbourhood is also to become a significant political jurisdiction. For there is no single definition of the neighbourhood; for some purposes, it is the block, for others, the elementary school, for others it is defined by shopping patterns. The desire to convert neighbourhood into community, to encourage fraternity, suggests an intimate neighbourhood, one where people can recognize each other, one, perhaps, whose residents might all fit into the school auditorium. And such a definition accords with the apparent desire to recreate smallness, to rediscover the virtues of the small town.

The difficulty here is that those virtues crumble under close inspection. If, in our earlier discussion of community, we emphasized the virtues of fraternity, it is now time to call attention to its dangers.

There is something about life in a small community that makes it less hospitable to divergent opinions than is the case in our urban centres.

In the anonymity of city life it is much easier for deviant behaviours to flourish than in the goldfish bowl of a small community. In the large community there are sometimes so many goldfish that nobody bothers to look at them. In the small town a lone exotic specimen can be viewed with careful, critical, and occasionally devastating concern.[2]

Thus, against the image of the sturdy cohesiveness and grass roots democracy of the small town we must juxtapose the image of the oppressive, censorial, anti-libertarian small town. Both sets of terms describe the same phenomenon; the choice depends largely on the perspective of the beholder rather than the character of the phenomenon. Nor is it possible to inquire productively as to which image is the more accurate. Both are accurate, for the small town involves a trade-off between certain values no less than does the metropolis. In general, the smaller the society, the less opportunity there is for deviance, whether political or cultural, the more the majority exercises subtle or explicit — tyranny. In return for a major sacrifice in liberty, a sacrifice which many people are perfectly willing, and even anxious, to make, the small community offers social support, a sense of belonging, an alternative to the uncertainties of autonomy. Yet those who would reflect nostalgically on the good old days of solidarity should bear in mind the treatment of eccentricity in those days, in those places. Solidarity was available only at a price.

The American political system has developed out of a very different perception. Since Madison, the system has been alert to the threat of tyranny, and has sought to defend against that threat. Let us recall the Madisonian argument: if we are concerned by a tyranny of the minority, a remedy is available in the principle of majority rule. But we need also to defend against majority tyranny. How can this be done?

Either the existence of the same passion or interest in a majority must be prevented, or the majority, having such coexistent passion or interest, must be rendered, by their number and local situation, unable to concert and carry into effect schemes of oppression. If the impulse and the opportunity be suffered to coincide, we well know that neither moral nor religious motives can be relied on as adequate control.

From this view of the subject it may be concluded that a pure democracy, by which I mean a society consisting of a small number of citizens, who assemble and administer the government in person, can admit of no cure for the mischiefs of fraction. A common passion

N

or interest will, in almost every case, be felt by a majority of the whole; a communication and concert result from the form of government itself; and there is nothing to check the inducements to sacrifice the weaker party or an obnoxious individual.[3]

Madison's argument is a classic of American political thought; it is likely the single most important document in the history of that thought, and one of the most widely taught, read, and accepted. Insofar as it is accepted, the suggestion that small communities be given political power is a violation of the general understanding. Insofar as it is valid, the vision of community schools is seriously tarnished. And, to make matters worse, we can no longer be quite so sanguine as was Madison about the problem of minority tyranny. Even if we discount the existence of apathy, which permits minorities to exercise disproportionate power, an increasing propensity to threaten physical violence suggests frightening possibilities Madison may well have not been required to consider.

But if we accept Madison's reasoning, and further compromise the community school by encouraging districts large enough to contain substantial diversity, have we not sacrificed almost completely the goal of rediscovering at least a limited fraternity? Organic community implies shared values; diversity implies value dissension. If diversity is required to defend against tyranny, then community is lost. If community is required to defend against impotence, tyranny is possible. And so it is that much of the attack against the community school has rested on the argument that small communities cannot be trusted to enforce the freedoms most of us hold central to the society. If, for example, the values of the community find a specific monthly magazine obnoxious, what is to prevent the community from removing that journal from the shelves of the school library? If a certain teacher is identified, outside the school, with an activity which offends a group vocal in the community, what is to prevent it from demanding that he be fired?

These kinds of questions can be answered, but it is important, before answering them, to acknowledge the degree to which they are put forward by serious people of honourable intent. They are not, as some would have it, merely a smokescreen for racism. Many people have long been concerned about the censorial policies of small town vigilantes, and they are, it seems to me, fully entitled to express equal concern for the possibility that community schools will encourage big city vigilantes. It is not sufficient to dismiss their argument by citing the persistence of vigilantism elsewhere, and it is unfair to imply that they seek to apply to the community-controlled school standards which are not operative elsewhere. From their perspective, those standards should apply everywhere.

Accordingly, the argument must be answered on its merits.

One kind of answer is, most simply, that it would be no great problem were the community to tyrannize. As Robert Dahl has shown, Madison's use of the concept 'tyranny' is very fuzzy, since it does not tell us which actions of a majority are to be viewed as tyrannical and which as benign.[4] If the values of a community are genuinely violated by a deviant journal or a deviant teacher, why should the community not be entitled to censor the one or censure the other? If it does not have that right, how can we pretend that schools are intended, even in part, to transmit the values of the community? Which community? The large, amorphous, lowest-common-denominator-oriented national community? What happens to diversity under such conditions? Surely, some defence against egregious violations of the national ethic, such as it is, or of the national interest, such as it is, may be developed. Beyond that, ought not communities be permitted their own standards?

A second answer argues not from theory, but from practice. It holds that the schools, as presently organized, are in fact the 'property' of a community — largely a middle-class community of college graduates who define the curriculum, the goals, the techniques of public education. In other words, the schools, as presently structured, do not insure that diversity which Madison sought; instead, they are of and by a specific group, a group with interests which may not match the interests of those whom they are ostensibly for. Community schools, the argument continues, would serve to open the system to a more diverse array of values, and not to close it. From the perspective of the system as a whole, options would be increased. And while, from the perspective of the individual school, there would be no increase in diversity, neither would there be a significant decrease. If majority tyranny is a real problem, then it is a problem which affects schools today. Worse, the majority that today tyrannizes is an alien majority; vis-à-vis the communities now seeking control over the schools their children attend, it is a minority.

The issues raised here speak not only to the question of scale, but also to the issue of district boundaries. Insofar as the system seeks to maintain some sort of balance between the competing values of liberty and fraternity, it must also seek a balance between social diversity and homogeneity. It is true, of course, that many urban neighbourhoods are socially homogeneous, and, therefore, that to base the school on the neighbourhood is to emphasize community. So, too, to require heterogeneous schools is to constrict community. Our problem is that we have powerful reasons to seek to maximize two values at once, and it is not at all clear that the two values are compatible.

Evidently, the concept of fraternity is more closely associated with the concept of society, while the concept of liberty is more closely associated with the concept of the polity. The one implies organic relationship, the other contractual relationship. The central theoretical dilemma of public education is precisely this: we have not made up our minds as to whether education is primarily a function of society or primarily a function of the state. If of the society, we would expect emphasis on affective relations, on community traditions, on particular truths. If of the state, we would expect emphasis on affective neutrality, on self-control, on universal truths. What we find, owing to our ambivalence, is a system full of internal contradictions, contradictions which tend to be solved by stressing organizational behaviours. Such behaviours inhibit both individual idiosyncracy, on the one hand, and meaningful human relationships, on the other. By avoiding the potential parochialism of fraternity and the potential eccentricity of liberty, they promote adaptive efficiency. And efficiency is both a common and a convenient replacement for genuine value commitment.

Clearly, education antedates the state, and is a primary means by which societies seek to ensure their survival. In the small society, the division between the agencies of the state and the agencies of the community was rarely clear, nor, if clear, was the state necessarily pre-eminent. But we are dealing now with large and complex societies, containing within themselves diverse communities, whose relations with one another tend to be governed and adjudicated by the state. In its efforts at managing diversity, the state has an obvious and major interest in the content of education, since it could not tolerate a situation in which the schools not only mirrored, but reinforced, the societal fragmentation.

There are, in general, two ways for the state to protect its interests. The one involves direct intervention in the management of the schools, a system preferred by most European countries, but rejected in the United States. The other is to rely on the diffusion of a national ethic powerful enough to insinuate itself into the private ethic of all, or most, subcultural groupings. There is, of course, the danger that what begins as insinuation will end up by overwhelming and destroying diversity in its wake, but between the threat of fragmentation and the threat of uniformity, the state is bound to opt for uniformity. The wonder is that substantial diversity remains for those who energetically pursue it. More correctly, for *some* of those who pursue it. Energy is not enough; resources, too, are required, including political and economic power, and a reasonably sure sense of what is being sought. Though the odds are with the state, the community is not without recourse, given the American tradition. But the question must not be seen as how the final victory of one side or the other can be ensured. Rather, the question is how balance can be maintained. And concern for balance points to specific diagnoses rather than general ones. Here the state seems overbearing, there the community seems stifling. Each instance, therefore, requires unique address.

These theoretical musings are, in part, given concrete shape in several sections of the Bundy Report.[5] At various places in that report, the following points are made:

1 The number and shape of new districts should be determined with great care in order to insure boundaries that are both educationally sensible and socially sound. The determination should take account of such factors as: sense of community (and) diversity in composition of student population.

2 The proposed reorganization would have built-in safeguards against movement towards still greater segregation of New York City schools. For example, if the central agency should reinstitute its open enrollment programme, Community School Districts with empty seats in mainly white schools would be required to receive Negro and Puerto Rican pupils from other districts.

3 The most important deterrent to segregation is quality education. Communities which achieve high levels of pupil performance – in schools that have a favourable climate for learning – will be the strongest possible magnet to draw all kinds of parents back to the city.

4 A major source of concern regarding the concept of community schools is the fear of provincialism. There are adequate defences against this. Moreover, within limits, fulfillment of highly localized interests may be a distinct advantage, giving residents a proprietary interest in the schools and enhancing the community climate and the motivation of children. Besides, it is not unreasonable that a district whose population is of predominantly Puerto Rican ancestry should spend additional school funds on Spanish-language instruction, or that a mainly Negro neighbourhood should give extra emphasis to African culture or the history of the American Negro .... Many students of education hold, in fact, that it is pedagogically desirable for the curriculum to contain subject matter that is immediately relevant to the learner.

There is obviously some tension between the stated goals of 'sense of community' and 'diversity in the composition of student population'. That tension is illustrated in citations 2 through 4 above. Let us suppose, for example, that the fourth point, endorsing community-oriented curricula, is taken seriously. Under such circumstances, is it likely that parents who have fled the city, a group made up predominantly of whites, will return to enroll their children in these schools, no matter how excellent their 'secular

357

education'? Or, suppose that not only Puerto Ricans and blacks, but many other racial and ethnic groups develop curricula 'immediately relevant to the learner' – to wit, we infer from the examples, ancestral languages, ethnic history, and so on. What happens, then, to the Negro and Puerto Rican pupils discussed in the second point, those who would be bussed into white districts? Shall they be encouraged to study Italian, or Chinese? And, if they are not so encouraged, and remain relatively few in number, will they not feel still more alien than they do today? For they will no longer be attending schools with curricula essentially interchangeable, as the curricula of state schools are. Rather, they will be attending schools with a definitive style, a style based on a communal solidarity they cannot share.

In confronting these questions, the New York State legislature has required heterogeneous districts; it has opted for diversity rather than community, an option wholly in keeping with the instinctive theoretical bias of the system, and the purposes of the state. For heterogeneous districts enable the system to avoid recognizing community as an educationally relevant phenomenon. But in the present climate, such a choice is likely to be interpreted by blacks as a violation of the entire thrust towards community control, which derives from very different purposes. In the end, it is not possible to discuss the virtues and liabilities of community control of the schools as an abstract theoretical question, as if it had nothing whatever to do with the racial crisis in America. When blacks urge community control, they do not do so because it is an appealing political philosophy, but because they see it as a solution to urgent problems their children face. And when they seek to solve those problems, the community they have in mind is the community of blacks. To appeal to other values, however compelling such values may be, is to subvert the special meaning which 'community' is coming to have for black people, and the special purposes for which they seek community control. Smaller school districts, with a greater opportunity for parental involvement, might help make the schools better in general, but if they were to include heterogeneous populations, they would not be blacker. Since, it is argued, the only way to ensure that the schools will be better specifically for blacks is to see to it that they are both blacker and controlled by the community, mere reduction in size is an inadequate response.

Perhaps the best that we can do to work our way out of the theoretical confusion is to adapt Berelson's view of the political system to the social system in general. *De facto*, society includes a great variety of communities, ranging from the highly organic to the highly incidental. Some people, perhaps, are trapped in a community they would not freely choose, yet cannot find the strength to leave. But there is no reason to suppose that most people do not get pretty much what they want. So long as the community is essentially a voluntary form of association, and so long as at least some communities are very loosely structured, and welcoming to newcomers, movement is possible. The liberal notion that organic communities are intrinsically bad reflects a very superficial understanding. If some people prefer neighbourhoods of limited liability, seeking more organic ties elsewhere than the neighbourhood or not at all, that is their business. And if others choose to live their lives within the bosom of the closed community, that is theirs.

The only issue that arises is whether the derivative freedom of groups to define themselves does not inevitably leave some people out in the cold. If it does, then the power of groups to draw their own boundaries must somehow be limited. The haunting spectre of walled neighbourhoods might be more frightening if the only bases of community in America were race and ethnicity. But the increasing propensity of people to define their communities in terms of cultural styles and income levels makes possible a greater flexibility. If, in short, powerful theoretical arguments can be raised on both sides of an issue, ought not the benefit of the theoretical doubt be given those whose stake is greatest and whose needs are most urgent – a position which points to ceding black people themselves the right to define the nature and boundaries of the community.

With one exception: if it can be shown that education cannot happen properly unless it is based on diversity – if black children cannot learn unless they learn together with whites, or if working class children do not learn unless they learn with middle class children – the justification for placing the schools under the authority of those organic communities which seek such authority fails. This is an important matter, and goes to the heart of the community control debate as a problem in educational theory.

Notes

1 Robert A. Nisbet (1966) *The Sociological Tradition*, New York: Basic Books, pp. 47–8.
2 Samuel Stouffer (1955) *Communism, Conformity, and Civil Liberties*, Garden City: Doubleday, p. 130.
3 James Madison, Federalist 10, in Alexander Hamilton, John Jay, and James Madison, *The Federalist*, New York: Modern Library College Edition p. 58.
4 See Robert A. Dahl (1956) *A Preface to Democratic Theory*, Chicago: University of Chicago Press, pp. 4–33.
5 The Mayor's Advisory Panel on Decentralization of New York City Schools (Bundy Report 1967). Reconnection for learning.

Index

Index

Bundy Report (on Decentralization of NY City Schools), determinants in number and shape of new districts, 359; built-in safeguards against greater segregation, 359; results of quality education, 359; endorsement of community-oriented curriculum, 359–60

Burke, Edmund, 150

Cabinet, the, final arbiter on public expenditure, 172, 197; restraints on general sector, 183, 203; gives guidance to Departments on financial decisions, 185; and defeat of Treasury ministers (1950s), 194

Capitalist system, place of trade unionism, 17; opposed by radical value systems, 21; and subordinate class, 22–3; and class stratified inequalities in education, 217

Central Advisory Council, cessation, 212

Central Policy Review Staff, and DES planning operations, 175; challenges spending departments, 175

Cheshire LEA, dirty books row (Kes and Billy Liar), 286

Child Poverty Action Group, children living below poverty line, 74

Children, position in society, 50; family membership, 50–1, 54; become occupationally mobile, 51; community interests after industrialization, 51; productivity potential, 51, 53; obligation towards educational system, 54, 57, 64; assumptions on their future in concepts of equality, 56, 58; shift in responsibility, 64; family and class origins determinants in educational achievement, 72, 73–4, 78; mental disturbance and school prospects, 74; and school's main objective, 243; educating them for socio/economic changes, 308; school input/output concept, 312 see also Black children

China, creation of mandarin class, 69

Civil Service, role of permanent officials in educational policy, 153, 154; professional neutrality, 153; safeguards against political patronage, 153; power in its own right, 153, 154; serves Government ministers of the day, 183; Ministerial expectations, 183

Civil Rights Act, 1964, creation of office of Education Survey of Educational Opportunity, 58, 60; definitions of inequality, 58–9, 61; dichotomy of definitions, 60–1; resulting controversy, 61; achievement in verbal skills by race and region, 62–3

Class consciousness, notions of 'them' and 'us'; alleged working class presence, 15–16; relationship to communal solidarity, 15; macro-social view of rewards system, 16; presents new view of meaning of inequality, 16; normative transformation experience, 16; existence in European socialist movements, 22

Class-culture paradigm, 217; of research, 239n3; and success of school, 238n3; work of Robson, 241n24

Class inequality, diverse and unitary theories of values, 7–8; differing moral interpretations, 9; meaning-systems used to perceive its nature and structure, 9ff., 24; acceptance of dominant value systems lessens conflict, 11; seen as part of social order, 12; variation in meaning in different societies, 14; effect of class consciousness, 16; relationship between class power and its moral framework, 20; role of political agencies in its apprehension, 21; radical view of its nature, 21–2; effect of decline in radicalism, 24; movement towards adaptation and accommodation, 24; non-political channels of resentment, 26; a determinant in educational achievement, 72

Class stratification, 'two nations' concept, 7; absence of unified moral order, 7; power distribution and legitimization of values relationship, 8; downward flow of moral assumptions, 8–9; three major meaning-systems, 9; effects of de-radicalization, 24; absence of radical opposition to socio/political order, 31; 'functional' theories of, 40, 41; an autonomous state, 40; duties of social scientists, 41; and educational

grammar school/secondary modern
school distinctions, 246; variation in
provision of learning opportunities, 261;
Rules of Management and its control
and conduct, 270, 276; public opinion
and 'modern' methods, 284; attitude to
a national model, 284; prescribed era,
284–5; feared use of for political ends,
285; position of RE, 285; Schools
Council proposals, 285–6; examples of
governing body involvement, 286–7;
retention of Latin, 296, 287; teacher
accountability, 287, 302, 306;
authorization in universities, 298, 299;
complex area of evaluation, 306;
relevance for a technical revolution,
308; determination by headmaster, 325
Curriculum (US), class oriented, 52;
diversification to meet needs of new
majority, 55; ability grouping (tracking)
and placement, 128–30; reflects present
distribution of power, 343; facts
involved in community oriented,
359–60
Curriculum resources, need to monitor
where they go and why, 242; fallacious
assumptions in their allocation, 242–3,
245; definition, 244; discriminatory
allocations, 245–6; revenue allocations
for teaching sciences, 246–7; principles
of revenue expenditure, 247–8; basis of
discriminatory allocations, 248–50

Dahl, Robert, 357
Dahrendorf, R., theory of class conflict, 15
Demographic factors, immigration, 51;
birth rates and school population, 160,
176, 208; teacher supply and declining
birthrate, 176; rise in pensioner
population, 194; staying on, 208, 209;
white outflow/black inflow in US cities,
335; population as basis for
apportionment of legislative districts,
350–1, 360
Department of Economic Affairs, 203
Department of Education and Science
(DES), position of power in total
educational sphere, 151–2, 153; role in
educational development, 152; position

and duties of Secretary of State, 153,
170, 185, 186, 276, 283, 291; privacy
of their deliberations, 155; concern with
scale and nature of educational
operations, 159, 174, 181–2; and
relationship between education and other
socio/economic objectives, 191; and
provisions for 16–19 age group, 161;
and binary HE provisions, 164; attitude
to research and experimentation, 164;
detachment from professional matters,
168; and resource allocation area of
planning, 170, 171–2, 174; importance
of contact with LEA thinking, 173, 177;
and 1972 White Paper, 174;
'programme budget', 175, 181; main
areas of responsibility, 178–9;
functional organization, 179–80;
involvement in financial decisions, 185,
190; duty to provide roofs over heads,
189–90; and school building projects,
207–8; loan sanction procedure,
208–9; and proposals made by specialist
committees, 212; cost per pupil and
school restrictions, 252; and role of
governing bodies, 281, 283; and
universities, 300
DES Circular : 'Local Authority
Expenditure in 1976–77 – forward
planning', 177
Department of Health and Social Security
(DHSS), 207
Departmental Planning Organization, scale
and distribution of resources, 174; and
decisions on educational objectives, 181;
not a backroom activity of specialists,
183
Disadvantaged children in EPA Schools,
ecological fallacy in Plowden, 83, 143; a
disappointing policy, 83–4, 89; children
at risk, 85–7; comparison with others,
87–8; analysis of their circumstances,
85–9; measurement of behaviour by
reading performance, 90–4, 96, 103;
geographical distribution, 94; effect of
school context and family circumstances,
94–5; of environmental disadvantage,
96–102; influence of father's socio/
economic status, 102, 104; numbers in
the schools, 103; need for new policies,

Index

105–6; area based theories, 143; numbers in and outside EPAs, 144; educational policy and, 156; finish education at compulsory stage, 160–1

Disadvantaged children (US), importance of cognitive skills in school social environment, 95; concept, 336; school failure to fulfil their needs, 336

Dominant class, legitimization of their value systems, 10, 11, 43; socio/political definitions become basis of entire social system, 10; provide socio/moral framework, 10; moral justification of reward system, 10, 11; results of institutional backing, 10, 11, 17; transform evaluative matter into factual, 11; interaction with subordinate class, 17; problematic appropriateness for less privileged, 17; introspective origin of abstract standards, 20; political/individual counterbalanced by socialist ideals, 22; opposition to a social policy based on incomes policy, 43 *see also* Value systems, dominant

Douglas, J.W.B., *The Home and the School*, 73

Durkheim, Emile, notion of anomie, 33, 35–6, 47n21; its relation to social inequality, 34, 36; distinction between restrictive reference groups and moral restraint, 35; his idea of 'external inequality', 42, 47n20, 49n37; on work of justice for advanced societies, 44; distinction between 'moral' discipline and one based on custom, 46n17; *The Division of Labour*, 44

'Early Leaving', 209

Education, attitudes of marginal members of subordinate class, 14; expresses dominant class values, 17; non-effect of egalitarian policy, 30, 70; UK/US comparison, 52; compulsory attendance laws, 54; can it effect social change? 66, 68, 69, 71, 138; a determinant in individual life and livelihood, 66; self-contained cures for ills, 68; self-generating shabby systems, 68; creation of meritocracy, 70; economic and

technical bases of development, 69; its purpose in an urban industrial society, 70–1, 75; position of relative deprivation, 140; collapse of belief in its redistributive virtues, 140, 143; rising share of public resources, 140, 308; relationship to upbringing, 141; instrument for achieving democratic affluence, 142; limited power of DES, 151; influence of competing ideologies, 156; and other socio/economic objectives, 161; recurrent or lifelong themes, 158, 162; academic/vocational dichotomy, 160–2; promotion v. selection view, 165; future planning needs, 169; mechanism of the advisory committees, 209–10; pre-empting of large % of social services resources, 211; call for a National Plan, 212; relationship between attainment and LEA resource provision, 216–18, 225, 256; difficulties of measuring its achievements, 239n6; assumed main aim, 243; idealist v. manpower supply concepts, 243–4; inequality in provisions for able and less able children, 256; peculiarities of British system, 301; hierarchical structure with management and inspection roles, 301; formal pupil/school/parent character, 307; as a social process, 322; primary social device for equalizing opportunity among socio/racial groups, 333; assumed potent power in society, 334; professional/non-professional roles, 348; need for external system of control, 348; society or state function? 358; to be based on diversity, 361

Education, adult, 158, 162–3, 250

Education, further, 160–2, 299, 301

Education, higher, restricted entry into, 52; economic sources of inequality, 53–4; anomalies in diversified curriculum, 55–6; college/non-college dichotomy, 56; period of expansion, 70; White Paper (1972) contribution, 163–4; reduction in student places, 163; binary split between university/polytechnic sectors, 163; influence of voluntary 'staying on', 209; collegiate

Index

search for an egalitarian system, 70, 71, 74; needs to be posed in new terms, 71; theory of non-educational determinants, 72–6; Plowden and, 74; unsolved issues, 75–6

Educational planning and decision-taking, part of pattern of accepted codes and mental habits, 150–1; role of DES, 151, 152, 155, 170; financial relationship between central and local government, 151, 152; autonomous bodies, 151; decentralization of authority, 151, 172; predominant role played by Civil Service and permanent staff, 152–4; separation from outside control and supervision, 155–6; dangers of accepting established goals and priorities, 156; allocation of resources programme, 156, 166; initiating structural changes, 156–7, 162; shared policy with whole of public administration, 157; dangers of closed procedure, 161; bases of White Paper (1972) recommendations, 166, 177; watershed position today, 167; essentially acquiescent to dominant opinion, 167; questions needing answers, 168–9; Rates Support Grant (RSG) system, 164, 171; proposed future course, 169; time-scale implementation, 171–2; Ministerial responsibilities, 172, 181–3; government/academic involvement, 172; development of consultation, 173, 211; local implementation of central decisions, 173; 'fly-wheel' effect of developments on the ground, 173–4; main concern with quantity of input, 177; and implementation of present policies, 180; assisting Ministers in deciding 'options', 'objectives' and 'priorities', 181–2, 183; political background, 181, 183, 202; part played by advisory *ad hoc* committees, 209–10; disjointed characteristics, 210–11; feedback process, 211; change to internal arrangements, 211–12; formal Departmental models, 212–3; resulting Planning Organization, 213–4; resource allocation for more able children, 242–56

Educational Priority Areas (EPAS), policy of positive discrimination, 68, 75–6, 141; recommended by Plowden, 68, 75–6, 78; educational/social deprivation, 74; development of community schools, 74; egalitarian policy, 76; formulation, 78, 79; identification, 81; fate of recommendations, 141; correlation between school and socio/economic deprivation, 143–4; numbers of deprived children in and outside, 144; low level of investment, 144

Elementary and Secondary Education Act 1965, 116

Eliot, T.S., 66, 76n1

Engels, Friedrich, 21; on proletariat/bourgeoisie dissimilarities, 7

Equiry One, research survey on variation in educational priorities, 286

Examinations, board/voluntary schools, 52; decision-making bodies, 151

Examinations, external (GCE, CSE), and staffing resources, 254, 255; in small schools, 254–5, 255; limitations in subjects offered, 255; value judgments, 255; and employment prospects, 255; public confusion, 284; diversity in schools participation, 287; basis of teacher accountability, 306

Family, the, 29; basic unit of social organization, 50; position of children, 50; patriarchal kinship system, 50; unit of economic production, 51; changes after industrialization, 51; inheritance of occupation, 54; white/middle class, Negro/lower class implications, 63; educative function, 69; a determinant in educational achievement, 72, 73, 74, 90, 95, 102–3, 141; influence of father's socio/economic status, 102, 104; pooling of incomes to reduce poverty, 138

Floud, J. and Halsey, A.H., on valid vocational aims, 244

Fox, and Flanders, analysis of state of industrial relations in UK, 33 ff.

France, attitude of subordinate class to inequality (*incivisme*), 11–12, 33;

political class consciousness, 23;
Napoleonic idea of education, 150;
public participation in school boards,
283–4; degree of autonomy, 306
Futurology, distinction between its use as
prediction and as design, 67; ends and
means in educational reform, 67–8

Galbraith, J.K., theme of public squalor
amid private affluence, 203
Gaitskell, Hugh, plan for social services,
140
Goldman, Sir Samuel, 'The developing
system of public expenditure
management control', 203, 204
Goldthorpe, J., discussion on futurology,
67
Government, 149; and costs of education,
151–2, 187–8; habits of secrecy and
confidentiality, 155; reforms to restrain
its growth, 192; and long-term surveys,
198, 201
Graduated Pension Scheme (1959), 193
Graham, Sir James, opposed appointment
of governors, 278, 279
Great Britain *see* United Kingdom
Guillebaud Committee, and state of NHS,
194

Hadow Report (1926), and role of school
managers, 278, 290
Handicapped, the, Warnock Report on
their education (forthcoming), 175
Haringey LEA, appointment of school
governors, 281–2
Harrison, Michael, 280–1
Haskins, Kenneth, definition of racism in
education, 341
Headteachers, headmasters, relationship
with managers, 275, 280; powers and
responsibilities conferred by Statute and
Rules of Management, 276;
appointment by governors, 276,
289–90; role on governing bodies, 288;
position in prime institutions, 298;
paternalistic idea, 309; use of
delegation, 323; and decision-making,
323; arguments for reducing his powers,

323–4; protection of school against
progressives, 324; direction of
deployment of his powers, 324, 331;
curricular determination, 325; financial
controls, 325; choice of staff, 325–6;
control of media of communication,
326; and administration, 327; assumed
autocratic powers, 330; antagonism
from fellow heads, 330; need for
participatory government, 331
Heath, Edward, and social security
expenditure, 207
Her Majesty's Inspectorate (HMI), 166,
180; role in decision-taking, 177; and
extended courses in non-grammar
schools, 253; and school's role in
statutory, 271; diagnostic and advisory
functions, 271–2
Hoggart, R., on subordinate value system,
14, 15–16 (*The Uses of Literacy*)
Horton, Peter, 281
House of Commons Expenditure
Committee, 201–2; and Treasury
policy, 206
Select Committee on Procedure ... and
scrutiny of expenditure, 198, 200
Housing, 206; reduction in council house
subsidies (1950s), 192, 194; LA role in
slum clearance, 192; Conservative
policy, 297; effect of overcrowding on
educational attainment, 233
'Human relations industry' movement,
47n20
Human resources, impact on school
performance, 95
Hyman, H.H., 'Value-systems of different
classes', 7–8

Immigrant children, in EPA Schools, 87;
reading scores by social class, 91–3, 99;
and overall reading performance, 97–8;
influence of home background, 102–3;
effect of discriminatory policy, 104;
additional teaching staff allowance, 259,
260 *see also* Black children (US)
Incomes policy, 34; lack of moral
regulations over individual needs, 33,
37; aims in a market economy, 371
involvement of ideals of social justice,

Index

Merton, R.K., *Social Theory and Social Structure*, 8

Middle class children (US), elementary schooling, 111; influence on blacks' test scores in segregated schools, 122, 124; effect of presence of black children, 125

Middle classes (UK), differing values from working classes, 7; lower class value change in response to, 18; and trade union power, 19; differentiated educational opportunities, 53; additional resources, 57; and grammar schools, 232; and community of limited liability (US), 354

Midwinter, Eric, and failure of uniform system of aid for EPAs, 76; promulgation of its ideas, 141

Military system (US), civilian/professional relations, 347, 348; MacArthur/Truman dispute, 347

Ministry of Education, Development Plan, 252–3

Morgan Community School, Columbia, gains in reading proficiency, 341

Morris, Henry, and role of school managers, 278

National Advisory Council on the Training and Supply of Teachers, 209; disbanded, 212

National Association of Governors and Managers (NAGM), achievement, 279–80; % teacher v. parent representation, 281

National Association of Schoolmasters (NAS), 280

National Child Development Study, parental interest/ school achievement relationship, 74

National Educational Association (NEA), 'cardinal principles' in report, 55; studies on use of teaching (ability grouping), 129

National Foundation for Educational Research, elementary teaching and cognitive inequality, 129; DES agent, 179

National Health Service (NHS), declining share of GNP (1950s), 192, 194;

Hospital Plan (1962), 197–8; private patients, 201; planned growth rate, 206; professionalism of consultants, 297

National Superannuation Scheme, time lag, 198

National Union of Teachers (NUT), and bias courses, 253–4; and membership of governing bodies, 280; and powers of curricular decision-making on content, 283, 284

Nationalized industries, 196

Negroes (US), exclusion from education, 52; differential systems, 53, 56, 59, 61; effect of input differences on achievement, 61, 62–3; comparison with whites, 62–3, 333; neglect of his cultural heritage, 334; dangers of ethnic-based communities, 352 *see also* Black Americans

Neighbourhoods, educative functions, 69; minor influence on school achievement, 74; racial mix and test scores, 122; distinguished from community, 349, 351–2; as a basis for the community school, 352–4; geographic mobility, 353, 354; and personal freedom v. genuine fraternity, 353–4; characteristics of residential segregation, 353; no single spatial definition, 354; conversion into communities ideas, 354

New York City, effects of school closure on reading scores, 109–10; staying on, 110; variation in elementary schools, 113; professional accountability in its schools, 310 ff; Bundy Report, 359–60

Newson Report, 1963, *Half our Future*, 70; and 15–18 age group, 209, 260

Newton, K., study of British C.P., 15

Normative systems, aspects of inequality, 7; class-differentiated view, 8; resulting from collective bargaining, 35–6; foundation on coercion or bargaining, 36; need for accepted moral basis, 36; difficulties of restoration in conditions of inequality, 36–7, 42

Northern Ireland, 180

Northumberland LEA and Nottinghamshire LEAs, provisions for less able children, 245, 249; curricular losses, 249; % grammar school entrants, 249; sex

372

Index

awareness in Britain, 32; use of educational means in achieving its ends, 66, 217; task of sociologists, 67; to be removed from education, 138

Polytechnics, 299; Departmental, similarity to universities, 301; three quality controls, 301; external examiners, 301

Popper, Sir Karl, distinction between holistic and piecemeal reform, 68

Poverty, 28; to be abolished by educational reform, 68; radical views of amelioration, 68; needs redistribution of effective social power, 68; numbers living below poverty line, 74; alleged not an hereditary state, 135; to be abolished by equal incomes policy, 138; geographical theory of, 142; origins in urban industrial areas, 143; theory of transatlantic passage, 143; origins in disadvantage and discrimination, 143; need for composite approach, 144

Preschooling (UK), point of entry for educational change, 69; and deprivation, 141, 142, 144; agreed priority in decision-taking, 173; Plowden recommendations, 210

Preschooling (US), effects of, 107, 336; on children still at school, 108; follow-up of alumni, 108–9; long term transitory effects, 108–9; failure to close socio/racial gaps between children, 109; little effect on cognitive development, 111; and needs of black children, 336

Prime institutions in education, 296; definition, 297; unitary philosophy, integrated curriculum and use of time, 297; submission to collective decision-making, 297–8; position of secondary schools as federations, 297–8; extent of autonomy and accountability, 299–304

Professional accountability (US), concept as applied to individual school as a unit, 310; areas of collective responsibility, 210–1, 217–8; staff towards children, 311; staff towards higher authority, 311; and educational accounting system, 311 (*see under*); identification of hard-to-change and easy-to-change conditions, 312–3; involves knowledge

of variables and their power to induce change, 313; use of 'school effectiveness indices' (SEIs), 313, *see under*; particularization of staff effort, 319; misuse of false analogies, 322; problems involved in development of objective criteria, 322

Professional associations, 270

Professionalism, analysis of concept, 296–7; in hierarchical state, 297–9; and LEA accountability, 303; involvement of loyalty, 307; and parent-child relationship, 307–8; low level among teachers, 309; attitude to community control (US), 347–8

Programme Analysis and Review on Higher Education and Schools Expenditure, evidence for 1972 White Paper, 155

Programme for Reform in Secondary Education (PRISE), 290

Progressivism, pedagogical assumptions, 141; and a 'national' curriculum, 284

Project Concern, reading scores study on bussing, 123

Public expenditure, 192; impact of Plowden, 194–8, 202; survey timetable, 199; 1972/73 budget, 200; ratio to GNP, 202–3; committed to unobtainable targets, 203; dominance of political over intellectual factor, 203; growth rate of public sector (1964ff), 203–5; (1952–74, Table 4), 205; political repercussions of holding back growth rate in services sector, 205; Conservative Government (1970–75), 206; economic crises and forward planning, 206

Public Expenditure Survey Committee (PESC), five year forecasts of expenditure, 171, 172, 196–7; Ministerial decisions on, 171, 185; responsibility for educational element, 171, 172; Examination of Witnesses, 182–91; machinery of operation, 183; Cabinet restrictions, 183, 184; role of Treasury, 184, 185–6; and LA spending, 184; RSG negotiations, 184, 187–8; government restraints, 184–5; time scale involved, 186; interim

Index

School buildings, DES control of projects, 152, 179, 207; MOE system of cost limits (1949), 208; forward planning policy, 208; elimination of 'all age' schools, 208; Building codes restraints, 252

School effectiveness indices (SEI), staff measurement of school's efficiency, 313–4; regression analysis technique, 314–7; differentiation from test score profile, 314; measurement of pupil development over a span of time, 314, 315; derivation from more fundamental measures, 315–6; use of reading test scores, 316, 317, 318; input/output measure under hard-to-change conditions, 317, 318; indication of specific corrective actions needed, 318; examination of educational process and easy-to-change condition variables, 318–9; stringent conditions of calculation, 321; misuse of 'basic skills' development, 321; avoiding false analogies, 322

School governors and managers, powers over conduct of school, 276; obligatory appointment, 276, 277; issue of model articles, 276; political appointments, 277, 281–2; historical origins, 277; distinction between, 278; a bastion against bureaucracy, 278, 279; links with the community, 278, 279; varying interpretations of their role, 278–9; parental and worker participation, 279, 281, 302; modern role, 279, 283, 287–9, 302; influence of Plowden, 279; influence of pressure groups, 279–80, 302; mandatory teacher membership, 280; overall membership, 281; LEA reforms, 280–2; issue of confidentiality, 281, 282, 292; coopted places, 282, 288, 289; opposition to individual bodies, 282–3; hostility of teachers organization on curriculum matters, 283; decision-making powers over the curriculum, 285–7; recommended membership, 287–8; role of political parties, 288; teacher, parent, pupil membership, 288, 302; advocated additional duties, 289; and finance,

289; appointment of senior staff, 289–90; use of external assessors, 290; need to be vocal and visible, 290; putting reforms into practice, 290–4; changing the law, 290–2; LEA backing and guidance, 292, 292; importance of training, 293; suggested rights in school organization, 308–9; and the powers of the head, 325 *see also* School managers *for specific items*

School leavers (16–19 age group), absence of educational/training provisions, 158, 159, 160–2; school role in finding jobs, 243; criticized by society, 308

School managers, extent of curriculum control, 270, 272, 273; political appointments, 272, 277; varied background, 272; relations with head teacher, 272–3; and quality of teaching provided, 273; actions to be taken in cases of disagreement, 273; conduct of visits, 273; call to LEA for full inspection, 274; and institution of Authority's Disciplinary Procedures, 274; intervention by Secretary of State, 274; mandatory appointment, 276; issue of model articles, 276

School resources, effects on student achievement, 115–8, 133n16, 135; allocation of non-capital, 258; use of virement, 258–9 *see also* AUR

Schools (UK general), passive role in educational opportunity, 54, 64; relation of inputs to effects on achievement, 61; failure to solve social problems, 72, 74; influence of its character on pupil attainment, 73–4, 95, 96–102, 312; effects on children's test scores, 111, 112–3, 128; contribution to cognitive inequality, 114–5, 137; achievement differences between and within, 128; alleged absence of relationship between quality and economic success, 135, 137; wide range in character and resources, 138–9; fallacious assumptions in allocation of resources, 242–3; and children's future employment, 243, 307; concept of 'viability', 252; possess public personalities, 297; hierarchical structure